The Editor

LYNN STALEY is Harrington and Shirley Drake Professor in the Humanities at Colgate University. She is the author of *The Powers of the Holy: Religion, Politics, and Gender in Late Medieval English Literature*, with David Aers (1996); *Margery Kempe's Dissenting Fictions* (1994); *The Shepheardes Calender: An Introduction* (1990); *The Voice of the Gawain-Poet* (1984); and editor of *The Book of Margery Kempe*, complete text, modernized spelling, and notes (1996). She is presently working on a book on Ricardian court culture.

A NORTON CRITICAL EDITION

THE BOOK
OF MARGERY KEMPE

A NEW TRANSLATION
CONTEXTS
CRITICISM

Translated and Edited by

LYNN STALEY
COLGATE UNIVERSITY

W • W • NORTON & COMPANY • *New York* • *London*

Copyright © 2001 by W. W. Norton & Company, Inc.

The text of this book is composed in Electra
with the display set in Bernhard Modern.
Composition by Publishing Synthesis.
Book design by Antonina Krass.

Library of Congress Cataloging-in-Publication Data

Kempe, Margery, b. ca. 1373.
  [Book of Margery Kempe. English]
  The book of Margery Kempe : a new translation, contexts, criticism /
translated and edited by Lynn Staley.
    p. cm—(A Norton critical edition)
  Includes bibliographical references.

  ISBN 0-393-97639-4 (pbk.)

    1. Kempe, Margery, b. ca. 1373. 2. Kempe, Margery, b. ca. 1373.
Book of Margery Kempe. 3. Authors, English—Middle English,
1100–1500—Biography. 4. Christian pilgrims and pilgrimages—Early
works to 1800. 5. Christian women—Religious life—England.
6. Mysticism—England—Early works to 1800. I. Staley, Lynn, 1947– II.
Title.

PR2007.K4 A199 2000
248.2′2′092–dc21
[B]   ·   00-055455

W. W. Norton & Company, Inc., 500 Fifth Avenue, New York, N.Y. 10110
www.wwnorton.com

W. W. Norton & Company Ltd., Castle House, 75/76 Wells Street,
London W1T 3QT

7 8 9 0

Contents

Introduction   vii
MAP: Medieval England   xx
A Kempe Lexicon   xxi

The Text of *The Book of Margery Kempe*   1

Contexts   185
From The Constitutions of Thomas Arundel   187
From Meditations on the Life of Christ   196
From The Shewings of Julian of Norwich   202
From The Book of Saint Bride   207
From The Life of Marie d'Oignies by Jacques de Vitry   218

Criticism   223
Clarissa W. Atkinson • Female Sanctity in the
   Late Middle Ages   225
Lynn Staley • Authorship and Authority   236
Karma Lochrie • From Utterance to Text   243
David Aers • The Making of Margery Kempe: Individual and
   Community   256
Kathleen Ashley • Historicizing Margery: *The Book of Margery*
   Kempe as Social Text   264
Gail McMurray Gibson • St. Margery: *The Book of*
   Margery Kempe   276
Sarah Beckwith • Margery Kempe's *Imitatio*   284
Caroline Walker Bynum • Late Medieval Eucharistic Doctrine   288
Nicholas Watson • Arundel's Constitutions   299

Selected Bibliography   303

Introduction[†]

The Book of Margery Kempe is an electrifying text. With its rich pictures of late medieval town life, its details of food and dress and travel, its look into the rituals of late medieval religion, its noisy, uncomfortable, and demonstrably pious protagonist, and its social and ecclesiastical critiques, the *Book* seems to belong to many genres without fitting precisely into the outlines of any. When the manuscript was discovered in the summer of 1934 by Colonel Butler-Bowdon among his family treasures and was identified and later announced by Hope Emily Allen in the London *Times* in December of that year, it was immediately seen as an invaluable find. The *Book* sets the account of one woman's spiritual development within the constrictions of a mercantile and status-conscious society, a society whose impulses and conflicts Margery herself seems to share, and, in many cases, to magnify.[1] Margery's narrative, which begins with a spiritual crisis that succeeded the birth of her first child, describes her increasingly successful efforts to carve out a degree of spiritual autonomy for herself, including accounts of her pilgrimages to Jerusalem, to Rome, and to shrines in Germany, and ends with a starkly simple long prayer which she was supposed to have composed. Though Margery describes herself as the mother of fourteen children, only one figures, albeit briefly, in the text. Her husband, John Kempe, has a more prominent role as the figure who initially supports her new way of life, then reluctantly grants her the physical freedom she desires, and ends by needing her to tend him in his declining age. The relationships that Margery has with her confessors and with other ecclesiastical officials are more vivid than those she has with her family. Most vivid yet are the conversations she has with the Virgin Mary and with the Godhead, first with the Jesus who appears to her in his humanity and, finally, with the Father. It is her intimacy with the Godhead that authorizes her to carve out a space for herself that public scorn, threats upon her safety, physical difficulties, and even episcopal inquiries into the nature of her faith cannot take from her.

Even the briefest account of *The Book of Margery Kempe* suggests the sorts of claims the text has upon our attention. The first of these con-

---

[†] See the Selected Bibliography to this volume (pp. 303–05) for publication information on many of the works cited in the notes to this introduction.
1. See Aers (1988); Beckwith (1986); Delany (1975).

cerns the version of social reality that we can find in Margery's purport-
edly dictated account of her own life. There is much in the *Book* that is
verifiable. Persons such as Thomas Arundel, archbishop of Canterbury
(1397, 1399–1414); Philip Repingdon, bishop of Lincoln (1405–19);
William Alnwick, bishop of Norwich (1426–36); the Carmelites Alan of
Lynn (b. 1348?) and William Sowthfeld (d. 1414); and Robert
Spryngolde, her confessor, were well known figures in the late medieval
English church.[2] Concerning the town of Bishop's Lynn (which is now
called King's Lynn), its religious foundations, guildhall, and topography
can be seen today and used to enlarge our understanding of Kempe's
handling of physical space in the *Book*.[3] Similarly, Margery's journeys
around England to towns like Bristol, Lincoln, and York, as well as her
visits to various religious foundations and shrines, are rooted in a physical reality the map of medieval England included in this volume (p. xx)
is meant to augment. Moreover, there are documents recording the
entry of one Margery Kempe into the Trinity Guild of Lynn (the most
prestigious of the town's religious guilds) in 1437–38 and entries in the
Lynn register both for John Brunham (Margery Kempe's father) and for
a John Kempe, junior, probably Margery Kempe's husband.[4] Other
events, like the death of Henry V in 1422, which is mentioned in Book
1, chapter 71, or the fire in the Guild Hall in Lynn in January, 1420–21,
which is mentioned in Book 1, chapter 67, can be used in attempts to
date the events of Margery's life. But we have no actual proof that the
Book is any "truer" than any fiction rooted in a social reality.

The *Book*, like Geoffrey Chaucer's *Canterbury Tales* or William
Langland's *Piers Plowman*, insists that we seek to discover not only what
that social and cultural reality may have been but the version of it that is
fundamental to the purposes of the *Book* itself. And, again like those two
great poems, the *Book* can serve as the most thorough of introductions
to the world it appears to capture and critique. To make a list of those
issues central to the *Book* is to make a list of those issues seen as central
to the study of fifteenth-century England: literacy and the transmission
of vernacular texts, religious heterodoxy, female and/or lay piety, gender
roles, episcopal control, the rise of nationalism, community, the making
of individual identities, and the nature of true authority.

The word concealed in *authority*, as in the Latin *auctoritas*, from
which it is drawn, is *author*, the figure whose conscious assumption of
authority drives the creation of any text. Here, too, the *Book* seems to
tease us with a reality that may or may not be actual. The two opening
proems, as well as numerous references within the text itself, describe
the *Book* as dictated episodically from memory by Margery Kempe ("this

---

2. See the copious notes provided by Allen and Meech in Meech (1961), to whose work on contemporary references I am indebted.
3. See Raguin and Stanbury, *Mapping Margery Kempe*.
4. For these, see Meech (1961), Appendix III; Owen (1984); Parker (1971).

creature") to two scribes. In so doing, the *Book* locates itself within the generic outlines of female sacred biography, accounts of the lives of holy women that were typically written by male clergy, such as Jacques de Vitry, author of the life of Marie d'Oignies, or the clerics who wrote out the life and Revelations of St. Bridget (ca. 1303–1373). Both women's lives are important to Kempe's design in the *Book*, and selections from each are included in this volume. Male ecclesiastical writers served not simply as narrators, but as authorizing voices for the texts of these women's lives, verifying their sanctity, which threw into sharp relief the worldliness of those who encountered and discounted the holy one in their midst. Sacred biography thus served two purposes—exemplary and hortatory, since it held up the Christ-like life as an example of what true devotion should be even as it castigated a world that worshipped Christ but failed to live as Christ. In the case of the lives of holy women, their devotion, as Caroline Walker Bynum's work has pointed out, was accompanied by a profound attachment to the humanity of Christ, frequently by tears or visions, and by a focus upon the sacrament of the Eucharist, or the Host, the visible, tastable *corpus Christi* (body of Christ) that was made available to the faithful in the Mass. However, the similarities between *The Book of Margery Kempe* and the lives of holy women to some extent point up the differences between them: Margery's life is not officially produced; it includes no account of her girlhood or of her death; it seems not to have generated any recognition aside from its endorsement by the Carthusian Abbey of Mount Grace in Yorkshire, which counted the manuscript among its holdings and whose readers probably wrote in its margins during the late fifteenth and early sixteenth centuries.[5] The short selection of extracts from the *Book* that was printed by Wynkyn de Worde in London around 1501 and reprinted by Henry Pepwell in 1521 omits any descriptions of the disruptive and challenging nature of Margery's life and travels, presenting her through her calmer mystical conversations with Jesus and the Blessed Virgin. Pepwell's reprint makes only one substantive change to the original edition by Wynken de Worde: in both the title and the ending he describes Margery Kempe as an "ancres," a female hermit. In so doing Pepwell gave her a recognizable place within late medieval society.[6]

When the *Book* was first discovered, it was taken as a sort of verbal diary, narrated by a possibly hysterical, certainly emotional, woman to a male scribe. More recently, it has been scrutinized for its depiction of female vulnerability and anxiety within a hegemonic society, where power and authority were wielded by men whose positions in church

---

5. The Carthusians were a strictly observant and contemplative order. For remarks about the annotations, see Lochrie (1991) 119–22; Staley (1996), Introduction. Meech and Allen (1940) note each of the annotations in their own notes and discuss them in their Introduction, xxxviii–xliv.
6. For the printed extracts, see Meech and Allen (1940) 353–57. For discussion of the extracts, see Meech and Allen (1940) xlvi–xlviii; Holbrook (1987).

and/or state allowed them to ignore or harass Margery for her passionate attachment to a Christ who bids her to dress in an unusual fashion, abstain from meat and wine, travel about Europe and England, and chastise others for swearing and lax living. Her constant praying, her boisterous and prolonged weeping, and her unwillingness to live as others live make her doubly vulnerable to the hostility of townspeople, as well as open to the charges of heterodoxy that put her in physical danger in London (chapter 16), Leicester (chapter 46), York (chapters 51–52), and Beverly (chapter 53). Hope Emily Allen, who was called upon to examine the manuscript when it was discovered and whose annotations of the scholarly edition of the *Book* produced by Sanford Brown Meech for the Early English Text Society in 1940 are still invaluable, saw the text as an authentic record of the social and religious conflicts of one woman's life in mid-fifteenth-century England. Meech and Allen went so far as to include a chronological table of contemporary events and of tentative dates for Margery's life in the introduction to the EETS edition, thus fixing the *Book* in the realm of fact.

But work since then has opened up new ways of seeing the account as at once rooted in a historical reality and creating a version of reality that, like Chaucer's and Langland's, must be seen as authored, as the product of a shaping imagination. If that imagination is Kempe's (as it well might be), she may have constructed a fictional scribe as an authorizing mediator between herself and the reader.[7] The genre of autobiography as we understand it today did not exist in the Middle Ages, but there was nonetheless a tradition extending back to St. Augustine's *Confessions* that made exemplary or didactic use of autobiographical narrative.[8] Though it is unlikely Kempe knew directly of the *Confessions* or of works like Abelard's *Story of My Calamities* or Guibert of Nogent's *Memoirs* or of the letters of St. Bernard, Peter the Venerable, or Abelard, which also contain examples of autobiographical writing, she had at hand an important and vigorous English tradition of life-writing. Richard Rolle, the mid-fourteenth-century Yorkshire mystic and hermit, whose English writings were addressed to a woman reader, presented his life as dramatizing a pattern of revolutionary spiritual growth. Rolle's use of himself as an example and his emphasis upon his own physical experience of feeling, hearing, and smelling the sweetness of God had a profound influence upon English devotional writing, as well as upon the "affective piety" of many in the late Middle Ages.[9] Rolle's writings are among those read to Margery by the priest in Lynn. The hearts and flames with which the late-fifteenth- and early-sixteenth-century Carthusian readers decorated the margins of the

---

7. Staley (1994), chapter 1. The entire study argues for the intentional and fictional nature of the *Book*.
8. See Vance (1973); Brown (1983).
9. For Rolle's account of his life, see "The Office of St. Richard Hermit," in Allen (1927). On Rolle, see Watson (1991).

manuscript of *The Book of Margery Kempe* are the conventional symbols associated with Rolle's intense and fervent spiritual love and vision. Julian of Norwich (ca. 1343–ca. 1415), whose *Book of Showings* was written probably in the last quarter of the fourteenth century and circulated in two versions during the fifteenth century, would have been the contemporary author most immediately available to Kempe. *The Book of Margery Kempe* describes Margery as visiting Julian (chapter 18). Though Julian of Norwich's *Showings* cannot be described as autobiography, it, like Rolle's writings and those of other mystics, is rooted in an experiential apprehension of the nature of God and derives its authority from the very experience the text seeks to describe and explicate.[1] Finally, there is *Piers Plowman*, the late-fourteenth-century poem that circulated in three revisions and many manuscripts throughout the fifteenth century. In it, William Langland, its author, makes a sophisticated use of autobiographical narrative that is at once exemplary, prophetic, and profoundly specific, serving to locate his spiritual message within a particular moment in English culture and history.[2] All of these texts would have been available to Kempe, and a strong argument can be made for linking her work to the vernacular autobiographical traditions represented by Richard Rolle, Julian of Norwich, and William Langland.

However, unlike their work, and indeed unlike all the autobiographical writings I have mentioned, Kempe's *Book* does not employ a first-person narrator, but presents Margery's life as an account of portions of the life of "this creature"; with one exception (see chapter 15), it maintains a third-person narration. In the second, longer, and more daring version of the *Showings*, Julian of Norwich omitted any references to her gender. If Julian's decision to present her visions and interpretations of them as detached from her personal circumstances indicates her sense that gender and authority were inextricably entwined, Kempe, too, may have felt that her work gained legitimacy if it was presented as issuing from a male writer. Moreover, by the 1430s, it was more dangerous to produce vernacular devotional prose. What Julian of Norwich could do (albeit carefully) in the late fourteenth century Kempe could not have done in the fifteenth without the danger of being suspected of heresy, possibly of treason. By distancing herself from her subject, Kempe thus screened herself from such charges, as well as from charges that she, a woman, had dared to set herself up as a figure of spiritual authority.[3] Gaining the safety of distance, she also gained the distance needed for the complicated fiction of

---

1. On Julian, see Aers and Staley (1996), chapters 3, 4.
2. See Justice and Kerby-Fulton (1997), especially Middleton's essay. There is, of course, a long and important secular tradition of writing concerned with the issues of authorial or social identity. In England, the two most important writers who employed the mode are Chaucer and Hoccleve. Hoccleve, like Kempe, emphasizes the self's relation to a defining community, whose morals may or may not be enough to sustain the self's quest for self-understanding.
3. For examples of the sorts of tensions with which women devotional writers grappled, see Newman (1995); Petroff (1986).

self and community achieved in the *Book*. Whether or not Margery actually did any of the things recorded in the *Book*, her life is "shown" to us as clearly as Margery "shows" her life to her confessors. And by such showings, she establishes her authority. Or perhaps Margery's life was written by someone else, a clerk or clerks who either recorded and shaped her memories or made of her a semi-fictional character.[4] In either case, we are confronted with a text whose sophistication is increasingly the subject of scholarly and critical attention. It demands that we attempt to understand it as having a purpose, an implied audience, as well as an author whose particular relationship to the political, social, and religious atmosphere of her world shaped her and was shaped by her into what is one of the most important of late-medieval prose works. Along with Thomas Malory's *Morte d'Arthur* and the four great cycles of *Corpus Christi* drama, *The Book of Margery Kempe* helps to define the century.

From remarks in the first proem and in the opening sentences of the second book, *The Book of Margery Kempe* appears to have been written between 1436 and 1438 and to describe events that belong to the reign of Henry V (1413–22) and the long minority of Henry VI. By that time, the Hundred Years' War, which officially began in 1340 when Edward III assumed the title of king of France, had lasted long enough to drain the resources of both countries. During the last years of Henry IV and the reign of Henry V, who asserted his claim to the French throne in 1413, the English forces had appeared to predominate. Henry's victory at Agincourt in 1415 and the signing of the Treaty of Troyes in 1420 signaled England's command of the field. Henry, however, died young in 1422, leaving an infant son and many debts which he did not have time to confront. After his death, England was ruled by a council of nobles, whose own factionalism produced a new set of problems and tensions. The *Book* is thus set in a period of English history when English prestige and prosperity were relatively high though already tested in France, where, after 1424, the English presence became less secure. (Not only did Joan of Arc inspire the French resurgence of the late 1420s, but the Normans grew restless, as did England's Breton and Burgundian allies.)[5] Though East Anglian towns like Bishop's Lynn maintained a high degree of wealth and stability, the potential for instability, or the fear of it, was deeply inscribed in Lancastrian England. Henry IV had usurped the throne from Richard II in 1399 and had sought to quell all rebellious motions throughout his reign by more closely linking ecclesiastical authority to the civil power to punish heresy as treason. Those followers of John

---

4. Ashley (1998); Voaden (1999), chapter 4.
5. See Ralph A. Griffiths, "The Later Middle Ages," in *The Oxford History of Britain*, ed. Kenneth O. Morgan (New York: Oxford UP, 1999) 228–31; A. R. Myers, *England in the Late Middle Ages, The Pelican History of England* (Harmondsworth, Middlesex: Penguin Books, 1952, rpt. 1985), Part II, chapter 1.

Wyclif, called Lollards, who espoused a proto-Protestant skepticism about the role of the priest, clerical celibacy, the doctrine of transubstantiation in the Eucharist (which specified that the bread and wine were physically changed during the Mass to the body and blood of Christ), and confession to a priest, were subjected to scrutiny and forced to recant publicly or risk the death by burning that William Sawtre in 1401 and John Badby in 1410 had endured for their beliefs.[6] The degree of fear and hostility aroused by Margery's behavior, as well as her claims to speak personally with Christ, her knowledge of scripture, her dislike of swearing, and her assumption of spiritual authority, cause her to be questioned by both spiritual and civic authorities, usually as to her beliefs about the Eucharist, probably the most notorious of Lollard heresies.

Not only does the picture of late-medieval English town life that we find in the *Book* seem to question the basis for the very prosperity, stability, and unity touted by Lancastrian propaganda, but Margery's female sanctity seems to rattle her countrymen and -women in ways that point up the flimsiness of the status quo the *Book* describes. The men of Beverly who warn her to forsake the life she leads and go "spin and card as other women do" (chapter 53), along with the famous preacher who cannot bear her loud cries of religious devotion during his sermons and banishes her from his presence (chapter 61) and her fellow pilgrims who do not wish to hear her speak of scripture, are all indications of a world called up for review in *The Book of Margery Kempe*. The social reality that Kempe describes serves as a context for Margery's anguished (and frequently irritating) attempts to live out the Christ-like life in a world where goods count more than good. As Margery's career demonstrates, the Gospel can be as unwelcome in Christian England as in Jerusalem and the one who proclaims it vulnerable to communal scorn. Her relative powerlessness—she is a woman, often alone, often without funds— is powerfully used to illustrate the insecurities of a world whose values are conformist and materialist. If many of the English discount or dislike Margery, there are others who cherish her for her prayers, for her acts of charity, and for her piety. There are enough glimpses of figures who communicate with her by signs or deeds or words, who help her, who read to her, or who give her money or clothing to see the outlines in the *Book* of another sort of community, one whose principles have little to do with the hierarchies of status or gender or power. That community is more than English; it contains all who love the Christ Margery attempts to imitate. If the Lancastrian kings—Henry IV, Henry V, and those who guided the young Henry VI—sought to create a version of England whose prosperity and peace depended upon its pristine orthodoxy, the

6. See McNiven (1987).

author of *The Book of Margery Kempe* provides an alternate view of community that dissents from official views.

Official English orthodoxy was prescribed in 1409 by Thomas Arundel, archbishop of Canterbury, in his Constitutions, which are included in this volume (p. 187) and commented upon by Nicholas Watson. The Constitutions were specifically formulated to combat the English heretics known as Lollards, who threatened the uniformity of the English church by preaching, teaching, or writing about their diverse beliefs. The emphasis in each of the thirteen constitutions is upon authority—Arundel mandates against unauthorized preaching, against preaching irregular doctrines, against schoolmasters teaching anything contrary to the Catholic faith, against unauthorized translation of any part of the scripture, against disputing the articles of the church, against any priest celebrating the Eucharist without his letters of orders, against dangerous beliefs or arguments at Oxford (where John Wyclif had been a scholar), and against violating the statutes themselves. By defining alternate beliefs as schismatic, Arundel established conformity as an official standard by which all should be judged. His focus upon the textuality of Lollardy reflects contemporary awareness that Lollardy was associated with literacy, particularly with unauthorized vernacular texts—sermons, translations of scripture, treatises— that opened private windows for their readers.[7] By reading the scriptures, thinking about them, and talking about them with others, a person might well arrive at a sense of personal authority that could do without priestly sacramental mediation. Nicholas Love's *Mirror of the Blessed Life of Jesus Christ*, which is a Middle English translation of the thirteenth-century Latin *Meditations on the Life of Christ*, was commissioned by Arundel to meet the needs of those who sought private vernacular devotional texts. The *Meditations*, which was falsely attributed to St. Bonaventure, offers a version of Jesus' life and ministry filled with intimate details of family life, all designed to underline the humanity of Christ. In addition, the narrator of the *Meditations* is careful to specify the ways in which the text might be used by the reader— what the reader should feel about certain scenes or where she should position herself as imaginative spectator. In sponsoring the translation, Arundel thus signaled his awareness of the demand for devotional texts in the vernacular, particularly for female readers who were probably not latinate, but also his judgment that such texts demanded the guidance supplied by an internal voice of counsel.[8]

Though Margery never imagines doing without her confessors and priests, the *Book* certainly describes her assumption of authority, an authority that is guaranteed, not by a representative of the church, but

7. See especially Aston (1984); Cross (1978); Hudson (1988).
8. See Sargent (1992).

by her personal conversations with Jesus and with God the Father. The very humanity of Christ so fundamental to officially sponsored late-medieval spirituality becomes the catalyst of Margery's increasing non-conformity. Beginning with Christ's appearance at her bedside as a young man in a flowing robe (a scene drawn from Love's *Mirror*), Margery comes to be guided by these private visions in ways possibly not foreseen by Archbishop Arundel and others who sought to curb the vagaries of private devotion. Her gender and her helplessness at some points in the narrative may diffuse our sense of her force, but, if read with care, the *Book* records her gradual trajectory toward a place that looks very like freedom. It is, however, carefully written to seem as though the text, like the life it recounts, is fully authorized. The intro-ductory material, the remarks scattered throughout about scribal medi-ation, about Margery's illiteracy, and about her dependence upon those who administer the sacraments to her, work to underline the orthodoxy of the book we read. Similarly, the manuscript itself, which is not the original but a copy made probably sometime before 1450 by someone who signed himself Salthows on the bottom portion of the last page, locates the text well within the boundaries of orthodox faith. Preserved at the Carthusian priory of Mount Grace in Yorkshire, the annotations by four hands in the margins of the manuscript, remark on elements of Margery's spiritual experience that link her to the conven-tions of late-medieval piety. In addition to demonstrating ways that late-medieval readers responded to texts, the annotations implicitly "authorize" the *Book* by authorizing Margery's life. No heretic Margery—her conflicts with the officials of church and state, the dis-like she arouses among staid townspeople, the sharp rebukes she levels at worldly churchmen and secularminded pilgrims are all subsumed into a narrative that can be set alongside the works of the fourteenth-century English mystic Richard Rolle and read as an account of mys-tical fervor!

This is not to say that Kempe's book is not about Margery's love of God, but it is to turn back to the artfulness of the *Book*, to its author's ability to create a text that is designed to appear as though it conformed to those contemporary standards of "uniformity." The very sense of iden-tity that Margery achieves in her sixty-odd years is the product of a con-tinuous conflict with figures of religious and communal authority. Thus the second book, which moves quickly through the deaths of Margery's oldest son and husband and the picaresque adventures she has when accompanying her daughter-in-law home to Germany, depicts Margery operating without benefit of clerical authority. In fact, she is expressly forbidden to leave the country by all but her inner voice, which is the voice of God in her. Upon returning to England, she meets in Shene, the Brigettine abbey founded by Henry V in 1415, the hermit who led her out of Lynn. He says to her:

I do you well to let you know your confessor has forsaken you because you went over the sea and would tell him no word thereof. You took leave to bring your daughter to the seaside; you asked no leave for any farther. There was no friend you had who knew of your counsel; therefore I suppose you shall find but little friendship when you come there. I pray you, get you fellowship where you can, for I was blamed for your default when I led you last; I will no more.

But Margery's triumph over censuring males is as sweet as any woman might wish:

She spoke fair and prayed, for God's love, that he would not be displeased, for those who loved her for God before she went out, they would love her for God when she came home. She offered to acquit his costs by the way homeward. So at the last he, consenting, brought her again to London and afterward home to Lynn, to the high worship of God and to the great merit of both of their souls. When she was come home to Lynn, she obeyed herself to her confessor. He gave her full sharp words, for she was his obediencer and had taken upon herself such a journey without his knowing. Therefore he was moved the more against her, but our Lord helped her so that she had as good love of him and of other friends afterward as she had before, worshipped be God.

The rich comedy of gender that brings the curtain down on Margery's extraordinary life barely conceals the gap the event opens up between priest and "obediencer." If Arundel's fears that "schism" would divide the English church and nation are the driving force behind the Constitutions, Margery's abilities to evade authorizing forces (all of whom are male) seem to beg the question of uniformity and, instead, point us in the direction of a world that looks more like our own than it does Arundel's.

Though *The Book of Margery Kempe* is certainly not a modern text and needs to be understood within the contexts of late-medieval England, the tensions it describes between Margery and her community, as well as her anguished questioning of her own "feelings," are material for fictions being written today. Margery's self-doubts are focused by her piety, a piety that is frequently expressed in the love language of medieval devotion or in the adoration of the humanity of Christ that is likewise central to late-medieval mysticism, especially female mysticism. She thus seeks to know if the voice she hears is a true voice, if it is God's voice. But those doubts, expressed in the secular language of later ages, have been shared by countless persons seeking to know if they can trust their consciences, their talents, or their passions. In each case, those private "feelings" will inevitably threaten an order that defines a world that must be left behind. It is perhaps in the works and lives of mystics and saints that we can find the beginnings of creative schism.

Earlier I suggested that, along with the works of Sir Thomas Malory and the four extant cycles of mystery plays, *The Book of Margery Kempe* can be used to define the fifteenth century. Both Malory and the authors of the plays employ figures of wholeness or unity as underlying rhetorical principles for their works. Beginning with the opening Creation pageants, where God defines himself in terms of inseparable unity, and continuing through pageants where figures like Lucifer, Cain, or Judas separate themselves from that unity, in their various ways each of the cycles elaborates upon the historic motion away from God that is countered by the offer of God to humankind through the Incarnation and Passion of Christ. The individual pageants in the drama cycles, though in many cases eloquently expressing the tensions and fissures submerged in late-medieval town-life, do so within an overall unity of design and theme that is centered—temporally and thematically—by the pageants enacting the Passion of Christ. Though the pageants certainly question the institutions, the civil and religious powers, out of which they emerge, in some cases quite sharply, their end effect does not scatter but regather the community around a renewed understanding of *corpus Christi*, the body of Christ.[9]

Writing during the chaos of the late fifteenth century, during the Wars of the Roses, Sir Thomas Malory does not feel his way toward a renewed understanding of community but laments a lost wholeness, a lament that is most powerfully expressed by King Arthur himself in *The Tale of the Sankgreal* as the knights prepare to depart the court for the series of individual quests that will finally and explicitly end all hopes of unity:

> 'Now,' seyde the king, 'I am sure at this quest of the Sangrail shall all ye of the Table Round depart, and never shall I see you again whole together; therefore I will see you all whole together in the meadow of Camelot to joust and to tourney, that after your death men may speak of it that such good knights were wholly together such a day.'[1]

9. See Sarah Beckwith, *Signifying God: Social Act and Symbolic Relation in York's Play of Corpus Christi* (forthcoming). For readings that emphasize the social valences of the vernacular *Corpus Christi* plays, see also Theresa Coletti, "Purity and Danger: The Paradox of Mary's Body and the En-gendering of the Infancy Narrative in the English Mystery Cycles," in L. Lomperis and S. Stanbury, eds., *Feminist Approaches to the Body in Medieval Literature* (Philadelphia: U of Pennsylvania P, 1993) 65–95; Gibson (1989); Mervyn James, "Ritual Drama and Social Body in the Late Medieval English Town," in *Society, Politics and Culture: Studies in Early Modern England* (Cambridge: Cambridge UP, 1989), chapter 1.

1. The quotation is from *Le Morte d'Arthur*, 2 vols., ed. Janet Cowan (New York: Penguin Books, 1969) 2:246. This edition is based on Caxton's printing of Malory's works. Vinaver's edition of Malory's works, based on the Winchester manuscript, contains the same passage. See *The Works of Sir Thomas Malory*, 3 vols., ed. Eugène Vinaver (Oxford: The Clarendon Press, 1967), vol. 1, Introduction, chapter 2, for remarks about the two versions of Malory's text—Caxton's and Malory's own. For an informed and lucid reading of the work, see Felicity Riddy, *Sir Thomas Malory* (New York: E. J. Brill, 1987), especially chapter 5.

The phrase "whole together" dominates the passage, and Arthur's grief over his divided fellowship reverberates through the final books. Later Arthur says, "'Wit you well my heart was never so heavy as it is now, and much more I am sorrier for my good knights' loss than for the loss of my fair queen; for queens I might have enow, but such a fellowship of good knights shall never be together in no company.'"[2]

Malory, like the authors of the drama cycles, speaks for the late-medieval citizen or reader, for whom unity was both a concrete and a theoretical good. For example, the Prologue to the Ordinances of the York Corpus Christi Guild, a guild devoted to the sacrament and open to any "worthy" person in the city of York, states, "From the beginning it must be evident that the unity of our confraternity is the unity of the Church, which, according to Augustine, is the unity of many sons in charity. . . . Unity is cause for rejoicing, and division by sin greatly to be lamented."[3] By identifying division, whereby what is one becomes many, with sin, the author effectively disallows any individual action that is not sanctioned by the whole. Kempe describes Margery as facing sharp rebukes from her pilgrim community when, on the way to Jerusalem, she refuses to eat, drink, and enjoy the idle talk of the group. Her clothing, habits, and devotedness are seen as divisive and, because she will not conform, she is "banned" from their "company."

However, Margery is described as living out triumphantly the shattering of community that Malory elegizes in his account of a world whose very inadequacies (adultery, treason, jealousy) rule out the possibility of creative change. Moreover, the Book seems to suggest that the quest for holiness (which is also the impetus for the search for the Grail) may well result in an identity that can no longer be fitted back into the community, or certainly not in the same way. The conflict that is a necessary crucible for identity-making must involve a break with a past life; otherwise, from where does self-consciousness come?[4] The conflicts Margery endures are all concerned with the concept of community that is outlined throughout the Book. It is a concept whose reality is perhaps most apparent in Margery herself, who, by internalizing it, has created even more anguish for herself. Her fears of public scorn, or her desire for public approval, as well as her unwillingness to give full credence to the voice of God in her, are those barriers to self-understanding and -acceptance that she must negotiate if she is to be as she wishes to be. The final sections of both the first and the second books of her history suggest just how successful she is. The end of the first book describes her as availing

---

2. Malory, ed. Cowan 2:473.
3. Paula Lozar, "The 'Prologue' to the Ordinances of the York Corpus Christi Guild," *Allegorica* 1 (1976): 94–113. The citation is on 107–08.
4. On this topic, see David Aers, "A Whisper in the Ear of Early Modernists; or, Reflections on Literary Critics Writing the 'History of the Subject,'" in *Culture and History 1350–1600. Essays on English Communities, Identities and Writing,* ed. David Aers (Detroit: Wayne State UP, 1992) 77–102.

herself of the freedom of the writer—she is more often to be found in her chamber with her "writer" (fictional or not!) than in church, *and*, during this period, she is more blessed with tears and other holy feelings than usual (see chapters 88, 89). Distinct from her community and filled with the tears that for her are creative grace ("But she thought there was no savor nor sweetness but when she might weep, for then she thought that she could pray"), Margery has redefined herself in terms of her vocation. Similarly, the end of the second book recounts her freedom from her confessor. In neither case does she abandon her community; she alters her relationship to it.

Finally, the last section of the *Book* records the prayer she "was known" to have said. In this prayer, which in the manuscript appears as a separate and third section of the *Book*, she recomposes the community—the body of Christ—by naming each of its members and praying for them. Rather than a prayer of exclusion, Margery's prayer is a prayer that includes archbishops, bishops, kings, lords, ladies, rich men, non-believers, lepers, friends, enemies, thieves, adulterers, common women, false tithers, and mischievous livers in one common plea for grace. Though she begins at the top—Pope, archbishops, bishops, king of England— the effect of the prayer as it increasingly mixes rich with poor and pure with impure is to democratize society by positioning all as needing God's mercy. The prayer itself is intercessory, so Margery offers it, as well as the grace she herself has known, for any and all. Distinct, and yet fully engaged, the *Book* ends with a picture of Margery kneeling before the Sacrament reciting this prayer that is then offered to the reader as a pattern for intercessory prayer and as a sign of the grace that abounds for all through her tumultuous life. The community broken is restored through Margery's prayer, and Margery's break with community is resolved through her act of charity. If Malory suggests that individual holiness and social wholeness cannot be mutually accommodated, Kempe seems to depict another ending for the solitary quest.

LYNN STALEY

My thanks go to Winthrop Wetherbee and Ralph Hanna for reading sections of the text and to Theresa Coletti for reading the Introduction, as well as a section of the text.

MEDIEVAL ENGLAND

SCOTLAND

NORTHUMBRIA

HADRIAN'S WALL

Tyne R.

CUMBRIAN MTS

THE PENNINES

ISLE OF MAN

IRISH SEA

Mt. Grace Priory

Ouse R.

York

Gawood

Beverly

Aire R.

Hessele

Hull

Mersey R.

Barton upon Humber

Lincoln

Trent R.

Yarmouth

Boston

The Wash

Leicester

King's Lynn

Norwich

CAMBRIAN MOUNTAINS

Severn R.

Thetford

EAST ANGLIA

Ely

Cambridge

Ouse R.

Bury St. Edmunds

CARDIGAN BAY

Hereford

ENGLAND

Ipswich

WALES

Gloucester

ESSEX

London

BRISTOL CHANNEL

Thames R.

Windsor

Bristol

Canterbury

KENT

W. ESSEX

SUSSEX

STRAIT OF DOVER

ISLE OF WIGHT

E N G L I S H   C H A N N E L

A Kempe Lexicon

These are words not translated in the text. Because they embrace multiple meanings, have meanings so idiosyncratic that to modernize them is to some extent impossible, or resonate throughout many late-medieval English texts, they are left in the original, as keys to Kempe's own use of her native tongue. For fuller definitions, see *The Middle English Dictionary* (Ann Arbor: U of Michigan P, 1956–), from which these are drawn.

bann (verb) curse, condemn, excommunicate, outlaw

buxom (adj) humble, gentle, obedient, submissive, gracious, helpful, kind, merciful

common (verb) to distribute in shares, deal out; to have something in common with, to conform; to associate with, act jointly; to have sexual intercourse with; to communicate with; to discuss; to administer or receive Holy Communion

compunction (noun) remorse, penitence

country (noun) both country or nation and used frequently to designate region within England

creature (noun) a created thing, used frequently in Lollard writing or in devotional prose to signify humankind's necessary relationship to God, the creator

dalliance (noun) [dally (verb)] polite, leisurely, intimate conversation; small talk; serious or spiritual conversation; amorous talk; sexual intercourse

draught (as noun) action of pulling; pulling in harnass; drawing of water; dragging of an offender through the streets; a motion or movement, course; a load for man or beast; a drink; a copy of a writing; a mystical ecstasy; (as verb) to draw, pull, attract, copy

ghost/ghostly (noun, adjective) spirit, spiritual

good/goods (noun) indicating both a spiritual and a worldly system of quantification or value

homely (as adj.) domestic; characteristic of a home; (as noun) members of one's household; (as adv.) intimately; privately; secretly; simply; without pretense

housel (verb) administer communion to

kind (as noun) having to do with nature or innate properties; (as adj.) kind; natural

meddle (verb) blend, mix; be concerned with, work on; to struggle with; to have sexual intercourse with; to include

meed (noun) gift, reward, compensation

mind (noun) mind, thought, consideration, memory

purchase (verb) common term used to define spiritual as well as economic exchange

show (verb) to see, to examine, to discover; to be visible; to exhibit; to make known; to teach; to disclose; to perform

stir (verb) to set in motion; to move; to agitate; to affect emotionally, or stir up someone's feelings; to be moved or excited; to trouble or frighten

treatise (noun) a formal discourse or written work expounding a topic

use (verb) use; have the use of; to employ (i.e., a treatment, someone else's words); to follow (advice, instruction); to associate with; to observe a custom; to possess, take control over; to take pleasure in, enjoy; to be accustomed

worship (noun) respect, honor, reverence—both worldly and spiritual

The Text of
THE BOOK OF MARGERY KEMPE

The base text for this translation of *The Book of Margery Kempe* is my own edition, originally published in 1996 in the TEAMS Middle English Texts series. It is here translated by permission of the Board of the Medieval Institute.

Book One

Here begins a short treatise and a comfortable for sinful wretches, wherein they may have great solace and comfort for themselves and understand the high and unspeakable mercy of our sovereign Savior Christ Jesus, whose name be worshiped and magnified without end, that now in our days to us, unworthy, deigns to exercise his nobleness and his goodness. All the works of our Savior are for our example and instruction, and what grace that he works in any creature is our profit if lack of charity be not our hindrance.

And therefore, by the leave of our merciful Lord Christ Jesus, to the magnifying of his holy name, Jesus, this little treatise shall treat somewhat piecemeal of his wonderful works, how mercifully, how benignly, and how charitably he moved and stirred a sinful caitif unto his love, which sinful caitif for many years was in will and in purpose through the stirring of the Holy Ghost to follow our Savior, making great promises of fastings with many other deeds of penance. And ever she was turned again aback in time of temptation, like the reed stalk which bows with every wind and never is stable unless no wind blows, until the time that our merciful Lord Christ Jesus, having pity and compassion for his handiwork and his creature, turned health into sickness, prosperity into adversity, worship into reproof, and love into hatred. Thus all these things turning upside down, this creature—who for many years had gone wayward and ever been unstable—was perfectly drawn and stirred to enter the way of high perfection, which perfect way Christ our Savior in his proper person exemplified. Steadily he trod it and dutifully he went before. Then this creature, of whom this treatise through the mercy of Jesus shall show in part the life, was touched by the hand of our Lord with great bodily sickness, where through she lost reason and her wits for a long time until our Lord by grace restored her again, as it shall more openly be showed afterward. Her worldly goods, which were plenteous and abundant on that day, in little while after were full barren and bare. Then was pomp and pride cast down and laid aside. Those who before had honored her, then full sharply reproved her; her kindred and those who had been friends were now her greatest enemies. Then she, considering this wonderful changing, seeking succor under the wings of her ghostly mother, Holy Church, went obediently to her ghostly father, accusing herself of her misdeeds, and afterwards did great bodily penance.

And in short time our merciful Lord visited this creature with plenteous tears of contrition day by day, in so much that some men said she might weep whenever she wanted and slandered the work of God. She was so used to being slandered and reproved, to being chided and rebuked by the world for the grace and virtue with which she was endued through the strength of the Holy Ghost that it was to her a manner of solace and comfort when she suffered any trouble for the love of God and for the grace that God wrought in her. For ever the more slander and reproof that she suffered, the more she increased in grace and in devotion of holy meditation, of high contemplation, and of wonderful speeches and dalliance which our Lord spoke and dallied to her soul, teaching her how she should be despised for his love, how she should have patience, setting all her trust, all her love, and all her affection in him only. She knew and understood many secret and privy things which should befall afterward, by the inspiration of the Holy Ghost. And often times, while she was kept with such holy speeches and dalliance, she should so weep and sob that many men were greatly awonder, for they knew full little how homely our Lord was in her soul. Neither could she herself ever tell the grace that she felt; it was so heavenly, so high above her reason and her bodily wits, and her body so feeble in the time of the presence of grace that she might never express it with her word as she felt it in her soul.

Then had this creature much dread for the illusions and deceits of her ghostly enemies. Then went she by the bidding of the Holy Ghost to many worshipful clerks, both archbishops and bishops, doctors and bachelors of divinity also. She spoke also with many anchorites[1] and showed them her manner of living and such grace as the Holy Ghost of his goodness wrought in her mind and in her soul, as her wit would serve her to express it. And they all that she showed her secrets unto said she was much bound to love our Lord for the grace that he showed unto her and counseled her to follow her movings and her stirrings and trustfully believe they were of the Holy Ghost and of no evil spirit. Some of these worthy and worshipful clerks took it, upon peril of their souls and as they would answer to God, that this creature was inspired with the Holy Ghost and bid her that she should have them write and make a book of her feelings and her revelations. Some offered to write her feelings with their own hands, and she would not consent in any way, for she was commanded in her soul that she should not write so soon.

And so it was twenty years and more from that time this creature had first feelings and revelations before she had any written. Afterward, when it pleased our Lord, he commanded her and charged her that she should have written her feelings and revelations and the form of her living so that his goodness might be known to all the world. Then had the creature no writer who would fulfill her desire nor give credence to her feelings until

1. Hermits.

the time that a man dwelling in Germany,[2] who was an Englishman in his
birth and had since wedded in Germany and had there both a wife and a
child, having good knowledge of this creature and of her desire, moved I
trust through the Holy Ghost, came into England with his wife and his
goods and dwelled with the foresaid creature until he had written as much
as she would tell him for the time that they were together. And, afterward,
he died. Then was there a priest for whom this creature had great affection, and so she commoned with him of this matter and brought him the
book to read. The book was so badly written that he could hardly understand it, for it was neither good English nor German, nor were the letters
shaped or formed as other letters are. Therefore the priest believed fully
there should never man read it, unless it were special grace. Nevertheless,
he promised her that, if he could read it, he would copy it out and write it
better with good will. Then was there so much evil spoken of this creature
and of her weeping that the priest dared not for cowardice speak with her
but seldom, nor would he write, as he had promised unto the foresaid
creature. And so he avoided and deferred the writing of this book well into
a fourth year, or else more, notwithstanding the creature spoke often to
him about it. At the last he said unto her that he could not read it, wherefore he would not do it. He would not, he said, put himself in peril thereof. Then he counseled her to go to a good man who had been much conversant with him who wrote first the book, supposing that he should best
be able to read the book, for he had once read letters of the other man's
writing that had been sent from beyond the sea while he was in Germany.
And so she went to that man, praying him to write this book and never to
reveal it as long as she lived, granting him a great sum of good for his labor.
And this good man wrote about a leaf, and yet it was little to the purpose,
for he could not well fare therewith—the book was so badly set and so
unreasonably written. Then the priest was vexed in his conscience, for he
had promised her to write this book, if he might come to the reading thereof, and he did not his part as well as he might have done, and prayed this
creature to get again the book if she kindly might. Then she got again the
book and brought it to the priest with right glad manner, praying him to
do his good will, and she would pray to God for him and purchase him
grace to read it and also to write it. The priest, trusting in her prayers,
began to read this book, and it was much easier, as he thought, than it was
the time before. And so he read it over before this creature, every word,
she sometimes helping where any difficulty was.

This book is not written in order, everything after the other as it was
done, but as the matter came to the creature in mind when it was written, for it was so long before it was written that she had forgotten the time
and the order when things befell. And therefore she had nothing written
but that she knew right well for very truth.

2. The term includes the Low Countries.

When the priest began first to write on this book, his eyes failed so that he might not see to make his letter, nor might he see to mend his pen. All other thing he might see well enough. He set a pair of spectacles on his nose, and then it was worse than it was before. He complained to the creature of his trouble. She said his enemy had envy at his good deed and would hinder him if he might, and she bade him do as well as God would give him grace and not leave off. When he came again to his book, he might see as well, he thought, as ever he did before, by daylight and by candlelight both. And because of this, when he had written a quire, he added a leaf onto it, and then wrote he this proem[3] to express more openly than does the next following, which was written before this one. Anno domini 1436.

A short treatise of a creature set in great pomp and pride of the world, who since was drawn to our Lord by great poverty, sickness, shames, and great reproofs in many divers countries[4] and places, of which tribulations some shall be showed afterward, not in order as they befell, but as the creature could have mind of them when it was written for it was twenty years and more from the time this creature had forsaken the world and diligently cleaved unto our Lord before this book was written, notwithstanding this creature had great counsel to have her tribulations and her feelings written, and a White Friar[5] freely offered to write if she wished. And she was warned in her spirit that she should not write so soon. And many years after, she was bidden in her spirit to write. And then it was written first by a man who could neither write good English nor German. So it was unable to be read except by special grace, for there was so much abuse and slander of this creature that few men would believe this creature. And so at the last, a priest was sorely moved to write this treatise, and he could not read it well for four years all together. And afterward, by the request of this creature and by the compulsion of his own conscience, he tried again to read it, and it was much easier than it was before. And so he began to write in the year of our Lord 1436, on the day next after Mary Magdalene[6] according to the information of this creature.

1. When this creature was twenty years of age or somewhat more, she was married to a worshipful burgess and was with child within a short time, as nature would. And, after she had conceived, she was labored with great attacks of illness until the child was born, and then, what for the labor she had in childing and for the sickness going before, she despaired of her life, thinking she might not live. And then she sent for her ghostly father, for she had a thing in conscience which she had never shown be-

---

3. Preface. "Quire": a collection of manuscript leaves.
4. In Middle English, *country* has the additional meaning of region.
5. Carmelite friar, a member of one of the four mendicant, or begging, orders.
6. The day of Mary Magdalene is July 22.

fore that time in all her life. For she was ever hindered by her enemy, the devil, evermore saying to her that, while she was in good health, she needed no confession but could do penance by herself alone,[7] and all should be forgiven, for God is merciful enough. And therefore this creature oftentimes did great penance in fasting on bread and water and other deeds of alms with devout prayers, except she would not show this sin in confession. And, when she was at any time sick or troubled, the devil said in her mind that she should be damned, for she was not shriven of that sin. Wherefore, after her child was born, she, not trusting her life, sent for her ghostly father, as was said before, in full will to be shriven[8] of all her lifetime as nearly as she could. And, when she came to the point to say that thing which she had so long concealed, her confessor was a little too hasty and began sharply to reprove her before she had fully said her intent, and so she would no more say for aught he might do.

And anon, for the dread she had of damnation on the one side and his sharp reproving on that other side, this creature went out of her mind and was wonderfully vexed and labored with spirits for half a year, eight weeks and some odd days. And in this time she saw, as she thought, devils open their mouths, all inflamed with burning flames of fire as if they should have swallowed her in, sometimes menacing her, sometimes threatening her, sometimes pulling her and hailing her both night and day during the foresaid time. And also the devils cried upon her with great threats and bade her that she should forsake her Christianity, her faith, and deny her God, his mother, and all the saints in heaven, her good works and all good virtues, her father, her mother, and all her friends. And so she did. She slandered her husband, her friends and her own self; she spoke many a reproving word and many a harsh word; she knew no virtue nor goodness; she desired all wickedness; just as the spirits tempted her to say and do, so she said and did. She would have killed herself many a time because of her stirrings and have been damned with them in hell. And as a witness thereof she bit her own hand so violently that it was seen all her life afterward. And also she tore the skin on her body against her heart grievously with her nails, for she had no other instruments, and worse she would have done, save she was bound and kept with strength both day and night so that she might not have her will.

And, when she had long been labored in these and many other temptations, so that men thought she should never have escaped nor lived, then on a time, as she lay alone and her keepers were away from her, our merciful Lord Christ Jesus, ever to be trusted, worshiped be his name, never forsaking his servant in time of need, appeared to his creature, who had forsaken him, in likeness of a man, most seemly, most beautiful, and

7. Auricular confession, or confessing to a priest, was central to the sacrament of penance, but some people, the Lollard followers of John Wyclif, who were seen as heretics, felt that the penitent needed no intermediary between the soul and God.
8. Confessed.

most amiable that ever might be seen with man's eye, clad in a mantle of purple silk, siting upon her bedside, looking upon her with so blessed a countenance that she was strengthened in all her spirits, said to her these words: "Daughter, why have you forsaken me, and I forsook never you?"

And anon, as soon as he had said these words, she saw verily how the air opened as bright as any lightning, and he rose up into the air, not right hastily and quickly, but fairly and easily so that she might well behold him in the air until it was closed again. And anon the creature was stabled in her wits and in her reason as well as ever she was before, and prayed her husband, as soon as he came to her, that she might have the keys of the buttery in order to take her meat and drink as she had done before. Her maidens and her keepers counseled him that he should deliver her no keys, for they said she would but give away such good as there was, for she knew not what she said, or so they thought. Nevertheless, her husband, ever having tenderness and compassion for her, commanded they should deliver to her the keys. And she took her meat and drink as her bodily strength would serve her and knew her friends and her household and all others who came to her to see how our Lord Jesus Christ had wrought his grace in her, so blessed may he be who ever is near in tribulation. When men think he is far from them, he is full near by his grace. Afterward, this creature did all other occupations that fell to her to do wisely and soberly enough, save she knew not verily the draught of our Lord.

2. And, when this creature was thus graciously come again to her mind, she thought she was bound to God and that she would be his servant. Nevertheless, she would not leave her pride nor her pompous array that she had used before that time, neither for her husband's nor for any other man's counsel. And yet she knew full well that men spoke much villainy of her, for she wore gold pipes on her head and her hoods with the tippets were dagged. Her cloaks also were dagged and laid with divers colors between the dags so that they should be more conspicuous to men's sight and she the more worshipped.[9]

And, when her husband would speak to her to leave her pride, she answered harshly and shortly and said that she was come of worthy kindred; he seemed never the man to have married her, for her father was sometime mayor of the town N.,[1] and since then he was an alderman of the high Guild of the Trinity in N.[2] And therefore she would save the worship of her kindred whatsoever any man said. She had full great envy of her neighbors, that they should be arrayed as well as she. All her desire was to be worshipped by the people. She would not beware of anyone's

9. The gold pipes are ornaments to a fashionable headdress. Again in the name of fashion, various parts of clothing were slashed and pointed (dagged) in arresting ways; sometimes colors were sewn in between the slashes.
1. Kempe uses N. as a sort of "wild card" designation.
2. The Guild of the Trinity was the most prestigious of the town of Lynn's parish fraternities.

chastising nor be content with the goods that God had sent her, as her husband was, but ever desired more and more.

And then, for pure covetousness and to maintain her pride, she began to brew and was one of the greatest brewers in the town N. for three or four years until she lost much good, for she had no experience of it.[3] For, though she had ever so good servants and cunning in brewing, yet it would never prove with them. For, when the ale was as fair standing under the barm[4] as any man might see, suddenly the barm would fall down so that all the ale was lost, every brewing after the other, so that her servants were ashamed and would not dwell with her. Then this creature thought how God had punished her before that time and she could not beware, and now again by the loss of her goods, and then she left off and brewed no more. And then she asked her husband mercy because she would not follow his counsel before, and she said that her pride and her sin were the causes of all her punishing, and she would amend where she had trespassed with a good will.

But yet she left not wholly the world, for now she thought of a new household occupation. She had a horse mill. She got herself two good horses and a man to grind men's corn, and thus she trusted to get her living. This provision endured not long, for in a short time afterward, on Corpus Christi Eve, befell this marvel.[5] This man was in good health of body and his two horses fat and in good condition and had drawn well in the mill before. Now he took one of the horses and put him in the mill as he had done before, and this horse would draw no draught in the mill for anything the man might do. The man was sorry and tried with all his wits how he should make this horse draw. Sometimes he led him by the head; sometimes he beat him, and sometimes he cherished him, and all availed not, for he would rather go backward than forward. Then this man set a sharp pair of spurs on his heels and rode on the horse's back in order to make him draw, and it was never the better. When this man saw it would be in no way, then he set up this horse again in the stable and gave him food, and he ate well and freshly. And then he took the other horse and put him in the mill. And just as his fellow did so did he, for he would not draw for anything that the man might do. And then this man forsook his service and would no longer abide with the foresaid creature.

Anon, as it was noised about the town of N. that neither man nor beast would do service to the said creature, then some said she was accursed; some said God took open vengeance upon her; some said one thing; and some said another. And some wise men, whose minds were more grounded in the love of our Lord, said it was the high mercy of our Lord Jesus Christ that had summoned and called her from the pride and van-

---

3. Brewing is one of the occupations associated with women.
4. The barm is the yeast formed on brewing liquors.
5. The feast of Corpus Christi was observed in England from 1318. It was celebrated on the Thursday after Trinity Sunday (in midsummer) and focused upon the Host, the body of Christ.

ity of the wretched world. And then this creature, seeing all these adversities coming on every side, thought they were the scourges of our Lord that would chastise her for her sin. Then she asked God mercy and forsook her pride, her covetousness, and the desire she had for the worships of the world, and did great bodily penance, and began to enter the way of everlasting life, as shall be said afterward.

3. On a night, as this creature lay in her bed with her husband, she heard a sound of melody so sweet and delectable, she thought, as if she had been in paradise. And therewith she started out of her bed and said, "Alas, that ever I did sin; it is full merry in heaven."

This melody was so sweet that it passed all the melody that ever might be heard in this world, without any comparison, and caused this creature when she heard any mirth or melody afterward to have full plenteous and abundant tears of high devotion with great sobbings and sighings after the bliss of heaven, not dreading the shames and the scorns of the wretched world. And ever after this draught she had in her mind the mirth and the melody that was in heaven, so much that she could not well restrain herself from the speaking thereof. For, where she was in any company, she would say oftentimes, "It is full merry in heaven." And they who knew her governance before that time and now heard her speak so much of the bliss of heaven said unto her, "Why speak you so of the mirth that is in heaven; you know it not, and you have not been there anymore than we," and were angry with her for she would not hear any speak of worldly things, as they did and as she did before.

And after this time she had never desire to common fleshly with her husband, for the debt of matrimony[6] was so abominable to her that she had rather, she thought, eat or drink the ooze, the muck in the channel, than to consent to any fleshly commoning, save only for obedience. And so she said to her husband, "I may not deny you my body, but the love of my heart and my affection is drawn from all earthly creatures and set only in God."

He would have his will, and she obeyed with great weeping and sorrowing because she might not live chaste. And oftentimes this creature lived chaste, counseled her husband to live chaste, and said that they oftentimes, she knew well, had displeased God by their inordinate love and the great delectation that they both had in using[7] one another, and now it was good that they should, by both their wills and the consent of them both, punish and chastise themselves willfully by abstaining from their lust of their bodies. Her husband said it was good to do so, but he might not yet; he should when God would.[8] And so he used her as he had done

---

6. Both partners in a marriage were officially described as owing one another the "debt" of matrimony, i.e., sexual relations, whereby children, one of the "goods" of marriage, were produced.
7. This is Kempe's term, and a common expression at the time; see the Lexicon.
8. I.e., when God wished it.

before; he would not spare. And ever she prayed to God that she might
live chaste, and three or four years after, when it pleased our Lord, he
made a vow of chastity, as shall be written after, by the leave of Jesus.

And also, after this creature heard this heavenly melody, she did great
bodily penance. She was shriven sometimes twice or three times a day,
and especially of that sin which she so long had concealed and covered,
as it is written in the beginning of the book. She gave herself to great fasting and to great waking. She rose at two or three o'clock and went to
church and was there in her prayers unto time of noon and also all the
afternoon. And then was she slandered and reproved by many people because she kept so straight a living. Then she got herself a hair cloth from
a kiln such as men use for drying malt and laid it in her kirtle[9] as subtly
and privily[1] as she might so that her husband should not spy it, nor did
he; and yet she lay by him every night in his bed, and wore the hair cloth
every day, and bore children during that time.

Then she had three years of great labor with temptations which she
bore as meekly as she could, thanking our Lord for all his gifts, and was as
merry when she was reproved, scorned, or mocked for our Lord's love,
and much more merry than she was before in the worship of the world.
For she knew right well she had sinned greatly against God and was worthy of more shame and sorrow than any man could do to her, and the
despite of the world was the right way toward heaven, since Christ himself
chose that way. All his apostles, martyrs, confessors, and virgins, and all
who ever come to heaven, passed by the way of tribulation, and she
desired nothing so much as heaven. Then was she glad in her conscience
when she believed that she was entering the way that would lead her to
the place that she most desired. And this creature had contrition and great
compunction[2] with plenteous tears and many violent sobbings for her sins
and for her unkindness against her maker. She recalled the unkindnesses
of her childhood as our Lord would bring them to her memory full many
a time. And then, she beholding her own wickedness, she might but sorrow and weep and ever pray for mercy and forgiveness. Her weeping was
so plenteous and so continuing that many people thought that she might
weep and leave off when she would, and therefore many men said she was
a false hypocrite and wept for the world for succor and for worldly good.
And then full many forsook her who had loved her before while she was
in the world and would not know her, and ever she thanked God for all,
nothing desiring but mercy and the forgiveness of sin.

4. The first two years when this creature was thus drawn to our Lord,
as for any temptations, she had great quiet of spirit. She might well endure fasting; it grieved her not. She hated the joys of the world. She felt

9. Woman's gown.
1. Secretly.
2. Remorse, penitence.

no rebellion in her flesh. She was strong, as she thought, so that she dreaded no devil in hell, for she did such great bodily penance. She thought that she loved God more than he her. She was smitten with the deadly wound of vain glory and felt it not, for she desired many times that the crucifix should loose his hands from the cross and embrace her in token of love.

Our merciful Lord Christ Jesus, seeing this creature's presumption, sent her, as is written before, three years of great temptation, of which one of the hardest I purpose to write for an example for those who come after, so that they should not trust in their own selves, nor have joy in themselves as this creature had; for without doubt, our ghostly enemy sleeps not, but he full busily searches our complexions and our dispositions, and wherever he finds us most frail, there, by our Lord's sufferance, he lays his snare, which may no man escape by his own power. And so he laid before this creature the snare of lechery when she thought that all fleshly lust had wholly been quenched in her. And for so long she was tempted with the sin of lechery for ought that she could do. And yet she was often shriven; she wore the hair cloth and did great bodily penance and wept many a bitter tear and prayed full often to our Lord that he would preserve her and keep her so she would not fall into temptation, for she thought she had rather be dead than consent thereto. And in all this time she had no lust to common with her husband, but it was very painful and horrible to her.

In the second year of her temptations it befell so that a man whom she loved well said unto her on Saint Margaret's Eve[3] before evensong that, despite anything, he would lie by her and have his lust of his body, and she should not withstand him, for, if he might not have his will that time, he said, he should else have it another time, she could not choose.

And he did it in order to prove her, what she would do; but she thought that he had meant it in full earnest at that time and said but little about it. So they parted asunder for then and went both to hear evensong, for their church was Saint Margaret's. This woman was so labored with the man's words that she might not hear her evensong,[4] nor say her Pater Noster,[5] or think any other good thought, but was more labored than ever she was before. The devil put in her mind that God had forsaken her, and else should she not have been so tempted. She believed the devil's persuasions and began to consent because she could think no good thought. Therefore thought she that God had forsaken her. And, when evensong was done, she went to the man before said so that he should have his lust,

---

3. St. Margaret's feast day was July 20. She was the virgin martyr tortured and killed for her espousal of Christian virginity by Olybrius, ruler of Antioch. The church of St. Margaret in Lynn, where Margery worshipped, was one of the town's main churches; it was attached to a priory of Benedictine monks. For views of the church, see Raguin and Stanbury, *Mapping Margery Kempe*.
4. The daily service of evening prayer.
5. "Our Father," the Lord's Prayer.

as she thought that he had desired, but he made such simulation that she could not know his intent, and so they parted asunder for that night.

This creature was so labored and vexed all that night that she knew never what she might do. She lay by her husband, and, whether to commmon with him, it was so abominable unto her that she might not endure it, and yet it was lawful unto her at a lawful time if she had wanted. But ever she was labored with the other man, whether to sin with him inasmuch he had spoken to her. At the last, through the inopportunity of temptation and the lack of discretion, she was overcome, and consented in her mind, and went to the man to learn if he would then consent to her. And he said he wouldn't for all the good in this world; he had rather been hewn as small as meat for the pot. She went away all shamed and confused within herself, seeing his stableness and her own unstableness.

Then thought she of the grace that God had given her before, how she had two years of great quiet of soul, repentance of her sin with many bitter tears of compunction, and a perfect will never to turn again to her sin, but rather, she thought, to be dead. And now she saw how she had consented in her will to do sin. Then she fell half in despair. She thought she would have been in hell for the sorrow that she had. She thought she was worthy of no mercy, for her consenting was so willfully done, nor never worthy to do him service because she was so false unto him. Nevertheless she was shriven many times and often, and did her penance, whatsoever her confessor would enjoin her to do, and was governed after the rules of the Church. That grace God gave this creature, blessed may he be, but he withdrew not her temptation but rather increased it, as she thought.

And therefore she knew that he had forsaken her and dared not trust to his mercy, but was labored with horrible temptations of lechery and of despair nearly all the next year following, save our Lord of his mercy, as she said herself, gave her each day for the most part two hours of compunction for her sins with many bitter tears. And afterward she was labored with temptations of despair as she was before and was as far from feeling grace as those who had never felt any. And that might she not bear, and therefore always she despaired. Save for the time that she felt grace, her labors were so wonderful that she could hardly fare with them, but ever mourned and sorrowed as though God had forsaken her.

5. Then on a Friday before Christmas Day, as this creature, kneeling in a chapel of Saint John[6] within a church of Saint Margaret in N., wept wonder sore, asking mercy and forgiveness for her sins and her trespasses, our merciful Lord Christ Jesus, blessed may he be, ravished her spirit and said unto her: "Daughter, why weep you so sorely? I am come to you, Jesus Christ, who died on the cross, suffering bitter pains and passions for

---

6. For a picture of St. Margaret's church, including the location of this chapel, see Raguin and Stanbury, *Mapping Margery Kempe*.

you. I, the same God, forgive you your sins to the utterest point. And you shall never come into hell nor into purgatory, but, when you shall pass out of this world, within the twinkling of an eye you shall have the bliss of heaven, for I am the same God who has brought your sins to your mind and made you to be shriven thereof. And I grant you contrition to your life's end. Therefore I bid you and command you, boldly call me Jesus, your love, for I am your love and shall be your love without end. And, daughter, you have a hair cloth upon your back. I want you to take it away, and I shall give you a hair cloth in your heart that shall please me much better than all the hair cloths in the world. Also, my worthy daughter, you must forsake what you love best in this world, and that is eating of meat. And instead of that flesh you shall eat my flesh and my blood, that is the very body of Christ in the sacrament of the altar.[7] This is my will, daughter, that you receive my body every Sunday,[8] and I shall flow so much grace into you that all the world shall marvel thereof. You shall be eaten and gnawed by the people of the world as any rat gnaws the stockfish.[9] Dread you not, daughter, for you shall have the victory of all your enemies. I shall give you grace enough to answer every clerk in the love of God. I swear to you by my majesty that I shall never forsake you in well nor in woe. I shall help you and keep you so that there shall never devil in hell part you from me, nor angel in heaven, nor man on earth, for devils in hell may not, angels in heaven will not, and man on earth shall not. And daughter, I want you to leave off your bidding of many beads[1] and think such thoughts as I will put into your mind. I shall give you leave to pray until six of the clock to say what you wish. Then shall you lie still and speak to me by thought, and I shall give to you high meditation and very contemplation. And I bid you go to the anchorite at the Friar Preachers,[2] and show him my secrets and my counsels which I show to you, and work after his counsel, for my spirit shall speak in him to you."

Then this creature went forth to the anchorite, as she was commanded, and showed him the revelations, such as were showed to her. Then the anchorite, with great reverence and weeping, thanking God, said, "Daughter, you suck even on Christ's breast,[3] and you have an earnest penny[4] of heaven. I charge you, receive such thoughts when God will give them as meekly and as devoutly as you can, and come to me and tell me what they are, and I shall, with the leave of our Lord Jesus Christ, tell you whether they are of the Holy Ghost or else of your enemy the devil."

---

7. The Eucharist.
8. It was unusual in the Middle Ages to receive Communion so often; once a year was mandated.
9. Salted and dried fish.
1. Saying many prayers.
2. Dominican priory at Lynn.
3. Late-medieval devotional literature frequently described Jesus using feminine, or nutritive, language. See Bynum [1987], 270–76.
4. Pledge penny.

6. Another day this creature gave herself to meditation, as she was bidden before, and she lay still, not knowing what she might best think. Then she said to our Lord Jesus Christ, "Jesus, what shall I think?" Our Lord Jesus answered to her mind, "Daughter, think on my mother, for she is the cause of all the grace that you have."

And then anon she saw Saint Anne[5] great with child, and then she prayed Saint Anne if she could be her maiden and her servant. And anon our Lady was born, and then she busied herself to take the child to herself and keep it until it was twelve years of age with good food and drink, with fair white clothes and white kerchiefs. And then she said to the blessed child, "Lady, you shall be the mother of God." The blessed child answered and said, "I would I were worthy to be the handmaiden of her who shall conceive the son of God." The creature said, "I pray you, Lady, if that grace fall on you, forsake not my service."

The blissful child passed away for a certain time, the creature being still in contemplation, and later came again and said, "Daughter, now am I become the mother of God."

And then the creature fell down on her knees with great reverence and great weeping and said, "I am not worthy, Lady, to do you service." "Yes, daughter," she said, "follow me, your service pleases me well."

Then she went forth with our Lady and with Joseph, bearing with her a vessel of sweetened and spiced wine. Then they went forth to Elizabeth, Saint John the Baptist's mother, and, when they met together, both of them worshipped each other, and so they dwelled together with great grace and gladness twelve weeks.[6]

And then Saint John was born, and our Lady took him up from the earth with all manner of reverence and gave him to his mother, saying of him that he would be a holy man, and blessed him. Afterward they took their leave of one another with compassionate tears. And then the creature fell down on her knees to Saint Elizabeth and asked her if she would pray for her to our Lady so that she might give her service and pleasure. "Daughter, it seems to me," said Elizabeth, "you do right well your duty."

And then went the creature forth with our Lady to Bethlehem and purchased her lodging every night with great reverence, and our Lady was received with a glad manner. Also she begged for our Lady fair white clothes and kerchiefs to swaddle her son when he was born, and, when Jesus was born, she prepared bedding for our Lady to lie in with her blessed son. And afterward she begged food for our Lady and her blessed child. Afterward she swaddled him with bitter tears of compassion, having mind of the sharp death that he should suffer for the love of sinful men, saying to him, "Lord, I shall fare fair with you; I shall not bind you sorely.[7] I pray you be not displeased with me."

---

5. St. Anne is the mother of the Virgin Mary.
6. For the Gospel account of this visit, see Luke 1.39–56.
7. Swaddle him tightly.

7. And after, on the Twelfth Day,[8] when the three kings came with their gifts and worshipped our Lord Jesus Christ, being in his mother's lap, this creature, our Lady's handmaiden, beholding all the process by contemplation, wept wonder sore. And, when she saw that they would take their leave to go home again into their country, she might not suffer that they should go from the presence of our Lord; and, for wonder that they would go away, she cried wonder sore.

And soon after, came an angel and bade our Lady and Joseph go from the country of Bethlehem into Egypt. Then went this creature forth with our Lady, day by day purveying her lodging with great reverence, with many sweet thoughts and high meditations and also high contemplations, sometimes enduring in weeping two hours and often longer in the mind of our Lord's Passion, without ceasing, sometimes for her own sin, sometimes for the sins of the people, sometimes for the souls in purgatory, sometimes for those who are in poverty or in any trouble, for she desired to comfort them all. Sometimes she wept full plenteously and full violently for desire of the bliss of heaven and because she was so long deferred therefrom. Then this creature coveted greatly to be delivered out of this wretched world. Our Lord Jesus Christ said to her mind that she should abide and languish in love. "For I have ordained you to kneel before the Trinity to pray for all the world, for many hundred thousand souls shall be saved by your prayers. And therefore, daughter, ask what you wish, and I shall grant you your asking." This creature said, "Lord, I ask mercy and preservation from everlasting damnation for me and for all the world; chastise us here however you wish and in purgatory, and keep us from damnation for your high mercy.

8. Another time, as this creature lay in her prayer, the Mother of Mercy, appearing to her, said, "Ah, daughter, blessed may you be, your seat is made in heaven before my son's knee, and that of whomever you will have with you."

Then asked her blessed son, "Daughter, whom will you have as your fellow with you?"

"My most worthy Lord, I ask for my ghostly father Master N."

"Why do you ask more for him than for your own father or for your husband?"

"For I may never requite him the goodness that he has done for me and the gracious labors that he has had about me in the hearing of my confession."

"I grant you your desire for him, and yet shall your father be saved and your husband also, and all your children."

Then this creature said, "Lord, since you have forgiven me my sin, I

---

8. The Feast of the Epiphany, twelve days after Christmas, which celebrates the coming of the Wise Men.

make you my executor of all the good works that you work in me. In praying, in thinking, in weeping, in pilgrimage going, in fasting, or in speaking any good word, it is fully my will that you give Master N. half to the increase of his merit as if he did them himself. And the other half, Lord, spread on your friends and your enemies and on my friends and my enemies, for I will have only you for my reward."

"Daughter, I shall be a true executor to you and fulfill all you wish, and for your great charity that you have to comfort your fellow Christians you shall have double reward in heaven."

9. Another time, as this creature prayed to God that she might live chaste by the leave of her husband, Christ said to her mind, "You must fast on Friday both from food and from drink, and you shall have your desire before Whitsunday, for I shall suddenly slay your husband."

Then on the Wednesday in Easter week, after her husband would have had knowledge of her as he was wont before, and when he came near her, she said, "Jesus, help me," and he had no power to touch her at that time in that way, nor never after with any fleshly knowing.

It befell on a Friday before Whitsunday Eve, as this creature was in a church of Saint Margaret at N., hearing her mass, she heard a great noise and a dreadful. She was sorely astonished, sorely dreading the voice of the people, who said God would take vengeance upon her. She kneeled upon her knees, holding down her head, her book in her hand, praying our Lord Christ Jesus for grace and for mercy. Suddenly there fell down from the highest part of the church vault, from under the foot of the rafter, on her head and on her back, a stone which weighed three pounds and a short end of a beam weighing six pounds, so that she thought her back broke asunder, and she fared as if she had been dead for a little while. Soon after she cried, "Jesus, mercy," and anon her pain was gone.

A good man who was called John of Wyreham, seeing this wonderful event and supposing that she was greatly distressed, came and pulled her by the sleeve and said, "Dame, how fare you?"

The creature, all whole and sound, thanked him for his manner and for his charity, much marveling and greatly wondering that she felt no pain and had felt so much a little before. Nor twelve weeks after she felt any pain. Then the spirit of God said to her soul, "Hold this for a great miracle, and, if the people will not believe this, I shall work many more."

A worshipful doctor of divinity who was called Master Alan, a White Friar,[1] hearing of this wonderful work, inquired of this creature all the form of this process. He, desiring the work of God to be magnified, got the same stone that fell upon her back and weighed it, and afterward he

---

9. Whitsunday is the Feast of the Pentecost, celebrating the gift of the Holy Ghost and thus the creation of the Church; it falls seven Sundays after Easter.
1. The Carmelite friar, Alan of Lynn.

got the beam's end that fell upon her head, which one of the wardens of the church had laid in the fire to burn it. And this worshipful doctor said it was a great miracle and our Lord was highly to be magnified for the preserving of this creature against the malice of her enemy, and told it to many people, and many people greatly magnified God in this creature. And also many people would not believe it, but rather believed it was a token of wrath and vengeance than they would believe it was any token of mercy or favor.

10. Soon after, this creature was moved in her soul to go visit certain places for ghostly health, inasmuch as she was under authority,[2] and could not go without the consent of her husband. She asked her husband to grant her leave, and, he, fully trusting it was the will of God, soon consenting, they went together to such places as she was moved. And then our Lord Christ Jesus said to her, "My servants desire greatly to see you."

Then was she welcomed and made much of in divers places. Wherefore she had great dread of vainglory and was much afraid. Our merciful Lord Christ Jesus, worshipped be his name, said to her, "Dread you not, daughter, I shall take vainglory from you. For those who worship you, they worship me; those who despise you, they despise me, and I shall chastise them therefore. I am in you, and you in me. And those who hear you, they hear the voice of God. Daughter, there is no sinful man on earth living, who, if he will forsake his sin and work after your counsel, such grace as you promise him, I will confirm for your love."

Then she and her husband went forth to York and to other divers places.

11. It befell upon a Friday on Midsummer Eve in right hot weather, as this creature was coming from York bearing a bottle with beer in her hand and her husband a loaf in his bosom, he asked his wife this question, "Margery, if there came a man with a sword and would smite off my head unless I should common naturally with you as I have done before, tell me the truth from your conscience—for you say you will not lie—whether would you suffer my head to be smote off or else suffer me to meddle with you again, as I did at one time?"

"Alas, sir," she said, "why move you this matter, and have we been chaste these eight weeks?"

"For I will know the truth of your heart."

And then she said with great sorrow, "Forsooth I had rather see you be slain than we should turn again to our uncleanness."

And he said again, "You are no good wife."

And then she asked her husband what was the cause that he had not

---

2. The Middle English term is "cured," meaning that she was under the authority of someone else, in this case, since she is married, her husband.

meddled with her eight weeks before, since she lay with him every night in his bed. And he said he was so made afraid when he would have touched her that he dared do no more.

"Now, good sir, amend yourself and ask God mercy, for I told you nearly three years since that you should be slain suddenly, and now is this the third year, and yet I hope I shall have my desire. Good sir, I pray you grant me what I shall ask, and I shall pray for you that you shall be saved through the mercy of our Lord Jesus Christ, and you shall have more reward in heaven than if you wore a hair cloth or a jacket of mail. I pray you, suffer me to make a vow of chastity in whatever bishop's hand that God will."

"No," he said, "that will I not grant you, for now may I use you without deadly sin and then might I not so."[3]

Then she said again, "If it be the will of the Holy Ghost to fulfill what I have said, I pray God you may consent thereto; and, if it be not the will of the Holy Ghost, I pray God you never consent thereto."

Then went they forth toward Bridlington in right hot weather, the aforesaid creature having great sorrow and great dread for her chastity. And, as they came by a cross, her husband set himself down under the cross, calling his wife unto him and saying these words unto her, "Margery, grant me my desire, and I shall grant you your desire. My first desire is that we shall lie still together in one bed as we have done before; the second, that you shall pay my debts before you go to Jerusalem; and the third, that you shall eat and drink with me on Fridays as you were wont to do."

"No, sir," she said, "to break the Friday I will never grant you while I live."

"Well," he said, "then shall I meddle you again."

She prayed him that he would give her leave to make her prayers, and he granted it well. Then she kneeled down beside a cross in the field and prayed in this manner with great abundance of tears, "Lord God, you know all things; you know what sorrow I have had to be chaste in my body to you all these three years, and now might I have my wish, and I dare not for love of you. For, if I would break that manner of fasting which you commanded me, to keep the Friday without food or drink, I should now have my desire. But, blessed Lord, you know I will not go against your will, and great now is my sorrow unless I find comfort in you. Now, blessed Jesus, make your will known to me, unworthy, so that I may follow thereafter and fulfill it with all my might."

And then our Lord Jesus Christ with great sweetness spoke to this creature, commanding her to go again to her husband and pray him to grant her what she desired. "And he shall have what he desires. For, my worthy daughter, this was the cause that I bade you to fast, for you should the

---

3. A vow of married chastity would sacramentally eliminate sexual union with marriage.

sooner obtain and get your desire, and now it is granted you. I wish no longer for you to fast, therefore I bid you in the name of Jesus eat and drink as your husband does."

Then this creature thanked our Lord Jesus Christ for his grace and his goodness, then rose up and went to her husband, saying unto him, "Sir, if it pleases you, you shall grant me my desire, and you shall have your desire. Grant me that you shall not come in my bed, and I grant you to requite your debts before I go to Jerusalem. And make my body free to God so that you never challenge me by asking the debt of matrimony after this day while you live, and I shall eat and drink on the Friday at your bidding."

Then said her husband again to her, "As free may your body be to God as it has been to me."

This creature thanked God greatly, rejoicing that she had her desire, praying her husband that they should say three Our Father's in the worship of the Trinity for the great grace that he had granted them. And so they did, kneeling under a cross, and afterward they ate and drank together in great gladness of spirit. This was on a Friday on Midsummer Eve. Then went they forth toward Bridlington and also to many other countries and spoke with God's servants, both anchorites and recluses and many other of our Lord's lovers, with many worthy clerks, doctors of divinity, and bachelors also in many different places. And this creature to divers of them showed her feelings and her contemplations, as she was commanded to do, to learn if any deceit were in her feelings.

12. This creature was sent by our Lord to divers places of religion, and among them she came to a place of monks where she was right welcome for our Lord's love, save there was a monk who bore great office in that place who despised her and set her at naught. Nevertheless she was set at table with the abbot, and many times during the meal she said many good words as God would put them in her mind, the same monk who had so despised her being present, and many others, to hear what she would say. And through her dalliance his affection began greatly to incline toward her and he began to have great savor in her words. So that afterward the aforesaid monk came to her and said, she being in church and he also at that time, "Damsel, I hear said that God speaks unto you. I pray you tell me whether I shall be saved or not and in what sins I have most displeased God, for I will not believe you unless you can tell me my sin."

The creature said to the monk, "Go to your Mass, and if I may weep for you, I hope to have grace for you."

He followed her counsel and went to his mass. She wept wonderfully for his sins. When Mass was ended, the creature said to our Lord Christ Jesus, "Blessed Lord, what answer shall I give to this man?"

"My worthy daughter, say in the name of Jesus that he has sinned in lechery, in despair, and in the keeping of worldly goods."[4]

"A, gracious Lord, this is hard for me to say. He shall cause me much shame if I tell him any lie."

"Dread you not, but speak boldly in my name, in the name of Jesus, for these are not lies."

And then she said again to our Lord Jesus Christ, "Good Lord, shall he be saved?"

"Yes," said our Lord Jesus, "if he will forsake his sin and work after your counsel. Charge him that he forsake his sin and be shriven thereof and also forsake the outside duties that he has."

Then came the monk again, "Margery, tell me my sins."

She said, "I pray you, sir, ask not thereafter, for I am surety for your soul. You shall be saved if you will work after my counsel."

"Forsooth, I will not believe you unless you tell me my sin."

"Sir, I understand that you have sinned in lechery, in despair, and in the keeping of worldly good."

Then stood the monk still, somewhat abashed, and afterward he said, "Whether have I sinned—with wives or with single women?"

"Sir, with wives."

Then said he, "Shall I be saved?"

"Yes, sir, if you will work after my counsel. Sorrow for your sin, and I shall help you to sorrow; be shriven thereof and forsake it voluntarily. Leave the outside duties that you have, and God shall give you grace because of my love."

The monk took her by the hand and led her into a fair building, made her a great dinner, and afterward gave her gold to pray for him. And so she took her leave at that time. Another time when the creature came again to the same place, the aforesaid monk had forsaken his duties on her counsel, and was turned from his sin, and was made sub-prior of the place, a well governed man and well disposed, thanked be God, and made this creature great comfort and highly blessed God that ever he saw her.

13. On a time, as this creature was at Canterbury in the church among the monks, she was greatly despised and reproved because she wept so hard, both by the monks and the priests and by secular men, nearly all day, both morning and afternoon, also in so much that her husband went away from her as if he had not known her and left her alone among them, choose her as she could, for other comfort had she none from him on that day. So an old monk, who had been treasurer with the Queen while he was in secular clothing, a rich man, and greatly feared by many people, took her by the hand, saying unto her, "What can you say of God?"[5]

---

4. These are the three classic vices of lust, pride (of which despair is a variety), and avarice.
5. Perhaps a reference to John Kynton, chancellor of Queen Joanna, wife of Henry IV.

"Sir," she said, "I will both speak of him and hear of him," telling the monk a story of scripture.

The monk said, "I would you were enclosed in a house of stone so no man could speak with you."

"A, sir," she said, "you should maintain God's servants, and you are the first who holds against them. Our Lord amend you."

Then a young monk said to this creature, "Either you have the Holy Ghost or else you have a devil within you, for what you speak here to us, it is Holy Writ, and that have you not of yourself."

Then said this creature, "I pray you, sir, give me leave to tell you a tale."

Then the people said to the monk, "Let her say what she will."

And then she said, "There was once a man who had sinned greatly against God, and, when he was shriven, his confessor enjoined him as part of penance that he should for one year hire men to chide him and reprove him for his sins, and he should give them silver for their labor. And on a day he came among many great men as now are here, God save you all, and stood among them as I do now among you, despising him as you do me, the man laughing or smiling and having good game at their words. The greatest master of them said to the man, 'Why do laugh you, wretch, since you are greatly despised?' 'A, sir, I have a great cause to laugh, for I have many days put silver out of my purse and hired men to chide me for the remission of my sin, and this day I may keep my silver in my purse. I thank you all.' Right so I say to you, worshipful sirs, while I was at home in my own country day by day with great weeping and mourning, I sorrowed because I had no shame, scorn, and despite as I was worthy. I thank you all, sirs, highly, for what in the morning and the afternoon I have had reasonably this day, blessed be God thereof."

Then she went out of the monastery, they following and crying upon her, "You shall be burnt, false Lollard.[6] There is a cartful of thorns ready for you and a tun,[7] to burn you with."

And the creature stood without the gates at Canterbury, for it was in the evening, many people wondering on her. Then said the people, "Take and burn her."

And the creature stood still, trembling and quaking full sorely in her flesh, without any earthly comfort, and knew not where her husband was gone. Then prayed she in her heart to our Lord, thinking in this manner, "Hither came I, Lord, for your love. Blessed Lord, help me and have mercy on me."

And anon, after she had made her prayers in her heart to our Lord,

---

6. Lollard, a follower of the beliefs of John Wyclif, the late-fourteenth-century theologian and preacher whose ideas were ruled heretical. He advocated purifying the Church of its ties to secular power and wealth and of its reliance upon the carnal world of images and saints. He also argued against transubstantiation and against the spiritual authority vested in worldly priests.
7. A large barrel.

there came two fair young men and said to her, "Damsel, are you neither heretic nor Lollard?"

And she said, "No, sirs, I am neither heretic nor Lollard."

Then they asked her where was her inn. She said she knew never in what street, nevertheless it should be at a German man's house.

Then these two young men brought her home to her hostel and made her great comfort, praying her to pray for them, and there found she her husband.

And many people in N. had said evil of her while she was out and slandered her in many things that she must have done while she was in that country. Then after this she was in great rest of soul a great while and had high contemplation day by day and many holy speeches and dalliance from our Lord Jesus Christ both morning and afternoon, with many sweet tears of high devotion so plenteously and continually that it was a marvel her eyes endured or her heart might last so that it was not consumed with the ardor of love, which was kindled by the holy dalliance from our Lord when he said to her many times, "Worthy daughter, love me with all your heart, for I love you with all my heart and with all the might of my Godhead, for you were a chosen soul without beginning in my sight and a pillar of Holy Church. My merciful eyes are ever upon you. It would be impossible for you to suffer the scorns and despites that you shall have were not my grace alone supporting you."

14. Then this creature thought it was full merry to be reproved for God's love. It was to her great solace and comfort when she was chided and scolded for the love of Jesus for reproving of sin, for speaking of virtue, for commoning in scripture, which she had learned from sermons and from commoning with clerks. She imagined to herself what death she might die for Christ's sake. She thought she would have been slain for God's love, but dreaded the point of death, and therefore she imagined for herself the softest death, as she thought, for dread of her lack of endurance—that was to be bound by her head and feet to a stock and her head to be smote off with a sharp axe for God's love.

Then said our Lord in her mind, "I thank you, daughter, what you would do for my love, for, as often as you think so, you shall have the same reward in heaven as though you suffered the same death. And yet shall no man slay you, nor fire burn you, nor water drench you, nor wind harm you; for I may not forget you, how you are written in my hands and my feet. It pleases me well the pains that I have suffered for you. I shall never be angry with you, but I shall love you without end. Though all the world be against you, dread you not, for they can have no knowledge of you. I swear to your mind, if it were possible for me to suffer pain again as I have done before, I would rather suffer as much pain as ever I did for your soul alone rather than you should part from me without end. And therefore, daughter, just as you see the priest take the child at the font stone and dip it in the water and wash it from original sin, just so shall I wash you in my precious blood from all your sin. And, though I withdraw sometimes the feeling of grace from you, either of speech or of weeping, dread you not thereof, for I am a hidden God in you so that you should have no vainglory and so that you should know well you may not have tears nor such dalliance but when God will send them to you, for they are the free gifts of God without your merit, and he may give them to whomever he will and do you no wrong. And therefore take them meekly and thankfully when I will send them, and suffer patiently when I withdraw them, and seek busily until you may get them, for tears of compunction, devotion, and compassion are the highest and surest gifts that I give on earth. And what should I do more for you unless I took your soul out of your body and put it in heaven, and that will I not yet.

"Nevertheless wheresoever God is, heaven is, and God is in your soul, and many an angel is about your soul, to keep it both night and day. For, when you go to church, I go with you. When you sit at your meal, I sit with you. When you go to your bed, I go with you. And when you go out of town, I go with you. Daughter, there was never a child so buxom to the father as I will be to you, to help you and keep you. I fare sometimes with my grace to you as I do with the sun. Sometimes you know well the sun shines all abroad so that many men may see it, and sometimes it is hidden under a cloud so that men may not see it, and yet is the sun never the less in his heat nor in his brightness. And right so fare I by you and by my chosen souls. Though it be so that you weep not always at your wish, my grace is nevertheless in you. Therefore I prove that you are a very daughter to me and a mother also, a sister, a wife, and a spouse, witnessing the gospel where our Lord said to his disciples, 'He that does the will of my Father in heaven, he is both mother, brother, and sister unto me.'[8] When you study to please me, then are you a true daughter. When you weep and mourn for my pain and for my passion, then are you a true mother to have compassion of her child. When you weep for other men's sins and for adversities, then are you a true sister. And, when you sorrow because you are so long from the bliss of heaven, then are you a true spouse and a wife, for it is fitting for a wife to be with her husband and to have no very joy until she comes to his presence."

15. This creature, when our Lord had forgiven her her sin as is written before, had a desire to see those places where he was born and where he suffered his passion and where he died, along with other holy places where he was in his life and also after his resurrection. While she was in these desires, our Lord bade her in her mind two years before she went that she should go to Rome, to Jerusalem, and to Saint James,[9] for she

---

8. Mark 3.35.
9. St. James of Compostella in Spain.

would fain have gone, but she had no good to go with. And then she said to our Lord, "Where shall I have good to go with to these holy places?"

Our Lord said again to her, "I shall send you friends enough in divers countries in England to help you. And, daughter, I shall go with you in every country and ordain for you; I shall lead you thither and bring you again in safety, and no Englishman shall die in the ship that you are in. I shall keep you from all wicked men's power. And, daughter, I say to you I will that you wear clothes of white[1] and no other color, for you shall be arrayed after my will."

"A, dear Lord, if I go arrayed in another manner than other chaste women do, I dread that the people will slander me. They will say I am a hypocrite and wonder upon me."

"Yes, daughter, the more wondering that you have for my love, the more you please me."

Then this creature dared not otherwise do than she was commanded in her soul. And so she went forth with her husband into the country, for he was ever a good man and an easy man to her. Though he sometimes for vain dread let her alone for a time, yet he resorted evermore again to her, and had compassion for her, and spoke for her as much as he dared for dread of the people. But all others who went with her forsook her, and full falsely they accused her through temptation by the devil of things that she was never guilty of. And so did one man on whom she trusted greatly and proferred himself to go with her into the country, wherethrough she was right glad, trusting he would well support her and help her when she had need, for he had been dwelling a long time with an anchorite, a doctor of divinity and a holy man, and that anchorite was this woman's confessor. And so his servant took leave by his own stirring to go with this creature into the country, and her own maiden went with her also, as long as they fared well and no man said anything against them. But, as soon as the people, through the enticing of our ghostly enemy and by the sufferance of our Lord, spoke against this creature because she wept so sorely, and said she was a false hypocrite and falsely deceived the people, and threatened to burn her, then the foresaid man, who was held so holy a man and whom she trusted so much upon, utterly reproved her, and foully despised her, and would no further go with her. Her maiden, seeing trouble on every side, waxed rude against her mistress. She would not obey nor follow her counsel. She let her go alone in many good towns and would not go with her. And ever her husband was ready when all others failed and went with her where our Lord would send her, always trusting that all was for the best and should come to a good end when God wanted.

And at this time he led her to speak with the Bishop of Lincoln, who was called Philip,[2] and they abode three weeks before they could speak

---

1. White clothing would be a sign of virginity.
2. Philip Repingdon was bishop of Lincoln from 1405 to 1419, when he resigned his see. At Oxford during the late 1370s and early 1380s, he had been a Wycliffite but later recanted.

with him, for he was not at home at his palace. When the Bishop was come home and heard said how such a woman had abided him so long to speak with him, anon he sent for her in great haste to learn her will. And then she came to his presence and saluted him, and he dearly welcomed her and said he had long desired to speak with her, and he was right glad of her coming. And so she prayed him that she might speak with him in counsel and show him the secrets of her soul, and he set her a time convenient thereto.

When the time came, she showed him her meditations and high contemplations and other secret things, both of the quick and of the dead as our Lord showed to her soul. He was right glad to hear them, and suffered her benignly to say what she wished, and commended greatly her feelings and her contemplations, saying they were high matters and full devout matters and inspired by the Holy Ghost, counseling her wisely that her feelings should be written down. And she said that it was not God's will that they should be written so soon, nor were they written for twenty years after or more.

And then she said furthermore, "My Lord, if it pleases you, I am commanded in my soul that you shall give me the mantle and the ring and clothe me all in white clothes.[3] And, if you clothe me on earth, our Lord Jesus Christ shall clothe you in heaven, as I understand by revelation."

Then the Bishop said to her, "I will fulfill your desire if your husband will consent thereto."

Then she said to the Bishop, "I pray you let my husband come to your presence, and you shall hear what he will say."

And so her husband came before the Bishop, and the Bishop asked him, "John, is it your will that your wife shall take the mantle and the ring and live chaste, and you also?"

"Yes, my Lord," he said, "and in token that we both vow to live chaste, here I offer my hands into yours," and he put his hands between the Bishop's hands.

And the Bishop did no more to us on that day, save he made us right good cheer and said we were right welcome.[4]

Another day this creature came to a meal at the request of the Bishop. And she saw him give with his hands, before he set himself at table, to thirteen poor men, thirteen pence and thirteen loaves, with other food. And so he did every day. This creature was stirred to high devotion by this sight and gave God praising and worshipping that he gave the Bishop grace to do these good deeds, with plenteous weeping, in so much that all the Bishop's household marveled at what ailed her.

And afterward she was set at table with many worthy clerks and priests

---

3. Margery refers to the ceremony through which she would take the vows and take on the habit of married chastity, vows normally associated with pious widowhood.
4. These are the only times Kempe uses first-person pronouns in the *Book*.

and squires of the Bishop's, and the Bishop himself sent her full graciously food from his own mess. The clerks asked this creature many hard questions, the which she by the grace of Jesus resolved, so that her answers pleased the Bishop right well, and the clerks had full great marvel of her because she answered so readily and pregnantly.

When the Bishop had eaten, he sent for this creature into his chamber, saying to her, "Margery, you and your husband spoke to me in order for me to give you the mantle and the ring, for which cause I have taken my counsel, and my counsel will not allow me to profess you in so singular a clothing without better advisement. And you say by the grace of God you will go to Jerusalem. Therefore pray to God that it may abide until you come from Jerusalem, in order that you be better proved and known.

On the next day this creature went to church and prayed to God with all her spirits that she might have knowledge how she should be governed in this matter and what answer she should give to the Bishop. Our Lord Jesus Christ answered to her mind in this manner, "Daughter, say to the Bishop that he dreads more the shames of the world than the perfect love of God. Say to him, 'I should as well have excused him if he had fulfilled your wish as I did the children of Israel when I bade them to borrow the goods of the people of Egypt and go away therewith.' Therefore, daughter, say to him, though he will not do it now, it shall be done another time when God wills."

And so she gave her message to the Bishop of Lincoln as she had in commandment. Then he prayed her to go to the Archbishop of Canterbury, Arundel,[5] and pray him to grant leave to me, the Bishop of Lincoln, to give her the mantle and the ring, inasmuch as she was not of his diocese.[6] This cause he feigned through the counsel of his clerks because they loved not this creature.

She said, "Sir, I will go to my Lord of Canterbury with right good will for other causes and matters which I have to show to his reverence. As for this cause, I shall not go, for God wills not that I ask him thereafter."

Then she took her leave of the Bishop of Lincoln, and he gave her twenty-six shillings and eight pence to buy her clothing with and to pray for him.

16. Then went this creature forth to London with her husband unto Lambeth,[7] where the Archbishop lay at that time. And, as they came into the hall in afternoon, there were many of the Archbishop's clerks and other reckless men, both squires and yeomen who swore many great oaths and spoke many reckless words, and this creature boldly rebuked them

---

5. Thomas Arundel, archbishop of Canterbury, 1397, 1399–1414, one of the most powerful men in England and a firm opponent of heterodox views.
6. Margery is a resident of King's Lynn and in the diocese of the bishop of Norwich.
7. Lambeth Palace, in London, the seat of the archbishop of Canterbury.

and said they should be damned unless they left off their swearing and other sins that they used. And with that came forth a woman of the same town in a pilche[8] and reviled this creature, banned her, and said full cursedly to her in this manner, "I would you were in Smithfield,[9] and I would bear a faggot to burn you with; it is a pity that you live."

This creature stood still and answered not, and her husband suffered with great pain and was full sorry to hear his wife so rebuked. Then the Archbishop sent for this creature to come into his garden. When she came to his presence, she saluted him as she could, praying him of his gracious lordship to grant her authority in choosing her confessor and to be houseled every Sunday, if God would dispose her thereto, under his letter and his seal through all his province.[1] And he granted it full benignly, all her desire without any silver or gold, nor would he let his clerks take anything for writing or for sealing the letter. When this creature found this grace in his sight, she was well comforted and strengthened in her soul, and so she showed this worshipful lord her manner of living and such grace as God wrought in her mind and in her soul, to learn what he would say thereto, if he found any default either in her contemplation or in her weeping. And she told him also the cause of her weeping and the manner of dalliance that our Lord dallied to her soul. And he found no default therein but approved her manner of living and was right glad that our merciful Lord Christ Jesus showed such grace in our days, blessed may he be.

Then this creature boldly spoke to him about the correction of his household, saying with reverence, "My Lord, our most high lord, almighty God, has not given you your benefice and great goods of the world to maintain traitors to him and those who slay him every day by swearing great oaths. You shall answer for them unless you correct them or else put them out of your service."[2]

Full benignly and meekly he suffered her to say her intent and gave a fair answer, she supposing it would be better. And so their dalliance continued until stars appeared in the firmament.

Then she took her leave and her husband also. Afterward they came again to London, and many worthy men desired to hear her dalliance and her communication, for her communication was so much of the love of God that the hearers were oftentimes stirred through it to weep right soberly. And so she had there right great welcome, and her husband because of her, as long as they would abide in the city.

8. A pilche is an outer garment of skin that is trimmed with the fur.
9. Smithfield was just northwest of the London city walls and the place where the first two Lollards were burned, William Sawtre in 1401 and John Badby in 1410.
1. Margery here is granted an extraordinary degree of choice. Moreover, most people received the sacrament once a year, though they went to church far more frequently, where they listened to services, prayed, and participated in the Mass by watching it.
2. Margery's dislike of swearing is one trait she shares with Lollards, and it causes some to suspect her of having Lollard sympathies.

Afterward they came again to Lynn, and then went this creature to the anchorite at the Friar Preachers[3] in Lynn and told him what welcome she had had and how she had sped while she was in the country. And he was right glad of her coming home and held it was a great miracle, her coming and her going to and fro. And he said to her, "I have heard much evil language of you since you went out, and I have been sorely counseled to leave you and no more to meddle with you and there are promised me great friendships upon condition that I leave you. And I answered for you thus: If you were in the same plight that you were when we parted asunder, I dare well say you were a good woman, a lover of God, and highly inspired with the Holy Ghost. And I will not forsake her for any lady in this realm in order to speak with the lady and leave her, for rather I should leave the lady and speak with her. If I might not do both, then I would do the contrary.'"

(Read first the twenty-first chapter and then this chapter after that.)[4]

17. On a day long before this time, while this creature was bearing children and she was newly delivered of a child, our Lord Christ Jesus said to her she should bear no more children, and therefore he bade her to go to Norwich.[5] And she said, "A, dear Lord, how shall I go? I am both faint and feeble."

"Dread you not, I shall make you strong enough. I bid you go to the vicar of Saint Stephen's[6] and say that I greet him well and that he is a high chosen soul of mine and tell him he pleases me much with his preaching and show him your secrets and my counsels such as I show you."

Then she took her way toward Norwich and came into his church on a Thursday a little before noon. And the vicar went up and down with another priest who was his ghostly father, who was alive when this book was made. And this creature was clad in black clothing at that time. She saluted the vicar, praying him that she might speak with him an hour or else two hours in the afternoon, when he had eaten, about the love of God.

He, lifting up his hands and blessing himself, said, "Benedicite![7] How could a woman occupy an hour or two hours in the love of our Lord? I shall never eat a meal until I learn what you can say of our Lord God for the time of one hour."

Then he set himself down in the church. She, sitting a little beside, showed him all the words which God had revealed to her in her soul. Afterward, she showed him all her manner of living from her childhood as nearly as it would come to her mind: how unkind she had been against

---

3. Dominican priory.
4. This sentence is one of the directives to a reader that is embedded in the text.
5. Norwich is about forty miles southeast of Lynn.
6. Richard Caister, known for his sanctity, was vicar of St. Stephen's in Norwich.
7. Bless you!

our Lord Jesus Christ, how proud and vain she had been in her bearing, how obstinate against the laws of God, and how envious against her fellow Christians, then, when it pleased our Lord Christ Jesus, how she was chastised with many tribulations and horrible temptations, and afterward how she was fed and comforted with holy meditations, especially in the mind of our Lord's Passion.

And, while she dallied in the Passion of our Lord Jesus Christ, she heard so hideous a melody that she could not bear it. Then this creature fell down as if she had lost her bodily strength and lay still a great while, desiring to put it away, and she might not. Then knew she well by her faith that there was great joy in heaven, where the least point of bliss passes without any comparison all the joy that ever might be thought or felt in this life. She was greatly strengthened in her faith and more bold to tell the vicar her feelings, which she had by revelations, both of the quick and of the dead and of his own self. She told him how sometimes the Father of heaven dallied in her soul as plainly and as verily as one friend speaks to another by bodily speech; sometimes the Second Person in Trinity;[8] sometimes all three Persons in Trinity and one substance in Godhead dallied in her soul and informed her in her faith and in his love how she should love him, worship him, and dread him—so excellently that she heard never a book, neither Hilton's book, nor Bridget's book, nor *Stimulus Amoris*, nor *Incendium Amoris*,[9] nor any other that ever she had heard read that spoke so highly of love of God but that she felt as highly about the working in her soul if she could or else might have showed what she felt.

Sometimes our Lady spoke to her mind. Sometimes Saint Peter, sometimes Saint Paul, sometimes Saint Katherine,[1] or what saint in heaven she had devotion for appeared to her soul and taught her how she should love our Lord and how she should please him. Her dalliance was so sweet, so holy, and so devout that this creature might not oftentimes bear it but fell down and twisted with her body and made wondrous faces and countenance with violent sobbings and great plenty of tears, sometimes saying "Jesus, mercy," sometimes "I die." And therefore many people slandered her, not believing it was the work of God but that some evil spirit vexed her in her body or else that she had some bodily sickness.

Notwithstanding the rumor and grudging of the people against her, this holy man, the vicar of Saint Stephen's church of Norwich, whom God had exalted and through marvelous works showed and proved as holy, ever held with her and supported her against her enemies, as he had

---

8. Jesus.
9. These are key devotional texts: Walter Hilton's *Scale of Perfection*; St. Bridget's *Liber Revelationum Celestium*; the *Stimulus Amoris*, a fourteenth-century mystical text falsely ascribed to St. Bonaventure; and the *Incendium Amoris*, a mystical work by the fourteenth-century English hermit Richard Rolle.
1. St. Katherine of Alexandria, the legendary fourth-century virgin martyr.

power, after the time that she by the bidding of God had showed him her manner of governance and living, for he trustfully believed that she was well learned in the law of God and endued with grace from the Holy Ghost, to whom it belongs to inspire wherever he will. And, though his voice be heard, it is not known by the world from whence it comes or whither it goes. This holy vicar after this time was always confessor to this creature when she came to Norwich and houseled her with his own hands. And, when she was on a time admonished to appear before certain officers of the bishop to answer to certain articles which would be put against her by the stirring of envious people, the good vicar, preferring the love of God before any shame of the world, went with her to hear her examination and delivered her from the malice of her enemies. And then it was revealed to this creature that the good vicar would live seven years afterwards and then he would pass hence with great grace, and he did as she had said.[2]

18. This creature was charged and commanded in her soul that she should go to a White Friar in the same city of Norwich, who was named William Sowthfeld,[3] a good man and an holy liver, to show him the grace that God wrought in her as she had done to the good vicar before. She did as she was commanded, and came to the friar before noon, and was with him in a chapel a long time, and showed him her meditations and such things as God wrought in her soul, to learn if she were deceived by any illusions or not.

This good man, the White Friar, ever while she told her feelings, holding up his hands, said, "Jesus, mercy and gramercy." "Sister," he said, "dread you not of your manner of living, for it is the Holy Ghost working plenteously his grace in your soul. Thank him highly for his goodness, for we all are bound to thank him for you who now in our days well inspires his grace in you to the help and comfort of us all who are supported by your prayers and by others such as you are. And we are preserved from many mischiefs and troubles which we would suffer—and worthily for our trespass—were not such good creatures among us. Blessed be almighty God for his goodness. And therefore, sister, I counsel you that you dispose yourself to receive the gifts of God as lowly and meekly as you can and put no obstacle nor objection against the goodness of the Holy Ghost, for he may give his gifts where he will, and of unworthy he makes worthy, of sinful he makes rightful. His mercy is ever ready unto us, unless the fault be in ourselves, for he dwells not in a body subject to sin. He flees all false feigning and falsehood; he asks of us a low, a meek, and a contrite heart with a good will. Our Lord says himself, My spirit shall rest upon a meek man, a contrite man, and one dreading my words.' Sis-

---

2. I have added this word—the word or words that ended this sentence have been destroyed.
3. William Sowthfield (d. 1414) was a Carmelite friar known for devotion.

ter, I trust to our Lord you have these conditions either in your will or in your affection or else in both, and I hold not that our Lord suffers them to be deceived endlessly who set all their trust in him and nothing seek or desire but him only, as I hope that you do. And therefore believe fully that our Lord loves you and works his grace in you. I pray God increase it and continue it to his everlasting worship for his mercy."

The before-said creature was much comforted both in body and in soul by this good man's words and greatly strengthened in her faith. And then she was bidden by our Lord to go to an anchoress in the same city, who was called Dame Julian.[4] And so she did and showed her the grace that God put in her soul of compunction, contrition, sweetness and devotion, compassion with holy meditation and high contemplation, and full many holy speeches and dalliances that our Lord spoke to her soul, and many wonderful revelations which she showed to the anchoress to learn if there were any deceit in them, for the anchoress was expert in such things and good counsel could give.

The anchoress, hearing the marvelous goodness of our Lord, highly thanked God with all her heart for his visitation, counseling this creature to be obedient to the will of our Lord God and fulfill with all her mights whatever he put in her soul if it were not against the worship of God and profit of her fellow Christians, for, if it were, then it were not the moving of a good spirit but rather of an evil spirit.

"The Holy Ghost moves never a thing against charity, and, if he did, he would be contrary to his own self, for he is all charity. Also he moves a soul to all chasteness, for chaste livers are called the temple of the Holy Ghost, and the Holy Ghost makes a soul stable and steadfast in the right faith and the right belief. And a double man in soul is ever unstable and unsteadfast in all his ways. He that is evermore doubting is like the flood of the sea, which is moved and borne about with the wind, and that man is not likely to receive the gifts of God. What creature that has these tokens, he must steadfastly believe that the Holy Ghost dwells in his soul. And much more, when God visits a creature with tears of contrition, devotion, or compassion, he may and ought to believe that the Holy Ghost is in his soul. Saint Paul says that the Holy Ghost asks for us with unspeakable mournings and weepings, that is to say, he makes us ask and pray with mournings and weepings so plenteously that the tears may not be numbered. There may no evil spirit give these tokens, for Jerome says that tears torment more the devil than do the pains of hell. God and the devil are evermore contrary, and they shall never dwell together in one place, and the devil has no power in a man's soul. Holy Writ says that the soul of a righteous man is the seat of God, and so I trust, sister, that you are. I pray God grant you perseverance. Set all your trust in God and fear

---

4. Julian of Norwich (ca.1343–ca.1415–16) was the anchorite, mystic, and author of the *Shewings*, a portion of which is included in this volume (pp. 202–07).

not the language of the world, for the more despite, shame, and reproof that you have in the world, the greater is your merit in the sight of God. Patience is necessary unto you for in that shall you keep your soul."

Much was the holy dalliance that the anchoress and this creature had by commoning in the love of our Lord Jesus Christ the many days that they were together.

This creature showed her manner of living to many a worthy clerk, to worshipful doctors of divinity, both religious men and others of secular habit, and they said that God wrought great grace with her and commanded that she should not be afraid; there was no deceit in her manner of living. They counseled her to be persevering, for her greatest dread was that she should turn and not keep her perfection. She had so many enemies and so much slander that it seemed she might not bear it without great grace and a mighty faith. Others, who had no knowledge of her manner of governance, save only by sight outwardly, or else by the jangling of other persons, perverting the judgment of truth, said full evil of her and caused her to have much enmity and much trouble, more than she should have otherwise had, had their evil language not been. Nevertheless the anchorite of the Friar Preachers in Lynn, who was the principal ghostly father to this creature as is written before, took it on charge of his soul that her feelings were good and sure and that there was no deceit in them. And he by the spirit of prophecy told her, when she should go toward Jerusalem, she should have much tribulation with her maiden and how our Lord would assay her sharply and prove her full straightly.

Then said she again, "A, good sir, what shall I then do when I am far from home and in a strange country and my maiden is against me? Then is my bodily comfort gone, and ghostly comfort from any confessor, as you are, I will not know where to find."

"Daughter, dread you not, for our Lord shall comfort you his own self, whose comfort passes all others, and, when all your friends have forsaken you, our Lord shall make a broken-backed man to lead you forth where you wish to be."

And so it befell as the anchorite had prophesied in every point, and, as I trust, shall be written more plainly afterward. Then this creature in a complaining manner said to the anchorite, "Good sir, what shall I do? He who is my confessor in your absence is right sharp unto me. He will not believe my feelings; he sets naught by them; he holds them but trifles and jokes. And that is a great pain unto me, for I love him well, and I would fain follow his counsel."

The anchorite, answering again to her, said, "It is no wonder, daughter, if he cannot believe in your feelings so soon. He knows well you have been a sinful woman, and therefore he thinks that God would not be homely with you in so short a time. After your conversion I would not for all this world be so sharp to you as he is. God for your merit has ordained him to be your scourge and fare with you as a smith with a file that makes the iron to be bright and clear to the sight which before appeared rusty, dark, evil-colored. The more sharp that he is to you the more clearly shines your soul in the sight of God, and God has ordained me to be your nurse and your comfort. Be you low and meek, and thank God both for one and for the other."

On a time before, this creature went to her prayers in order to learn what answer she should give to the widow.[5] She was commanded in her spirit to bid the widow leave her confessor that was at that time, if she would please God, and go to the anchorite at the Friar Preachers in Lynn and show him her life. When this creature gave this message, the widow would not believe her words, nor her ghostly father either, unless God would give her the same grace that he gave this creature, and she charged this creature that she should no more come in her place. And because this creature told her that she had to feel love of affection for her ghostly father, therefore the widow said it had been good for this creature if her love and her affection were set as hers was. Then our Lord told this creature to have a letter written and send it to her. A master of divinity wrote a letter at the request of this creature and sent it to the widow with these clauses that follow. One clause was that the widow should never have the grace that this creature had. Another was, though this creature came never in her house, it pleased God right well. Our Lord said again to this creature, "It was better for her than all this world if her love were set as yours is. And I bid you go to her ghostly father and tell him, for he will not believe your words, they shall be parted asunder before he is aware, and those who are not of her counsel shall know it before he does, whether he will it or not. Lo, daughter, here may you see how hard it is to part a man from his own will."

And all this process was fulfilled in truth as the creature had said before, twelve years afterward. Then this creature suffered much tribulation and great heaviness, for she said these words as our Lord bade her say. And ever she increased in the love of God and was bolder than she was before.

19. Before this creature went to Jerusalem, our Lord sent her to a worshipful lady so that she should speak with her in counsel and do his errand unto her. The lady would not speak with her unless her ghostly father were present, and she said she was well pleased. And then when the lady's ghostly father was come they went into a chapel all three together, and then this creature said with great reverence and many tears, "Madam, our Lord Jesus Christ bade me tell you that your husband is in purgatory, and that you shall be saved but it shall be long before you come to heaven."

And then the lady was displeased and said her husband was a good man; she believed not that he was in purgatory. Her ghostly father held

---

5. This incident seems rather to belong to the end of chapter 19, which recounts Margery's difficult relationship with a widow concerned about the state of her husband's soul.

with this creature and said it might right well be so as she said and confirmed her words with many holy tales. And then this lady sent her daughter, with other members of the household with her, to the anchorite who
was the principal confessor to this creature so that he should forsake her
or else he would lose her friendship. The anchorite said to the messen-
gers that he would not forsake this creature for any man on earth, for to
such creatures as would inquire of him her manner of governance and
how he held of her he said she was God's own servant, and also he said
she was the tabernacle of God. And the anchorite said unto her own person in order to strengthen her in her faith, "Though God took from you
all tears and dalliance, believe nevertheless that God loves you and that
you shall be right sure of heaven for what you have had before, for tears
with love is the greatest gift that God may give on earth, and all men who
love God ought to thank him for you."

Also there was a widow who prayed this creature to pray for her husband
and learn if he had any need of help. And, as this creature prayed for him,
she was answered that his soul should be thirty years in purgatory unless
he had better friends on earth. Thus she told the widow and said, "If you
will give alms for him—three pounds or four in masses and almsgiving to
poor folk—you shall highly please God and give the soul great ease."

The widow took little heed at her words and let it pass forth. Then this
creature went to the anchorite and told him how she had felt, and he said
the feeling was of God and the deed in itself was good, though the soul
had no need thereof, and counseled it should be fulfilled. Then this creature told this matter to her ghostly father in order that he should speak to
the widow, and so it was a long time that this creature heard anymore of
this matter. Afterward our Lord Jesus Christ said to this creature, "That
thing I bade that should have been done for the soul, it is not done. Ask
now your ghostly father."

And so she did, and he said it was not done. She said again, "My Lord
Jesus Christ told me so right now."

20. One day as this creature was hearing her Mass, a young man and a
good priest holding up the sacrament in his hands over his head, the sacrament shook and flickered to and fro as a dove flickers with her wings. And,
when he held up the chalice with the precious sacrament, the chalice
moved to and fro as though it should have fallen out of his hands. When
the consecration was done, this creature had great marvel about the stirring
and moving of the blessed sacrament, desiring to see more consecrations,
looking if it would do so again. Then said our Lord Jesus Christ to the creature, "You shall no more see it in this manner, therefore thank God that
you have seen. My daughter, Bridget,[6] saw me never in this manner."

6. St. Bridget of Sweden (ca. 1303–1373) was a major figure in late-medieval English devotional
life. Both her life and her Revelations are important to Margery's account of her experience.
Bridget, like Margery, was married with many children. She spent the last twenty-four years of her

Then said this creature in her thought, "Lord, what does this betoken?"
"It betokens vengeance."

"A, good Lord, what vengeance?"

Then said our Lord again to her, "There shall be an earthquake; tell it to whom you wish in the name of Jesus. For I tell you forsooth, right as I spoke to Saint Bridget, right so I speak to you, daughter, and I tell you truly it is true, every word that is written in Bridget's book, and by you it shall be known for very truth. And you shall fare well, daughter, in spite of all your enemies. The more envy they have for you because of my grace, the better shall I love you. I were not a rightful God unless I proved you, for I know you better than you know yourself, whatever men say of you. You say I have great patience for the sin of the people, and you say the truth, but, if you saw the sin of the people as I do, you would have much more marvel in my patience and much more sorrow in the sin of the people than you have."

Then the creature said, "Alas, worthy Lord, what shall I do for the people?"

Our Lord answered, "It is enough for you to do as you do."

Then she prayed, "Merciful Lord Christ Jesus, in you is all mercy and grace and goodness. Have mercy, pity, and compassion for them. Show your mercy and your goodness upon them. Help them; send them very contrition, and let them never die in their sin."

Our merciful Lord said, "I may no more, daughter, for my rightfulness, do for them than I do. I send them preaching and teaching, pestilence and battles, hunger and famine, loss of their goods with great sickness, and many other tribulations, and they will not believe my words, nor will they know my visitation. And therefore I shall say to them that I made my servants to pray for you, and you despised their works and their living."

21. During the time that this creature had revelations, our Lord said to her, "Daughter, you are with child."

She said again, "A, Lord, how shall I then do for keeping of my child?"

"Our Lord said, "Daughter, dread you not, I shall ordain for a keeper."

"Lord, I am not worthy to hear you speak and thus to common with my husband. Nevertheless, it is to me a great pain and great distress."

"Therefore is it no sin to you, daughter, for it is to you rather reward and merit, and you shall have never the less grace, for I will that you bring me forth more fruit."

Than said the creature, "Lord Jesus, this manner of living belongs to your holy maidens."

"Yes, daughter, believe right well that I love wives also, and specially those wives who would live chaste, if they might have their will, and do

---

life in Rome; in 1370 her new order, the Brigittine Order, was confirmed by Pope Urban V. She was canonized in 1391.

their business to please me as you do, for, though the state of maidenhood is more perfect and more holy than the state of widowhood, and the state of widowhood more perfect than the state of wedlock; yet daughter I love you as well as any maiden in the world. There may no man hinder me from loving whom I will and as much as I will; for love, daughter, quenches all sin. And therefore ask of me the gifts of love. There is no gift so holy as is the gift of love, nor nothing to be so much desired as love; for love may purchase what it can desire. And therefore, daughter, you may no better please God than continually to think on his love."

Then this creature asked our Lord Jesus how she should best love him.

And our Lord said, "Have mind of your wickedness and think on my goodness."

She said again, "I am the most unworthy creature that ever you showed grace unto on earth."

"A, daughter," said our Lord, "fear you not. I take no heed what a man has been, but I take heed what he will be. Daughter, you have despised yourself; therefore you shall never be despised by God. Have mind, daughter, what Mary Magdalene was, Mary the Egyptian, Saint Paul,[7] and many other saints who are now in heaven; for of unworthy I make worthy, and of sinful I make rightful. And so have I made you worthy to me, once loved and evermore loved with me. There is no saint in heaven whom you will speak with but he will come to you. Whom God loves, they love. When you please God, you please his mother and all the saints in heaven. Daughter, I take witness of my mother, of all the angels in heaven, and of all the saints in heaven that I love you with all my heart, and I may not forego your love."

Our Lord said then to his blissful mother, "Blessed Mother, tell my daughter of the greatness of love I have unto her."

Then this creature lay still all in weeping and sobbing as though her heart should have burst for the sweetness of speech that our Lord spoke unto her soul. Quickly after, the Queen of Mercy, God's mother, dallied to the soul of this creature, saying, "My worthy daughter, I bring you sure tidings, witnessing my sweet son Jesus, with all angels and all saints in heaven who love you full highly. Daughter, I am your mother, your lady, and your mistress to teach you in all manner how you shall please God best."

She taught this creature and informed her so wonderfully that she was abashed to speak it or tell it to any—the matters were so high and so holy—save only to the anchorite who was her principal confessor; for he had the most knowledge of such things. And he charged this creature by virtue of obedience to tell him what ever she felt, and so she did.

---

7. St. Paul began as Saul, one of the great persecutors of Christians. His dramatic conversion is described in Acts 9. "Mary Magdalene": New Testament follower of Jesus; she was among the first witnesses of the Resurrection; she is linked to passionate love of Jesus, to penitential grief and to revelation. "Mary the Egyptian": Mary of Egypt, legendary fifth-century courtesan from Alexandria, who, upon conversion, left her life of luxury and sin for one of relentless penance and poverty.

22. As this creature lay in contemplation, sorely weeping in her spirit, she said to our Lord Jesus Christ, "A, Lord, maidens dance now merrily in heaven. Shall not I do so? For, because I am no maiden, lack of maidenhood is to me now great sorrow. It seems to me I wish I had been slain when I was taken from the font stone[8] so that I should never have displeased you, and then should you, blessed Lord, have had my maidenhead without end. A, dear God, I have not loved you all the days of my life, and that sorely rues me. I have run away from you, and you have run after me. I would fall into despair, and you would not allow me."

"A, daughter, how often have I told you that your sins are forgiven you and that we are joined together without end? You are to me a singular love, daughter, and therefore I promise you you shall have a singular grace in heaven, daughter, and I promise you I shall come to your end at your dying with my blessed mother and my holy angels and twelve apostles, Saint Katherine, Saint Margaret, Saint Mary Magdalene, and many other saints who are in heaven, who give great worship to me for the grace that I give to you, God, your Lord Jesus.

"You need dread no grievous pains in your dying, for you shall have your desire, that is to have more mind of my Passion than of your own pain. You shall not dread the devil of hell, for he has no power in you. He dreads you more than you do him. He is angry with you, for you torment him more with your weeping than does all the fire in hell; you win many souls from him with your weeping. And I have promised you that you should no other purgatory have than slander and speech from the world, for I have chastised you myself as I wished, by many great dreads and torments that you have had with evil spirits, both sleeping and waking for many years. And therefore I shall preserve you at your end through my mercy so that they shall no power have over you, neither in body nor in soul. It is great grace and miracle that you have your bodily wits for the vexation that you have had with them before. I have also, daughter, chastised you with the dread of my Godhead, and many times have I frightened you with great tempests of winds so that you thought vengeance would have fallen on you for sin. I have proved you by many tribulations, many great sorrows, and many grievous sicknesses in so much that you have been anointed for dead; and all through my grace have you escaped.

"Therefore dread you not, daughter, for with my own hands, which were nailed to the cross, I shall take your soul from your body with great mirth and melody, with sweet smells and good odors, and offer it to my Father in heaven. There you shall see him face to face, dwelling with him without end. Daughter, you shall be right welcome to my Father and to my mother and to all my saints in heaven, for you have given them drink full many times with tears of your eyes. All my holy saints shall enjoy your coming home. You shall be fulfilled of all manner of love that you covet.

8. I.e., at baptism.

Then shall you bless the time that you were wrought and the body that has you bought.[9] He shall joy in you and you in him without end. Daughter, I promise you the same grace that I promised Saint Katherine, Saint Margaret, Saint Barbara,[1] and Saint Paul, in so much that what creature on earth, until the day of judgment, asks you any boon and believes that God loves you, he shall have his boon, or else a better thing. Therefore, those who believe that God loves you, they shall be blessed without end.

"The souls in purgatory shall joy in your coming home, for they know well that God loves you specially. And men on earth shall joy in God for you, for he shall work much grace for you and make all the world to know that God loves you. You have been despised for my love, and therefore you shall be worshipped for my love. Daughter, when you are in heaven, you shall be able to ask what you will, and I shall grant you all your desire. I have told you before that you are a singular lover, and therefore you shall have a singular love in heaven, a singular reward, and a singular worship. And, forasmuch as you are a maiden in your soul, I shall take you by the one hand in heaven and my mother by the other hand, and so shall you dance in heaven with other holy maidens and virgins, for I may call you dearly bought and my own worthy darling. I shall say to you, my own blessed spouse, 'Welcome to me with all manner of joy and gladness, here to dwell with me and never to depart from me without end, but ever to dwell with me in joy and bliss, which no eye may see, nor ear hear, nor tongue tell, nor heart think; that I have ordained for you and for all my servants who desire to love me and please me as you do.'"

23. There came once a vicar to this creature, praying her to pray for him and learn whether he should more please God to leave his curacy and his benefice[2] or to keep it still, for he thought he profited not among his parishioners. The creature, being in her prayers, having mind of this matter, Christ said unto her spirit, "Bid the vicar keep still his curacy and his benefice and do his diligence in preaching and teaching to them in his own person and sometimes procure another to teach them my laws and my commandments so that there be no default on his part, and, if they do never the better, his meed shall never be the less."

And so she gave her message as she was commanded, and the vicar kept still his curacy.

As this creature was in a church of Saint Margaret in the choir, where a body was present, and he, who was husband of the same body while she lived, was there in good health in order to offer her mass penny after the custom of the place, our Lord said to the foresaid creature, "Lo, daughter, the soul of this body is in purgatory, and he who

9. This is one of several couplets in the text.
1. St. Barbara, third-century virgin persecuted by her father for her conversion to Christianity.
2. A curacy is a priest's responsibility for the souls in his parish; a benefice is his ecclesiastical appointment and hence his living.

was her husband is now in good health; and yet he shall be dead in a short time."

And so it befell, as she felt by revelation.

Also, as this creature lay in the choir in her prayers, a priest came to her and prayed her to pray for a woman who lay in point of death. As this creature began to pray for her, our Lord said to her, "Daughter, it is great need to pray for her, for she has been a wicked woman, and she shall be dead."

And she said again, "Lord, as you love me, save her soul from damnation," and then she wept with plenteous tears for that soul. And our Lord granted her mercy for the soul, commanding her to pray for her.

This creature's ghostly father came to her, moving her to pray for a woman who lay in point of death to man's sight. And anon our Lord said she should live and fare well, and so she did.

A good man who was a great friend to this creature and helpful to the poor people was strongly sick many weeks together. And much moan was made for him, for men thought he should never have lived; his pain was so wonderful in all his joints and in all his body. Our Lord Jesus said to her spirit, "Daughter, be not abashed for this man, he shall live and fare right well."

And so he lived many years after in good health and prosperity.

Another good man who was a clerk[3] lay sick also, and, when this creature prayed for him, it was answered to her mind that he would linger a while and afterward he should be dead with that same sickness. And so he was in short time after.

Also a worshipful woman and, as men believed, a holy woman, who was a special friend to this creature, was right sick, and many people thought she should have been dead. Then, this creature praying for her, our Lord said, "She shall not die these ten years, for you shall after this make full merry together and have full good communications as you have had before."

And so it was in truth; this holy woman lived many years after.

Many more such revelations this creature had in feeling; to write them all should perhaps be a hindrance to more profit. These are written to show the homeliness and the goodliness of our merciful Lord Christ Jesus and for no commendation of the creature. These feelings and such others, many more than are written, both of the living and of the dying, of some to be saved, of some to be damned, were to this creature great pain and punishing. She had rather have suffered any bodily penance than these feelings, and she might have put them away for the dread that she had of illusions and deceits from her ghostly enemies. She had sometimes so great trouble with such feelings when it fell not true to her understanding, that her confessor feared that she should have fallen into de-

---

3. The word is *lyster*, meaning a clerk who read and explained the scriptures.

spair therewith. And then after her trouble and her great fear, it would be showed unto her soul how the feelings should be understood.

24. The priest who wrote this book, in order to prove this creature's feelings, many times and divers times he asked her questions and demands about things that were to come, unsure, and uncertain at that time to any creature what should be the end, praying her, though she was loathe and not willing to do such things, to pray to God therefore and learn, when our Lord would visit her with devotion, what should be the end, and truly without any feigning tell him how she felt, else he would not gladly have written the book. And so this creature, somewhat for dread that he would else not have followed her intent to write this book, compelled, did as he prayed her and told him her feelings about what should befall in such matters, as he asked her if her feelings were truth. And thus he proved them for very truth. And yet he would not always give credences to her words, and that hindered him in this manner that follows.

It befell on a time that there came a young man to this priest, which young man the priest never saw before, complaining to the priest of poverty and trouble that he was fallen in by misfortune, explaining the cause of misfortune, saying also he had taken holy orders to be a priest. For a little hastiness, defending himself, since he might not choose unless he would have been dead through the pursuit of his enemies, he struck a man or else two, wherethrough, as he said, were dead or else like to be dead. And so he was fallen into irregularity and might not execute his orders without dispensation of the court of Rome, and for this cause he fled from his friends and dared not come into his country for dread of being taken for their death.

The foresaid priest, giving credence to the young man's words, inasmuch as he was an amiable person, fair featured, well favored in manner and in countenance, sober in his language and dalliance, priestly in his gesture and vesture, having compassion of his trouble, purposing to get him friends for his relief and comfort, went to a worshipful burgess in Lynn, a mayor's peer and a merciful man, who lay in great sickness and a long time had done, complaining to him and to his wife, a full good woman, of the misfortune of this young man, trusting to have fair alms as he oftentimes had for others whom he asked for.

It happened the creature of whom this book is written was there present and heard how the priest complained for the young man and how the priest praised him. And she was sorely moved in her spirit against that young man, and said they had many poor neighbors which they knew well enough had great need to be helped and relieved, and it was more charitable to help those who they knew well as well-disposed folk and their own neighbors than other strangers which they knew not; for many speak and show full fair outward to the sight of the people—God knows what they are in their souls.

The good man and his wife thought that she said right well, and therefore they would grant him no alms. At that time the priest was evil pleased with this creature, and, when he met with her alone, he repeated how she had hindered him so that he might no alms get for the young man, who was a well disposed man, as he thought, and commended much his governance.

The creature said, "Sir, God knows what his governance is; for, what I know, I saw him never, and yet I have understanding what his governance should be, and therefore, sir, if you will act by my counsel and after what I feel, let him choose and help himself as well as he can and meddle you not with him, for he shall deceive you at the last."

The young man resorted always to the priest, flattering him and saying that he had good friends in other places who should help him if they knew where he was, and that in short time; and also they would thank those persons that had supported him in his distress.

The priest, trusting it should be as this young man told him, lent him silver with a good will to help him. The young man prayed the priest to have him excused if he saw him not for two days or three, for he should go a little way and come again in a short time and bring him again his silver right well and truly. The priest, having confidence in his promise, was well content, granting him good love and leave unto the day on which he had promised to come again. When he was gone, the foresaid creature having understanding by feeling in her soul that our Lord would show that he was an untrue man and no more would come again, she, in order to prove whether her feeling was true or false, asked the priest whither the young man was whom he had praised so much. The priest said he walked a little way and trusted that he would come again. She said she supposed that he would no more see him; no more he did ever after. And then he repented that he had not acted after her counsel.

In short time after this was passed, came another false scoundrel, an old man, to the same priest and offered to sell him a portable breviary, a good little book. The priest went to the foresaid creature, praying her to pray for him and learn whether God wished he should buy the book or not, and, while she prayed, he cared for the man as well as he could, and afterward he came again to this creature and asked how she felt.

"Sir," she said, "buy no book from him, for he is not to trust upon, and that shall you well know if you meddle with him."

Then the priest prayed the man if he might see this book. The man said he had it not upon him. The priest asked how he came thereby. He said he was executor to a priest who was of his kindred, and he charged him to sell it and dispose it for him.

"Father," said the priest (because of reverence), "why proffer you me this book, rather than other men or other priests, when there are many more prosperous, richer, priests in this church than I am, and I well know you had never any knowledge of me before this time?"

"Forsooth, sir," he said, "no more I had, nevertheless I have good will with your person, and also it was his will who owned it before that: if I knew any young priest whom I thought sober and well disposed, that he should have this book before any other man and for less price than any other man, so that he might pray for him. And these causes move me to come to you rather than to another man."

The priest asked where his dwelling was.

"Sir," he said, "but five miles from this place, in Pentney Abbey."[4]

"There I have been," said the priest, "and I have not seen you."

"No sir," he said again, "I have been there but a little while and now have I there a livery,[5] thanked be God."

The priest prayed him that he might have a sight of the book and see if they might agree. He said, "Sir, I hope to be here again the next week and bring it with me, and, sir, I promise you, you shall have it before any other man if you like it."

The priest thanked him for his good will, and so they parted asunder, but the man would never come near the priest afterward, and then the priest knew well that the foresaid creature's feeling was true.

25. Furthermore there follows a right notable matter of the creature's feeling, and it is written here for convenience, inasmuch as it is in feeling similar to the matters that are written before, notwithstanding it befell long after the matters that follow.

It happened in a worshipful town where there was one parish church and two chapels annexed, the chapels having and administering all the sacraments, except for christening and purifications,[6] through the sufferance of the parson, who was a monk of Saint Benedict's Order, sent from the house at Norwich, keeping residence with three of his brothers in the worshipful town before written. Through some of the parishioners desiring to make the chapels like the parish church, pursuing a bull from the court of Rome, there fell great legal action and great heaviness between the prior who was their parson and curate[7] and the foresaid parishioners who desired to have fonts[8] and purifications in the chapels, as were in the parish church. And especially in the one chapel that was the greater and the fairer they would have a font.

There was pursued a bull, in which was granted a font to the chapel if it were no detraction to the parish church. The bull was appealed, and divers days were kept by form of law to prove whether the font, if it were

<hr />

4. Major Augustinian priory in Norfolk, about seven miles southeast of Bishop's Lynn.
5. I.e., a position and sustenance as though he were a member of the community.
6. The rite of "churching" women after childbirth, designating their re-entry into the community. Kempe here describes a dispute about privileges between a parish church and two of its chapels. Such a dispute indeed occurred in Lynn, but it has a greater than local relevance to all parish life.
7. In Lynn during Margery's time, this was John Derham, prior of St. Margaret's.
8. Baptismal fonts.

had, should be a detraction to the parish church or not. The parishioners who pursued were right strong and had great help from lordship, and also, most of all, they were rich men, worshipful merchants, and had gold enough, which may speed in every need, and that is a pity that meed should speed rather than truth. Nevertheless the prior who was their parson, though he was poor, manfully he withstood them through the help of some of his parishioners who were his friends and loved the worship of their parish church. So long this matter was in plea that it began to irk them on both sides, and it was never the nearer an end. Then the matter was put before my lord of Norwich, Alnwick,[9] to see if he might by negotiation bring it to an end. He labored this matter diligently, and, in order to establish rest and peace, he offered the foresaid parishioners much of their desire with certain conditions, in so much that those who held with the parson and with their parish church were full sorry, dreading greatly that those who sued in order to have a font should obtain and get their intent and so make the chapel equal to the parish church.

Then the priest who afterward wrote this book went to the creature of whom this treatise makes mention, as he had done before in the time of legal action, and asked her how she felt in her soul in this matter, whether they should have a font in the chapel or not.

"Sir," said the creature, "dread you not, for I understand in my soul, though they would give a bushel of nobles,[1] they should not have it."

"Ah, mother," said the priest, "my lord of Norwich has offered it to them with certain conditions, and they have a time of advisement in order to say no or yes, whether they will, and therefore I am afraid they will not deny it but be right glad to have it."

This creature prayed to God that his will might be fulfilled. And, forasmuch as she had by revelation that they should not have it, she was the more bold to pray our Lord to withstand their intent and to slake their boasting. And, so as our Lord would, they obeyed not nor liked not the means that were offered them, for they trusted fully to have their intent by lordship and by process of law; and, as God would, they were deceived of their intent, and because they would have had all, they lost all. And so, blessed may God be, the parish church stood still in its worship and its degree as it had done two hundred years before and more, and the inspiration of our Lord was, by experience, proved for very truth and surety in the foresaid creature.

26. When the time came that this creature should visit those holy places where our Lord was quick and dead, as she had by revelation years before, she prayed the parish priest of the town where she was dwelling to say for her in the pulpit that, if any man or woman claimed any debt

---

9. William Alnwick, bishop of Norwich (1426–36).
1. The noble was a gold coin equal to six shillings and eight pence.

of her husband or of her, they should come and speak with her before she went, and she, with the help of God, should make compensation to each of them so that they should hold themselves content. And so she did. Afterward she took her leave of her husband and of the holy anchorite, who had told her before the process of her going and much trouble that she should suffer by the way, and, when all her fellowship forsook her, how a broken-backed man should lead her forth in safety through the help of our Lord. And so it befell in deed, as it shall be written afterward. Then she took her leave of Master Robert[2] and prayed him for his blessing, and so forth from other friends. And then she went forth to Norwich and offered at the Trinity,[3] and after she went to Yarmouth, and offered at an image of our Lady, and there she took her ship.

And the next day they came to a great town called Zierikzee,[4] where our Lord of his high goodness visited this creature with abundant tears of contrition for her own sins and sometimes for other men's sins also. And specially she had tears of compassion in the mind of our Lord's Passion. And she was houseled each Sunday where there was time and place convenient for it, with great weepings and violent sobbings so that many men marveled and wondered about the great grace that God wrought in his creature.

This creature had eaten no meat nor drunk any wine for four years before she went out of England. And now her ghostly father charged her by virtue of obedience that she should both eat meat and drink wine, and so she did a little while. Afterward, she prayed her confessor if he would hold her excused though she ate no meat, and suffer her to do as she wanted for a time that pleased him. And soon after, through the moving of some of her company, her confessor was displeased because she ate no meat, and so was much of all the company. And they were most displeased because she wept so much and spoke always of the love and goodness of our Lord, as well at the table as in other places. And therefore shamefully they reproved her and greatly chided her and said they would not suffer her as her husband did when she was at home and in England. And she said meekly again unto them, "Our Lord almighty God is as great a lord here as in England, and as great cause have I to love him here as there, blessed may he be."

For these words her fellowship was angrier than they were before, whose wrath and unkindness to this creature was a matter of great heaviness, for they were held right good men, and she desired greatly their love if she might have had it by the pleasure of God. And then she said to one of them specially, "You do me much shame and great grievance."

He answered again anon, "I pray God that the devil's death may overcome you soon and quickly." And many more cruel words he said to her than she could rehearse.

And soon after some of the company on whom she trusted best, and

2. Robert Spryngolde, parish priest of St. Margaret's church and Margery's chief confessor.
3. Cathedral of the Holy Trinity, Norwich.
4. In the Netherlands.

her own maiden also, said she should no longer go in their fellowship, and they said they would take away her maiden from her so that she should be no strumpet in her company. And then one of them, who had her gold in his keeping, with great anger left her a noble to go where she would and help herself as well as she might, for with them, they said, she should no longer abide, and forsook her that night.

Then on the next morning there came to her one of her company, a man who loved her well, praying her that she would go to his fellows and meek herself unto them and pray them that she might go still in their company until she came to Constance.[5] And so she did, and went forth with them until she came to Constance with great distress and great trouble, for they caused her much shame and much reproof as they went in divers places. They cut her gown so short that it came but a little beneath her knee and made her put on a white canvas in the manner of a sackcloth garment, for she would be taken as a fool, and the people should not make much of her nor hold her in reputation. They made her sit at the table's end, beneath all the others so that she dared hardly speak a word. And, notwithstanding all their malice, she was held in more worship than they wherever they went. And the good man of the house where they were hosteled, though she sat lowest at the table's end, would always take care of her before all of them if he could and might, and sent her from his own meal such service as he had, and that grieved her fellowship badly.

As they went by the way toward Constance, it was told them they should be harmed and have great distress unless they had great grace. Then this creature came by a church and went in to make her prayer, and she prayed with all her heart, with great weeping and many tears, for help and succor against her enemies. Anon our Lord said to her mind, "Dread you not, daughter, your fellowship shall no harm have while you are in their company."

And so, blessed may our Lord be in all his works, they went forth in safety to Constance.

27. When this creature and her fellowship were come to Constance, she heard tell of an English friar, a master of divinity and the Pope's legate, who was in that city. Then she went to that worshipful man and showed him her life from the beginning unto that hour, as nearly as she might in confession, because he was the Pope's legate and a worshipful clerk. And after she told him what trouble she had with her fellowship. She told him also what grace God gave her—of contrition and compunction, of sweetness and devotion, and of many divers revelations that our Lord had revealed unto her—and the dread that she had of illusions and deceits of her ghostly enemies, wherefore she lived in great dread, desiring to put them away and to feel none if she might withstand them.

5. In Germany, on Lake Constance (in German, it is *Konstanz*).

And, when she had spoken, the worshipful clerk gave her words of great comfort and said it was the work of the Holy Ghost, commanding and charging her to obey them and receive them when God would give them and have no doubts, for the devil has no power to work such grace in a soul. And also he said he would support her against the evil will of her fellowship.

Afterward, when it pleased her fellowship, they prayed this worthy doctor to dinner. And the doctor told the foresaid creature, warning her to sit at the meal in his presence as she did in his absence and keep the same manner of governance that she kept when he was not there. When the time was come that they should sit at the meal, every man took his place as he pleased, the worshipful legate and doctor first sat, and afterward the others, and at the last the said creature at the table's end sitting and no word speaking, as she was wont to do when the legate was not there. Then the legate said unto her, "Why are you no merrier?"

And she sat still and answered not, as he himself had commanded her to do. When they had eaten, the company made great complaint about this creature to the legate, and said utterly she should no longer be in their company unless he would command her to eat meat as they did and leave her weeping and that she should not speak so much of holiness.

Then the worshipful doctor said, "Nay, sirs, I will not make her eat meat while she may abstain herself and be the better disposed to love our Lord. If one of you all made a vow to go to Rome barefoot, I would not absolve him of his vow while he might fulfill it; neither will I bid her eat meat while our Lord gives her strength to abstain. As for her weeping, it is not in my power to restrain it, for it is the gift of the Holy Ghost. As for her speaking, I will ask her to cease until she comes where men will hear her with a better will than you do."

The company was wroth and in great anger. They gave her over to the legate and said utterly they would no more meddle with her. He full benignly and goodly received her as though she had been his mother and received her gold—about twenty pounds—and yet one of them withheld wrongfully about sixteen pounds. And they withheld also her maiden and would not let her go with her mistress, notwithstanding she had promised her mistress and assured her that she should not forsake her for any need. And the legate ordained for this creature and made her exchange as if she had been his mother.

Then this creature went into a church and prayed our Lord to ordain her a leader. And anon our Lord spoke to her and said, "You shall have right good help and a good leader."

And quickly after there came to her an old man with a white beard. He was of Devonshire, and he said, "Damsel, will you pray me for God's love and for our Lady's to go with you and be your guide, for your countrymen have forsaken you?"

She asked what was his name.

He said, "My name is William Weaver."

She prayed him for the reverence of God and of our Lady that he would help her in her need, and she should well reward him for his labor. And so they were accorded.

Then she went to the legate and told him how well our Lord had ordained for her, and took her leave of him and of her company that so unkindly had refused her and also of her maiden, who was bound to have gone with her. She took her leave with a full heavy manner and mournful, having great heaviness, inasmuch as she was in a strange country and did not know the language, nor the man who should lead her either.

And so the man and she went forth together in great dread and heaviness. As they went together, the man said unto her, "I am afraid you shall be taken from me, and I shall be beaten for you and forebear my tabard."[6]

She said, "William, dread you not; God shall keep us right well."

And this creature had every day mind of the Gospel which tells of the woman who was taken in adultery and brought before our Lord.[7] And then she prayed, "Lord, as you drove away her enemies, so drive away my enemies, and keep well my chastity that I vowed to you, and let me never be defiled, for if I am, Lord, I make my vow I will never come in England while I live."

Then went they forth day by day and met with many jolly men. And they said no evil word to this creature but gave her and her man food and drink, and the good wives where they were at inn laid her in their own beds for God's love in many places where they came. And our Lord visited her with great grace of ghostly comfort as she went by the way. And so God brought her forth until she came to Bologna. And, after she came thither, came her other fellowship, which had forsaken her before, thither also. And, when they heard say that she was come to Bologna before them, then had they great wonder, and one of their fellowship came to her, praying her to go to his fellowship and try to see if they would received her again into their fellowship. And so she did.

"If you will go in our fellowship, you must make a new covenant, and that is this: you shall not speak of the Gospel where we come, but you shall sit still and make merry, as we do, both at the midday meal and at supper."

She consented and was received again into their fellowship. Then went they forth to Venice, and they dwelled there thirteen weeks. And this creature was houseled every Sunday in a great house of nuns and had great welcome among them, where our merciful Lord Christ Jesus visited this creature with great devotion and plenteous tears so that the good ladies of the place were much astonished thereof.

Afterward, it happened, as this creature sat at table with her fellowship, that she repeated a text from a Gospel just as she had learned before,

6. Outer garment.
7. John 8.3–11.

along with other good words. And anon her fellowship said she had broken covenant. And she said, "Yes, sirs, forsooth I may no longer hold you in covenant, for I must needs speak of my Lord Jesus Christ though all this world had forbidden it to me."

And then she took to her chamber and ate alone six weeks until the time that our Lord made her so sick that she thought to have been dead, and afterward, suddenly, he made her whole again. And all the time her maiden left her alone and made the company's food and washed their clothes, and to her mistress, to whom she had promised service, she would not at all attend.

28. Also this company, which had put the foresaid creature from their table so that she should no longer eat among them, ordained a ship for themselves to sail in.[8] They bought vessels for their wine and ordained bedding for themselves, but nothing for her. Then she, seeing their unkindness, went to that same man where they had been, and purveyed her bedding, as they had done, and came where they were and showed them what she had done, purposing to sail with them in that ship that they had ordained. Afterward, as this creature was in contemplation, our Lord warned her in her mind that she should not sail in that ship, and he assigned her another ship, a galley, that she should sail in. Then she told this to some of the company, and they told it forth to their fellowship, so then they dared not sail in the ship which they had ordained. And so they sold away their vessels which they had ordained for their wines and were right fain to come to the galley where she was, and so, though it was against their will, she went forth with them in their company, for they dared not otherwise do.

When it was time to make their beds, they locked up her clothes, and a priest who was in their company took away a sheet from the foresaid creature and said it was his. She took God to witness that it was her sheet. Then the priest swore a great oath, and by the book in his hand, that she was as false as she might be and despised her and greatly rebuked her. And so she had ever much tribulation until she came to Jerusalem.

And, before she came there, she said to them that she supposed they were grieved with her. "I pray you, sirs, be in charity with me, for I am in charity with you; forgive me if I have grieved you by the way. And, if any of you have in anything trespassed against me, God forgive it you as I do."

And so they went forth into the Holy Land till they might see Jerusalem. And, when this creature saw Jerusalem, riding on an ass, she

8. Medieval English pilgrims to Jerusalem who intended to take the sea route would have taken about six weeks to arrive in a Mediterranean port. They then booked passage with a shipping company in the pilgrimage business. Some of these ships were quite large, and accommodations were minimal, so the pilgrim had to provide his or her own bedding. If the pilgrim had signed on with a tour, meals would be provided. Once in the Holy Land, travel was strictly regulated, and pilgrims were charged admission fees to important sites. See *Guide to the Holy Land* (1986) and the Introduction by Musto for accounts of medieval pilgrims' experiences.

thanked God with all her heart, praying him for his mercy that, as he had brought her to see this earthly city Jerusalem, he would grant her grace to see the blissful city Jerusalem above, the city of heaven. Our Lord Jesus Christ, answering to her thought, granted her to have her desire. Then, for joy that she had and the sweetness that she felt in the dalliance of our Lord, she was in point to have fallen off her ass, for she might not bear the sweetness and grace that God wrought in her soul. Then two German pilgrims went to her and kept her from falling, of which one was a priest. And he put spices in her mouth to comfort her, thinking she had been sick. And so they helped her forth to Jerusalem.

And, when she came there, she said, "Sirs, I pray you be not displeased though I weep sorely in this holy place where our Lord Jesus Christ was quick and dead."

Then went they to the temple in Jerusalem, and they were let in on the one day at evensong time and abided therein till the next day at evensong time.[9]

Then the friars[1] lifted up a cross and led the pilgrims about from one place to another where our Lord had suffered his pains and his passions, every man and woman bearing a wax candle in their hand. And the friars always, as they went about, told them what our Lord suffered in every place. And the foresaid creature wept and sobbed so plenteously as though she had seen our Lord with her bodily eye suffering his Passion at that time. Before her in her soul she saw him verily by contemplation, and that caused her to have compassion. And when they came up onto the Mount of Calvary, she fell down so that she might not stand or kneel but wallowed and twisted with her body, spreading her arms abroad, and cried with a loud voice as though her heart should have burst asunder, for in the city of her soul she saw verily and freshly how our Lord was crucified. Before her face she heard and saw in her ghostly sight the mourning of our Lady, of Saint John and Mary Magdalene, and of many others who loved our Lord. And she had so great compassion and so great pain to see our Lord's pain that she might not keep herself from crying and roaring though she should have died from it.

And this was the first cry that ever she cried in any contemplation. And this manner of crying endured many years after this time for aught that any man might do, and therefore suffered she much despite and much reproof. The crying was so loud and so wonderful that it made the people astonished unless they had heard it before or else they knew the cause of the crying. And she had them so often that they made her right weak in her bodily mights, and, namely, if she heard of our Lord's Passion. And

---

9. Entrance to the Church of the Holy Sepulcher was limited to between six and twelve pilgrims at a time. They were brought in one door, charged admission, locked in for the time of their vigils, and let out by another.
1. The Franciscans enjoyed the most prominent presence of any order in the Holy Lands. They had a convent that joined the Church of the Holy Sepulcher.

sometimes, when she saw the crucifix, or if she saw a man or a beast, whether it were, had a wound or if a man beat a child before her or smote a horse or another beast with a whip, if she might see it or hear it, she thought she saw our Lord being beaten or wounded just as she saw in the man or in the beast, as well in the field as in the town, and by herself alone, as well as among the people.

First when she had her cryings at Jerusalem, she had them often times, and in Rome also. And, when she came home into England, first at her coming home it came but seldom, as it were once in a month, afterward once in the week, afterward daily, and once she had fourteen on one day, and another day she had seven, and so as God would visit her, sometime in the church, sometime in the street, sometime in the chamber, sometime in the field when God would send them, for she knew never time nor hour when they should come. And they came never without passing great sweetness of devotion and high contemplation.

And, as soon as she perceived that she should cry, she would keep it in as much as she might, so that the people should not have heard it, for it annoyed them. For some said it was a wicked spirit vexed her; some said it was a sickness; some said she had drunk too much wine; some banned her; some wished she had been in the harbor; some would she had been in the sea in a bottomless boat; and so each man as he thought. Other ghostly men loved her and favored her the more. Some great clerks said our Lady cried never so, nor no saint in heaven, but they knew full little what she felt, nor would they not believe that she might have abstained from crying if she wished. And therefore, when she knew that she should cry, she kept it in as long as she might and did all that she could to withstand it or else to put it away until she waxed as blueish gray as any lead, and ever it should labor her mind more and more, unto the time that it broke out. And, when the body might no longer endure the ghostly labor but was overcome with the unspeakable love that wrought so fervently in the soul, then fell she down and cried wonder loud. And the more that she would labor to keep it in or to put it away, much the more should she cry and the louder.

And thus she did in the Mount of Calvary, as it is written before. She had such very contemplation in the sight of her soul, as if Christ had hung before her bodily eye in his manhood. And, when through dispensation of the high mercy of our sovereign savior Christ Jesus, it was granted this creature to behold so verily his precious tender body, completely rent and torn with scourges, more full of wounds than ever was a dove house of holes, hanging upon the cross with the crown of thorns upon his head, his blissful hands, his tender feet nailed to the hard tree, the rivers of blood flowing out plenteously from every member, the grisly and grievous wound in his precious side shedding out blood and water for her love and her salvation, then she fell down and cried with loud voice, wonderfully turning and twisting her body on every side, spreading her arms abroad as if she should have died, and could not keep herself from crying or from these bodily movings, for the fire of love that burnt so fervently in her soul with pure pity and compassion.

It is not to be marveled at if this creature cried and made wonderful face and countenance, when we may see each day with our eyes both men and women, some for loss of worldly good, some for affection of their kindred or for worldly friendships through over much study and earthly affection, and most of all for inordinate love and fleshly affection if their friends are parted from them, they will cry and roar and wring their hands as if they had no wit nor any mind, and yet know they well enough that they displease God. And, if a man counsel them to leave off or cease their weeping or crying, they will say that they may not; they loved their friend so much and he was so gentle and so kind to them that they may in no way forget him. How much more might they weep, cry, and roar if their most beloved friends were with violence taken in their sight and with all manner of reproof brought before the judge, wrongfully condemned to the death, and namely so spiteful a death as our merciful Lord suffered for our sake? How should they suffer it? No doubt but they should both cry and roar and avenge themselves if they might, else men would say they were no friends. Alas, alas, for sorrow, that the death of a creature who had often sinned and trespassed against its maker shall be so unmeasurably mourned and sorrowed. And it is offense to God and hindrance to the souls on each side. And the compassionate death of our Savior, by which we are all restored to life, is not had in mind by us unworthy and unkind wretches, nor will we support our Lord's own secretaries[2] whom he has endued with love, but rather detract them and hinder them as much as we may.

29. When this creature with her fellowship came to the grave where our Lord was buried, anon, as she entered that holy place, she fell down with her candle in her hand as though she should have died for sorrow. And afterward she rose up again with great weeping and sobbing as though she had seen our Lord buried even before her. Then she thought she saw our Lady in her soul, how she mourned and how she wept her son's death, and then was our Lady's sorrow her sorrow.

And so over all where that ever the friars led them in that holy place she always wept and sobbed wonderfully, and especially when she came where our Lord was nailed on the cross. There cried she and wept without measure so that she might not restrain herself. Also they came to a stone of marble that our Lord was laid on when he was taken down from the cross, and there she wept with great compassion, having mind of our Lord's Passion. Afterward she was houseled on the Mount of Calvary, and then she wept, she sobbed, she cried so loud that it wonder was to hear

2. I.e., the holy men and women who mark out the Christlike life.

it. She was so full of holy thoughts and meditations and holy contemplations on the Passion of our Lord Jesus Christ and holy dalliance that our Lord Jesus Christ dallied to her soul that she could never express them afterward, so high and so holy they were.

Great was the grace that our Lord showed to this creature while she was three weeks in Jerusalem. Another day, early in the morning, they went again to the great hills. And their guides told where our Lord bore the cross on his back, and where his Mother met with him, and how she swooned, and how she fell down and he fell down also. And so they went forth all the morning until they came to the Mount Syon. And ever this creature wept abundantly all the way that she went for compassion of our Lord's Passion. In Mount Syon is the place where our Lord washed his disciples' feet, and a little later he made his Last Supper with his disciples. And therefore this creature had great desire to be houseled in that holy place where our merciful Lord Christ Jesus first consecrated his precious body in the form of bread and gave it to his disciples. And so she was, with great devotion, with plenteous tears, and with violent sobbings, for in this place is plenary remission.[3]

And so is it in four other places in the temple. One is in the Mount of Calvary; another at the grave where our Lord was buried; the third is at the marble stone that his precious body was laid on when it was taken from the cross; the fourth is where the holy cross was buried, and in many other places in Jerusalem.

And, when this creature came into the place where the apostles received the Holy Ghost, our Lord gave her great devotion. Afterward she went to the place where our Lady was buried,[4] and as she kneeled on her knees for the time of hearing two masses, our Lord Jesus Christ said unto her, "You come not hither, daughter, for any need but for merit and for meed, for your sins were forgiven you before you came here, and therefore you come hither for the increase of your meed and of your merit. And I am well pleased with you, daughter, for you stand under the obedience of Holy Church and because you will obey your confessor and follow his counsel, which through the authority of Holy Church has pardoned you of your sins and absolved you so that you should not go to Rome or to Saint James unless you yourself want to. Notwithstanding all this, I command you in the name of Jesus, daughter, that you go visit these holy places and do as I bid you, for I am above all Holy Church and I shall go with you and keep you right well."

Then our Lady spoke to her soul in this manner, saying, "Daughter, well are you blessed, for my son Jesus shall flood so much grace into you that all the world shall wonder at you. Be not ashamed, my worthy daughter, to receive the gifts that my son shall give you, for I tell you in truth

3. Complete remission of all sins.
4. This is where the Church of St. Mary was founded, in a garden near Cedron Brook (*Guide to the Holy Land*, p. 37).

they shall be great gifts that he shall give you. And therefore, my worthy daughter, be not ashamed of him that is your God, your Lord, and your love, no more than I was when I saw him hang on the cross, my sweet son, Jesus, to cry and to weep for the pain of my sweet son, Jesus Christ; nor was Mary Magdalene ashamed to cry and weep for my son's love. And therefore, daughter, if you will partake in our joy, you must partake in our sorrow."

This sweet speech and dalliance this creature had at our Lady's grave, and much more than she could ever rehearse. Afterward she rode on an ass to Bethlehem[5] and when she came to the temple and to the crib where our Lord was born, she had great devotion, much speech, and dalliance in her soul, and high ghostly comfort with much weeping and sobbing so that her fellows would not let her eat in their company. And therefore she ate her meals by herself alone.

And then the Gray Friars[6] who had led her from place to place received her into them and set her with them at meals so that she should not eat alone. And one of the friars asked one of her fellowship if that was the woman of England whom they had heard spoke with God. And, when this came to her knowledge, she knew well that it was truth that our Lord said to her before she went out of England, "Daughter, I shall make all the world to wonder at you, and many men and many women shall speak of me for love of you and worship me in you."

30. Another time this creature's fellowship would go to the River Jordan and would not let her go with them. Then this creature prayed our Lord that she might go with them, and he bade that she should go with them whether they would or not. And then she went forth by the grace of God and asked them no permission. When she came to the River Jordan, the weather was so hot that she thought her feet should have burnt for the heat that she felt. Afterward, she went forth with her fellowship to the Mount Quarentyne,[7] where our Lord fasted forty days.[8] And there she prayed her fellowship to help her up onto the Mount. And they said no, for they could not well help themselves. Then she had much sorrow, for she might not go on the hill. And anon happened a Saracen, a comely man, to come by her, and she put a groat[9] in his hand, making to him a sign to bring her onto the Mount. And quickly the Saracen took her under his arm and led her up onto the high Mount where our Lord fasted forty days.

Then was she sorely athirst and had no comfort of her fellowship. Then God of his high goodness moved the Gray Friars with compassion, and

---

5. The Church of the Nativity, whose high altar was dedicated to Mary.
6. Franciscans.
7. Near Jericho.
8. After his baptism, Jesus went into the wilderness and fasted for forty days. Afterward, he was tempted by the devil. See Matthew 3.13–4.3.
9. A silver coin worth four pennies.

they comforted her when her countrymen would not know her. And so she was evermore strengthened in the love of our Lord and the more bold to suffer shames and reproofs for his sake in every place where she came for the grace that God wrought in her of weeping, sobbing, and crying, the which grace she might not withstand when God would send it.

And ever she proved her feelings true. And those promises that God had promised her while she was in England and in other places also, they fell to her in effect just as she had felt before, and therefore she dared better receive such speeches and dalliances and the more boldly work thereafter.

Afterward, when this creature was come down from the Mount, as God would, she went forth to the place where Saint John the Baptist was born. And afterward she went to Bethany where Mary and Martha dwelled and to the grave where Lazarus was buried and raised from death into life.[1] And she went also into the chapel where our blessed Lord appeared to his blissful mother, first of all others, on Easter Day in the morning.[2] And she stood in the same place where Mary Magdalene stood when Christ said to her, "Mary, why do you weep?"[3]

And so she was in many more places than are written, for she was three weeks in Jerusalem and in the countries thereabout. And she had ever great devotion as long as she was in that country. And the Friars of the Temple[4] made her great welcome and gave her many great relics, desiring that she should have dwelled still among them, if she had wished, for the faith they had in her. Also the Saracens made much of her and conveyed her and led her about in the country where she wished to go. And she found all people good unto her and gentle, save only her own countrymen. And, as she came from Jerusalem toward Ramleh,[5] then would she have turned again to Jerusalem for the great grace and ghostly comfort that she felt when she was there and in order to purchase herself more pardon.

And then our Lord commanded her to go to Rome, and so forth home into England, and said unto her, "Daughter, as oftentimes as you say or think, 'Worshipped be all those holy places in Jerusalem that Christ suffered bitter pain and passion in,' you shall have the same pardon as if you were there with your bodily presence, both for yourself and for all those that you will give it to."

And, as she went forth to Venice, much of her fellowship was right sick, and ever our Lord said to her, "Dread you not, daughter, no man shall die in the ship that you are in."

---

1. John 11.1–44.
2. This event is apocryphal; it is memorialized in a chapel within the Church of the Holy Sepulcher.
3. For this scene, which is crucial to medieval devotional literature and particularly important to Margery's spirituality, see John 20.1–18.
4. Franciscans of the convent of the Holy Sepulcher.
5. Town outside Jerusalem on the road to Jaffa.

And she found her feelings right true.

And, when our Lord had brought them again to Venice in safety, her countrymen forsook her and went away from her, leaving her alone. And some of them said that they would not go with her for a hundred pounds. And, when they were gone away from her, then our Lord Jesus Christ, who ever helps at need and never forsakes his servant who truly trusts to his mercy, said to his creature, "Dread you not, daughter, for I shall ordain for you right well and bring you in safety to Rome and home again into England without any villainy to your body if you will be clad in white clothes and wear them as I said to you while you were in England."

Then this creature, being in great heaviness and great doubt, answered again in her mind, "If you are the spirit of God that speaks in my soul and I may prove you for a true spirit with counsel of the church, I shall obey your will, and, if you bring me to Rome in safety, I shall wear white clothes, though all the world should wonder on me, for your love."

"Go forth, daughter, in the name of Jesus, for I am the spirit of God, the which shall help you in all your needs, go with you, and support you in every place, and therefore mistrust me not. You found me never deceiving, nor do I bid you do anything but that which is worship to God and profit to your soul if you will do thereafter, and I shall flood on you great plenty of grace."

Then anon, as she looked on the one side, she saw a poor man sitting, who had a great hump on his back. His clothes were all patched, and he seemed a man of fifty winters age. Then she went to him and said, "Good man, what ails your back?"

He said, "Damsel, it was broken in a sickness."

She asked what was his name and what countryman he was.

He said his name was Richard, and he was of Ireland. Then she thought of her confessor's words (who was a holy anchorite, as is written before), who said to her while she was in England, in this manner, "Daughter, when your own fellowship has forsaken you, God shall ordain a broken backed man to lead you forth where you will be."

Then she with a glad spirit said unto him, "Good Richard, lead me to Rome, and you shall be rewarded for your labor."

"No, damsel," he said, "I know well your countrymen have forsaken you, and therefore it would be hard for me to lead you. For your countrymen have both bows and arrows, with which they might defend both you and themselves, and I have no weapon except a cloak full of patches. And yet I fear that my enemies shall rob me and perhaps take you away from me and defile your body, and therefore I dare not lead you, for I would not for a hundred pounds that you had shame in my company."

And then she said again, "Richard, dread you not; God shall keep us both right well, and I shall give you two nobles for your labor."

Then he consented and went forth with her.

Soon after there came two Gray Friars and a woman who came with them from Jerusalem, and she had with her an ass, which bore a chest and an image therein made after our Lord. And then said Richard to the foresaid creature, "You shall go forth with these two men and women, and I shall meet with you at morning and at evening, for I must attend to my purchase and beg my living."

And so she did after his counsel and went forth with the friars and the woman. And none of them could understand her language, and yet they ordained for her every day food, drink, and lodging as well as they did for themselves, and rather better, so that she was ever bound to pray for them. And every evening and morning Richard with the broken back came and comforted her as he had promised. And the woman who had the image in the chest, when they came into good cities, she took the image out of her chest and set it in worshipful wives' laps. And they would put shirts thereupon and kiss it as though it had been God himself. And, when the creature saw the worship and the reverence that they gave to the image, she was taken with sweet devotion and sweet meditations so that she wept with great sobbing and loud crying. And she was moved in so much the more as, while she was in England, she had high meditations on the birth and the childhood of Christ, and she thanked God forasmuch as she saw these creatures had such great faith in that she saw with her bodily eye just as she had before with her ghostly eye. When these good women saw this creature weep, sob, and cry so wonderfully and mightily that she was nearly overcome therewith, then they ordained a good soft bed and laid her thereupon and comforted her as much as they might for our Lord's love, blessed may he be.

31. The foresaid creature had a ring which our Lord had commanded her to have made while she was at home in England and had her engrave thereupon, "Jesus est amor meus."[6] She had much thought how she should keep this ring from thieves and stealing as she went through the countries, for she thought she would not have lost the ring for a thousand pounds, and much more, because she had it made at the bidding of God. And also she wore it by his bidding, for she purposed before, before she had it by revelation, never to have worn a ring. And, as it happened, she was lodged in a good man's house, and many neighbors came in to welcome her for her perfection and her holiness, and she gave them the measure of Christ's grave, which they received full kindly, having great joy thereof, and thanked her highly for it. Afterward this creature went to her chamber and let her ring hang by her purse string which she bore at her breast. In the morning on the next day, when she would have taken her ring, it was gone; she might not find it. Then she had much heaviness and complained to the good wife of the house, saying in this manner,

6. "Jesus is my love."

"Madam, my good marriage ring to Jesus Christ, as one might say, it is lost."

The good wife, understanding what she meant, prayed her to pray for her, and she changed her manner and her countenance wonderfully, as though she had been guilty. Then this creature took a candle in her hand and sought all about her bed where she had lain all night, and the good wife of the house took another candle in her hand and busied herself to seek also about the bed. And at the last she found the ring under the bed on the boards, and with great joy she told the good wife that she had found her ring. Then the good wife, obeying her, prayed this creature for forgiveness as she could, "Good Christian, pray for me."

Afterward this creature came to Assisi and there she met with a Friar Minor, an Englishman, and he was held as a solemn clerk. She told him of her manner of living, of her feelings, of her revelations, and of the grace that God wrought in her soul by holy inspirations and high contemplations, and how our Lord dallied to her soul, in a manner of speaking. Then the worshipful clerk said that she was much beholden to God, for he said he had never heard of anyone living in this world to be so homely with God by love and homely dalliance as she was, thanked be God of his gifts, for it is his goodness and no man's merit.

Upon a time when this creature was in church at Assisi, our Lady's veil which she wore here on earth was shown with great light and great reverence.[7] Then this creature had great devotion. She wept, she sobbed, she cried with great plenty of tears and many holy thoughts. She was there also on Lammas Day,[8] when there is great pardon of plenary remission, in order to purchase grace, mercy, and forgiveness for herself, for all her friends, for all her enemies, and for all the souls in purgatory. And there was a lady come from Rome to purchase her pardon. Her name was Margaret Florentine, and she had with her many Knights of Rhodes,[9] many gentlewomen, and much good conveyance. Then Richard, the broken backed man, went to her, praying her that this creature might go with her to Rome and himself also, in order to be kept from the peril of thieves. And then that worshipful lady received them into her company and let them go with her to Rome, as God would.

When the foresaid creature was come into Rome, and those who were her fellows before—and had put her out of their company—were in Rome also and heard tell such a woman was come thither, they had great wonder how she came there in safety. And then she went and ordered herself white clothes and was clad all in white, just as she was

---

7. The lower church of St. Francis holds the Veil of Our Lady. "Great light": i.e., large candles, which were expensive.
8. August 1, the feast of St. Peter in Chains, commemorating Peter's freeing from chains and thus our own freedom from the "chains" of sin. In England, Lammas was a day on which quarter rents were collected, and it was associated with agricultural harvest.
9. One of the military orders of the Church.

commanded to do years before in her soul by revelation, and now it was fulfilled in effect.

Then was this creature received into the hospice of Saint Thomas of Canterbury[1] in Rome, and there was she houseled every Sunday with great weeping, violent sobbing, and loud crying and was highly beloved of the master of the hospice and by all his brothers. And then through the stirring of her ghostly enemy there came a priest who was held a holy man in the hospice and also in other places of Rome, who was one of her fellows and one of her own countrymen. And notwithstanding his holiness, he spoke so evilly of this creature and slandered so her name in the hospice that through his evil language she was put out of the hospice so that she might no longer be shriven nor houseled therein.

32. When this creature saw she was forsaken and put from among the good men, she was full heavy, mostly because she had no confessor nor might not be shriven then as she wished. Then prayed she our Lord of his mercy that he would dispose for her as was most pleasing unto him, with great plenty of tears. And afterward she called unto her the foresaid Richard with the broken back, praying him to go over to a church against the hospice and inform the parson of the church of her manner of governance, and what sorrow she had, and how she wept because she might not be shriven nor houseled, and what compunction and contrition she had for her sins. Then Richard went to the parson and informed him of this creature, and how our Lord gave her contrition and compunction with great plenty of tears, and how she desired to be houseled every Sunday if she might, and she had no priest to be shriven to. And then the parson, hearing of her contrition and compunction, was right glad and bade she should come to him in the name of Jesus and say her confession of sins, and he should housel her his own self, for he could not understand any English.

Then our Lord sent Saint John the Evangelist[2] to hear her confession, and she said "Benedicite." And he said "Dominus"[3] verily in her soul so that she saw him and heard him in her ghostly understanding as she should have another priest by her bodily wits. Then she told him all her sins and all her heaviness with many sorrowful tears, and he heard her full meekly and benignly. And afterward he enjoined her penance that she should do for her trespass and assoiled her of her sins with sweet words and meek words, highly strengthening her to trust in the mercy of our Lord Jesus Christ, and bade her that she should receive the sacrament of the altar in the name of Jesus. And afterward he passed away from her. When he was gone, she prayed with all her heart all the time as she heard

1. The hospice of St. Thomas of Canterbury in Rome was for English pilgrims to the city.
2. St. John, the beloved disciple, who also appeared to St. Elizabeth of Hungary. "Benedicite": bless you.
3. Lord.

her mass, "Lord, as surely as you are not angry with me, grant me a well of tears, wherethrough I may receive your precious body with all manner of tears of devotion to your worship and the increase of my merit, for you are my joy, Lord, my bliss, my comfort, and all the treasure that I have in this world, for other wordly joy covet I none but only you. And therefore, my worthy Lord and my God, forsake me not."

Then our blissful Lord Christ Jesus answered to her soul and said, "My worthy daughter, I swear by my high majesty that I shall never forsake you. And, daughter, the more shame, despite, and reproof that you suffer for my love, the better I love you, for I fare like a man who loves well his wife, the more envy that men have toward her the better he will array her, in despite of her enemies. And right so, daughter, shall I fare with you. In no thing that you do, daughter, or say, you may no better please God than believe that he loves you, for, if it were possible that I might weep with you, I would weep with you, daughter, for the compassion that I have of you. Time shall come when you shall hold yourself right well pleased, for it shall be verified in you the common proverb that men say, 'He is well blessed who may sit on his well stool and tell of his woe stool.' And so shall you do, daughter, and all your weeping and your sorrow shall turn into joy and bliss, which you shall never miss."

33. Another time, as this creature was at Saint John's Church Lateran,[4] before the altar hearing the mass, she thought that the priest who said mass seemed a good man and devout. She was sorely moved in spirit to speak with him. Then she prayed her man with the broken back to go to the priest and ask him to speak with her. Then the priest understood no English nor knew what she said, and she knew no other language than English, and therefore they spoke through an interpreter, a man who told either what the other said. Then she prayed the priest in the name of Jesus if he would make his prayers to the blissful Trinity, to our Lady, and to all the blessed saints in heaven, also stirring others who loved our Lord to pray for him, so that he might have grace to understand her language and her speech about such things as she through the grace of God would say and show unto him. The priest was a good man, and by his birth he was a German, a good clerk, and a well learned man, highly beloved, well cherished, and much trusted in Rome, and had one of the greatest offices of any priest in Rome. Desiring to please God, he followed the counsel of this creature and made his prayers to God as devoutly as he could every day that he might have grace to understand what the foresaid creature would say to him, and also he made other lovers of our Lord to pray for him. Thus they prayed thirteen days. And after thirteen days, the priest came again to her in order to prove the effect of their prayers, and then he understood what she said in English to him, and she understood what

---

4. The church of St. John Lateran.

he said. And yet he understood not the English that other men spoke; though they spoke the same words that she spoke, yet he understood them not, unless she spoke herself. Then she was confessed to this priest of all her sins, as nearly as her mind would serve her from her childhood unto that hour and received her penance full joyfully.

And afterward she showed him the secret things of revelations and of high contemplations, and how she had such mind of his Passion and so great compassion when God would give it that she fell down therewith and might not bear it. Then she wept bitterly, she sobbed violently and cried full loudly and horribly so that the people were oftentimes afraid and greatly astonished, believing she had been vexed with some evil spirit, not believing it was the work of God but rather some evil spirit, or a sudden sickness, or else simulation and hypocrisy falsely feigned by her own self. The priest had great trust that it was the work of God, and, when he would mistrust, our Lord sent him such tokens by the foresaid creature of his own misgovernance and his living, which no man knew but God and himself, as our Lord showed to her by revelation and bade her tell him, so that he knew well thereby her feelings were true.

And then this priest received her full meekly and reverently, like his mother and his sister, and said he would support her against her enemies. And so he did as long as she was in Rome and suffered many evil words and much tribulation. And also he forsook his office because he would support her in her sobbing and in her crying when all her countrymen had forsaken her, for they were ever her greatest enemies and caused her much heaviness in every place where they came, for they wished that she should neither have sobbed nor cried. And she might not choose, but that would they not believe. And they were ever against her and against the good man who supported her.

And then this good man, seeing this woman so wonderfully sobbing and crying, and especially on Sundays when she should be houseled among all the people, purposed himself to prove whether it was the gift of God, as she said, or else her own feigning by hypocrisy, as the people said, and took her alone another Sunday into another church when mass was done and all the people were home, no man knowing thereof, save himself and the clerk only. And, when he should housel her, she wept so plenteously and sobbed and cried so loudly, that he was astonished himself, for it seemed to his hearing that she cried never so loudly before that time. And then he believed fully that it was the working of the Holy Ghost and neither feigning nor hypocrisy by her.

And then afterward he was not abashed to hold with her and to speak against those who would defame her and speak evil of her until he was detracted by the enemies of virtue nearly as much as she, and that pleased him well to suffer tribulation for God's cause. And many people in Rome who were disposed to virtue loved him much the more, and her also, and often prayed her to a meal and made her right great welcome, praying her to pray for them. And ever her own countrymen were obstinate, and specially a priest who was among them. He stirred many people against her and said much evil of her, for she wore white clothing more than others did, who they thought were holier and better than ever she was. The cause of his malice was because she would not obey him. And she knew well it was against the health of her soul to obey him as he wished that she should have done.

34. Then the good man, the German priest to whom she was shriven, through the stirring of the English priest who was her enemy, asked her if she would be obedient unto him or not. And she said, "Yes, sir."

"Will you do then as I shall bid you do?"

"With right good will, sire."

"I charge you then that you leave your white clothes, and wear again your black clothes."

And she did his commandment. And then had she feeling that she pleased God with her obedience. Then she suffered many scorns from the wives of Rome. They asked her if highwaymen had robbed her, and she said, "No, Madame."

Afterward, as she went on pilgrimage, it happened that she met with the priest who was her enemy, and he delighted greatly that she was put from her will and said unto her, "I am glad that you go in black clothing as you used to do."

And she said again to him, "Sir, our Lord was not displeased though I wore white clothes, for he willed that I do so."

Then the priest said to her again, "Now know I well that you have a devil within you, for I hear him speak in you to me."

"A, good sir, I pray you drive him away from me, for God knows I would right fain do well and please him if I could."

And then he was right angry and said full many sharp words. And she said to him, "Sir, I hope I have no devil within me, for, if I had a devil within me, know well I should be angry with you and, sir, I think that I am not angry with you for any thing that you can do unto me."

And then the priest parted away from her with a heavy countenance.

And then our Lord spoke to this creature in her soul and said, "Daughter, dread you not whatever he says unto you; for, though he ran every year to Jerusalem, I have no delight in him; for as long as he speaks against you, he speaks against me, for I am in you and you are in me. And hereby may you know that I suffer many sharp words, for I have often said to you that I should be new crucified in you by sharp words, for you shall not otherwise be slain than by suffering sharp words. For this priest who is your enemy, he is but a hypocrite."

Then the good priest her confessor bade her by virtue of obedience and also as part of penance that she should serve an old woman who was a poor creature in Rome. And she did so six weeks. She served her as she would have done our Lady. And she had no bed to lie in nor any clothes to be covered with save her own mantle. And then she was full of vermin and suffered great pain therewith. Also she fetched home water and sticks on her neck for the poor woman and begged food and wine both for her. And, when the poor woman's wine was sour, this creature herself drank that sour wine and gave the poor woman good wine that she had bought for her own self.

35. As this creature was in the Apostle's Church at Rome on St. John Lateran's Day,[5] the Father of Heaven said to her, "Daughter, I am well pleased with you, inasmuch as you believe in all the sacraments of Holy Church and in all faith that belongs to it, and specially because you believe in the manhood of my son and because of the great compassion that you have for his bitter Passion."

Also the Father said to this creature, "Daughter, I will have you wedded to my Godhead, for I shall show you my secrets and my counsels, for you shall dwell with me without end."[6]

Then the creature kept silence in her soul and answered not thereto, for she was full sore afraid of the Godhead, and she had no knowledge of the dalliance of the Godhead, for all her love and all her affection was set on the manhood of Christ and thereof had she good knowledge, and she would for no thing have parted therefrom. She was so much affected by the manhood of Christ that when she saw women in Rome bearing children in their arms, if she might learn that there were any men children, she should then cry, roar, and weep as though she had seen Christ in his childhood. And, if she might have had her will, oftentimes she would have taken the children out from the mothers' arms and have kissed them in the place of Christ. And, if she saw a seemly man, she had great pain to look on him in case she might have seen him who was both God and man. And therefore she cried many times and often when she met a seemly man and wept and sobbed full sorely in the manhood of Christ as she went in the streets at Rome, so that those who saw her wondered full much on her, for they knew not the cause.

And therefore it was no wonder if she were still and answered not the Father of Heaven when he told her that she should be wedded to his Godhead. Then said the second person, Christ Jesus, whose manhood she loved so much, to her, "What say you, Margery, daughter, to my Father of these words that he speaks to you? Are you well pleased that it is so?"

And then she would not answer the second person but wept wonder sore, desiring to have still himself and in no way to be parted from him.

Then the second person in the Trinity answered to his Father f

---

5. The feast celebrating the dedication of the church of St. John Lateran.
6. This speech implies that attachment to the manhood of Jesus was pre
the first person of the Trinity, God the Father.

and said, "Father, have her excused, for she is yet but young and not fully learned as to how she should answer."

And then the Father took her by the hand in her soul before the Son and the Holy Ghost and the Mother of Jesus and all the twelve apostles and Saint Katherine and Saint Margaret and many other saints and holy virgins, with a great multitude of angels, saying to her soul, "I take you, Margery, for my wedded wife, for fairer, for fouler, for richer, for poorer, so that you be buxom and obedient to do what I bid you do. For, daughter, there was never a child so buxom to the mother as I shall be to you, both in well and in woe, to help you and comfort you. And thereto I make you surety."

And then the Mother of God and all the saints that were there present in her soul prayed that they might have much joy together. And then the creature with high devotion, with great plenty of tears, thanked God for this ghostly comfort, holding herself in her own feeling right unworthy of any such grace as she felt, for she felt many great comforts, both ghostly comforts and bodily comforts. Sometimes she felt sweet smells with her nose; it was sweeter, she thought, than ever was any sweet earthly thing that she smelled before, nor might she ever tell how sweet it was, for she thought she might have lived thereby if they would have lasted.

Sometimes she heard with her bodily ears such sounds and melodies that she might not well hear what a man said to her in that time unless he spoke the louder. These sounds and melodies had she heard nearly every day for the term of twenty-five years when this book was written, and especially when she was in devout prayer, also many times while she was at Rome and in England both.

She saw with her bodily eye many white things flying all about her on every side, as thick in a manner as motes in the sun; they were right delicate and comfortable, and the brighter that the sun shone, the better she might see them. She saw them many different times and in many different places, both in church and in her chamber, at her meal and in her prayers, in field and in town, both going and sitting. And many times she was afraid what they might be, for she saw them as well in nights in darkness as in daylight. Then, when she was afraid of them, our Lord said unto her, "By this token, daughter, believe it is God that speaks in you, for whereso God is, heaven is, and where God is there are many angels, and God is in you and you are in him. And therefore be not afraid, daughter, for this betokens that you have many angels about you to keep you both day and night so that no devil shall have power over you nor no evil man harm you."

Then from that time forward she used to say when she saw them come, "Benedictus qui venit in nomine domini."[7]

---

7. "Blessed is he who comes in the name of the Lord" are the words used by the priest to welcome Christ's entrance into the elements of the Mass; they here suggest Margery's own sacramental areness.

Also our Lord gave her another token, which endured about sixteen years, and it increased ever more and more, and that was a flame of fire wonderfully hot and delectable and right comfortable, not wasting but ever increasing of flame, for, though the weather was never so cold, she felt the heat burning in her breast and at her heart, as verily as a man should feel the material fire if he put his hand or his finger therein.[8]

When she felt first the fire of love burning in her breast, she was afraid thereof, and then our Lord answered to her mind and said, "Daughter, be not afraid, for this heat is the heat of the Holy Ghost, which shall burn away all your sins, for the fire of love quenches all sins. And you shall understand by this token that the Holy Ghost is in you, and you know well wherever the Holy Ghost is, there is the Father, and where the Father is, there is the Son, and so you have fully in your soul all the Holy Trinity. Therefore you have great cause to love me right well, and yet you shall have greater cause than ever you had to love me, for you shall hear what you never heard, and you shall see what you never saw, and you shall feel what you never felt.

For, daughter, you are as sure of the love of God as God is God. Your soul is more sure of the love of God than of your own body, for your soul shall part from your body, but God shall never part from your soul, for they are joined together without end. Therefore, daughter, you have as great cause to be merry as any lady in this world, and, if you knew, daughter, how much you please me when you suffer me willfully to speak in you, you should never do otherwise, for this is a holy life, and the time is right well spent. For, daughter, this life pleases me more than wearing of the jacket of mail or of the hair shirt or fasting on bread and water, for, if you said every day a thousand Pater Noster's,[9] you should not please me as well as you do when you are in silence and suffer me to speak in your soul.

36. "Fasting, daughter, is good for young beginners and discreet penance, namely that their ghostly father gives them or enjoins them to do. And to bid many beads,[1] it is good to those who can do no better, and yet it is not perfect. But it is a good way toward perfection. For I tell you, daughter, those who are great fasters and great doers of penance, they would that it should be held the best life; also those who give themselves to say many devotions, they would have that the best life, and those who give many alms, they would that that was held the best life. And I have oftentimes, daughter, told you that thinking, weeping, and high contemplation is the best life on earth. And you shall have more merit in heaven for one year of thinking in your mind than for a hundred years of praying

---

8. This sensation of inward burning is one commonly reported by medieval mystics such as Richard Rolle.
9. "Our Father's"; i.e., the Lord's Prayer.
1. I.e., say many prayers.

with your mouth, and yet you will not believe me, for you will bid many beads whether I will or not.

"And yet, daughter, I will not be displeased with you whether you think, say, or speak, for I am always pleased with you. And, if I were on earth as bodily as I was before I died on the cross, I should not be ashamed of you as many other men are, for I should take you by the hand among the people and make you great welcome so that they should well know that I loved you right well. For it is suitable for the wife to be homely with her husband. Be he never so great a lord and she so poor a woman when he wedded her, yet they must lie together and rest together in joy and peace. Right so must it be between you and me, for I take no heed what you have been but what you would be. And oftentimes have I told you that I have clean forgiven you all your sins. Therefore must I needs be homely with you and lie in your bed with you. Daughter, you desire greatly to see me, and you may boldly, when you are in your bed, take me to you as your wedded husband, as your most worthy darling, and as your sweet son, for I will be loved as a son should be loved by the mother and will that you love me, daughter, as a good wife ought to love her husband. And therefore you may boldly take me in the arms of your soul and kiss my mouth, my head, and my feet as sweetly as you will.[2]

"And, as often as you think on me or would do any good deed to me, you shall have the same reward in heaven as if you did it to my own precious body which is in heaven, for I ask no more of you but your heart to love what loves you, for my love is ever ready for you."

Then she gave thanks and praise to our Lord Jesus Christ for the high grace and mercy that he showed unto her, an unworthy wretch.

This creature had divers tokens in her bodily hearing. One was a manner of sound as if it had been a pair of bellows blowing in her ear. She, being abashed thereof, was warned in her soul no fear to have, for it was the sound of the Holy Ghost. And then our Lord turned that sound into the voice of a dove, and afterward he turned it into the voice of a little bird which is called a red breast that sang full merrily oftentimes in her right ear. And then should she evermore have great grace after she heard such a token. And she had been used to such tokens about twenty-five years at the writing of this book.

Then our Lord Jesus Christ said to his creature, "By these tokens may you well know that I love you, for you are to me a very mother, and to all the world, because of that great charity that is in you, and yet I myself am the cause of that charity, and you shall have great reward therefore in Heaven.

37. "Daughter, because you are so buxom to my will and cleave as sorely unto me as to a man's hands cleaves the skin of dried fish when it

---

2. The language of intimate physical love was used both by male and by female mystics to express spiritual desire and ecstacy.

is boiled, and will not forsake me for any shame that any man can do to you, and you say also that though I stood before you in my own person and said to you that you should never have my love, nor ever come into heaven, nor ever see my face, yet say you, daughter, that you would never forsake me on earth, nor never love me the less, nor ever do the less business to please me, though you should lie in hell without end, for you may not forbear my love on earth, nor can you have any other comfort but me only, which I am, your God, and am all joy and all bliss to you. Therefore I say to you, worthy daughter, it is impossible that any such soul which has so great meekness and charity toward me should be damned or parted from me. And therefore, daughter, dread you never, for all the great promises that I have promised to you and to all of yours and to all your ghostly fathers shall ever be true and truly fulfilled when the time comes. Have no doubt thereof."

Another time while she was in Rome, a little before Christmas, our Lord Jesus Christ commanded her to go to her ghostly father, Wenslawe by name, and bid him give her leave to wear again her white clothes, for he had put her therefrom by virtue of obedience, as is written before. And, when she told him the will of our Lord, he dared not once say no. And so she wore white clothes ever after.

Then our Lord bade her that she should at Christmas go home again to her host's house where she was at hostel before. And then she went to a poor woman whom she served at that time by the bidding of her confessor, as is before written, and told the poor woman how she must go from her. And then the poor woman was right sorry and made great moan for her departing. And then this creature told her how it was the will of God that it should be so, and then she took it the more easily.

Afterward, as this creature was in Rome, our Lord bade her give away all her goods and make herself bare for his love. And anon she, with a fervent desire to please God, gave away such goods as she had and such as she had borrowed also from the broken-backed man who went with her. When he knew how she had given away his goods, he was greatly moved and evil pleased for she gave away his goods, and spoke right sharply to her.

And then she said unto him, "Richard, by the grace of God we shall come home into England right well. And you shall come to me in Bristol in Whitsun week, and there shall I pay you right well and truly, by the grace of God, for I trust right well that he who bade me give it away for his love will help me to pay it again." And so he did.

38. After this creature had thus given away her goods and had neither penny nor halfpenny to help herself with, as she lay in Saint Marcello's Church in Rome, thinking and studying where she should have her living, inasmuch as she had no silver to sustain herself withal, our Lord answered to her mind and said, "Daughter, you are not yet so poor as I was when I hung naked on the cross for your love, for you have clothes on

your body, and I had none. And you have counseled other men to be poor for may sake, and therefore you must follow your own counsel. But dread you not, daughter, for there is gold toward you, and I have promised you before that I would never fail you. And I shall pray my own mother to beg for you, for you have many times begged for me and for my mother also. And therefore dread you not. I have friends in every country and shall make my friends comfort you."

When our Lord had thus sweetly dallied to her soul, she thanked him for this great comfort, having good trust it should be as he said.

Afterward she, rising up, went forth in the street and met casually with a good man. And so they fell into good communication as they went together by the way. With him she had many good tales and many good exhortations till God visited him with tears of devotion and of compunction, to his high comfort and consolation. And then he gave her money, by which she was well relieved and comforted a good while.

Then on a night she saw in vision how our Lady, she thought, sat at a meal with many worshipful persons and asked food for her. And then thought this creature that our Lord's words were fulfilled ghostly in that vision, for he promised this creature a little before that he should pray his mother to beg for her.

And in a short time after this vision she met with a worshipful lady, Dame Margaret Florentine, the same lady who brought her from Assisi into Rome. And neither of them could well understand the other but by signs or tokens and in a few common words. And then the lady said unto her, "Margerya in poverté?"[3]

She, understanding what the lady meant, said again, "Yes, great poverty, Madam."

Then the lady commanded her to eat with her every Sunday and set her at her own table above herself and laid her meal with her own hands. Then this creature sat and wept full sorely, thanking our Lord that she was so cared for and cherished for his love by those who could not understand her language. When they had eaten, the good lady used to take her a hamper with other stuff that she might make her soup therewith, as much as would serve her for a two days' meal, and filled her bottle with good wine. And sometimes she gave her eight bolendines[4] as well.

And then another man in Rome, who was called Marcelle, whose wife was great with child, highly desiring to have had this creature as godmother to her child when it had been born (and she abode not so long in Rome), asked her to a meal two days in the week. And also there was a holy maiden who gave this creature her food on Wednesday. Other days when she was not purveyed she begged her food from door to door.

---

3. An attempt to capture broken English, i.e., "Margery, are you in poverty?"
4. Roman coin.

39. Another time, right as she came by a poor woman's house, the poor woman called her into her house and had her sit by her little fire, giving her wine to drink in a cup of stone. And she had a little man child sucking on her breast. He sucked one while on the mother's breast; another while he ran to this creature, the mother sitting full of sorrow and sadness. Then this creature burst all into weeping, as though she had seen our Lady and her son in the time of his Passion, and had so many holy thoughts that she might never tell the half, but ever sat and wept plenteously a long time so that the poor woman, having compassion for her weeping, prayed her to cease, not knowing why she wept. Then our Lord Jesus Christ said to the creature, "This place is holy."

And then she rose up and went forth in Rome and saw much poverty among the people. And then she thanked God highly for the poverty that she was in, trusting through it to be partner with him in merit.

Then was there a great gentlewoman in Rome, praying this creature to be godmother of her child and named it after Saint Bridget,[5] for they had knowledge of her in her lifetime. And so she did.

Afterward God gave her grace to have great love in Rome, both from men and from women, and great favor among the people. When the master and brother of the hospice of Saint Thomas, where she was refused before, as is written before, heard tell what love and what favor she had in the city, they prayed her that she would come again to them, and she should be more welcome than ever she was before, for they were right sorry that they had put her away from them. And she thanked them for their charity and did their bidding. And, when she was come again to them, they made her right good welcome and were right glad of her coming.

Then found she there her who was her maiden before, and with right should have been so still, dwelling in the hospice in much wealth and prosperity, for she was keeper of their wine. And this creature went sometimes to her out of meekness and prayed her for food and drink, and the maiden gave them to her with a good will, and sometimes a groat also. Then she complained to her maiden and said that she felt great sorrow at her departing and what slander and evil words men said of her because they were asunder; but would she never be again with her.

Afterward this creature spoke with Saint Bridget's maiden in Rome, but she could not understand what she said. Then she had a man who could understand her language, and that man told Saint Bridget's maiden what this creature said and how she asked after Saint Bridget, her lady. Then the maiden said that her lady, Saint Bridget, was goodly and meek to every creature and that she had a laughing countenance. And also the good man where this creature was at hostel told her that he knew her himself, but he little knew that she had been as holy a woman as she

5. See above, p. 35, n. 6.

was, for she was ever homely and goodly to all creatures who would speak with her. She was in the chamber that Saint Bridget died in, and heard a German priest preach of her therein and of her revelations and of her manner of living. And she kneeled also on the stone on which our Lord appeared to Saint Bridget and told her on what day she should die. And this was one of Saint Bridget's days that this creature was in her chapel, which before was her chamber that she died in.[6]

Our Lord sent such tempests of winds and rains and divers disturbances of the air that those who were in the fields and in their labors outside were compelled to enter houses for relief of their bodies to avoid divers perils. Through such tokens this creature supposed that our Lord wanted his holy saint's day to be hallowed and the saint held in more worship than she was at that time.

And sometimes, when this creature would have made the Stations,[7] our Lord warned her at night in her bed that she should not go out far from her hostel, for he should send great tempests that day of lightning and thunder. And so it was in deed. There were such great tempests that year of thunder and lightning, of great rains and divers stormy weather, that right old men at that time dwelling in Rome said they had never seen such before. The lightning was so plenteous and so bright shining within their houses that they thought verily it should have burnt their houses along with the contents. Then cried they to the foresaid creature to pray for them, fully trusting that she was the servant of almighty God and through her prayers they should be helped and succored. This creature at their request praying our Lord for mercy, he answered in her soul, saying, "Daughter, be not afraid, for there shall no weather nor tempest harm you, and therefore mistrust me not, for I shall never deceive you."

And our merciful Lord Christ Jesus, as it pleased him, withdrew the tempests, preserving the people from all troubles.

40. Then through the provision of our merciful Lord Christ Jesus there came a priest, a good man, out of England into Rome with other fellowship, asking and inquiring diligently after the said creature whom he had never seen before, nor she him. But while he was in England he heard tell that such a woman was at Rome with whom he longed highly to speak if God would grant him grace. Wherefore, while he was in his own land, he, purposing to see this creature when he through the sufferance of our Lord might come where she was, purveyed gold to bring her for her relief if she had need. Then by inquiring, he came to the place where she was, and full humbly and meekly he called her mother, praying her out of charity to receive him as her son.

6. There were three days sacred to St. Bridget: July 23, the feast of her death; May 28, the feast of her translation; and October 7, the medieval date for her canonization. Meech, pp. 304–05, feels the latter date is the one referred to here.
7. Stations of Rome—visiting and praying in a sequence of Roman churches.

She said that he was as welcome to God and to her as to his own mother. So by holy dalliance and communication she felt well that he was a good man. And then she, disclosing the secret of her heart, revealed what grace God wrought in her soul through his holy inspiration and somewhat of her manner of living. Then he would no longer suffer her to beg her food from door to door, but prayed her to eat with him and his fellowship, unless good men and women by the way of charity and for ghostly comfort would pray her to meals. Then he wished that she should take it in the name of our Lord, and otherwise she should eat with him and with his fellowship every day, and he gave her gold sufficient to come home with into England. And then was fulfilled what our Lord said to her a little before, "Gold is to theeward."[8] And so it was indeed, thanked be almighty God.

Then some of her fellows with whom she had been at Jerusalem came to this good priest, newly come to Rome, complaining of her, and said that she was shriven by a priest who could not understand her language nor her confession. Then this good priest, trusting to her as to his mother, desiring the health of her soul, asked of her if her confessor understood her when she spoke to him or not.

"Good son, I beseech you ask him to dine with you and with your fellows and let me be present, and then shall you know the truth."

Her confessor was asked to a meal and, when the time came, set and served with this good priest and his fellowship, the said creature being present, the good priest of England dallying and commoning in her own language, English. The German priest, a worthy clerk, as is written before confessor to the said creature, sat all still in a manner of heaviness because he understood not what they said in English unless they spoke it in Latin. And they did it on purpose, he unknowing, in order to prove if he understood English or not. At the last, the said creature, seeing and well understanding that her confessor understood not their language and that it was tedious to him, then, in part to comfort him and in part or else much more to prove the work of God, she told in her own language in English a story of Holy Writ which she had learned from clerks while she was at home in England, for she would speak of no vanity nor of fantasies.

Then they asked her confessor if he understood what she had said, and he anon in Latin told them the same words that she said before in English, for he could neither speak English nor understand English, save only after her tongue. And then they had great marvel, for they knew well that he understood what she said and she understood what he said, and he could understand no other Englishman. So blessed may God be that made an alien to understand her when her own countrymen had forsaken her and would not hear her confession unless she would have left her weeping and speaking of holiness.

8. "Gold is toward you."

And yet she might not weep but when God gave it to her. And oftentimes he gave it so plenteously that she could not withstand it. But the more that she would have withstood it or put it away, the more strongly it wrought in her soul with such holy thoughts that she should not cease. She should sob and cry full loudly, all against her will, so that many men and women also wondered on her therefore.

41. Sometimes, when the foresaid creature was at sermons where Germans and other men preached, teaching the laws of God, sudden sorrow and heaviness occupying her heart caused her to complain with a mourning countenance for lack of understanding, desiring to be refreshed with some crumb of ghostly understanding of her most trusted and entirely beloved sovereign, Christ Jesus, whose melodious voice, sweetest of all savors softly sounding in her soul, said, "I shall preach you and teach you myself, for your will and your desire is acceptable unto me."

Then was her soul so delectably fed with the sweet dalliance of our Lord and so fulfilled by his love that, like a drunken man, she turned herself, first on the one side and then on the other, with great weeping and great sobbing, unable to keep herself in stableness for the unquenchable fire of love that burnt full sorely in her soul. Then many people wondered upon her, asking her what ailed her, to whom she, as a creature all wounded with love and as reason had failed, cried with a loud voice, "The Passion of Christ slays me."

The good women, having compassion for her sorrow and greatly marveling at her weeping and at her crying, much the more they loved her. And therefore they, desiring to make her solace and comfort after her ghostly labor, by signs and tokens, for she understood not their speech, prayed her and in a manner compelled her to come home with them, willing that she should not go from them.

Then our Lord sent her grace to have great love and great favor from many persons in Rome, both from religious men and from others. Some religious came to such persons of her countrymen that loved her and said, "This woman has sown much good seed in Rome since she came hither, that is to say, shown a good example to the people, wherethrough they love God more than they did before."

On a time, as this creature was in a church at Rome where the body of Saint Jerome lies buried[9] (which was miraculously translated from Bethlehem to that place and there now is had in great worship beside the place where Saint Lawrence[1] lies buried), to this creature's ghostly sight appearing, Saint Jerome said to her soul, "Blessed are you, daughter, in the weeping that you weep for the people's sin, for many shall be saved

9. St. Jerome's remains were in the church of Santa Maria Maggiore; Jerome had lived and worked in Bethlehem.
1. The relics of St. Lawrence are in the church of San Lorenzo, two miles from Santa Maria Maggiore.

thereby. And, daughter, dread you not, for it is a singular and a special gift that God has given you, a well of tears which man shall never take from you."

With such manner of dalliance he highly comforted her spirits. And also he made great praising and thanking to God for the grace that he wrought in her soul, for, unless she had had such ghostly comforts, it had been impossible for her to have borne the shames and wonderings which she suffered patiently and meekly for the grace that God showed in her.

42. When the time of Easter or else Paske[2] was come and gone, this creature with her fellowship purposing to go again into their own native land, it was told them that there were many thieves by the way who would spoil them of their goods and perhaps slay them. Then the said creature with many a bitter tear from her eye prayed to our Lord Jesus Christ, saying, "Christ Jesus, in whom is all my trust, as you have promised me many times before that there should no man be distressed in my company, and I was never deceived nor defrauded by your promise as long as I fully and truly trusted unto you, so hear the prayers of your unworthy servant, all wholly trusting in your mercy. And grant that I and my fellowship without hindering of body or of goods—for over our souls, Lord, have they no power—may go home again into our land just as we came hither, for your love, and let never our enemies have any power over us, Lord, if it please you. As you will, so may it be."

Then our Lord Jesus Christ said to her mind, "Dread you not, daughter, for you and all who are in your company shall go as safely as if they were in Saint Peter's Church."

Then thanked she God with all her spirits, and was bold enough to go where God wished, and took her leave of her friends in Rome, and most specially of her ghostly father, who, for our Lord's love, had supported her and succored her full tenderly against the wicked winds of her envious enemies, whose parting was full lamentable as was witnessed well by the pure water drops running down their cheeks. She, falling on her knees, received the favor of his blessing, and so parted asunder those whom charity joined both in one, through which they trusted to meet again, when our Lord wished, in their natural country when they had passed this wretched worldly exile. And thus she and her fellowship passed forth toward England.

And when they were a little way out of Rome, and the good priest, who as is before written this creature had received as her own son, had great dread of enemies. Wherefore he said unto her, "Mother, I dread to be dead and slain by enemies."

She said, "Nay, son, you shall fare right well and go safely by the grace of God."

2. In the Middle Ages, *Paske* (Pasch = the Passover) was another name for Easter.

And he was well comforted by her words, for he trusted much in her feelings and made her as good comfort by the way as if he had been her own son born of her body.

And so they came forth to Middelburg,[3] and then her fellowship would take their journey into England on the Sunday. Then the good priest came to her, saying, "Mother, will you go with your fellowship or not on this good day?"

And she said, "Nay, son, it is not my Lord's will that I should go so soon hence."

And so she abode still with the good priest and some other of the fellowship until the Saturday after. And much of her fellowship went to ship on the Sunday. On the Friday after, this creature went to disport herself in the field and men of her own nation with her, whom she informed in the laws of God as well as she could; and sharply she spoke against them for they swore great oaths and broke the commandment of our Lord God. And as she went thus dallying with them, our Lord Jesus Christ bade her to go home in haste to her hostel, for there should come great weather and perilous. Then she hied herself homeward with her fellowship, and, as soon as they came home to their hostel, the weather befell as she felt by revelation.

And many times, as she went by the way and in the fields, there befell great lightning with hideous thunderclaps, ghastly and grievous, so that she feared that it should have smote her to death, and many great rains, which caused in her great dread and heaviness. Then our Lord Jesus Christ said to her, "Why are you afraid while I am with you? I am as mighty to keep you here in the field as in the strongest church in all this world."

And after that time she was not so greatly afraid as she was before, for ever she had great trust in his mercy, blessed may he be that comforted her in every sorrow. And afterward, it happened that an Englishman came to this creature and swore a great oath. She, hearing that oath, wept, mourned, and sorrowed without measure, not having power to restrain herself from weeping and sorrowing, forasmuch as she saw her brother offend our Lord God almighty and little heed would take to his own fault.

43. On the next day early, came to this creature the good priest, who was as her son, and said, "Mother, good tidings. We have good wind, thanked be God."

And anon she gave praise to our Lord and prayed him of his mercy to grant them good perseverance of wind and weather so that they might come home in safety.

---

3. In Zeeland, a province in the southwest Netherlands.

And it was answered and commanded in her soul that they should go their way in the name of Jesus. When the priest knew that she would go forth anyway, he said, "Mother, there is no ship; there is but a little vessel."

She answered again, "Son, God is as mighty in a little ship as in a great ship, for I will go therein by the leave of God."

And, when they were in the little ship, great tempests and dark weather began to wax. Then they cried to God for grace and mercy, and anon the tempests ceased, and they had fair weather and sailed all the night on end and the next day until evensong time, and then they came to land. And, when they were on the land, the foresaid creature fell down on her knees kissing the ground, highly thanking God who had brought them home in safety.

Then had this creature neither penny nor halfpenny in her purse. And so they happened to meet with other pilgrims who gave her three half-pennies, inasmuch as she had, in commoning, told them good tales. And then was she right glad and merry, for she had some good that she might offer in the worship of the Trinity when she came to Norwich, as she did when she went out of England. And so, when she came there, she offered with right good will and afterward went she with her fellowship to the vicar of Saint Stephen's, Master Richard Caister, who lived at that time. And he led them with him to the place where he went to board and made them right good welcome. And he said to the foresaid creature, "Margery, I marvel how you can be so merry and have had such great labor and been so far hence."

"Sir, for I have great cause to be merry and delight in our Lord who has helped me and succored me and brought me again in safety, blessed and worshipped may he be."

And so they dallied in our Lord a good while and had full goodly comfort. And then they took their leave, and she went to an anchorite who was a monk from a far country and dwelled in the chapel of the field. He bore a name of great perfection and beforetime had loved this creature right much. And afterward through evil language that he heard of her he turned all against her. And therefore she went to him on purpose to meek herself and draw him to charity if she might. When she was come to him, he welcomed her home shortly and asked where she had left her child which was begotten and born while she was out, as he had heard said.

And she said, "Sir, the same child that God sent me I have brought home, for God knows I did nothing since I went out wherethrough I should have a child."

And he would not believe her for anything that she could say. And nevertheless yet she lowly and meekly showed him for the trust that she had in him how it was our Lord's will that she should be clad in white clothing.

And he said, "God forbid it," for she should then make all the world to wonder on her.

And she said again, "Sir, I take no heed so that God is pleased therewith."

Then he bade her come again to him and be governed by him and by a good priest called Sir Edward. And she said she should learn first if it was the will of God or not, and therewith she took her leave at that time. And, as she went from him, by the way, our Lord said to her soul, "I will not that you be governed by him."

And she sent him word what answer she had from God.

44. And then prayed she to God, saying, "As surely, Lord, as it is your will that I should be clad in white, so grant me a token of lightning, thunder, and rain—so that it doesn't hinder or annoy any thing—in order that I, unworthy, may the better fulfill your will."

Then our Lord answered and said unto his unworthy servant, "Daughter, doubt it not, you shall have that token by the third day."

And so it was. On the Friday next following, early in the morning, as she lay in her bed, she saw great lightning, she heard great thunder and great rain following, and as quickly it passed away and was fair weather again. And then she purposed herself fully to wear white clothes, except she had neither gold nor silver to buy herself clothing. And then our Lord said to her soul, "I shall ordain for you."

Then went she forth to a worshipful man in Norwich to whom she was right welcome and had great comfort. And, as they sat together telling good tales, ever our Lord said in her soul, "Speak to this man, speak to this man."

Then she said to that worshipful man, "Would God, sir, that I might find a good man who would lend me two nobles, until I might pay him again, to buy myself clothes with."

And he said, "That I will do, damsel, gladly. What clothes will you wear?"

"Sir," she said, "white clothes, with the leave of God."

So this good man bought white cloth and had made for her a gown thereof and a hood, a kirtle, and a cloak. And on the Saturday, which was the next day, at evening he brought her this clothing and gave it to her for God's love, and much more goodness did for her for our Lord's love, Christ Jesus be his reward and have mercy upon his soul and on all Christians.

And on the Trinity Sunday[4] next following she was houseled all in white, and afterward she suffered much despite and much shame in many divers countries, cities, and towns, thanked be the God of all.

And soon after her husband came from Lynn into Norwich to see how she fared and how she had sped, and so they went home together to Lynn.

---

4. Trinity Sunday was the Patron's Day of Norwich Cathedral. It is the Sunday next after Whitsunday, which is the seventh Sunday and fiftieth day after Easter. Margery's appearance in the white clothing of the professional virgin on such an important date is provocative.

And she in short time after fell into great sickness, in so much that she was anointed for fear of death. And she desired, if it were the will of God, that she might seek Saint James[5] before she died and suffer more shame for his love, as he had promised her before that she should do. And then our Lord Jesus Christ said to her in her soul that she should not die yet, and she thought to herself that she should not have lived for her pain was so great. And hastily afterward she was hale and whole.

And then it drew in toward winter, and she had so much cold that she knew not what she might do, for she was poor and had no money, and also she was in great debt. Then suffered she shames and reproofs for wearing her white clothes and because she cried so loudly when our Lord gave her mind of his Passion. And for the compassion that she had of our Lord's Passion, she cried so wonder loud, and they had never heard her crying beforetime, and it was the more marvel unto them. For she had her first cry at Jerusalem, as it written before.

And many said there was never a saint in heaven who cried so as she did, wherefore they would conclude that she had a devil within her which caused that crying. And so they said plainly, and much more evilly. And all she took patiently for our Lord's love, for she knew well that the Jews said much worse of his own person than men did of her. And therefore she took it the more meekly. Some said that she had the falling evil, for she with the crying twisted her body, turning from the one side into the other, and waxed all blue and all gray, like the color of lead. And then folk spitted at her for horror of the sickness, and some scorned her and said that she howled like a dog and banned her and cursed her and said that she did much harm among the people. And then those who beforetime had given her both food and drink for God's love now put her away and bade her that she should not come in their places because of the sharp tales that they heard of her.

And afterward, when time came that she would go to Saint James, she went to the best friends that she had in Lynn and told them her intent, how she purposed to go to Saint James if she might have good to go with, but she was poor and owed much debt. And her friends said to her, "Why have you given away your good and other men's also? Where shall you now have as much good as you owe?"

And she said again, "Our Lord God shall help right well, for he failed me never in any country, and therefore I trust him right well."

And suddenly came a good man and gave her forty pence, and with some thereof she bought herself a pilche.[6]

And ever our Lord said to her, "Daughter, study you for no goods, for I shall ordain for you, but ever study to love me and keep your mind on me, for I shall go with you wherever you go, as I have promised you before."

5. St. James of Compostela in Spain.
6. See p. 28, n. 8.

And afterward there came a woman, a good friend to this creature, and gave her seven marks because she should pray for her when she came to Saint James.

And then she took her leave of her friends in Lynn, purposing herself forward in all the haste that she might. And then it was said in Lynn that there were many thieves by the way. Then had she great dread that they should rob her and take her gold away from her. And our merciful Lord, comforting her, said unto her, "Go forth, daughter, in the name of Jesus, there shall no thief have power over you."

Then she went forth and came to Bristol on the Wednesday in Whitsun week,[7] and there found she ready the broken backed man who had been with her at Rome, whom she left in Rome when she came thence two years before this time. And, while they were in Rome, she borrowed certain gold from him and at the bidding of God she gave away to poor people all the money that she had, and that she had borrowed from him also, as is written before. And then, while she was in Rome, she promised him to pay him again in Bristol at this time, and so he was come thither for his payment. And our Lord Jesus Christ had so ordained for her, as she went toward Bristol, that there was given her so much money that she might well pay the foresaid man all that she owed him. And so she did, blessed be our Lord therefore.

And then she lay still in Bristol by the bidding of God six weeks in order to abide shipping, inasmuch as there were no English ships that might sail thither, for they were arrested and taken up for the king.[8] And other pilgrims who were at Bristol, desiring to speed their journey, went about from port to port and sped never the more. And so they came again to Bristol, while she lay still and sped better than they for all their labor.

And while she was thus still in Bristol after the bidding of God, our merciful Lord Christ Jesus visited his creature with many holy meditations and many high contemplations and many sweet comforts. And there she was houseled every Sunday with plenteous tears and violent sobbings, with loud cryings and shrill shriekings. And therefore many men and many women wondered upon her, scorned her and despised her, banned her and cursed her, said much evil of her, slandered her, and accused her of saying things which she never said. And then wept she full sorely for her sins, praying God for mercy and forgiveness for them, saying to our Lord, "Lord, as you said hanging on the cross for your crucifiers, 'Father, forgive them; they know not what they do,' so I beseech you, forgive the people all scorn and slanders and all that they have trespassed, if it be your will, for I have deserved much more and of much more am I worthy."

---

7. Whitsunday is the Feast of Pentecost, celebrating the descent of the Holy Spirit (see Acts 2), which comes seven Sundays and fifty days after Easter.
8. Henry V's second expedition to France in 1417 placed great demands on English ships.

45. On Corpus Christi Day[9] afterward, as the priests bore the Sacrament about the town with solemn procession, with many candles and great solemnity, as was worthy to be done, the foresaid creature followed, full of tears and devotion, with holy thoughts and meditation, sore weeping and violent sobbing. And then there came a good woman by this creature and said, "Damsel, God give us grace to follow the steps of our Lord Jesus Christ."

Then that word wrought so sorely in her heart and in her mind that she might not bear it, so that she was fain to take to a house. And there she cried, "I die, I die," and roared so wonderfully that the people wondered upon her, having great marvel what ailed her. And yet our Lord made some to love her and cherish her right much and had her home both for food and for drink and had full great gladness to hear her dally in our Lord.

And so there was a man of New Castle, his name was Thomas Marchale, who oftentimes bade this creature to a meal in order to hear her dalliance. And he was so drawn by the good words that God put in her to say of contrition and compunction, of sweetness and of devotion, that he was all moved, as if he had been a new man, with tears of contrition and compunction, both days and nights, as our Lord would visit his heart with grace, so that sometimes when he went into the fields he wept so sorely for his sins and his trespasses that he fell down and might not bear it and told the foresaid creature that he had been a full reckless man and misgoverned, and that sorely rued him, thanked be God. And then he blessed the time that he knew this creature and purposed himself fully to be a good man. Also he said to the said creature, "Mother, I have here ten marks.[1] I pray you that it be like your own, for I will help you to Saint James with God's grace. And whatever you bid me give to any poor man or woman I will do your bidding, always one penny for you another for myself."

Then, as it pleased our Lord, he sent a ship out of Brittany into Bristol, which ship was made ready and arrayed in order to sail to Saint James. And then the said Thomas Marchale went and paid the master for himself and for the said creature. Then was there a rich man of Bristol who would not let the said creature sail in that ship, for he held her no good woman. And then she said to that rich man, "Sir, if you put me out of the ship, my Lord Jesus shall put you out of heaven, for I tell you, sir, our Lord Jesus has no delight in a rich man unless he will be a good man and a meek man."

And so she said many sharp words unto him without any glossing or

9. Corpus Christi Day, instituted relatively late, was observed in England from 1318. It was celebrated on the Thursday after Trinity Sunday. The day honored the Host, which was carried in processions, and the feast rapidly became the focus for medieval civic ceremonies, including the cycle plays performed in many English cities.
1. Silver coins each worth thirteen shillings and four pence.

flattering. And then our Lord said to her in her soul, "You shall have your will and go to Saint James at your desire."

And anon afterward she was put up before the bishop of Worcester[2] who was staying three miles beyond Bristol and admonished her to appear before him where he stayed. She rose up early on the next day and went to the place where he stayed, he being yet in bed, and she happened to meet one of his most worshipful men in the town, and so they dallied of God. And, when he had heard her dallying a good while, he prayed her to a meal and afterward he brought her into the bishop's hall. And, when she came into the hall, she saw many of the bishop's men greatly ragged and dagged[3] in their clothing. She, lifting up her hands, blessed herself. And then they said to her, "What devil ails you?"

She said again, "Whose men are you?"

They answered again, "The bishop's men."

And then she said, "Nay, forsoothe, you are more like the devil's men." Then they were angry and chided her and spoke angrily unto her, and she suffered them well and meekly. And afterward she spoke so soberly against sin and their misgovernance that they were in silence and held themselves well pleased with her dalliance, thanked be God, before she left.

And then she went into the church and abode the coming of the bishop. And when he came, she kneeled down and asked what was his will and why she was summoned to come before him; it was to her a great annoyance and hindrance, inasmuch as she was a pilgrim purposing by the grace of God toward Saint James.

Then the bishop said, "Margery, I have not summoned you, for I know well enough you are John Brunham's[4] daughter from Lynn. I pray you, be not angry, but fare fair with me, and I shall fare fair with you, for you shall eat with me this day."

"Sir," she said, "I pray you have me excused, for I have promised a good man in town to eat with him today."

And then he said, "You shall both eat with me."

And so she abode with him until God sent wind so that she might sail and had great welcome of him and of his household also. And afterward she was shriven by the bishop. And then he prayed her to pray for him so that he might die in charity, for it was warned him by a holy man, who had it by revelation, that this bishop should be dead within the term of two years. And it befell so indeed. And therefore he complained to this creature and prayed her to pray for him so that he might die in charity. At the last she took her leave of him, and he gave her gold and his bless-

---

2. Thomas Peverel, bishop of Worcester (1407–18/19).
3. Their clothes were fashionably slashed and pointed.
4. John Brunham was a prominent citizen of King's Lynn who held a number of public offices. He died sometime between 1412 and 1413. For documents relating to him, see Meech, Appendix III.

ing and commanded his household to lead her forth on her way. And also he prayed her, when she came from Saint James again, that she would come unto him. And so she went forth to her ship.

Before she entered the ship, she made her prayers that God should keep them and preserve them from vengeance, tempests, and perils in the sea so that they might go and come in safety, for it was told her, if they had any tempest, they would cast her into the sea, for they said it was for her, and they said the ship was the worse because she was therein. And therefore she in her prayer said in this manner, "Almighty God, Christ Jesus, I beseech you for your mercy, if you will chastise me, spare me until I come again into England. And, when I come again, chastise me right as you will."

And then our Lord granted her her boon. And so she took her ship in the name of Jesus and sailed forth with her fellowship, to whom God sent fair wind and weather so that they came to Saint James on the seventh day. And then those who were against her when they were at Bristol, now they made her good welcome. And so they abode there fourteen days in that land, and there had she great comfort, both bodily and ghostly, high devotion, and many great cries in the mind of our Lord's Passion, with plenteous tears of compassion. And afterward they came home again to Bristol in five days. And she abode not long there but went forth to the Blood of Hailes,[5] and there was shriven and had loud cries and violent weepings. And then the religious men had her in among them and made her good welcome, save they swore many great oaths and horrible. And she rebuked them thereof according to the Gospel, and thereof had they great wonder. Nevertheless some were right well pleased, thanked be God of his goodness.

46. Afterward went she forth to Leicester,[6] and a good man also, Thomas Marchale, of whom is written before. And there she came into a fair church where she beheld a crucifix, which was piteously decorated and lamentable to behold. Through beholding it, the Passion of our Lord entered her mind, wherethrough she began to melt and completely dissolve into tears of pity and compassion. Then the fire of love kindled so quickly in her heart that she might not keep it secret, for, whether she would or not, it caused her to break out with a loud voice and cry marvelously and weep and sob full hideously so that many a man and woman wondered on her therefore.

When it was overcome, she going out at the church door, a man took her by the sleeve and said, "Damsel, why weep you so sorely?"

"Sir," she said, "it is not meant to tell you."

And so she and the good man, Thomas Marchale, went forth and

5. The blood of Christ held at the Cistercian Abbey of Hailes in Gloucestershire.
6. Margery's route is northeast from Bristol.

found their hostel and there ate their meal. When they had eaten, she prayed Thomas Marchale to write a letter and send it to her husband so that he might fetch her home. And, while the letter was being written, the hostler came up to her chamber in great haste and took away her scrip[7] and bade her come quickly and speak with the mayor. And so she did. Then the mayor asked her of what country[8] she was and whose daughter she was.

"Sir," she said, "I am of Lynn in Norfolk, a good man's daughter of the same Lynn, who has been mayor five times of that worshipful town and alderman also many years, and I have a good man, also a burgess of the said town, Lynn, for my husband."

"A," said the mayor, "Saint Katherine[9] told what kindred she came of and yet you are not like her, for you are a false strumpet, a false Lollard, and a false deceiver of the people, and therefore I shall have you in prison."

And she said again, "I am as ready, sir, to go to prison for God's love as you are ready to go to church."

When the mayor had long chided her and said many evil and horrible words unto her and she, by the grace of Jesus, had reasonably answered him in all that he could say, then he commanded the jailer's man to lead her to prison. The jailer's man, having compassion for her with weeping tears, said to the mayor, "Sir, I have no house to put her in unless I put her among men."

Then she, moved with compassion for the man who had compassion on her, praying for grace and mercy for that man as for her own soul, said to the mayor, "I pray you, sir, put me not among men, so that I may keep my chastity and my bond of wedlock to my husband, as I am bound to do."

And then said the jailer himself to the mayor, "Sir, I will be bound to keep this woman in safekeeping until you will have her again."

Then was there a man from Boston,[1] and he said to the good wife where she was at hostel, "Forsoothe," he said, "in Boston this woman is held a holy woman and a blessed woman."

Then the jailer took her into his keeping and led her home into his own house and put her in a fair chamber, shutting the door with a key and commending his wife to keep the key. Nevertheless he let her go to church when she wished and had her eat at his own table and made her right good welcome for our Lord's love, thanked be almighty God thereof.

47. Then the steward of Leicester,[2] a seemly man, sent for the said creature to the jailer's wife, and she, because her husband was not at home,

---

7. A small bag or wallet.
8. In medieval England, "country" was used to designate region.
9. St. Katherine was of noble kindred.
1. Boston is southeast of Lincoln, just across the Wash from Bishop's Lynn.
2. I.e., the steward of the earl of Leicester.

would not let her go to any man, steward nor other. When the jailer knew thereof, he came in his own proper person and brought her before the steward. The steward, as soon as he saw her, spoke Latin to her, many priests standing about to hear what she should say, and other people also. She said to the steward, "Speak English, if you please, for I understand not what you say."[3]

The steward said unto her, "You lie falsely in plain English."

Then said she unto him again, "Sir, ask what question you will in English, and through the grace of my Lord Jesus Christ I shall answer you reasonably thereto."

And then asked he many questions, to which she answered readily and reasonably so that he could find no cause against her. Then the steward took her by the hand and led her into his chamber and spoke many foul ribald words unto her, purposing and desiring, as it seemed to her, to oppress her and lie with her. And then had she much dread and much sorrow, crying him mercy.

She said, "Sir, for the reverence of almighty God, spare me, for I am a man's wife."

And then said the steward, "You shall tell me whether you have this speech from God or from the devil, or else you shall go to prison."

"Sir," she said, "as far as going to prison, I am not afraid for my Lord's love, who suffered much more for my love than I may for his. I pray you do as you think best."

The steward, seeing her boldness that she did not dread prison, he wrestled with her, making unclean tokens and ungoodly countenance, wherethrough he frightened her so much that she told him how she had her speech and her dalliance from the Holy Ghost and not from her own cunning.

And then he, all astonished at her words, left his business and his lewdness, saying to her as many men had done before, "Either you are a right good woman or else a right wicked woman," and delivered her again to her jailer.

And he led her home again with him.

Afterward they took two of her fellows who went with her on pilgrimage—one was Thomas Marchale before said, the other, a man of Wisbeach[4]—and put them both in prison because of her. Then was she heavy and sorry for their distress and prayed to God for their deliverance. And then our merciful Lord Christ Jesus said to his creature, "Daughter, I shall, for your love, so dispose for them that the people shall be right fain to let them go and not long to keep them."

And, on the next day following, our Lord sent such weather of light-

---

3. If Margery spoke Latin, she might well be suspected of a dangerous literacy and thus capable of reading heretical Wycliffite texts. By speaking to her in Latin, the steward hopes to trap her into an admission.
4. In Cambridgeshire.

nings, thunders, and rains continuing that all the people in the town were so afraid they knew not what to do. They feared it was because they had put the pilgrims in prison. And then the governors of the town went in great haste and took out those two pilgrims who had lain in prison all the night before, leading them to the guild hall, there to be examined before the mayor and the worshipful men of the town, compelling them to swear if the foresaid creature were a woman of the right faith and right belief, continent and clean of her body, or not. As far as they knew, they swore, as surely God should help them at the day of judgment, that she was a good woman of the right faith and right belief, clean and chaste in all her governance as far as they could know, in manner, countenance, in word, and in work. And then the mayor let them go whether they would. And anon the tempest ceased, and it was fair weather, worshipped be our Lord God.

The pilgrims were glad that they were delivered and dared no longer abide in Leicester but went ten miles thence and abode there so that they might have knowledge what should be done with the said creature, for, when they both were put in prison, they had told her themselves that they supposed, if the mayor might have his will, he would have her burnt.[5]

48. On a Wednesday, the said creature was brought into a church of All Hallows in Leicester, in which place before the high altar was set the abbot of Leicester[6] with some of his canons, the dean of Leicester, a worthy clerk. There were also many friars and priests, also the mayor of the same town with many other lay people. There were so many people that they stood upon stools in order to behold her and wonder upon her. The said creature lay on her knees, making her prayers to almighty God that she might have grace, wit, and wisdom to answer that day as might be most pleasant and worshipful to him, the most profit to her soul, and the best example to the people.

Then there came a priest to her and took her by the hand and brought her before the abbot and his assessors who were sitting at the altar. He made her swear on a book that she should answer truly to the articles of the faith just as she felt them.[7] And first they rehearsed the blissful sacrament of the altar, charging her to say right as she believed therein. Then she said, "Sirs, I believe in the sacrament of the altar in this manner, that whatever man has taken the order of priesthood, be he never so vicious a man in his living, if he says duly those words over the bread that our Lord Jesus Christ said when he made his Last Supper among his disciples

---

5. Heretics could be burnt.
6. Richard Rothley, the abbot of the house of Augustinian Canons in Leicester; Margery has been brought into the Church of All Saints in Leicester.
7. What follows is an official inquiry into the nature of Margery's beliefs, beginning with the Eucharist. The belief in transubstantiation—whereby the elements of the Mass become the body and blood of Christ—was a key subject for a suspected heretic. Wyclif had argued that the bread and wine were spiritually rather than physically changed. Margery's answer is carefully worded and perfectly orthodox.

where he sat at the supper, I believe that it is his very flesh and his blood and no material bread nor ever may be unsaid be it once said."

And so she answered forth to all the articles, as many as they would ask her, so that they were well pleased. The mayor, who was her deadly enemy, he said, "In faith, she means not with her heart as she says with her mouth."

And the clerks said to him, "Sir, she answers right well to us."

Then the mayor greatly rebuked her and repeated many reproving and ungoodly words, which are more expedient to conceal than to express.

"Sir," she said, "I take witness of my Lord Jesus Christ, whose body is here present in the sacrament of the altar, that I never had part of a man's body in this world in actual deed by way of sin, but only of my husband's body, whom I am bound to by the law of matrimony, and by whom I have born fourteen children. For I want you to know, sir, that there is no man in this world that I love so much as God, for I love him above all thing, and, sir, I tell you truly I love all men in God and for God."

Also furthermore she said plainly to his own person, "Sir, you are not worthy to be a mayor, and that shall I prove by Holy Writ, for our Lord God said himself before he would take vengeance on the cities, 'I shall come down and see.' And yet he knew all things. And that was nothing else, sir, but for to show men as you are that you should make no execution in punishing unless you know before that it were worthy to be done. And, sir, you have done all the contrary to me this day, for, sir, you have caused me much vexation for a thing that I am not guilty in. I pray God forgive you it."

Then the mayor said to her, "I will learn why you go in white clothes, for I believe you are come hither to take away our wives from us and lead them with you."

"Sir," she said, "you shall not learn from my mouth why I go in white clothes; you are not worthy to learn it. But, sir, I will tell it to these worthy clerks with good will in the manner of confession. Let them consider if they will tell it to you."

Then the clerks prayed the mayor to go down away from them, with the other people. And, when they were gone, she kneeled on her knees before the abbot, and the dean of Leicester, and a Friar Preacher, a worshipful clerk, and told these three clerks how our Lord by revelation warned her and bade her wear white clothes before she came to Jerusalem. "And so have I told my ghostly fathers. And therefore they have charged me that I should go thus, for they dare not go against my feelings for dread of God, and, if they dared, they would do so full gladly. And therefore, sirs, if the mayor will learn why I go in white, you may say, if you like, that my ghostly fathers bid me go so, and then shall you make no lies nor shall he know the truth."

So the clerks called up again the mayor and told him in counsel that her ghostly fathers had charged her to wear white clothes, and she had bound herself to their obedience. Then the mayor called her to him, saying, "I will not let you go hence for anything that you can say unless you will go to my Lord of Lincoln for a letter, inasmuch as you are in his jurisdiction, so that I may be discharged of you."[8]

She said, "Sir, I dare speak to my Lord of Lincoln right well, for I have had of him right good welcome before this time."

And then other men asked her if she were in charity with the mayor, and she said, "Yes, and with all creatures."

And then she, obeying herself to the mayor, prayed him to be in charity with her with weeping tears and to forgive her anything that she had done to displease him. And he gave her goodly words for a while so that she thought all had been well and he had been her good friend, but afterward she knew well it was not so. And thus she had leave of the mayor to go to my Lord of Lincoln and fetch a letter by which the mayor should be excused.

49. So she went first to the Abbey of Leicester, into the church, and, as soon as the Abbot had spied her, he, of his goodness, along with many of his brothers, came to welcome her. When she saw them coming, anon in her soul she beheld our Lord coming with his apostles, and she was so ravished into contemplation with sweetness and devotion that she might not stand against their coming as courtesy would but leaned on a pillar in the church and held herself strongly thereby for dread of falling, for she would have stood, and she might not for the plenty of devotion, which was the cause that she cried and wept full sorely. When her crying was overcome, the Abbot prayed his brothers to have her in with them and comfort her, and so they gave her right good wine and made her right good welcome.

Then she got herself a letter from the abbot to my Lord of Lincoln to record what conversation she had had during the time she was in Leicester. And the Dean of Leicester was ready to record and witness for her also, for he had great confidence that our Lord loved her, and therefore he cherished her full highly in his own place. And so she took leave of her said son, purposing forth toward Lincoln with a man called Patrick, who had been with her at Saint James before. And at this time he was sent by Thomas Marchale, before said, from Melton Mowbray[9] to Leicester to inquire and see how it stood with the same creature. For the foresaid Thomas Marchale feared greatly that she should have been burnt, and therefore he sent this man Patrick to prove the truth. And so she and Patrick, with many good folk of Leicester come to welcome her, thanking God who had preserved her and given her the victory of her enemies, went forth out at the town's end, and they made her right good welcome,

---

8. Philip Repingdon, bishop of Lincoln.
9. In Leicestershire.

promising her if ever she came again, she should have better comfort among them than ever she had before.

Then had she forgotten and left in the town a staff from a Moses yard which she had brought from Jerusalem,[1] and she would not have lost it for forty shillings. Then went Patrick again into the town for her staff and her scrip and happened to meet with the mayor, and the mayor would have put him in prison. So at the last he hardly escaped and left there her scrip.

Then the foresaid creature waited for this man in a blind woman's house in great heaviness, dreading what was befallen of him, for he was so long. At the last this man came riding past where she was. When she saw him she cried, "Patrick, son, where have you been so long from me?"

"Yes, yes, mother," he said, "I have been in great peril for you. I was in a point to have been put in prison for you, and the mayor has greatly tormented me for you, and he has taken away your scrip from me."

"A, good Patrick," said she, "be not displeased, for I shall pray for you, and God shall reward your labor right well; it is all for the best."

Then Patrick set her upon his horse and brought her home into Melton Mowbray into his own house, where Thomas Marchale (before written) was, and took her down from the horse, highly thanking God that she was not burnt. So they delighted in our Lord all that night.

And afterward she went forth to the Bishop of Lincoln, where he lay at that time. She, not verily knowing where he was, met a worshipful man with a furred hood, a worthy officer of the bishop's, who said unto her, "Damsel, know you not me?"

"No, sir," she said, "forsooth."

"And yet you were beholden," he said, "for I have sometimes made you good welcome."

"Sir, I trust that you did what you did for God's love, and therefore I hope he shall right well reward you. And I pray you hold me excused, for I take little heed of a man's beauty or of his face, and therefore I forget him much the sooner."

And then he told her kindly where she should find the bishop. And so she got herself a letter from the bishop to the mayor of Leicester, admonishing him that he should not vex her nor hinder her from going and coming whenever she wished.

Then there befell great thunders and lightnings and many rains so that the people thought it was for vengeance of the said creature, greatly desiring that she had been out of that country. And she would in no way go thence until she had her scrip again. When the said mayor received the foresaid letter, he sent her her scrip and let her go in safety where she would. Three weeks she was hindered from her journey by the mayor of Leicester before he would let her go out of that district. Then she hired

1. A relic from the Holy Land.

the foresaid man Patrick to go with her through the country, and so they went forth to York.

50. When she was come into York, she went to an anchoress, who had loved her well before she went to Jerusalem, in order to have knowledge of her ghostly increase, and also desiring more ghostly communication, to eat with the anchoress that day, nothing except bread and water, for it was on our Lady's Eve.[2] And the anchoress would not receive her, for she had heard so much evil told of her.

So she went forth to other strange folk, and they made her right good welcome for our Lord's love. On a day, as she sat in a church of York, our Lord Jesus Christ said in her soul, "Daughter, there is much tribulation toward you."

She was somewhat heavy and abashed thereof, and therefore she, sitting still, answered not. Then said our blessed Lord again, "What, daughter, are you badly paid to suffer more tribulation for my love? If you will suffer no more, I shall take it away from you."

And then she said again "No, good Lord, let me be at your will and make me mighty and strong to suffer all that ever you will that I suffer, and grant me meekness and patience therewith."

And so, from that time forward that she knew it was our Lord's will that she should suffer more tribulation, she received it well when our Lord would send it and thanked him highly thereof, being right glad and merry on that day that she suffered any trouble. And by process of time, that day on which she suffered no tribulation she was not as merry or glad as on that day when she suffered tribulation. Afterward, as she was in the foresaid Minster[3] at York, a clerk came to her, saying, "Damsel, how long will you abide here?"

"Sir," she said, "I purpose to abide these fourteen days."

And so she did. And in that time many good men and women prayed her to meals and made her right good comfort and were right glad to hear her dalliance, having great marvel at her speech, for it was fruitful.

And also she had many enemies who slandered her, scorned her, and despised her, of whom one priest came to her while she was in the said Minster and, taking her by the collar of the gown, said, "You wolf, what is this cloth that you have on?"

She stood still and would not answer in her own cause. Children of the monastery[4] who were going beside said to the priest, "Sir, it is wool."

The priest was annoyed because she would not answer and began to swear many great oaths. Then she began to speak for God's cause; she was

---

2. The Nativity of the Virgin is celebrated on September 8; thus September 7.
3. A church belonging to a monastery or any large church.
4. Children were sent to monasteries for schooling and sometimes donated to the monastic life by their parents.

not afraid. She said, "Sir, you should keep the commandments of God and not swear so negligently as you do."

The priest asked her who kept the commandments.

She said, "Sir, those who keep them."

Then said he, "Keep you them?"

She said again, "Sir, it is my will to keep them, for I am bound thereto, and so are you and every man who will be saved at the last."

When he had long jangled with her, he went away secretly, before she was aware, so that she knew not where he went.

51. Another time there came a great clerk unto her, asking how these words should be understood, "Crescite et multiplicamini."[5] She, answering, said, "Sir, these words are not understood only for the begetting of bodily children, but also for the purchasing of virtue, which is ghostly fruit, as by hearing the words of God, by giving a good example, by meekness and patience, charity and chastity, and such other, for patience is more worthy than working miracles."

And she through the grace of God answered so that clerk that he was well pleased. And our Lord of his mercy ever he made some men to love her and support her. And so in this city of York there was a doctor of divinity, Master John Aclom, also a Canon of the Minster, Sir John Kendale, and another priest who sung by the bishop's grave.[6] These were her good friends of the spirituality.

So she dwelled still in that city fourteen days, as she had said before, and somewhat more, and on the Sundays she was houseled in the Minster with great weeping, violent sobbing, and loud crying so that many man marveled greatly what ailed her. So afterward there came a priest, a worshipful clerk he seemed, and said unto her, "Damsel, you said when you first came hither that you would abide here but fourteen days."

"Yes, sir, with your leave, I said that I would abide here fourteen days, but I said not that I should neither abide more here nor less. But as now, sir, I tell you truly I go not yet."

Then he set her a day, commanding her to appear before him in the chapter-house. And she said that she would obey his admonition with a good will. She went then to Master John Aclom, the foresaid doctor, praying him to be there in her part. And so he was, and he found great favor among them all. Also another master of divinity had promised her to have been there with her, but he held back till he knew how the cause should go, whether with her or against her. There were many people that day in the chapter-house of the Minster to hear and see what should be said or done to the foresaid creature.

---

5. "Be fruitful and multiply" (Genesis 1.22). Margery's interpretation of this injunction points up its spiritual rather than literal meaning and is completely orthodox. For another view, see Chaucer's Wife of Bath's prologue to her tale in *The Canterbury Tales*.
6. These men were distinguished members of the Yorkshire episcopate.

When the day came, she was all ready in the Minster to come to her answering. Then came her friends to her and bade her be of good cheer. She, thanking them, said so she should. And quickly came a goodly priest and took her by the arm to help her through the press of the people and brought her before a worshipful doctor, who had admonished her before to appear before him in the chapter-house on this day in York Minster. And with this doctor sat many other clerks, full reverend and worshipful, of which clerks some loved the said creature right well. Then the said worshipful doctor to her, "Woman, what do you here in this country?"

"Sir, I come on pilgrimage to offer here at Saint William."[7]

Then said he again, "Have you a husband?"

She said, "Yes."

"Have you any letter of record?"

"Sir," she said, "my husband gave me leave with his own mouth. Why fare you thus with me more than you do with other pilgrims that are here, who have no letter any more than I have? Sir, them you let go in peace and quiet and in rest, and I may no rest have among you. And, sir, if there be any clerk among you all who can prove that I have said any word otherwise than I ought to do, I am ready to amend it with good will. I will maintain neither error nor heresy, for it is my full will to hold as the Holy Church holds and fully to please God."

Then the clerks examined her in the Articles of the Faith and in many other points as they wished, to which she answered well and truly so that they might have no occasion in her words to trouble her, thanked be God.

And then the doctor who sat there as a judge summoned her to appear before the Archbishop of York and told her what day at a town called Cawood,[8] commanding her to be kept in prison until the day of her appearing came. Then the secular people answered for her and said she should not go into prison, for they would themselves be surety for her and go to the Archbishop[9] with her. And so the clerks said no more to her at that time, for they rose up and went wherever they would and let her go where she would, worship to Jesus. And soon after there came a clerk unto her—one of the same who had sought against her—and said, "Damsel, I pray you are not displeased with me, though I sat with the doctor against you; he cried so upon me that I dared not do otherwise."

And she said, "Sir, I am not displeased with you therefore."

Then said he, "I pray you, then, pray for me."

"Sir," she said, "I will, readily."

52. There was a monk who should preach in York, who had heard much slander and much evil language of the said creature. And, when

7. Shrine in York Minster of William Fitzherbert, archbishop of York (d. 1154).
8. A town in Yorkshire, south of York.
9. Henry Bowet was archbishop of York from 1407 to 1423. He was notorious for his stern stand against lollardy.

he should preach, there was a great multitude of people to hear him, and she was present with them. And so, when he was in his sermon, he rehearsed many matters so openly that the people conceived well it was because of her, wherefore her friends that loved her well were full sorry and heavy thereof, and she was much the more merry, for she had matter to prove her patience and her charity wherethrough she trusted to please our Lord Christ Jesus. When the sermon was done, a doctor of divinity who loved her well, with many others also, came to her and said, "Margery, how have you done this day?"

"Sir," she said, "right well, blessed be God. I have cause to be right merry and glad in my soul that I may suffer anything for his love, for he suffered much more for me."

Anon after came a man of good will who loved her right well, with his wife and others, and led her seven miles thence to the Archbishop of York, and brought her into a fair chamber, where came a good clerk, saying to the good man who had brought her thither, "Sir, why have you and your wife brought this woman hither? She shall steal away from you, and then shall you have shame of her."

The good man said, "I dare well say she will abide and be at her answering with good will."

On the next day she was brought into the Archbishop's chapel, and there came many of the Archbishop's household, despising her, calling her "lollard" and "heretic," and swearing many a horrible oath that she should be burnt. And she, through the strength of Jesus, said again to them, "Sirs, I fear you shall be burnt in hell without end unless you amend yourselves of your swearing of oaths, for you keep not the commandments of God. I would not swear as you do for all the good of this world."

Then they went away as if they were ashamed. She then, making her prayer in her mind, asked grace so to conduct herself that day as was most pleasant to God and profit to her own soul and good example to her fellow Christians. Our Lord, answering her, said it should be right well. At the last, the said Archbishop came into the chapel with his clerks, and sharply he said to her, "Why go you in white? Are you a maiden?"

She, kneeling on her knees before him, said, "No, sir, I am no maiden; I am a wife."

He commanded his household to fetch a pair of fetters and said she should be fettered, for she was a false heretic. And then she said, "I am no heretic, nor shall you prove me one."

The Archbishop went away and let her stand alone. Then she made her prayers to our Lord God almighty to help her and succor her against all her enemies, ghostly and bodily, a long while, and her flesh trembled and quaked wonderfully so that she was fain to put her hands under her clothes so that it should not be espied.

Afterward the Archbishop came again into the chapel with many worthy clerks, among which was the same doctor who had examined her before and the monk who had preached against her a little time before in York. Some of the people asked whether she were a Christian woman or a Jew; some said she was a good woman, and some said no. Then the Archbishop took his seat, and his clerks also, each of them in his degree, many people being present. And in the time while the people were gathering together and the Archbishop taking his seat, the said creature stood all behind, making her prayers for help and succor against her enemies with high devotion, so long that she melted all into tears. And at the last she cried loudly therewith, so that the Archbishop and his clerks and many people had great wonder of her, for they had not heard such crying before. When her crying was passed, she came before the Archbishop and fell down on her knees, the Archbishop saying full roughly unto her, "Why weep you so, woman?"

She, answering, said, "Sir, you shall wish some day that you had wept as sorely as I."

And then anon, after the Archbishop put to her the Articles of our Faith, to which God gave her grace to answer well and truly and readily without any great study so that he might not blame her, then he said to the clerks, "She knows her faith well enough. What shall I do with her?"

The clerks said, "We know well that she knows the Articles of the Faith, but we will not suffer her to dwell among us, for the people have great faith in her dalliance, and perhaps she might pervert some of them."

Then the Archbishop said unto her, "I am badly informed of you; I hear said you are a right wicked woman."

And she said again, "Sir, so I hear said that you are a wicked man. And, if you are as wicked as men say, you shall never come into heaven unless you amend yourself while you are here."

Then he said full roughly, "Why, you, what say men of me?"

She answered, "Other men, sir, can tell you well enough."

Then said a great clerk with a furred hood, "Peace, you speak of yourself and let him be."

Afterward said the Archbishop to her, "Lay your hand on the book here before me and swear that you shall go out of my diocese as soon as you may."

"No, sir," she said, "I pray you, give me leave to go again into York to take my leave of my friends."

Then he gave her leave for one day or two. She thought it was too short a time, wherefore she said again, "Sir, I may not go out of this diocese so hastily, for I must tarry and speak with good men before I go, and I must, sir, with your leave, go to Bridlington[1] and speak with

---

1. Bridlington was the site of the cult of St. John of Bridlington (d. 1379), who was prior of the house of Augustinian Canons there.

my confessor, a good man, who was the good prior's confessor, who is now canonized."[2]

Then said the Archbishop to her, "You shall swear that you shall neither teach nor challenge the people in my diocese."[3]

"No, sir, I shall not swear," she said, "for I shall speak of God and reprove those who swear great oaths wheresoever I go, unto the time that the pope and holy church have ordained that no man shall be so hardy to speak of God, for God almighty forbids not, sir, that we shall speak of him. And also the gospel makes mention that, when the woman had heard our Lord preach, she came before him with a loud voice and said, 'Blessed be the womb that bore you and the teats that gave you suck.'[4] Then our Lord said again to her, 'Forsooth so are they blessed that hear the word of God and keep it.' And therefore, sir, I think that the gospel gives me leave to speak of God."

"A, sir," said the clerks, "here know we well that she has a devil within her, for she speaks of the gospel."[5]

Immediately a great clerk brought forth a book and laid Saint Paul for his part against her that no woman should preach.[6]

She, answering thereto, said, "I preach not, sir, I go in no pulpit. I use but communication and good words, and that will I do while I live."

Then said a doctor who had examined her beforetime, "Sir, she told me the worst tales of priests that ever I heard."

The bishop commanded her to tell that tale.

"Sir, by your reverence, I spoke but of one priest by way of example, who as I have learned went wayward in a wood through the sufferance of God for the profit of his soul until the night came upon him. He, destitute of his lodging, found a fair garden, in which he rested that night, having a fair pear tree in the midst all flourished with flowers and embellished, and blooms full delectable to his sight, where came a bear, great and violent, ugly to behold, shaking the pear tree and knocking down the flowers. Greedily this grievous beast ate and devoured those fair flowers. And, when he had eaten them, turning his tail end in the priest's presence, voided them out again at the shameful part.

"The priest, having great abomination of that loathly sight, conceiving great heaviness for doubt of what it might mean, on the next day wandered forth on his way all heavy and pensive and fortuned to meet with a seemly aged man, like a palmer or a pilgrim, who inquired of the priest the cause of his heaviness. The priest, rehearsing the matter before written, said he conceived great dread and heaviness when he beheld that

---

2. William Sleighholme (see also the reference to Sleytham in chapter 53, p. 95) was confessor to St. John of Bridlington.
3. Women were prohibited from preaching. Julian of Norwich draws a careful distinction between teaching and preaching.
4. Luke 11.27–28.
5. Lollards were known as "Bible men and women."
6. 1 Corinthians 14.34–35.

loathly beast befoul and devour such fair flowers and blooms and afterward so horribly devoid them before him at his tail end, and he not understanding what this might mean.

"Then the palmer, showing himself the messenger of God, thus addressed him, 'Priest, you yourself are the pear tree, somewhat flourishing and flowering through saying your service and administering the sacraments, though you do so undevotedly, for you take full little heed how you say your matins[7] and your service, just so it is blabbered to an end. Then go you to your mass without devotion, and for your sin have you full little contrition. You receive there the fruit of everlasting life, the sacrament of the altar, in full feeble disposition. Afterward all the day after you mis-spend your time, you give yourself to buying and selling, chopping and changing, as if you were a man of the world. You sit at the ale, giving yourself to gluttony and excess, to lust of your body, through lechery and uncleanness. You break the commandments of God through swearing, lying, detraction, and backbiting, and the use of other such sins. Thus by your misgovernance, like the loathly bear, you devour and destroy the flowers and blooms of virtuous living to your endless damnation and many men's hindering unless you have grace from repentance and amending.'"

Then the Archbishop liked well the tale and commended it, saying it was a good tale. And the clerk who had examined her beforetime, in the absence of the Archbishop, said, "Sir, this tale smites me to the heart."

The foresaid creature said to the clerk, "A, worshipful doctor, sir, in the place where my dwelling is mostly, is a worthy clerk, a good preacher, who boldly speaks against the misgovernance of the people and will flatter no man. He says many times in the pulpit, 'If any man is evil pleased with my preaching, note him well, for he is guilty.' And right so, sir," said she to the clerk, "fare you by me, God forgive it you."

The clerk knew not well what he might say to her. Afterward the same clerk came to her and prayed her for forgiveness that he had been so against her. Also he prayed her specially to pray for him. And then anon after, the Archbishop said, "Where shall I find a man who might lead this woman from me?"

Quickly many young men started up, and every man said, "My Lord, I will go with her."

The Archbishop answered, "You are too young; I will not have you."

Then a good sober man from the Archbishop's household asked his Lord what he would give him if he should lead her. The Archbishop offered him five shillings, and the man asked for a noble. The Archbishop, answering, said, "I will not spend so much on her body."

"Yes, good sir," said the said creature, "our Lord shall reward you right well again."

---

7. The service that, with lauds, is the first of the canonical hours of morning prayer.

Then the Archbishop said to the man, "See, here is five shillings, and lead her fast out of this country."

She, kneeling down on her knees, asked his blessing. He, praying her to pray for him, blessed her and let her go.

Then she, going again to York, was received by many people and by full worthy clerks, who delighted in our Lord who had given her, not lettered, wit and wisdom to answer so many learned men without villainy or blame. Thanks be to God.

53. Afterward that good man who was her leader brought her out of the town and then went they forth to Bridlington to her confessor, who was named Sleytham,[8] and spoke with him and with many other good men who had comforted her beforetime and done much for her.

Then she would not abide there but took her leave to walk forth on her journey. And then her confessor asked her if she dared not abide because of the Archbishop of York, and she said, "No, forsooth."

Then the good man gave her silver, beseeching her to pray for him. And so she went forth unto Hull. And there on a time, as they went in procession, a great woman greatly despised her, and she said no word thereto. Many other folk said that she should be set in prison and made great threats. And notwithstanding all their malice, yet a good man came and prayed her to a meal and made her right good welcome. Then the malicious people, who had despised her before, came to this good man and bade him that he should do her no good, for they held that she was no good woman.

On the next day at morn her host led her out at the town's end, for he dared no longer keep her. And so she went to Hessle and would have gone over the water at Humber. Then she happened to find there two Friar Preachers and two yeomen of the Duke of Bedford.[9] The friars told the yeomen what woman she was, and the yeomen arrested her as she would have taken her boat, and arrested a man who went with her also.

"For our Lord," they said, "the Duke of Bedford has sent for you. And you are held the greatest Lollard in all this country or about London either. And we have sought you in many a country, and we shall have a hundred pounds for bringing you before our Lord."

She said to them, "With good will, sirs, I shall go with you wherever you will lead me."

Then they brought her again into Hessle, and there men called her Lollard, and women came running out of their houses with their distaffs, crying to the people, "Burn this false heretic."

So, as she went forth toward Beverly with the said yeomen and the friars before said, they met many times with men of the country, who said

---

8. I.e., William Sleightholme.
9. John, duke of Bedford, third son of Henry IV, and at this time lieutenant of the kingdom during Henry V's absence abroad. "Humber": the Humber river in Yorkshire.

unto her, "Damsel, forsake this life that you have, and go spin and card as other women do, and suffer not so much shame and so much woe. We would not suffer so much for any good on earth."

Then she said to them, "I suffer not so much sorrow as I would do for our Lord's love, for I suffer but sharp words, and our merciful Lord Christ Jesus, worshipped be his name, suffered hard strokes, bitter scourgings, and shameful death at the last for me and for all mankind, blessed may he be. And therefore it is right naught what I suffer in regard to what he suffered."

And so, as she went with the foresaid men, she told them good tales until one of the duke's men who had arrested her said unto her, "I regret that I met with you, for it seems to me that you say right good words."

Then said she unto him, "Sir, regret nor repent you not that you met with me. Do your lord's will, and I trust all shall be for the best, for I am right well pleased that you met with me."

He said again, "Damsel, if ever you are a saint in heaven, pray for me."

She answered, saying to him again, "Sir, I hope you shall be a saint yourself and every man who shall come to heaven."

So they went forth until they came into Beverly, where dwelled the wife of one of the men who had arrested her. And thither they led her and took away from her her scrip and her ring. They ordained her a fair chamber and an honest bed therein with the necessaries, locking the door with the key and bearing away the key with them. Afterward they took the man whom they arrested with her, who was the Archbishop of York's man, and put him in prison. And soon after, that same day came tidings that the Archbishop was come into the town where his man was put in prison. It was told the Archbishop of his man's imprisonment, and anon he had him let out. Then that man went with an angry manner to the said creature, saying, "Alas that ever I knew you. I have been imprisoned for you."

She, comforting him, said again, "Have meekness and patience, and you shall have great reward in heaven for it."

So went he away from her. Then she stood looking out of a window, telling many good tales to those who would hear her, in so much that women wept sorely and said with great heaviness of their hearts, "Alas, woman, why shall you be burnt?"

Then she prayed the good wife of the house to give her drink, for she was badly off for thirst. And the good wife said her husband had born away the key, wherefore she might not come to her nor give her drink. And then the women took a ladder and set it up to the window and gave her a pint of wine in a pot and took her a wine cup, beseeching her to set away the pot secretly and the wine cup, so that when the good man came he might not spy it.

54. The said creature, lying in her bed the next night following, heard with her bodily ears a loud voice calling, "Margery."

With that voice she woke, greatly afraid, and, lying still in silence, she made her prayers as devoutly as she could for the time. And soon our merciful Lord, overall present, comforting his unworthy servant, said unto her, "Daughter, it is more pleasing unto me that you suffer despites and scorns, shames and reproofs, wrongs and troubles than if your head were smote off three times a day every day for seven years. And therefore, daughter, fear not what any man can say unto you, but in my goodness and in your sorrows that you have suffered therein have you great cause to rejoice, for, when you come home into heaven, then shall every sorrow turn you to joy."

On the next day she was brought into the chapter house at Beverley, and there was the Archbishop of York and many great clerks with him, priests, canons, and secular men. Then said the Archbishop to the said creature, "What, woman, are you come again? I would fain be delivered of you."

And then a priest brought her forth before him, and the Archbishop said, all who were present hearing, "Sirs, I had this woman before me at Cawood, and there I, with my clerks, examined her in her faith and found no default in her. Furthermore, sirs, I have since that time spoken with good men who hold her a perfect woman and a good woman. Notwithstanding all this, I gave one of my men five shillings to lead her out of this country for the quieting of the people. And, as they were going on their journey, they were taken and arrested, my man put in prison for her, also her gold and her silver was taken away from her with her beads and her ring, and she is brought here again before me. Is there any man who can say anything against her?"

Then other men said, "Here is a friar who knows many things against her."

The friar came forth and said that she disproved all men of holy church and much ill language he uttered that time of her. Also he said that she should have been burnt at Lynn, had his order, that was the Friar Preachers,[1] not been there. "And, sir, she says that she may weep and have contrition when she wishes."

Than came those two men who had arrested her, saying with the friar that she was Cobham's daughter[2] and was sent to bear letters about the country. And they said she had not been at Jerusalem nor in the Holy Land nor on other pilgrimages, just as she had been in truth. They denied all truth and maintained the wrong, as many others had done before. When they had said enough for a great while and a long time, they were in peace.

Than the Archbishop said to her, "Woman, what say you hereto?"

---

1. The Dominicans.
2. This is probably a reference to Sir John Oldcastle, who was Lord Cobham, the Herefordshire Lollard who had escaped from the Tower and remained in hiding from 1413 to 1417, when he was captured, tried, and executed.

She said, "My Lord, save your reverence, all the words that they say are lies."

Then said the Archbishop to the friar, "Friar, the words are not heresy; they are slanderous words and erroneous."

"My Lord," said the friar, "she knows her faith well enough. Nevertheless, my Lord of Bedford is angry with her, and he will have her."

"Well, friar," said the Archbishop, "and you shall lead her to him."

"No, sir," said the friar, "it falls not for a friar to lead a woman about."

"And I will not," said the Archbishop, "that the Duke of Bedford be angry with me for her."

Then said the Archbishop to his men, "Take heed of the friar till I will have him again," and commanded another man to keep the said creature also, till he would have her again another time when he liked.

The said creature prayed him of his lordship that she should not be put among men, for she was a man's wife. And the Archbishop said, "Nay, you shall no harm have."

Then he who was charged with her took her by the hand and led her home to his house and had her sit with him at meat and drink, showing her goodly welcome. Thither came many priests and other men again to see her and speak with her, and many people had great compassion that she was so badly fared with.

In a short time after, the Archbishop sent for her, and she came into his hall. His household was at a meal, and she was led into his chamber, even to his bedside. Then she, obeying, thanked him for his gracious lordship that he had showed to her beforetime.

"Yes, yes," said the Archbishop, "I am worse informed of you than ever I was before."

She said, "My Lord, if it pleases you to examine me, I shall confess the truth, and, if I am found guilty, I will obey your correction."

Then came forth a Friar Preacher who was suffragen[3] to the Archbishop, to whom the Archbishop said, "Now, sir, as you said to me when she was not present, say now while she is present."

"Shall I so?" said the suffragen.

"Yes," said the Archbishop.

Then said the suffragen to the said creature, "Damsel, you were at my Lady Westmorland's."[4]

"When, sir?" said she.

"At Easter," said the suffragen.

She, not replying, said, "Well, sir?"

Then said he, "My Lady her own person was well pleased with you and liked well your words, but you counseled my Lady Greystoke, who is a

---

3. Assistant.
4. Lady Westmorland was Joan de Beaufort, the daughter of John of Gaunt and Catherine Swynford (his longtime mistress and third wife); she was married to Ralph Neville, the earl of Westmorland.

baron's wife and daughter to my lady of Westmorland,[5] to forsake her husband, and now have you said enough to be burnt for."

And so he multiplied many sharp words before the Archbishop; it is not expedient to rehearse them. At the last she said to the Archbishop, "My Lord, if it be your will, I saw not my Lady Westmorland these two years and more, Sir, she sent for me before I went to Jerusalem and, if it pleases you, I will go again to her for record that I moved no such matter."

"Nay," said those who stood about, "let her be put in prison, and we shall send a letter to the worshipful lady, and, if it be truth that she says, let her go free without danger."

And she said she was right well satisfied that it was so. Then said a great clerk who stood a little beside the Archbishop, "Put her for forty days in prison, and she shall love God the better while she lives."

The Archbishop asked her what tale it was that she told the Lady of Westmorland when she spoke with her. She said, "I told her a good tale of a lady who was damned because she would not love her enemies and of a bailiff who was saved because he loved his enemies and forgave it that they had trespassed against him, and yet he was held an evil man."

The Archbishop said it was a good tale. Then his steward and many more with him said, crying with a loud voice to the Archbishop, "Lord, we pray you let her go hence at this time, and, if ever she comes again, we shall burn her ourselves."

The Archbishop said, "I believe there was never woman in England so treated as she is and has been." Then he said to the said creature, "I know not what I shall do with you."

She said, "My Lord, I pray you let me have your letter and your seal as a record that I have excused myself against my enemies and nothing is charged against me, neither error nor heresy, that may be proved upon me, thanked be our Lord, and John, your man, again to bring me over the water."

And the Archbishop full kindly granted her all her desire, our Lord reward him his meed, and delivered her scrip with her ring and her beads, which the Duke's men of Bedford had taken from her before. The Archbishop had great marvel where she had good to go with about the country, and she said good men gave it to her in order that she should pray for them. Then she, kneeling down, received his blessing and took her leave with right glad countenance, going out of his chamber. And the Archbishop's household prayed her to pray for them, but the steward was angry because she laughed and made good cheer, saying to her, "Holy folk should not laugh."

She said, "Sir, I have great cause to laugh, for the more shame and despite I suffer, the merrier may I be in our Lord Jesus Christ."

---

5. Lady Greystoke was the daughter of Joan de Beaufort by her first husband and the wife of John de Greystoke.

Then she came down into the hall, and there stood the Friar Preacher who had caused her all that woe. And so she passed forth with a man of the Archbishop's, bearing the letter which the Archbishop had granted her for a record, and he brought her to the water of Humber, and there he took his leave of her, returning to his lord and bearing the said letter with him again, so was she left alone, without knowledge of the people. All the foresaid trouble befell her on a Friday, thanked be God of all.

55. When she had passed the water of Humber, anon she was arrested as a Lollard and led toward prison. There happened to be a person who had seen her before the Archbishop of York and got her leave to go where she would and excused her against the bailiff and undertook for her that she was no Lollard. And so she escaped away in the name of Jesus.

Then met she with a man of London and his wife with him. And so went she forth with them till she came to Lincoln, and there suffered she many scorns and many annoying words, answering again in God's cause without any hindrance, wisely and discreetly so that many men marveled at her cunning. There were men of law who said unto her, "We have gone to school many years, and yet are we not sufficient to answer as you do. Of whom have you this cunning?"

And she said, "Of the Holy Ghost."

Then asked they, "Have you the Holy Ghost?"

"Yes, sirs," said she, "there may no man say a good word without the gift of the Holy Ghost, for our Lord Jesus Christ said to his disciples, 'Study not what you shall say, for it shall not be your spirit that shall speak in you, but it shall be the spirit of the Holy Ghost.'"

And thus our Lord gave her grace to answer them, worshipped may he be.

Another time there came great lords' men unto her, and they swore many great oaths, saying, "It is given us to know that you can tell us whether we shall be saved or damned."

She said, "Yes, forsooth I can, for, as long as you swear such horrible oaths and break the commandment of God knowingly as you do and will not leave your sin, I dare well say you shall be damned. And, if you will be contrite and shriven of your sin, willfully do penance and leave it while you may, in will no more to turn again thereto, I dare well say you shall be saved."

"What, can you nothing otherwise tell us but thus?"

"Sirs," she said, "this is right good, I think."

And then they went away from her. After this she came homeward again till she came to West Lynn.[6] When she was there, she sent into Bishop's Lynn after her husband, after Master Robert, her confessor, and after Master Alan, a doctor of divinity, and told them in part of her tribulation. And afterward she told them that she might not come home to

6. The parish of West Lynn is opposite the parish of King's Lynn.

Bishop's Lynn from the time that she had been to the Archbishop of Canterbury for his letter and his seal.[7]

"For, when I was before the Archbishop of York," she said, "he would give no credence to my words inasmuch as I had not my lord's letter and seal of Canterbury. And so I promised him that I should not come into Bishop's Lynn till I had my lord's letter and the seal of Canterbury."

And then she took her leave of the said clerks, asking their blessing, and passed forth with her husband to London. When she came there, she was helped quickly about her letter from the Archbishop of Canterbury. And so she dwelled in the city of London a long time and had right good welcome of many worthy men.

Afterward she came toward Ely in order to have come home into Lynn, and when she was three miles from Ely, there came a man riding after at a great speed and arrested her husband and her also, purposing to lead them both into prison. He cruelly rebuked them and greatly reviled them, repeating many reproving words. And at the last she prayed her husband to show him my Lord's letter of Canterbury. When the man had read the letter, then he spoke fair and kindly unto them, saying, "Why showed me not your letter before?"

And so they parted away from him and then came into Ely and, from thence, home into Lynn, where she suffered much despite, much reproof, many a scorn, many a slander, many a banning, and many a cursing. And on a time a reckless man, little caring for his own shame, with will and with purpose, cast a bowlful of water on her head as she came in the street. She, nothing moved therewith, said, "God make you a good man," highly thanking God thereof, as she did many more other times.

56. Afterward God punished her with many great and divers sicknesses. She had the flux[8] a long time till she was anointed, thinking to have been dead. She was so feeble that she might not hold a spoon in her hand. Then our Lord Jesus Christ spoke to her in her soul and said that she should not die yet. Then she recovered again for a little while. And anon after, she had a great sickness in her head and afterward in her back so that she feared to have lost her wit from it. Afterward, when she was recovered from all these sicknesses, in short time followed another sickness which was set in her right side, enduring the term of eight years, save eight weeks, at different times. Sometimes she had it once in a week, continuing sometimes thirty hours, sometimes twenty, sometimes ten, sometimes eight, sometimes four, and sometimes two, so hard and so sharp that she must void what was in her stomach as bitter as though it had been gall, neither eating nor drinking while the sickness endured but ever groaning till it was gone.

7. This is probably an allusion to Henry Chichele, who succeeded Thomas Arundel as archbishop of Canterbury (1414–43).
8. Dysentery.

Then would she say to our Lord, "A, blissful Lord, why would you become man and suffer so much pain for my sins and for all men's sins who shall be saved, and we are so unkind, Lord, to you, and I, most unworthy, cannot suffer this little pain? A, Lord, for your great pain have mercy on my little pain. For the great pain that you suffered give me not so much as I am worthy, for I may not bear so much as I am worthy. And, if you will, Lord, that I bear it, send me patience, for else I may not suffer it. A, blissful Lord, I had rather suffer all the sharp words that men might say of me and all clerks preach against me for your love, so it were no hindering to any man's soul, than this pain that I have. For sharp words to suffer for your love, it hurts me right naught, Lord, and the world may take nothing from me but worship and worldly good, and by the worship of the world I set right naught. And all manner of goods and worships and all manner of loves on earth, I pray you, Lord, forbid me, namely all those loves and goods of any earthly thing which should decrease my love toward you, or lessen my merit in heaven; and all manner of loves and goods which you know in your Godhead should increase my love toward you, I pray you, grant me for your mercy to your everlasting worship."

Sometimes, notwithstanding, the said creature had great bodily sickness, yet the Passion of our merciful Lord Christ Jesus worked so in her soul that for the time she felt not her own sickness but wept and sobbed in the mind of our Lord's Passion as though she saw him with her bodily eye, suffering pain and passion before her.

Afterward, when eight years were passed, her sickness went away so that it came not week by week as it did before, but then increased her cries and her weepings, insomuch that priests dared not housel her openly in the church but privately in the prior's chapel at Lynn, away from the people's hearing. And in that chapel she had such high contemplation and so much dalliance from our Lord, inasmuch as she was put out of church for his love, that she cried whatever time she should be houseled as if her soul and her body should have parted asunder, so that two men held her in their arms till her crying was ceased, for she might not bear the abundance of love that she felt in the precious sacrament, which she steadfastly believed was very God and man in the form of bread.

Then our blissful Lord said unto her mind, "Daughter, I will not have my grace hidden that I give you, for the more busy that the people are to hinder it, the more shall I spread it abroad and make it known to all the world."

57. Then it happened there came another monk to Lynn at the time of removing,[9] as the custom was among them, who loved not the said creature nor would suffer her to come in their chapel as she had done before he came thither. Then the prior of Lynn, Daun Thomas

---

9. Day when clergy were moved to new locations.

Hevingham, meeting with the said creature and Master Robert Spryngolde,[1] who was her confessor at that time, prayed them to hold him excused if she was no more houseled in his chapel, "For there is come," he said, "a new brother of mine who will not come in our chapel as long as she is therein. And therefore provide you another place, I pray you."

Master Robert answered, "Sir, we must then housel her in the church; we may not choose, for she has my lord's letter of Canterbury and his seal, in which we are commanded, by virtue of obedience, to hear her confession and administer to her the sacrament as often as we are required."[2]

Then was she houseled after this time at the high altar in Saint Margaret's Church, and our Lord visited her with such great grace when she should be houseled that she cried so loudly that it might be heard all about the church and out of the church, as if she should have died therewith, so that she might not receive the sacrament from the priest's hands, the priest turning himself again to the altar with the precious sacrament, till her crying was ceased. And then he, turning again to her, should administer her as he ought to do. And thus it happened many a time when she should be houseled. And sometimes she should weep full softly and stilly in receiving the precious sacrament, without any violence, as our Lord would visit her with his grace.

On a Good Friday, as the said creature beheld priests kneeling on their knees and other worshipful men with torches burning in their hands before the Sepulcher,[3] devoutly representing the lamentable death and doleful burying of our Lord Jesus Christ after the good custom of Holy Church, the mind of our Lady's sorrows, which she suffered when she beheld his precious body hanging on the Cross and afterward buried before her sight, suddenly occupied the heart of this creature, drawing her mind all wholly into the Passion of our Lord Christ Jesus, whom she beheld with her ghostly eye in the sight of her soul as verily as though she had seen his precious body beaten, scourged, and crucified with her bodily eye, which sight and ghostly beholding wrought by grace so fervently in her mind, wounding her with pity and compassion, so that she sobbed, roared, and cried, and, spreading her arms abroad, said with a loud voice, "I die, I die," so that many men wondered at her and marveled what ailed her. And the more she busied herself to keep herself from crying, the louder she cried, for it was not in her power to take it or leave it, but as God would send it.

---

1. Robert Spryngolde was parish priest of St. Margaret's and Margery's main confessor. Thomas Hevingham was prior of St. Margaret's.
2. Margery has received unusual permission to receive the sacrament as often as she wishes it.
3. The Sepulcher was the recessed place in the wall of the chancel or, more simply, a prepared timber-frame hearse, where, on Good Friday, the Host, along with the Crucifix, was "buried." A watch was then kept until Easter. For the ceremonies of Eastertide, see Duffy (1992), pp. 22–36.

Then a priest took her in his arms and bore her into the Prior's Clois-ter[4] in order to let her take the air, supposing she should not otherwise have endured, her labor was so great. Then waxed she all blue as if she had been lead and sweated full sorely. And this manner of crying endured for the term of ten years, as it is written before. And every Good Friday in all the foresaid years she was weeping and sobbing five or six hours to-gether and therewith cried full loudly many times, so that she might not restrain herself therefrom, which made her full feeble and weak in her bodily mights.

Sometimes she wept on Good Friday an hour for the sin of the people, having more sorrow for their sins than for her own, inasmuch as our Lord forgave her her own sin before she went to Jerusalem. Nevertheless she wept for her own sins full plenteously when it pleased our Lord to visit her with his grace. Sometimes she wept another hour for the souls in Pur-gatory; another hour for those who were in trouble, in poverty, or in any distress; another hour for Jews, Saracens, and all false heretics that God for his great goodness should put away their blindness so that they might, through his grace, be turned to the faith of Holy Church and be children of salvation.

Many times, when this creature should make her prayers, our Lord said unto her, "Daughter, ask what you will, and you shall have it."

She said, "I ask right naught, Lord, but what you may well give me, and that is mercy, which I ask for the people's sin. You say oftentimes in the year to me that you have forgiven me my sins. Therefore I ask now mercy for the sin of the people, as I would do for my own, for, Lord, you are all charity, and charity brought you into this wretched world and caused you to suffer full hard pains for our sins. Why should I not then have charity for the people and desire forgiveness for their sins? Blessed Lord, I think that you have showed right great charity to me, unworthy wretch. You are as gracious to me as though I were as clean a maiden as any is in this world and as though I had never sinned. Therefore, Lord, I would I had a well of tears to constrain you with so that you should not take utter vengeance on man's soul in order to part him from you without end, for it is a hard thing to think that any earthly man should ever do any sin wherethrough he should be parted from your glorious face without end. If I might as well, Lord, give the people contrition and weeping as you give me for my own sins, and other men's sins also, and as easily as I might give a penny out of my purse, soon should I fulfill men's hearts with contrition so that they might cease from their sin. I have great marvel in my heart, Lord, that, I, who have been so sinful a woman and the most unwor-thy creature that ever you showed your mercy unto in all this world,

---

4. The Prior's Cloister was to one side of St. Margaret's Church. The Prior's Chapel was on one side of the Cloister.

that I have such great charity toward my fellow Christian souls that I think, though they had ordained for me the most shameful death that ever might any man suffer on earth, yet would I forgive it them for your love, Lord, and have their souls saved from everlasting damnation. And therefore, Lord, I shall not cease, when I may weep, to weep for them plenteously, prosper if I may. And, if you will, Lord, that I cease from weeping, I pray you take me out of this world. What should I do therein unless I might profit? For, though it were possible that all this world might be saved through the tears of my eyes, I would not be thankworthy. Therefore, all praising, all honor, all worship may be to the Lord. If it were your will, Lord, I would for your love and for the magnifying of your name be hewn as small as meat for the pot."

58. On a time, as the foresaid creature was in her contemplation, she hungered right sorely after God's word and said, "Alas, Lord, as many clerks as you have in this world, that you would not send me one of them who might fulfill my soul with your word and with reading of Holy Scripture, for all the clerks who preach may not fulfill, for I think that my soul is ever alike hungry. If I had gold enough, I would give every day a noble to have every day a sermon, for your word is more worthy to me than all the good in this world. And therefore, blessed Lord, take pity on me, for you have taken away the anchorite from me who was to me a singular solace and comfort and many times refreshed me with your holy word."

Then answered our Lord Jesus Christ in her soul, saying, "There shall come one from far who shall fulfill your desire."

So, many days after this answer, there came a priest newly to Lynn, who had never known her before, and, when he saw her go in the streets, he was greatly moved to speak with her and inquired of other folk what manner woman she was. They said they trusted to God that she was a right good woman. Afterward the priest sent for her, praying her to come and speak with him and with his mother, for he had hired a chamber for his mother and for himself, and so they dwelled together. Then the said creature came to learn his will and spoke with his mother and with him and had right good welcome of them both.

Then the priest took a book and read therein how our Lord, seeing the city of Jerusalem, wept thereupon, relating the troubles and sorrows that should come thereto, for she knew not the time of her visitation.[5] When the said creature heard read how our Lord wept, then wept she sorely and cried loudly, the priest nor his mother knowing no cause of her weeping. When her crying and her weeping was ceased, they joyed and were right merry in our Lord. Afterward she took her leave and parted from them at that time.

5. See Luke 19.41–44.

When she was gone, the priest said to his mother, "I marvel much at this woman, why she weeps and cries so. Nevertheless I think she is a good woman, and I desire greatly to speak more with her."

His mother was well pleased and counseled that he should do so.

And afterward, the same priest loved her and trusted her full much and blessed the time that ever he knew her, for he found great ghostly comfort in her and she caused him to examine much good scripture and many a good doctor which he would not have looked at at that time had she not been. He read to her many a good book of high contemplation and other books, such as the Bible with doctors thereupon, Saint Bride's book, Hilton's book, Bonaventure, *Stimulus Amoris*, *Incendium Amoris*, and such other[6] And then knew she that it was a spirit sent from God which said to her, as is written a little before, when she complained for lack of reading, these words, "There shall come one from far who shall fulfill your desire." And thus she knew by experience that it was a right true spirit.

The foresaid priest read her books the most part of seven years or eight years to the great increase of his knowledge and of his merit, and he suffered many an evil word for her love inasmuch as he read her so many books and supported her in her weeping and her crying. Afterward he waxed beneficed[7] and had great cure of souls, and then it pleased him full well that he had read so much before.

59. Thus, through the hearing of holy books and through the hearing of holy sermons, she ever increased in contemplation and holy meditation. It would be in manner impossible to write all the holy thoughts, holy speeches, and the high revelations which our Lord showed unto her, both of herself and of other men and women, also of many souls, some to be saved and some to be damned, which was to her a great punishing and a sharp chastising. For to know of those who should be saved she was full glad and joyful, for she desired in as much as she dared all men to be saved. And, when our Lord showed to her of any who should be damned, she had great pain. She would not hear it nor believe that it was God who showed her such things and put it out of her mind as much as she might.

Our Lord blamed her therefore and bade her believe that it was his high mercy and his goodness to show her his privy counsels, saying to her mind, "Daughter, you must as well hear of the damned as of the saved."

She would give no credence to the counsel of God but rather believed it was some evil spirit deceiving her. Then for her forwardness and her unbelief our Lord drew from her all good thoughts and

---

6. For these texts, see the notes for chapter 17 (p. 30). "The Bible with doctors thereupon": This is either a Latin Bible or a vernacular Bible, most likely a Wycliffite translation with marginal glosses (interpretation) by the Doctors of the Church near difficult verses. Archbishop of Canterbury Thomas Arundel had in the *Constitutions* of 1409 forbidden laypeople to read the Bible privately.
7. Received a benefice in which he had the care of many souls.

all good minds of holy speeches and dalliance and the high contemplation which she had been used to beforetime, and suffered her to have as many evil thoughts as she had before of good thoughts. And this vexation endured twelve days together. And, just as beforetime she had four hours of the morning in holy speeches and dalliance with our Lord, so had she now as many hours of foul thoughts and foul minds of lechery and all uncleanness, as though she should have been common to all manner of people. And so the devil deceived her, dallying unto her with cursed thoughts, just as our Lord dallied unto her beforetime with holy thoughts. And, as she before had many glorious visions and high contemplation in the manhood of our Lord, in our Lady, and in many other holy saints, right even so had she now horrible sights and abominable, for any thing that she could do, of the beholding of men's members and such other abominations. She saw, as she thought verily, divers men of religion, priests, and many others, both heathen and Christian, coming before her sight so that she might not avoid them nor put them out of her sight, showing their bare members unto her. And therewith the devil bade her in her mind choose whom she would have first of them all, and she must be common to them all. And he said she liked better some one of them than all the others. She thought that he said the truth; she could not say no; and she must needs do his bidding, and yet would she not have done it for all this world. But yet she thought that it should be done, and she thought that these horrible sights and cursed minds were delectable to her against her will. Wherever she went or whatever she did, these cursed minds abided with her. When she should see the sacrament, make her prayers, or do any other good deed, ever such cursedness was put in her mind. She was shriven and did all that she might, but she found no releasing till she was nearly at despair. It cannot be written what pain she felt and the sorrow that she was in.

Then she said, "Alas, Lord, you have said beforetime that you should never forsake me. Where is now the truth of your word?"

And anon after came her good angel unto her, saying, "Daughter, God has not forsaken you nor ever shall forsake you, as he has promised you, but, because you believe not that it is the spirit of God that speaks in your soul and shows you his privy counsels of some who shall be saved and some who shall be damned, therefore God chastised you in this way and manner, and this chastising shall endure twelve days till you will believe that it is God who speaks to you and no devil."

Then she said to her angel, "A, I pray you, pray for me to my Lord Jesus Christ so that he will vouchsafe to take from me these cursed thoughts and speak to me as he did beforetime, and I shall make a promise to God that I shall believe that it is God who has spoken to me aforetime, for I may no longer endure this great pain."

Her angel said again to her, "Daughter, my Lord Jesus will not take it away from you till you have suffered it twelve days, for he wills that you know thereby whether it is better that God speaks to you or the devil. And my Lord Christ Jesus is never the angrier with you, though he suffers you to feel this pain."

So she suffered that pain till twelve days were passed, and then had she as holy thoughts, as holy minds, and as holy desires, as holy speeches and dalliance of our Lord Jesus Christ as ever she had before, our Lord saying to her, "Daughter, believe now well that I am no devil."

Then was she filled with joy, for she heard our Lord speak to her as he was wont to do. Therefore she said, "I shall believe that every good thought is the speech of God, blessed may you, Lord, be, that you deign not to comfort me again. I would not, Lord, for all this world suffer such another pain as I have suffered these twelve days, for I thought I was in hell, blessed may you be that it is passed. Therefore, Lord, now will I lie still and be buxom to your will; I pray you, Lord, speak in me whatever is most pleasing to you."

60. The good priest, of whom it is written before, who was her reader, fell into great sickness, and she was stirred in her soul to take care of him in God's service. And, when she lacked such as was needful for him, she went about to good men and good women and got such thing as was necessary unto him. He was so sick that men trusted nothing for his life, and his sickness was long continuing. Then on a time, as she was in the church hearing her mass and prayed for the same priest, our Lord said to her that he should live and fare right well. Then was she stirred to go to Norwich to Saint Stephen's Church where is buried the good vicar, who died but little before that time, for whom God showed high mercy to his people, and thank him for the recovery of this priest.[8]

She took leave of her confessor, going forth to Norwich. When she came in the churchyard of Saint Stephen's, she cried, she roared, she wept, she fell down to the ground, so fervently the fire of love burnt in her heart. Afterward she rose up again and went forth weeping into the church to the high altar, and there she fell down with violent sobbings, weepings, and loud cries beside the grave of the good vicar, all ravished with ghostly comfort in the goodness of our Lord who wrought so great grace for his servant who had been her confessor and many times heard her confession of all her living, and administered to her the precious sacrament of the altar at divers times. And in so much was her devotion the more increased in that she saw our Lord work such special grace for such a creature as she had been conversant with in his lifetime. She had such holy thoughts and such holy minds that she might not measure her weeping nor her crying. And therefore the people had great marvel of her, supposing that she had wept for some fleshly or earthly affection, and

---

8. This would be the grave of Richard Caister (d. 1420), vicar of St. Stephen's.

said unto her, "What ails you, woman? Why do you fare thus with your-self? We knew him as well as you."[9]

Then were there priests in the same place who knew her manner of working, and they full charitably led her to a tavern and made her drink and made her full high and goodly comfort. Also there was a lady who desired to have the said creature to a meal. And therefore, as honest would, she went to the church where the lady heard her service, where this creature saw a fair image of our Lady called a *pity*.[1] And through the beholding of that *pity*, her mind was all wholly occupied in the Passion of our Lord Jesus Christ and in the compassion of our Lady, Saint Mary, by which she was compelled to cry full loudly and weep full sorely, as though she should have died.

Then came to her the lady's priest, saying, "Damsel, Jesus is dead long since."

When her crying was ceased, she said to the priest, "Sir, his death is as fresh to me as if he had died this same day, and so I think it ought to be to you and to all Christian people. We ought ever to have mind of his kindness and ever think of the doleful death that he died for us."

Then the good lady, hearing her communication, said, "Sir, it is a good example to me, and to other men also, the grace that God works in her soul."

And so the good lady was her advocate and answered for her. Afterward she had her home with her to meat and showed her full glad and goodly comfort as long as she would abide there. And soon after, she came home again to Lynn, and the foresaid priest, for whom she went most specially to Norwich, who had read to her for about seven years, recovered and went about where he wished, thanked be almighty God for his goodness.

61. Then came there a friar to Lynn who was held a holy man and a good preacher. His name and his perfection of preaching spread and sprung wonder wide. There came good men to the said creature out of good charity and said, "Margery, now shall you have preaching enough, for there is come one of the most famous friars in England to this town, in order to be here in the convent."

Then was she merry and glad and thanked God with all her heart that so good a man was coming to dwell among them. In short time after, he said a sermon in a chapel of Saint James[2] in Lynn, where there were many people gathered to hear the sermon.

And, before the friar went to the pulpit, the parish priest of the same place where he should preach went to him and said, "Sir, I pray you, be not displeased. There shall come a woman to your sermon who often times, when she hears of the Passion of our Lord or of any high devotion,

9. The people speak here of Caister; Margery weeps for Christ.
1. A *pieta*, an image of Mary with the dead Christ.
2. Chapel of ease in St. Margaret's parish.

she weeps, sobs, and cries, but it lasts not long. And therefore, good sir, if she makes any noise at your sermon, suffer it patiently and be not abashed thereof."

The good friar went forth to say the sermon and said full holily and full devoutly and spoke much of our Lord's Passion so that the said creature might no longer bear it. She kept herself from crying as long as she might, and then at the last she burst out with a great cry and cried wonder sore. The good friar suffered it patiently and said no word thereto at that time. In a short time after he preached again in the same place. The said creature being present, and, beholding how fast the people came running to hear the sermon, she had great joy in her soul, thinking in her mind, "A, Lord Jesus, I believe if you were here to preach in your own person, the people should have great joy to hear you. I pray you, Lord, make your holy word settle in their souls as I would that it should do in mine, and as many might be turned by his voice as should be by your voice if you preached yourself."

And with such holy thoughts and holy minds she asked grace for the people at that time, and afterward, what through the holy sermon and what through her meditation, the grace of devotion wrought so sorely in her mind that she fell into a violent weeping.

Then said the good friar, "I would this woman were out of the church; she annoys the people."

Some who were her friends answered again, "Sir, have her excused. She may not withstand it."

Then many people turned against her and were full glad that the good friar held against her. Then said some men that she had a devil within her. And so had they said many times before, but now they were more bold, for they thought that their opinion was well strengthened or else fortified by this good friar. Nor would he suffer her to hear his sermon unless she would leave her sobbing and her crying. There was then a good priest who had read to her much good scripture and knew the cause of her crying. He spoke to another good priest, who had known her many years, and told him his conceit, how he was purposed to go to the good friar and try to humble his heart. The other good priest said he would with good will go with him to get grace if he might. So they went, both priests together, and prayed the good friar as entirely as they could that he would suffer the said creature quietly to come to his sermon and suffer her patiently if she happened to sob or cry as other good men had suffered her before.

He said shortly again, if she came in any church where he should preach and she made any noise as she was wont to do, he should speak sharply against her; he would not suffer her to cry in any way.

Afterward a worshipful doctor of divinity, a White Friar,[3] a solemn clerk and old doctor, and well approved, who had known the said creature

3. Carmelite friar.

many years of her life and believed the grace that God wrought in her, took with him a worthy man, a bachelor of law, a well grounded man in scripture and long exercised, who was confessor to the said creature, and went to the said friar as the good priests did before and sent for wine to cheer him, praying him of his charity to favor the works of our Lord in the said creature and grant her his benevolence in support of her if she happened to cry or sob while he was in his sermon. And these worthy clerks told him that it was a gift of God and that she could not have it but when God would give it, nor might she withstand it when God would send it, and God should withdraw it when he willed, for that had she by revelation, and that was unknown to the friar.

Then he, giving credence neither to the doctor's words nor to the bachelor's, trusting much in the favor of the people, said he would not favor her in her crying for aught that any man might say or do, for he would not believe that it was a gift of God. But he said, if she might not withstand it when it came, he believed it was a heart disease or some other sickness, and, if she would be so known, he said, he would have compassion on her and steer the people to pray for her, and under this condition he would have patience with her and suffer her to cry enough, if she should say that it was a natural sickness.

And she knew well by revelation and by experience of its working that it was no sickness, and therefore she would not for all this world say otherwise than she felt. And therefore they might not accord. Then the worshipful doctor and her confessor counseled her that she should not come to his sermon, and that was to her a great pain.

Then went another man, a worshipful burgess, who a few years after was mayor of Lynn, and prayed him as the worthy clerks had done before, and he was answered as they were.

Then was she charged by her confessor that she should not come where he preached, but when he preached in one church, she should go into another. She had so much sorrow that she knew not what she might do, for she was put from the sermon, which was to her the highest comfort on earth when she might hear it, and right so the contrary was to her the greatest pain on earth when she might not hear it. When she was alone by herself in one church and he preaching to the people in another, she had as loud and as marvelous cries as when she was among the people. It was years that she might not be suffered to come to his sermon because she cried so when it pleased our Lord to give her mind and very beholding of his bitter Passion.

But she was not excluded from any other clerk's preaching, but only from the good friar's, as is said before, notwithstanding in the meantime there preached many worshipful doctors and other worthy clerks, both religious and seculars, at whose sermons she cried full loudly and sobbed full violently many times and often. And yet they suffered it full patiently, and some who had spoken with her before and had knowledge of her manner of living excused her to the people when they heard any rumor or grudging against her.

62. After, on Saint James' Day[4] the good friar preached in Saint James chapel yard at Lynn—he was at that time neither bachelor nor doctor of divinity—where were many people and a great audience, for he had a holy name and great favor of the people, in so much that some men, if they knew that he should preach in the country, they would go with him or else follow him from town to town, so great delight they had to hear him and so, blessed may God be, he preached full holily and full devoutly. Nevertheless, on this day he preached much against the said creature, not expressing her name, but so he explained his conceits that men understood well that he meant her. Then was there much rumor among the people, for many men and many women trusted her and loved her right well and were right heavy and sorrowful because he spoke so much against her as he did, desiring that they had not heard him that day. When he heard the murmur and grudging of the people, supposing to be gainsaid another day by those who were her friends, he, smiting his hand on the pulpit, said, "If I hear any more these matters repeated, I shall so smite the nail on the head," he said, "that it shall shame all her maintainers."

And then many of those who pretended their friendship turned back for a little vain dread that they had of his words and dared not well speak with her, of which the same priest was one, he who afterward wrote this book and was in purpose never to have believed her feelings afterward. And yet our Lord drew him again in a short time, blessed may he be, so that he loved her more and trusted more to her weeping and her crying than ever he did before, for afterward he read of a woman called Mary of Oignies[5] and of her manner of living, of the wonderful sweetness that she had in hearing the word of God, of the wonderful compassion that she had in thinking of his Passion, and of the plenteous tears that she wept, which made her so feeble and so weak that she might not endure to behold the cross, nor hear our Lord's Passion rehearsed, so she was resolved into tears of pity and compassion. Of the plenteous grace of her tears he treats specially in the book before written, the eighteenth chapter, that begins, "Bonus es, domine, sperantibus in te,"[6] and also in the nineteenth chapter where he tells how she, at the request of a priest that he should not be troubled nor distraught in his mass with her weeping and her sobbing, went out of the church door, with a loud voice crying that she might not restrain herself therefrom. And our Lord also visited the priest in his mass with such grace and with such devotion when he should read the

---

4. The feast of St. James the Greater is July 25.
5. Marie d'Oignies (ca. 1177–1213), whose passionate devotion to Christ and life of poverty and service made her a special figure of female piety. Jacques de Vitry, her friend and confessor, wrote her life, which influenced the spirituality of the later Middle Ages.
6. "He is good, Lord, whose hope is in you."

Holy Gospel that he wept wonderfully, so that he wet his vestment and
ornaments of the altar and might not measure his weeping nor his sobbing, it was so abundant, nor might he restrain it nor stand well therewith
at the altar. Then he believed well that the good woman, whom he had
before little affection toward, might not restrain her weeping, her sobbing, or her crying and felt much more plenty of grace than ever did he,
without any comparison. Then knew he well that God gave his grace to
whom he would.

Then the priest who wrote this treatise through the stirring of a worshipful clerk, a bachelor of divinity, had seen and read the matter before
written much more seriously and expressively than it is written in this
treatise (for here is but a little of the effect thereof, for he had not a right
clear mind of the said matter when he wrote this treatise, and therefore
he wrote the less thereof), then he drew again and inclined more soberly
to the said creature, whom he had fled and eschewed through the friar's
preaching, as is before written.

Also the same priest read afterward in a treatise which is called "The
Prykke of Lofe,"[7] the two chapters that Bonaventure wrote of himself,
these words following, "A, Lord, of what shall I more noise or cry? You
tarry and you come not, and I, weary and overcome through desire,
begin to madden, for love governs me and not reason. I run with hasty
course wherever you will. I bow, Lord. Those who see me are irked
and pity me, not knowing me drunk with your love. Lord, they say 'Lo,
yon mad man cries in the streets,' but how great is the desire of my
heart they perceive not." (And chapter from the *Stimulus Amoris* and
chapter as above.) He read also of Richard Hampole, hermit, in
Incendio Amoris like matter that moved him to give credence to the
said creature. Also, Elizabeth of Hungary[8] cried with a loud voice, as
is written in her treatise.

And many others who had forsaken her through the friar's preaching
repented and turned again unto her by process of time, notwithstanding
the friar kept his opinion. And always he would in his sermon have a part
against her, whether she were there or not, and caused many people to
think evil of her many a day and long.

For some said that she had a devil within her, and some said to her own
mouth that the friar should have driven two devils out of her. Thus was
she slandered, eaten, and gnawed by the people for the grace that God
wrought in her of contrition, of devotion, and of compassion, through the
gift of which graces she wept, sobbed, and cried full sorely against her

---

7. This is the fourteenth-century devotional work entitled *Stimulus Amoris* that was falsely attributed to St. Bonaventure.
8. St. Elizabeth of Hungary (1207–1231) also wept copiously in devotion; her legend was popular
in England in the fifteenth century. *Incendio Amoris* was the mid-fourteenth-century treatise by
Richard Rolle of Hampole, the important English mystic and author. It was translated into English as *The Fire of Love* by Richard Misyn in 1435.

will; she might not choose, for she had rather have wept softly and secretly than openly if it had been in her power.

63. Then some of her friends came to her and said it was more ease for her to go out of the town than abide therein, so many people were against her. And she said she should abide there as long as God wished. "For here," she said, "in this town have I sinned. Therefore it is worthy that I suffer sorrow in this town there again. And yet have I not so much sorrow or shame as I have deserved, for I have trespassed against God. I thank almighty God for whatever he sends me, and I pray God that all manner of wickedness that any man shall say of me in this world may stand for remission of my sins, and any goodness that any man shall say of the grace that God works in me may turn to God, to worship and to praising and magnifying of his holy name without end, for all manner of worship belongs to him, and all despite, shame, and reproof belongs to me, and that have I well deserved."

Another time her confessor came to her in a chapel of our Lady, called the Gesine,[9] saying, "Margery, what shall you now do? There is no more against you but the moon and seven stars. Hardly is there any man who holds with you but I alone."

She said to her confessor, "Sir, be of a good comfort, for it shall be right well at the last. And I tell you truly, my Lord Jesus gives me great comfort in my soul, and else should I fall into despair. My blissful Lord Christ Jesus will not let me despair for any holy name that the good friar has, for my Lord tells me that he is angry with him, and he says to me it were better he were never born, for he despises his works in me."

Also our Lord said to her, "Daughter, if he be a priest who despises you, knowing well wherefore you weep and cry, he is accursed."

And on a time, as she was in the prior's cloister and dared not abide in the church for disturbing of the people with her crying, our Lord said unto her, being in great heaviness, "Daughter, I bid you go again into church, for I shall take away from you your crying so that you shall no more cry so loud, nor in that manner of way as you have done before, though you would."

She did the commandment of our Lord and told her confessor just as she felt, and it fell in truth as she felt. She cried no more after so loudly nor in that manner as she had done before; but afterward she sobbed wonderfully and wept as sorely as ever she did before, sometimes loud and sometimes still, as God would measure it himself. Then many people believed that she dared no longer cry because the good friar preached so against her and would not suffer her in any manner. Then they held him a holy man and her a false feigned hypocrite. And, as some spoke evil of her before because she cried, so some spoke now evil of her because she

---

9. This is a chapel in St. Margaret's Church in which was a picture of the birth of Jesus.

cried not. And so slander and bodily anguish fell to her on every side, and all was an increasing of her ghostly comfort.

Then our merciful Lord said unto his unworthy servant, "Daughter, I must needs comfort you, for now you have the right way to heaven. By this way came I to heaven and all my disciples, for now you shall know better what sorrow and shame I suffered for your love, and you shall have the more compassion when you think on my Passion. Daughter, I have told you many times that the friar should say evil of you. Therefore I warn you that you tell him not of the privy counsel that I have showed to you, for I will not that he hear it of your mouth. And, daughter, I tell you, forsoothe he shall be chastised sharply. As his name is now, it shall be thrown down and yours shall be raised up. And I shall make as many men to love you for my love as have despised you for my love. Daughter, you shall be in church when he shall be without. In this church you have suffered much shame and reproof for the gifts that I have given you and for the grace and goodness that I have wrought in you, and therefore in this church and in this place I shall be worshiped in you. Many a man and woman shall say 'it is well seen that God loved her well.' Daughter, I shall work so much grace for you that all the world shall wonder and marvel at my goodness."

Then the said creature said unto our Lord with great reverence, "I am not worthy that you should show such grace for me. Lord, it is enough to me that you save my soul from endless damnation by your great mercy."

"It is my worship, daughter, that I shall do, and therefore I will that you have no will but my will. The less price that you set by yourself, the more price set I by you, and the better will I love you, daughter. Look you have no sorrow for earthly good. I have tried you in poverty, and I have chastised you as I would myself, both within your soul and without, through slander of the people. Lo, daughter, I have granted you your own desire, for you should no other purgatory have but in this world only. Daughter, you say often to me in your mind that rich men have great cause to love me well, and you say right soothe, for you say I have given them much good wherewith they may serve me and love me. But, good daughter, I pray you, love you me with all your heart, and I shall give you good enough to love me with, for heaven and earth should rather fail than I should fail you. And, if other men fail, you shall not fail. And, though all your friends forsake you, I shall never forsake you. You made me once steward of your household and executor of all your good works, and I shall be a true steward and a true executor unto you, fulfilling all your will and all your desire. And I shall provide for you, daughter, as for my own mother and as for my own wife."

64. The creature said unto her Lord Christ Jesus, "A, blissful Lord, I would I knew wherein I might best love you and please you and that my love were as sweet to you as I think that your love is unto me."

Then our sweet Lord Jesus, answering his creature, said, "Daughter, if you knew how sweet your love is unto me, you should never do another thing but love me with all your heart. And therefore believe well, daughter, that my love is not so sweet to you as your love is to me. Daughter, you know not how much I love you, for it may not be known in this world how much it is, nor be felt as it is, for you should fail and burst and never endure it for the joy that you should feel. And therefore I measure it as I will to your greatest ease and comfort. But, daughter, you shall well know in another world how much I loved you on earth, for there you shall have great cause to thank me. There you shall see without end every good day that ever I gave you on earth of contemplation, of devotion, and of all the great charity that I have given to you to the profit of your fellow Christians. For this shall be your food when you come home into heaven.

"There is no clerk in all this world who can, daughter, teach you better than I can do, and, if you will be buxom to my will, I shall be buxom to your will. Where is a better charity than to weep for your Lord's love? You know well, daughter, that the devil has no charity, for he is full angry with you and he might outwardly hurt you, but he shall not harm you save a little in this world in order to make you afraid sometimes, so that you should pray the mightier to me for grace and steer your charity the more toward me. There is no clerk who can speak against the life which I teach you, and, if he does, he is not God's clerk; he is the devil's clerk. I tell you right forsooth that there is no man in this world, if he would suffer as much despite for my love willfully as you have done and cleave as sorely unto me, not willing for anything that may be done or said against him to forsake me, but I shall fare right fair with him and be right gracious unto him, both in this world and in the other."

Than said the creature, "A, my worthy Lord, this life should you show to religious men and to priests."

Our Lord said again to her, "Nay, nay, daughter, for that thing that I love best they love not, and that is shames, despites, scorns, and reproofs from the people, and therefore shall they not have this grace. For, daughter, I tell you, he who dreads the shames of the world may not perfectly love God. And, daughter, under the habit of holiness is covered much wickedness. Daughter, if you saw the wickedness that is wrought in the world as I do, you should have great wonder that I take not utter vengeance on them. But, daughter, I spare for your love. You weep so every day for mercy that I must needs grant it you, and the people will not believe the goodness that I work in you for them. Nevertheless, daughter, there shall come a time when they shall be right fain to believe the grace that I have given you for them. And I shall say to them when they are passed out of this world, 'Lo, I ordained her to weep for her sins, and you had her in great despite, but her charity would never cease for you.' And therefore, daughter, those who are good souls shall highly thank me for the grace and goodness that I have given you, and those who are wicked shall grudge and have great pain to suffer the grace that I show to you. And therefore I shall chastise them as it were for myself."

She prayed, "Nay, worthy Lord Jesus, chastise no creature for me. You know well, Lord, that I desire no vengeance, but I ask mercy and grace for all men if it be your will to grant it. Nevertheless, Lord, rather than they should be parted from you without end, chastise them as you yourself will. It seems, Lord, in my soul that you are full of charity, for you say you will not the death of a sinful man. And you say also you will all men be saved. Then, Lord, since you would all men should be saved, I must will the same, and you say yourself that I must love my fellow Christians as my own self. And, Lord, you know that I have wept and sorrowed many years because I would be saved, and so must I do for my fellow Christians."

65. Our Lord Jesus Christ said unto the said creature, "Daughter, you shall well see when you are in heaven with me that there is no man damned but he who is well worthy to be damned, and you shall hold yourself well pleased with all my works. And therefore, daughter, thank me highly for this great charity that I work in your heart, for it is myself, almighty God, who makes you to weep every day for your own sins, for the great compassion that I give you for my bitter Passion and for the sorrows that my mother had here on earth, for the anguishes that she suffered and for the tears that she wept, also, daughter, for the holy martyrs in heaven (when you hear of them, you give me thankings with crying and weeping for the grace that I have showed to them, and, when you see any lepers, you have great compassion for them, yielding me thankings and praisings that I am more favorable to you than I am to them), and also, daughter, for the great sorrow that you have for all this world that you might help them as well as you would help yourself, both ghostly and bodily, and furthermore for the sorrows that you have for the souls in purgatory that you wished so gladly that they were out of their pain so that they might praise me without end. And all this is my own goodness that I give to you, wherefore you are greatly bound to thank me. And nevertheless yet I thank you for the great love you have toward me and because you have such great will and such great desire that all men and women should love me right well, for, as you think, holy and unholy, all of them would have good to live with as is lawful for them, but all will not busy themselves to love me as they do to get themselves temporal goods.

"Also, daughter, I thank you because you think it so long that you are out of my blessed presence. Furthermore, I thank you, daughter, especially because you may suffer no man to break my commandments nor to swear by me without it being a great pain to you and because you are always ready for my love to rebuke them for their swearing. And therefore have you suffered many a sharp word and many a reproof, and you shall therefore have many a joy in heaven. Daughter, I sent once Saint Paul unto you to strengthen you and comfort you so that you should boldly speak in my name from that day forward. And Saint Paul said unto you that you had suffered much tribulation because of his writing, and he promised you that you should have as much grace in return for his love as ever you had shame or reproof for his love. He told you also of many joys of heaven and of the great love that I had toward you.

"And, daughter, I have oftentimes said to you that there is no saint in heaven but, if you will speak with him, he is ready toward you, to comfort you and speak to you in my name. My angels are ready to offer your holy thoughts and your prayers to me, and the tears of your eyes also, for your tears are angels' drink, and they are truly sweetened and spiced wine to them.

"Therefore, my worthy daughter, be not weary of me on earth to sit alone by yourself and think of my love, for I am not weary of you and my merciful eye is ever upon you. Daughter, you may boldly say to me 'Jesus est amor meus,' that is to say, 'Jesus is my love.' Therefore, daughter, let me be all your love and all the joy of your heart. Daughter, if you will bethink you well, you have right great cause to love me above all thing for the great gifts that I have given you beforetime. And yet you have another great cause to love me, for you have your wish of chastity as if you were a widow, your husband living in good health. Daughter, I have drawn the love of your heart from all men's hearts into my heart. Sometimes, daughter, you thought it had been in a manner impossible to be so, and that time suffered you full great pain in your heart with fleshly affections. And then could you well cry to me, saying, 'Lord, for alle thi wowndys smert, drawe al the lofe of myn hert into thyn hert.'[1] Daughter, for all these causes and many other causes and benefits which I have shown you on this half of the sea and on yon half of the sea, you have great cause to love me.

66. "Now, daughter, I will that you eat meat again as you were wont to do, and that you be buxom and obedient to my will and to my bidding and leave your own will and bid your ghostly fathers that they let you act after my will. And you shall have never the less grace, but so much the more, for you shall have the same reward in heaven as though you fasted still after your own will. Daughter, I bade you first that you should leave off flesh food and not eat it, and you have obeyed my will for many years and abstained yourself after my counsel. Therefore now I bid you resort again to flesh food."

The said creature with reverent dread said, "A, blissful Lord, the people, who have known of my abstinence for so many years and see me now return and eat flesh food, they will have great marvel and, as I suppose, despise me and scorn me therefore."

---

1. "Lord, for all your wounds smart, draw all the love of my heart into your heart." This couplet is
   repeated in chapter 88 (p. 158).

Our Lord said to her again, "You shall no heed take of their scorns but let every man say what he will."

Then went she to her ghostly fathers and told them what our Lord had said unto her. When her ghostly fathers knew the will of God, they charged her by virtue of obedience to eat flesh food as she had done many years before. Then had she many a scorn and much reproof because she ate flesh again.

Also she had made a vow, while she lived, to fast one day in the week for worship of our Lady, which vow she kept for many years. Our Lady, appearing to her soul, bad her go to her confessor and say that she would have her discharged of her vow so that she should be mighty to bear her ghostly labors; for without bodily strength they might not be endured. Then her confessor, seeing by the eye of discretion it was expedient to be done, commanded her by the virtue of obedience to eat as other creatures did, measurably wherever God would she had her food. And her grace was not decreased but rather increased, for she had rather have fasted than have eaten, if it had been the will of God.

Furthermore, our Lady said to her, "Daughter, you are weak enough from weeping and from crying, for those make you feeble and weak enough. And I can the more thank you to eat your food for my love than to fast, so that you may endure your perfection of weeping."

67. On a time there happened to be a great fire in Bishop's Lynn, which fire burnt up the guild hall of the Trinity[2] and, in the same town, a hideous fire and grievous, full likely to have burnt the parish church, dedicated to the honor of Saint Margaret, a solemn place and richly honored, and also all the town, had there not been grace or miracle. The said creature being there present and seeing the peril and misfortune of all the town, cried full loudly many times that day and wept full abundantly, praying for grace and mercy for all the people. And, notwithstanding in other times they might not endure her crying and weeping for the plenteous grace that our Lord wrought in her, on this day, in order to avoid their bodily peril, they might suffer her to cry and weep as much as ever she would, and no man would bid her cease, but rather prayed her for continuation, full trusting and believing that through her crying and weeping our Lord would take them to mercy.

Then came her confessor to her and asked if it were best to bear the sacrament to the fire or not.

She said, "Yes, sir, yes, for our Lord Jesus Christ told me it shall be right well."

So her confessor, parish priest of Saint Margaret's Church, took the precious sacrament and went before the fire as devoutly as he could and afterward brought it in again to the church, and the sparks of the fire flew

2. The Guild Hall in Lynn was burned on January 23, 1420/21.

about the church. The said creature, desiring to follow the precious sacrament to the fire, went out at the church door, and, as soon as she beheld the hideous flames of the fire, anon she cried with a loud voice and great weeping, "Good Lord, make it well."

These words wrought in her mind, inasmuch as our Lord had said to her before that he should make it well, and therefore she cried, "Good Lord, make it well and send down some rain or some weather that may through your mercy quench this fire and ease my heart."

Afterward she went again into the church, and then she beheld how the sparks came into the choir through the lantern of the church.[3] Then had she a new sorrow and cried full loudly again for grace and mercy with great plenty of tears. Soon after, came to her three worshipful men with white snow on their clothes, saying unto her, "Lo, Margery, God has wrought great grace for us and sent us a fair snow to quench the fire. Be now of good cheer and thank God therefore."

And with a great cry she gave praising and thanking to God for his great mercy and his goodness, and specially because he had said to her before that it should be right well, when it was full unlikely to be well save only through miracle and special grace. And now she saw it was well indeed, she thought that she had great cause to thank our Lord.

Then came her ghostly father unto her and said he believed that God granted them, because of her prayers, to be delivered out of their great perils, for it might not be, without devout prayers, that the air being bright and clear should be so soon changed into cloudiness and darkness and send down great flakes of snow, through the which the fire was hindered of its natural working, blessed may our Lord be.

Notwithstanding the grace that he showed toward her, yet, when the perils were ceased, some men slandered her because she cried, and some said to her that our Lady cried never, "Why cry you in this manner?"

And she said because she might not otherwise do. Than she fled the people into the prior's cloister so that she should give them no occasion. When she was there, she had such great mind of the Passion of our Lord Jesus Christ and of his precious wounds and how dearly he bought her that she cried and roared wonderfully, so that she might be heard a great way and might not restrain herself therefrom. Then had she great wonder how our Lady might suffer or endure to see his precious body be scourged and hanged on the cross. Also it came to her mind how men had said to her before that our Lady, Christ's own mother, cried not as she did, and that caused her to say in her crying, "Lord, I am not your mother. Take away this pain from me, for I may not bear it. Your passion will slay me."

So there came a worshipful clerk by her, a doctor of divinity, "I had rather than twenty pounds that I might have such a sorrow for our Lord's Passion."

---

3. The lantern is an open structure upon the roof that gives light to the interior.

Then the said doctor sent for her to speak with him where he was, and she with good will went to him with weeping tears to his chamber. The worthy and worshipful clerk caused her to drink and made her right good welcome. Afterward he led her to an altar and asked what was the reason that she cried and wept so sorely. Then she told him many great causes of her weeping, and yet she told him of no revelation. And he said she was much bound to love our Lord for the tokens of love that he showed to her in various ways.

Afterward there came a parson who had taken a degree in school, who should preach both before noon and after noon. And, as he preached full holily and devoutly, the said creature was moved by devotion in his sermon, and at the last she burst out with a cry. And the people began to grudge at her crying, for it was in the time that the good friar preached against her, as is written before, and also before our Lord took her crying from her. (For, though the matter be written before this, nevertheless it befell after this.)[4] Then the parson ceased a little of his preaching and said to the people, "Friends, be still and grudge not at this woman, for each of you may sin deadly in her and she is not the cause but your own thinking; for, though this manner of working may seem both good and ill, yet ought you to think the best in your hearts, and I doubt it not it is right well. Also I dare well say it is a right gracious gift of God, blessed may he be."

Then the people blessed him for his goodly words and were the more stirred to believe his holy works. Afterward, when the sermon was ended, a good friend of the said creature met with the friar who had preached so sorely against her and asked how he thought of her. The friar, answering sharply again, said, "She has a devil within her," nothing moved from his opinion, but rather defending his error.

68. Soon after there was at Lynn held the chapter of the Friar Preachers,[5] and thither came many worshipful clerks of that holy order, of which it belonged to one to say a sermon in the parish church. And there was come among the others to the said chapter a worshipful doctor who was called Master Custawns,[6] and he had known the foresaid creature many years before. When the creature heard it said that he was come thither, she went to him and showed him why she cried and wept so sorely, to learn if he might find any default in her crying or in her weeping. The worshipful doctor said to her, "Margery, I have read of a holy woman to whom God had given great grace of weeping and crying as he has done unto you. In the church where she dwelled was a priest who had no conceit in her weeping and caused her through his stirring to go out of the church. When she was in the churchyard, she prayed God that the priest might have feeling of the grace that she felt, as surely as it lay not in her

4. Another remark about the order of the events the *Book* records.
5. Chapter is the provincial assembly of the Dominicans.
6. There was a Thomas Constans, a Dominican, in Norwich about this time.

power to cry or weep but when God would. And so suddenly our Lord sent him devotion at his mass so that he might not measure himself, and then would be no more despise her after that, but rather comfort her." Thus the said doctor, confirming her crying and her weeping, said it was a gracious and a special gift of God, and God was highly to be magnified in his gift.[7]

And then the same doctor went to another doctor of divinity who was assigned to preach in the parish church before all the people, praying him that if the said creature cried or wept at his sermon that he would suffer it meekly and not be abashed thereof nor speak against it. So afterward, when the worshipful doctor should preach and worthily was brought to the pulpit, as he began to preach full holily and devoutly of our Lady's Assumption, the said creature, lifted up in her mind by high sweetness and devotion, burst out with a loud voice and cried full loudly and wept full sorely. The worshipful doctor stood still and suffered well meekly till it was ceased and afterward said forth his sermon to an end. In the afternoon he sent for the same creature into the place where he was and made her right glad welcome. Then she thanked him for his meekness and his charity that he showed in support of her crying and her weeping before noon at his sermon. The worshipful doctor said again to her, "Margery, I would not have spoken against you though you had cried till evening. And, if you would come to Norwich, you shall be right welcome and have such comfort as I can make you."

Thus God sent her good mastership of this worthy doctor to strengthen her against her detractors, worshipped be his name.

Afterward in Lent preached a good clerk, an Austin Friar in his own house at Lynn, and had a great audience, where that time was the said creature present. And God of his goodness inspired the friar to preach much of his Passion so compassionately and so devoutly that she might not bear it. Then fell she down weeping and crying so sorely that many of the people wondered upon her and banned and cursed her full sorely, supposing that she might have left off her crying if she had wished, inasmuch as the good friar had so preached against it, as is before written. And then this good man who preached as now at this time said to the people, "Friends, be still, you know full little what she feels."

And so the people ceased and were still and listened to the sermon with quiet and rest of body and soul.

69. Also on a Good Friday at Saint Margaret's Church the prior[8] of the same place and the same town, Lynn, should preach. And he took for his theme, "Jesus is dead." Then the said creature, all wounded with pity and compassion, cried and wept as if she had seen our Lord dead with her bodily eye. The worshipful prior and doctor of divinity suffered her full

7. This story probably refers to Marie d'Ognies.
8. Thomas Hevingham, see chapter 57 (p. 103).

meekly and moved nothing against her. Another time Bishop Wakering, Bishop of Norwich,[9] preached at Lynn in the said church of Saint Margaret, and the foresaid creature cried and wept full violently in the time of his sermon, and he suffered it full meekly and patiently and so did many a worthy clerk, both regular and secular, for there was never a clerk who preached openly against her crying but the Gray Friar, as is written before.

So our Lord of his mercy, just as he had promised the said creature that he should ever provide for her, stirring the spirits of two good clerks, who long and many years had known her conversation and all her perfection, made them mighty and bold to speak for his part in excusing the said creature, both in the pulpit and, in addition, wherever they heard anything moved against her, strengthening their arguments by authority of Holy Scripture sufficiently, of which clerks one was a White Friar, a doctor of divinity. The other clerk was a bachelor of canon law, a well-labored man in scripture.[1]

And then some envious persons complained to the Provincial[2] of the White Friars that the said doctor was too conversant with the said creature, forasmuch as he supported her in her weeping and in her crying and also informed her in questions of Scripture when she would ask him any. Then was he admonished by virtue of obedience that he should no more speak with her nor inform her in any texts of Scripture, and that was to him full painful, for, as he said to some persons, he had rather have lost a hundred pounds, if he had had it, than her communication; it was so ghostly and fruitful. When her confessor perceived how the worthy doctor was charged by obedience that he should not speak or common with her, then he, in order to exclude all occasion warned her also by virtue of obedience that she should no more go to the friars, nor speak with the said doctor, nor ask him questions as she had done before. And then her thoughts were full of great sorrow and heaviness, for she was put from much ghostly comfort. She had rather had lost any earthly good than his communication, for it was to her great increase of virtue.

Then long afterward it happened that she went in the street and met with the said doctor and neither of them spoke one word to the other. And then she had a great cry with many tears. After, when she came to her meditation, she said in her mind to our Lord Jesus Christ, "Alas, Lord, why may I no comfort have of this worshipful clerk, who has known me so many years and oftentimes strengthened me in your love? Now have you, Lord, taken from me the anchorite, I trust to your mercy, the most special and singular comfort that ever I had on earth, for he ever loved me for your love and would never forsake me for anything that any man could do or say while he lived. And Master Alan is put from me and I

9. John Wakering, bishop of Norwich (1416–25).
1. Robert Spryngolde, Margery's chief confessor. "Doctor of divinity": Master Alan, Alan of Lynn.
2. Thomas Netter was elected provincial prior of the English Carmelites in 1414.

from him. Sir Thomas Andrew and Sir John Amy are beneficed and out of town. Master Robert dares never speak with me. Now have I in a manner no comfort neither of man nor of child."

Our merciful Lord Christ Jesus, answering in her mind, said, "Daughter, I am more worthy for your soul than ever was the anchorite and all those whom you have related, or all the world may be, and I shall comfort you myself, for I would speak to you more often than you will let me. And, daughter, I will have you know that you shall speak to Master Alan again as you have done before."

And then our Lord sent by provision of the prior of Lynn a priest to be keeper of a chapel of our Lady, called the Jesyn, within the Church of Saint Margaret, which priest many times heard her confession in the absence of her principle confessor. And to this priest she showed all her life as nearly as she could from her young age, both her sins, her labors, her vexations, her contemplations, and also her revelations and such grace as God wrought in her through his mercy, and so that priest trusted right well that God wrought right great grace in her.

70. On a time God visited the foresaid doctor, Master Alan, with great sickness so that no man who saw him promised him life. And so it was told the said creature of his sickness. Then she was full heavy for him, and especially for as much as she had by revelation that she should speak with him again as she had done before, and, if he had died of this sickness, her feeling had not been true. Therefore she ran into the choir at Saint Margaret's Church, kneeling down before the Sacrament and saying in this manner, "A, Lord, I pray you, for all goodness that you have showed to me and as surely as you love me, let this worthy clerk never die till I may speak with him as you have promised me that I should do. And you, glorious Queen of Mercy, have mind what he was wont to say of you in his sermons. He was wont to say, Lady, that he was well blessed that had you for his friend, for, when you prayed, all the company of heaven prayed with you. Now for the blissful love that you had for your Son, let him live till the time that he has leave to speak with me and I with him, for now we are put asunder by obedience."

Then she had answer in her soul that he should not die before the time that she had leave to speak with him and he with her as they had done years before. And, as our Lord would, in a short time after, the worthy clerk recovered and went about hale and whole and had leave of his sovereign to speak with the said creature. And she had leave of her confessor to speak with him.

So it happened that the foresaid doctor should dine in town with a worshipful woman who had taken the mantle and the ring,[3] and he sent for

---

3. This is what Margery wished to be granted early in her spiritual life, the mantle and ring that would signify her state of married chastity.

the said creature to come and speak with him. She, having great marvel thereof, took leave and went to him. When she came into the place where he was, she might not speak for weeping and for joy that she had in our Lord, inasmuch as she found her feeling true and not deceitful that he had leave to speak to her and she to him. Then the worshipful doctor said to her, "Margery, you are welcome to me, for I have long been kept from you, and now has our Lord sent you hither so that I may speak with you, blessed may he be."

There was a dinner of great joy and gladness, much more ghostly than bodily, for it was sauced and savored with tales of Holy Scripture. And then he gave the said creature a pair of knives in token that he would stand with her in God's cause, as he had done before time.

71. On a day there came a priest to the said creature, who had great trust in her feelings and in her revelations, desiring to prove them in divers times, and prayed her to pray to our Lord that she might have understanding if the prior of Lynn, who was a good master to the said priest, should be removed or not and, as she felt, make him a true account. She prayed about the foresaid matter, and, when she had answer thereof, she told the priest that the prior of Lynn, his master, should be called home to Norwich and another of his brothers should be sent to Lynn in his stead. And so it was in deed. But he[4] who was sent to Lynn abode there but a little while before he was called home to Norwich again, and he who had been prior of Lynn before was sent again to Lynn and dwelled there well about four years till he died. And in the mean time the said creature had often a feeling that he who was last called home to Norwich and abode but a little while at Lynn should yet be prior of Lynn again. She would give no credence thereto, inasmuch as he had been there and was in a little time called home again. Then, as she went up and down on a time in the White Friars' Church[5] at Lynn, she felt a wonderfully sweet and heavenly savor so that she thought she might have lived thereby without food or drink if it would have continued. And in that time our Lord said unto her, "Daughter, by this sweet smell you may well know that there shall in a short time be a new prior in Lynn, and that shall be he who was last removed thence."

And soon after the old prior died, and then our Lord said to her as she lay in her bed, "Daughter, as loath as you are to believe my stirrings, yet shall you see him of whom I showed you before, the prior of Lynn, before the seventh day."

And so our Lord rehearsed to her this matter each day until the seventh till she saw it was so in deed, and then was she full glad and joyful that her feeling was true. Afterward, when this worshipful man, who

4. John Derham briefly succeeded Thomas Hevingham.
5. This is the church of the Carmelites in Lynn.

was a most worshipful clerk, a doctor of divinity, was come to Lynn and had dwelled there but a little while, he was appointed to go over the sea to the King in France, and other clerks also, of the worthiest in England. Then a priest who had an office under the said prior came to the foresaid creature and beseeched her to have this matter in mind when God would administer his holy dalliance to her soul and learn about this matter whether the prior should go over the sea or not. And so she prayed to have understanding of this matter, and she had answer that he should not go. Nevertheless he thought he would have gone and was all purveyed therefore and with great heaviness had taken leave of his friends, supposing never to have come again, for he was a full weak man and feeble of complexion.

And in the meantime the king died,[6] and the prior bode at home. And so her feeling was true without any deceit. Also it was voiced that the Bishop of Winchester[7] was dead, and, notwithstanding, she had feeling that he lived. And so it was in truth. And so had she feelings of many more than are written, which our Lord of his mercy revealed to her understanding, though she were unworthy by her merits.

72. So by process of time her mind and her thought were so joined to God that she never forgot him, but continually had mind of him and beheld him in all creatures. And ever the more that she increased in love and in devotion, the more she increased in sorrow and in contrition, in lowness, in meekness, and in the holy dread of our Lord, and in knowledge of her own frailty, so that, if she saw a creature be punished or sharply chastised, she should think that she had been more worthy to be chastised than that creature was for her unkindness against God. Then should she cry, weep, and sob for her own sin and for compassion of the creature whom she saw so punished and sharply chastised. If she saw a prince, a prelate, or a worthy man of state and degree whom men worshipped and reverenced with lowness and meekness, anon her mind was refreshed unto our Lord, thinking what joy, what bliss, what worship and reverence he had in heaven among his blessed saints, since a deadly man had such great worship on earth. And most of all when she saw the precious sacrament born about the town with light and reverence, the people kneeling on their knees, then had she many holy thoughts and meditations, and then oftentimes should she cry and roar as though she should have burst for the faith and the trust that she had in the precious sacrament.

Also the said creature was desired by many people to be with them at their dying and to pray for them, for, though they loved not her weeping nor her crying in their lifetime, they desired that she should both weep

---

6. King Henry V died on August 31, 1422.
7. The bishop of Winchester was Henry Beaufort, half-brother to Henry IV.

and cry when they should die, and so she did. When she saw folk be anointed, she had many holy thoughts, many holy meditations, and, if she saw them die, she thought she saw our Lord die and sometimes our Lady, as our God would illumine her ghostly sight with understanding. Then should she cry, weep, and sob full wonderfully as if she had beheld our Lord in his dying or our Lady in her dying. And she thought in her mind that God took many out of this world who would full fain have lived, "and I, Lord," thought she, "would full fain come to you, and after me you have no yearning," and such thoughts increased her weeping and her sobbing.

On a time a worshipful lady sent for her for the purpose of commoning, and, as they were in their communication, the lady gave to her a manner of worship and praising, and it was to her great pain to have any praising. Nevertheless, anon she offered it up to our Lord—for she desired no praising but his only—with a great cry and many devout tears.

So there was neither worship nor praising, love nor lacking, shame nor despite that might draw her love from God, but, after the sentence of Saint Paul, "To them that love God all things turn into goodness,"[8] so it fared with her. Whatever she saw or heard, always her love and her ghostly affection increased toward our Lord, blessed may he be, who wrought such grace in her for many men's profit.

Another time there sent for her another worshipful lady who had a great household about her, and great worship and great reverence was done unto her. When the said creature beheld all her household about her and the great reverence and worship that was done her, she fell on a great weeping and cried therewith right sadly. There was a priest who heard how she cried and how she wept, and he was a man not savoring ghostly things, who banned her full fast, saying unto her, "What devil ails you? Why weep so? God give you sorrow."

She sat still and answered no word. Then the lady had her into a garden by themselves alone and prayed her to tell why she cried so sorely. And then she, supposing it was expedient to do so, told her in part the cause. Then the lady was ill pleased with her priest who had so spoken against her and loved her right well, desiring and praying her to abide still with her. Then she excused herself and said she might not accord with the array and the governance that she saw there among her household.

73. On the Holy Thursday, as the said creature went in procession with other people, she saw in her soul our Lady, Saint Mary Magdalene,[9] and

---

8. Romans 8.28.
9. Mary Magdalene was one of the female followers of Jesus, whose penitence and fervent love for her lord made her a focus for late-medieval devotion to the humanity of Jesus. "Holy Thursday": Thursday of Holy Week, Maundy Thursday, the day on which Jesus washed the feet of his disciples, instituted the Last Supper, prayed in the Garden of Gethsemane, and was betrayed by Judas and arrested. With Holy Thursday begins an intense period of penance and devotion that ends with the joy of Easter.

the twelve apostles. And then she beheld with her ghostly eye how our Lady took her leave of her blissful Son, Christ Jesus, how he kissed her and all his apostles and also his true lover, Mary Magdalene. Then she thought it was a sorrowful parting and also a joyful parting. When she beheld this sight in her soul, she fell down in the field among the people. She cried, she roared, she wept as though she should have burst therewith. She might not measure herself nor rule herself, but cried and roared so that many men wondered at her. But she took no heed what any man said or did, for her mind was occupied in our Lord. She felt many a holy thought in that time which she never afterward knew. She had forgotten all earthly things and only attended to ghostly things. She thought that all her joy was gone. She saw her Lord rise up into heaven, but she could not forgo him on earth. Therefore she desired to have gone with him, for all her joy and all her bliss was in him, and she knew well that she should never have joy or bliss till she came to him. Such holy thoughts and such holy desires caused her to weep, and the people knew not what ailed her.

Another time the said creature beheld how our Lady was, she thought, at her death and all the apostles kneeling before her and asking grace. Then she cried and wept sorely. The apostles commanded her to cease and be still. The creature answered to the apostles, "Would you I should see the Mother of God die and I should not weep? It may not be, for I am so full of sorrow that I may not withstand it. I must needs cry and weep."

And then she said in her soul to our Lady, "A, blessed Lady, pray for me to your Son that I may come to you and no longer be tarried from you, for, Lady, this is all too great a sorrow, to be both at your son's death and at your death and not die with you but live still alone and no comfort have with me."

Then our gracious Lady answered to her soul, promising her to pray for her to her son, and said, "Daughter, all these sorrows that you have had for me and for my blessed son shall turn for you to great joy and bliss in heaven without end. And doubt you not, daughter, that you shall come to us right well and be right welcome when you come. But you may not come yet, for you shall come in right good time. And, daughter, know you well you shall find me a very mother to you to help you and succor you as a mother ought to do with her daughter and purchase for you grace and virtue. And the same pardon that was granted you beforetime, it was confirmed on Saint Nicholas Day,[1] that is to say, plenary remission, and it is not only granted to you but also to all those who believe and to all those who shall believe unto the world's end that God loves you and shall thank God for you. If they will forsake their sin and be in full will no more to turn again thereto but be sorry and heavy for what they have done and will do due penance therefore, they shall have the same pardon that is granted to

---

1. There are no events for St. Nicholas Day recorded in the *Book*.

you, and that is all the pardon that is in Jerusalem, as was granted you when you were at Rafnys," as is written before.[2]

74. The said creature on a day, hearing her mass and revolving in her mind the time of her death, sorely sighing and sorrowing because it was so long delayed, said in this manner, "Alas, Lord, how long shall I thus weep and mourn for your love and for desire of your presence?"

Our Lord answered in her soul and said, "All these fifteen years."

Then said she, "A, Lord, I shall think it many thousand years."

Our Lord answered to her, "Daughter, you must bethink you of my blessed mother who lived after me on earth for fifteen years, also Saint John the Evangelist, and Mary Magdalene, who loved me right highly."

"A, blissful Lord," said she, "I would I were as worthy to be sure of your love as Mary Magdalene was."

Then said our Lord, "Truly, daughter, I love you as well, and the same peace that I gave to her, the same peace I give to you. For, daughter, there is no saint in heaven displeased if I love a creature on earth as much as I do them. Therefore they will not otherwise than I will."

Thus our merciful Lord Christ Jesus drew his creature into his love and into the mind of his passion so that she might not endure to behold a leper or another sick man, especially if he had any wounds appearing on him. So she cried and so she wept as if she had seen our Lord Jesus Christ with his wounds bleeding. And so she did in the sight of her soul, for through beholding the sick man, her mind was all taken into our Lord Jesus Christ. Then had she great mourning and sorrowing because she might not kiss the lepers when she saw them or met with them in the streets for the love of Jesus. Now began she to love what she had most hated beforetime, for there was no thing more loathful nor more abominable to her while she was in the years of worldly prosperity than to see or behold a leper, whom now through our Lord's mercy she desired to embrace and kiss for the love of Jesus, when she had time and place convenient. Then she told her confessor how great a desire she had to kiss lepers, and he warned her that she should kiss no men, but, if she would kiss anyhow, she should kiss women. Then was she glad, for she had leave to kiss the sick women and went to a place where sick women dwelled, who were right full of the sickness, and fell down on her knees before them, praying them that she might kiss their mouth for the love of Jesus. And so she kissed there two sick women, with many a holy thought and many a devout tear, and, when she had kissed them and told them full many good words and stirred them to meekness and patience so that they should not grudge about their sickness but highly thank God therefore and they should have great bliss in heaven through the mercy of our Lord

---

2. Margery stayed at Rafnes when she went to Jerusalem; there she received plenary remission for her sins.

Jesus Christ, then the one woman had so many temptations that she knew not how she might best be governed. She was so labored with her ghostly enemy that she dared not bless herself nor do any worship to God for dread that the devil should have slain her. And she was labored with many foul and horrible thoughts,[3] many more than she could tell. And, as she said, she was a maid. Therefore the said creature went to her many times to comfort her and prayed for her, also especially that God should strengthen her against her enemy, and it is to be believed that he did so, blessed may he be.

75. As the said creature was in the church of Saint Margaret to say her devotions, there came a man kneeling at her back, wringing his hands and showing tokens of great heaviness. She, perceiving his heaviness, asked what ailed him. He said it stood right hard with him, for his wife was newly delivered of a child and she was out of her mind. "And, dame," he said, "she knows not me nor any of her neighbors. She roars and cries so that she makes folk terribly afraid. She will both smite and bite, and therefore is she manacled on her wrists."

Then asked she the man if he would that she went with him and saw her, and he said, "Yes, dame, for God's love."

So she went forth with him to see the woman. And, when she came into the house, as soon as the sick woman who was aliened from her wit saw her, she spoke to her soberly and well and said she was right welcome to her. And she was right glad of her coming and greatly comforted by her presence, "For you are," she said, "a right good woman, and I behold many fair angels about you, and therefore, I pray you, go not from me, for I am greatly comforted by you."

And, when other folk came to her, she cried and gaped as if she would have eaten them and said that she saw many devils about them. She would not, by her good will, suffer them to touch her. She roared and cried so, both night and day, that, for the most part, men would not suffer her to dwell among them; she was so irritating to them. Then was she taken to the furthest end of the town, into a chamber, so that the people should not hear her cry. And there was she bound hands and feet with chains of iron so that she should smite nobody. And the said creature went to her each day, once or twice at the least, and, while she was with her, she was meek enough and heard her speak and dally with a good will, without any roaring or crying. And the said creature prayed for this woman every day, that God should, if it were his will, restore her to her wits again. And our Lord answered in her soul and said, "She should fare right well."

Then was she more bold to pray for her recovering than she was before, and each day, weeping and sorrowing, prayed for her recovery till

3. Leprosy and lechery were thought to be related to one another.

God gave her her wit and her mind again. And then was she brought to church and purified[4] as other women are, blessed may God be. It was, as they thought who knew it, a right great miracle, for he who wrote this book had never before that time seen man or woman, as he thought, so far out of herself as this woman was, nor so evil to rule or to govern, and afterward he saw her sad and sober enough, worship and praising be to our Lord without end for his high mercy and his goodness that ever helps at need.

76. It happened on a time that the husband of the said creature, a man of great age passing three score years,[5] as he would have come down from his chamber barefoot and bare-leg, he slithered or else failed of his footing and fell down to the ground from the steps, with his head under him grievously broken and bruised, insomuch that he had in his head five rolls of soft material in the wounds[6] for many days while his head was healing. And, as God would, it was known to some of his neighbors how he had fallen down the steps, perhaps through the din and the rushing of his falling. And so they came to him and found him lying with his head under him, half on life, all streaked with blood, never likely to have spoken with priest nor with clerk unless by high grace and miracle. Then the said creature, his wife, was sent for, and so she came to him. Then was he taken up and his head was sewn, and he was sick a long time after, so that men thought that he should have been dead. And then the people said, if he died, his wife was worthy to be hanged for his death, forasmuch as she might have kept him and did not.

They dwelled not together; they lay not together, for, as is written before, they both with one assent and with free will of the other had made a vow to live chaste. And therefore to avoid all perils they dwelled and sojourned in divers places where no suspicion should be had of their incontinence,[7] for first they dwelled together after they had made their vow, and then the people slandered them and said they used their lust and their liking as they did before their vow-making. And, when they went out on pilgrimage or to see and speak with other ghostly creatures, many evil folk whose tongues were their own, lacking the dread and love of our Lord Jesus Christ, thought and said that they went rather to woods, groves, or valleys to use the lust of their bodies so that the people should not espy it nor know it. They, having knowledge how prone the people were to think evil of them, desiring to avoid all occasion, inasmuch as they might goodly, by their good will and their mutual consent, they parted asunder as touching their board and their chambers, and went to

4. Kempe here refers to the ceremony of "churching," or purification, which took place some weeks after childbirth and signified a woman's re-entry into parish life.
5. A score is twenty years.
6. The material distended the wounds, allowing them to drain.
7. I.e., incontinence to their mutual vow of married chastity.

board in divers places. And this was the cause that she was not with him and also that she should not be hindered from her contemplation.

And therefore, when he had fallen and grievously was hurt, as is said before, the people said, if he died, it was worthy that she answer for his death. Then she prayed to our Lord that her husband might live a year and she delivered from slander if it were his pleasure. Our Lord said to her mind, "Daughter, you shall have your boon, for he shall live, and I have wrought a great miracle for you that he was not dead. And I bid you take him home and keep him for my love."

She said, "No, good Lord, for I shall then not tend to you as I do now."

"Yes, daughter," said our Lord, "you shall have as much meed for keeping him and helping him in his need at home as if you were in church to make your prayers. And you have said many times that you would fain keep me. I pray you now keep him for the love of me, for he has sometime fulfilled your will and my will both, and he has made your body free to me so that you should serve me and live chaste and clean, and therefore I will that you be free to help him at his need in my name."

"A, Lord," said she, "for your mercy grant me grace to obey your will and fulfill your will and let never my ghostly enemies have any power to hinder me from fulfilling your will."

Then she took home her husband with her and kept him years after, as long as he lived, and had full much labor with him, for in his last days he turned childish again and lacked reason so that he could not do his own easement by going to a stool, or else he would not, but, as a child, voided his natural digestion in his linen clothes where he sat by the fire or at the table, whether it were, he would spare no place. And therefore was her labor much the more in washing and wringing and her expense in making fires and hindered her full much from her contemplation, so that many times she should have been irked at her labor save she bethought herself of how she in her young age had full many delectable thoughts, fleshly lusts, and inordinate loves for his person. And therefore she was glad to be punished with the same person and took it much the more easily and served him and helped him, as she thought, as she would have done Christ himself.

77. When the said creature had first her wonderful cries and on a time was in ghostly dalliance with her sovereign Lord Christ Jesus, she said, "Lord, why will you give me such crying so that the people wonder on me therefore, and they say that I am in great peril, for, as they say, I am the cause that many men sin through me. And you know, Lord, that I would give no man cause nor occasion of sin if I might, for I had rather, Lord, be in a prison of ten fathoms deep, there to cry and weep for my sin and for all men's sins and especially for your love, all my lifetime than I should give the people occasion to sin willfully through me. Lord, the world may not suffer me to do your will nor to follow after your stirring,

and therefore I pray you, if it be your will, take these cryings from me in the time of sermons so that I cry not at your holy preaching and let me have them by myself alone so that I be not put from the hearing of your holy preaching and of your holy words, for greater pain may I not suffer in this world than be put from hearing your holy word. And, if I were in prison, my greatest pain should be the forbearing of your holy words and of your holy sermons. And, good Lord, if you will anyway that I cry, I pray you give me it alone in my chamber as much as ever you will and spare me among the people, if it please you."

Our merciful Lord Christ Jesus answering to her mind said, "Daughter, pray not therefore; you shall not have your desire in this though my mother and all the saints in heaven pray for you, for I shall make you buxom to my will so that you shall cry when I will, and where I will, both loud and still, for I told you, daughter, you are mine and I am yours, and so shall you be without end. Daughter, you see how the planets are buxom to my will, so that sometimes there come great thunderclaps and make the people full sorely afraid. And sometimes, daughter, you see how I send great lightning bolts that burn churches and houses. Also sometimes you see that I send great winds that blow down steeples, houses, and trees from the earth and do much harm in many places, and yet the wind may not be seen but it may well be felt.

"And right so, daughter, I fare with the might of my Godhead; it may not be seen with man's eye, and yet it may well be felt in a simple soul where it likes to work grace, as I do in your soul. And, as suddenly as the lightning comes from heaven, so suddenly come I into your soul and illumine it with the light of grace and of understanding, and set it all on fire with love, and make the fire of love to burn therein and purge it full clean from all earthly filth. And sometimes, daughter, I make earthquakes in order to frighten the people so that they should dread me. And so, daughter, ghostly have I done with you and with other chosen souls that shall be saved, for I turn the earth of their hearts upside down and make them sorely afraid, so that they dread vengeance should fall on them for their sins. And so did you, daughter, when you turned first to me, and it is needful that young beginners do so, but now, daughter, you have great cause to love me well, for the perfect charity that I give you puts away all dread from you.

And, though other men set little by you, I set but the more price by you. As sure as you are of the sun when you see it shine brightly, just so sure are you of the love of God at all times. Also, daughter, you know well that I send sometimes many great rains and sharp showers, and sometimes but small and soft drops. And right so I fare with you, daughter, when it pleases me to speak in your soul; I give you sometimes small weepings and soft tears for a token that I love you, and sometimes I give you great cries and roarings to make the people afraid of the grace that I put in you, as a token that I will that my mother's sorrow be known by you so that men and women might have more compassion for her sorrow that she suffered for me. And the third token is this, daughter, that whatever creature will take as much sorrow for my passion as you have done many a time and will cease from their sins they shall have the bliss of heaven without end. The fourth token is this: that any creature on earth, has he been ever so horrible a sinner, he will never fall into despair if he will take example of your living and work somewhat thereafter as he may do. Also, daughter, the fifth token is that I will you know in yourself, by the great pain that you feel in your heart when you cry so sorely for my love, that it shall be the cause that you shall no pain feel when you are come out of this world and also that you shall have the less pain in your dying, for you have so great compassion for my flesh that I must need have compassion for your flesh. And therefore, daughter, suffer the people to say what they will of your crying, for you are not the cause of their sin. Daughter, the people sinned on me, and yet was I not the cause of their sin."

Then she said, "A, Lord, blessed may you be, for I think you do yourself all that you bid me do. In Holy Writ, Lord, you bid me love my enemies, and I know well that in all this world was never so great an enemy to me as I have been to you. Therefore, Lord, though I were slain a hundred times on a day, if it were possible, for your love, yet could I never yield you the goodness that you have showed to me."

Then answered our Lord to her and said, "I pray you, daughter, give me not else but love. You may never please me better than have me ever in your love, nor shall you never in any penance that you may do on earth please me so much as to love me. And, daughter, if you will be high in heaven with me, keep me always in your mind as much as you may and forget me not at your meals, but think always that I sit in your heart and know every thought that is therein, both good and ill, and that I perceive the least thinking and twinkling of your eye."

She said again to our Lord, "Now truly, Lord, I would I could love you as much as you might make me to love you. If it were possible, I would love you as well as all the saints in heaven love you and as well as all the creatures on earth might love you. And I would, Lord, for your love be laid naked on a hurdle, all men to wonder on me, for your love, if it were no peril to their souls, and they to cast slurry and sludge on me, and be drawn from town to town every day of my lifetime, if you were pleased thereby and no man's soul hindered. May your will be fulfilled and not mine."

78. For many years on Palm Sunday,[8] as this creature was at the procession with other good people in the churchyard and beheld how the

---

8. Palm Sunday is the Sunday before Easter, the day that celebrates Jesus' triumphal entry into Jerusalem when he was hailed by crowds bearing palm branches. In the Middle Ages, worshippers carrying palms would process behind the priest and the sacrament out of the church and then around it from east to south to west, entering again into the church by the west door (Duffy [1992], pp. 23–27).

priests made their observance, how they kneeled to the sacrament, and the people also, it seemed to her ghostly sight as though she had been that time in Jerusalem and seen our Lord in his manhood received by the people, as he was while he went here on earth. Then had she so much sweetness and devotion that she might not bear it, but cried, wept, and sobbed full violently. She had many a holy thought of our Lord's passion and beheld him in her ghostly sight as verily as if he had been before her in her bodily sight. Therefore might she not withstand weeping and sobbing, but she must needs weep, cry, and sob when she beheld her Savior suffer such great pains for her love. Then should she pray for all the people that were living on earth that they might do our Lord due worship and reverence that time and all times and that they might be worthy to hear and understand the holy words and laws of God and meekly obey and truly fulfill them within their power.

And it was custom in the place where she was dwelling to have a sermon on that day, and then, as a worshipful doctor of divinity was in the pulpit and said the sermon, he repeated oftentimes these words, "Our Lord Jesus languishes for love." Those words wrought so in her mind when she heard spoken of the perfect love that our Lord Jesus Christ had for mankind and how dearly he bought us with his bitter Passion, shedding his heart's blood for our redemption, and suffered so shameful a death for our salvation, then she might no longer keep the fire of love close within her breast, but, whether she would or not, it would appear without forth such as was closed within forth. And so she cried full loudly and wept and sobbed full sorely, as though she should have burst for pity and compassion that she had for our Lord's passion. And sometimes she was all in a sweat with the labor of the crying; it was so loud and so violent, and many people wondered on her and banned her full fast, supposing that she had feigned herself for to cry.

And soon after our Lord said unto her, "Daughter, this pleases me right well, for the more shame and more despite that you have for my love, the more joy shall you have with me in heaven, and it is rightful that it be so."

Sometimes she heard great sounds and great melodies with her bodily ears, and then she thought it was full merry in heaven and had full great languishing and full great longing thitherward, with many a still mourning. And then many times our Lord Jesus Christ would say to her, "Daughter, here is this day a fair people, and many of them shall be dead before this day twelvemonth," and told her before when pestilence should fall. And she found it indeed as she had felt before, and that strengthened her much in the love of God.

Our Lord would say also, "Daughter, those who will not believe the goodness and the grace that I show unto you in this life, I shall make them to know the truth when they are dead and out of this world. Daughter, you have a good zeal of charity in that you would all men were saved, and so would I. And they say that so would they, but you may well see that they will not themselves be saved, for all they will sometimes hear the word of God, but they will not always do thereafter, and they will not sorrow themselves for their sins, nor will they suffer any other to suffer for them. Nevertheless, daughter, I have ordained you to be a mirror among them, to have great sorrow so that they should take example by you in order to have some little sorrow in their hearts for their sins so that they might through it be saved, but they love not to hear of sorrow nor of contrition. But, good daughter, do you your duty and pray for them while you are in this world, and you shall have the same meed and reward in heaven as if all the world were saved by your good will and your prayer. Daughter, I have many times said to you that many thousand souls shall be saved through your prayers, and some who lie on the point of death shall have grace through your merits and your prayers, for your tears and your prayers are full sweet and acceptable unto me."

Then she said in her mind to our Lord Jesus Christ, "A, Jesus, blessed may you be without end, for I have many a great cause to thank you and love you with all my heart, for it seems to me, Lord, that you are all charity to the profit and health of man's soul. A, Lord, I believe that he shall be right wicked who shall be parted from you without end. He shall neither will good, nor do good, nor desire good. And therefore, Lord, I thank you for all goodness that you have showed unto me, right unworthy wretch."

And then on the same Sunday, when the priest took the cross staff and smote on the church door[9] and the door opened against him, and then the priest entered with the sacrament and all the people following into church, then thought she that our Lord spoke to the devil and opened hell gates, confounding him and all his host and what grace and goodness he showed to those souls, delivering them from everlasting prison, in spite of the devil and all his. She had many a holy thought and many a holy desire which she could never tell nor repeat, nor might her tongue ever express the abundance of grace that she felt, blessed be our Lord for all his gifts.

When they were come into the church and she beheld the priests kneeling before the crucifix, and, as they sang, the priest who executed the service that day drew up a cloth before the crucifix three times, every time higher than the other, so that the people should see the crucifix, then was her mind all wholly taken out of all earthly things and set all in ghostly things, praying and desiring that she might at the last have the full sight of him in heaven who is both God and man in one person.[1] And

---

9. This is the point in the ceremony when the Palm Sunday procession prepared to re-enter the church, a moment that re-enacted both Jesus' entry into Jerusalem and his breaking down of Hell's gates on Holy Saturday.
1. Throughout Lent the Crucifix was hidden by a painted veil suspended on the rood screen, the carved screen that separated lay worshippers from the altar. At the climax of the Palm Sunday ceremony, the worshippers gathered in front of the rood screen and knelt as the veil was drawn up on pulleys, the anthem "Ave Rex Noster" was sung, and the priests venerated the Crucifix (Duffy [1992], p. 27).

then should she, all the mass time after, weep and sob full plenteously; and sometimes while crying right fervently she thought that she saw our Lord Christ Jesus as verily in her soul with her ghostly eye as she had seen before the crucifix with her bodily eye.

79. Then she beheld in the sight of her soul our blissful Lord Christ Jesus coming toward his Passion, and, before he went, he kneeled down and took his mother's blessing.[2] Then she saw his mother falling down in swooning before her son, saying unto him, "Alas, my dear Son, how shall I suffer this sorrow and have no joy in all this world but you alone. A, dear Son, if you will die anyway, let me die before you and let me never suffer this day of sorrow, for I may never bear this sorrow that I shall have for your death. I would, Son, that I might suffer death for you so that you should not die, if man's soul might so be saved. Now, dear son, if you have no pity on yourself, have pity on your mother, for you know full well there can no man in all this world comfort me but you alone."

Then our Lord took up his mother in his arms and kissed her full sweetly and said to her, "A, blessed mother, be of a good cheer and of a good comfort, for I have told you full often that I must needs suffer death, otherwise no man should be saved nor ever come into bliss. And mother, it is my father's will that it be so, and therefore I pray you let it be your will also, for my death shall turn me to great worship and you and all mankind to great joy and profit, whomever trusts in my passion and works thereafter. And therefore, blessed mother, you must abide here after me, for in you shall rest all the faith of Holy Church, and by your faith Holy Church shall increase in her faith. And therefore I pray you, worthy mother, cease from your sorrowing, for I shall not leave you comfortless. I shall leave here with you John, my cousin, to comfort you instead of me; I shall send my holy angels to comfort you on earth; and I shall comfort you in your soul my own self, for, mother, you know well I have promised you the bliss of heaven and that you are sure thereof. A, worthy mother, what would you better than where I am king you be queen, and all angels and saints shall be buxom to your will?

"And what grace you ask me I shall not deny your desire. I shall give you power over the devils so that they shall be afraid of you and you not of them. And also, my blessed mother, I have said to you beforetime that I shall come for you my own self when you shall pass out of this world with all my angels and all my saints that are in heaven and bring you before my father with all manner of music, melody, and joy. And there shall I set you in great peace and rest without end. And there shall you be crowned as Queen of Heaven, as lady of all the world, and as Empress of

---

2. Kempe's extrabiblical account of the Passion, which emphasizes the relationships between Jesus and those who loved and followed him, is indebted to Nicholas Love's influential treatise *Mirror of the Blessed Life of Jesus Christ*. Margery imaginatively places herself in these scenes.

Hell. And therefore, my worthy mother, I pray you bless me and let me go do my father's will, for therefore I came into this world and took flesh and blood from you."

When the said creature beheld this glorious sight in her soul and saw how he blessed his mother and his mother him, and then his blessed mother might not speak one word more to him but fell down to the ground, and so they parted asunder, his mother lying still as if she had been dead, then the said creature thought she took our Lord Jesus Christ by the clothes and fell down at his feet, praying him to bless her, and therewith she cried full loudly and wept right sorely, saying in her mind, "A, Lord, where shall I become? I had far rather that you would slay me than let me abide in the world without you, for without you I may not abide here, Lord."

Then answered our Lord to her, "Be still, daughter, and rest with my mother here, and comfort you in her, for she who is my own mother must suffer this sorrow. But I shall come again, daughter, to my mother and comfort her and you both and turn all your sorrow into joy."

And then she thought our Lord went forth his way, and she went to our Lady and said, "A, blessed Lady, rise up and let us follow your blessed son as long as we may see him so that I may look enough upon him before he dies. A, dear Lady, how may your heart last and see your blissful son see all this woe? Lady, I may not endure it, and yet am I not his mother."

Then our Lady answered and said, "Daughter, you hear well it will not otherwise be, and therefore I must needs suffer it for my son's love."

And then she thought that they followed forth after our Lord and saw how he made his prayers to his father in the Mount of Olives and heard the goodly answer that came from his father and the goodly answer that he gave his father again.[3] Then she saw how our Lord went to his disciples and bade them wake; his enemies were near. And then came a great multitude of people with much light and many armed men with staves, swords, and poleaxes to seek our Lord Jesus Christ. Our merciful Lord as a meek lamb saying unto them, "Whom seek you?"

They answered with a sharp spirit, "Jesus of Nazareth."

Our Lord said again, "Ego sum."[4]

And then she saw the Jews fall down on the ground; they might not stand for dread, but anon they rose again and sought as they had done before. And our Lord asked, "Whom seek you?"

And they said again, "Jesus of Nazareth."

Our Lord answered, "I it am."

---

3. After the Last Supper, Jesus took his disciples to the Mount of Olives, where he prayed in the Garden of Gethsemane. He prayed that his cup of suffering might be taken from him if it was God's will. The disciples were not able to stay awake during Jesus' agony though he asked them to pray with him. Shortly afterward he was betrayed by Judas and arrested. See Luke 22.39–54 for a Gospel account.
4. I am he.

And then anon she saw Judas come and kiss our Lord, and the Jews laid hands upon him full violently.

Then had our Lady and she much sorrow and great pain to see the lamb of innocence so contemptibly be held and drawn by his own people that he was specially sent unto. And immediately the said creature beheld with her ghostly eye the Jews putting a cloth before our Lord's eye, beating him and buffeting him in the head and bobbing him before his sweet mouth, crying full cruelly unto him, "Tell us now who smote you."

They spared not to spit in his face in the most shameful way that they could. And then our Lady and she her unworthy handmaiden for the time wept and sighed full sorely, for the Jews fared so foul and so venomously with her blissful Lord. And they would not spare to pull his blissful ears and draw the hair of his beard. And anon after she saw them draw off his clothes and make him all naked and then draw him forth before them as if he had been the greatest malefactor in all the world. And he went forth full meekly before them, all mother-naked as he was born, to a pillar of stone and spoke no word against them but let them do and say what they would. And there they bound him to the pillar as straight as they could and beat him on his fair white body with switches, with whips, and with scourges. And then she thought our Lady wept wonderfully sorely. And therefore the said creature must needs weep and cry when she saw such ghostly sights in her soul as freshly and as verily as if it had been done in deed in her bodily sight, and she thought that our Lady and she were always together to see our Lord's pains. such ghostly sights had she every Palm Sunday and every Good Friday, and in many other ways for many years together. And therefore cried she and wept full sorely and suffered full much despite and reproof in many a country.

And then our Lord said to her soul, "Daughter, these sorrows and many more suffered I for your love, and divers pains, more than any man can tell on earth. Therefore, daughter, you have great cause to love me right well, for I have bought your love full dearly."

80. Another time she saw in her contemplation our Lord Jesus Christ bound to a pillar, and his hands were bound above his head. And then she saw sixteen men with sixteen scourges, and each scourge had eight lead-tipped lashes on the end, and every metal tip was full of sharp prickles as if it had been the rowels[5] of a spur. And those men with the scourges made covenant that each of them should give our Lord forty strokes. When she saw this piteous sight, she wept and cried right loudly as if she should have burst for sorrow and pain. And, when our Lord was utterly beaten and scourged, the Jews unloosed him from the pillar and gave him his cross to bear on his shoulder.

And then she thought that she and our Lady went by another way in

5. The rowel is the part of a spur that is a small wheel with several rotating sharp points.

order to meet with him, and, when they met with him, they saw him bear the heavy cross with great pain; it was so heavy and so rough that hardly he might bear it. And then our Lady said unto him, "A, my sweet son, let me help to bear that heavy cross." And she was so weak that she might not but fell down and swooned and lay still as a dead woman.

Then the creature saw our Lord fall down by his mother and comfort her as he might with many sweet words. When she heard the words and saw the compassion that the mother had of the son and the son of his mother, then she wept, sobbed, and cried as though she should have died for the pity and compassion that she had of that piteous sight and the holy thoughts that she had in the meantime, which were so delicate and heavenly that she could never tell them afterward as she had them in feeling.

Afterward she went forth in contemplation through the mercy of our Lord Jesus Christ to the place where he was nailed to the cross. And then she saw the Jews with great violence rend from our Lord's precious body a cloth of silk, which had cleaved and hardened with his precious blood so completely and straightly to our Lord's body that it drew away all the hide and all the skin from his blessed body and renewed his precious wounds and made the blood to run down all about on every side. Then that precious body appeared to her sight as raw, as a thing that was newly flayed out of the skin, full piteous and rueful to behold. And so had she a new sorrow so that she wept and cried right sorely.

And anon after she beheld how the cruel Jews laid his precious body to the cross and afterward took a long nail, rough and huge, and set it to his one hand and with great violence and cruelness they drove it through his hand. His blissful mother and this creature beholding how his precious body shrunk and drew together with all the sinews and veins in that precious body for the pain that it suffered and felt, they sorrowed and mourned and sighed full sorely. Then saw she with her ghostly eye how the Jews fastened ropes on the other hand, for the sinews and veins were so shrunken with pain that it might not come to the hole that they had marked for it, and drew thereon to make it meet with the hole. And so her pain and her sorrow ever increased. And afterward they drew his blissful feet in the same manner.

And then she thought in her soul she heard our Lady say to the Jews, "Alas, you cruel Jews, why fare you so with my sweet son and did he you never any harm? You fill my heart full of sorrow.[6]

And then she thought the Jews spoke again violently to our Lady and put her away from her son. Then the foresaid creature thought that she cried out on the Jews and said, "You cursed Jews, why slay you my Lord Jesus Christ? Slay me rather, and let him go."

6. The anti-Judaism of the *Book* should be compared to other Middle English treatments of the Passion, which are often more intensely expressed. For remarks about Kempe's use of contemporary anti-Judaism as a critique of Margery's fellow Christians, see Staley (1994), pp. 68–71.

And then she wept and cried passingly sore so that many of the people in the church wondered on her body. And anon she saw them take up the cross with our Lord's body hanging thereon and made a great noise and a great cry and lifted it up from the earth a certain distance and afterwards let the cross fall down into the hole. And then our Lord's body shook and shuddered, and all the joints of that blissful body burst and went asunder, and his precious wounds ran down with rivers of blood on every side. And so she had ever more cause of more weeping and sorrowing. And then she heard our Lord hanging on the cross say these words to his mother, "Woman, see your son, Saint John, the Evangelist."

Then she thought our Lady fell down and swooned, and Saint John took her up in his arms and comforted her with sweet words as well as he could or might.

The creature said then to our Lord, as it seemed to her, "Alas, Lord, you leave here a care-full mother. What shall we now do and how shall we bear this great sorrow that we shall have for your love?"

And then she heard the two thieves speak to our Lord, and our Lord said to the one thief, "This day you shall be with me in paradise."

Then was she glad of that answer and prayed our Lord, for his mercy, that he would be as gracious to her soul when she should pass out of this world as he was to the thief; for she was worse, she thought, than any thief.

And then she thought our Lord commended his spirit into his father's hands and therewith he died. Then she thought she saw our Lady swoon and fall down and lie still as if she had been dead. Then the creature thought that she ran all about the place as if she had been a mad woman, crying and roaring. And afterward she came to our Lady and fell down on her knees before her, saying to her, "I pray you, Lady, cease from your sorrowing, for your son is dead and out of pain, for I think you have sorrowed enough. And, Lady, I will sorrow for you, for your sorrow is my sorrow."

Then she thought she saw Joseph of Arimethea take down our Lord's body from the cross and lay it before our Lady on a marble stone. Our Lady had then a manner of joy when her dear son was taken down from the cross and laid on the stone before her. And then our blissful Lady bowed down to her son's body and kissed his mouth and wept so plenteously over his blessed face that she washed away the blood from his face with the tears of her eyes. And then the creature thought she heard Mary Magdalene say to our Lady, "I pray you, Lady, give me leave to handle and kiss his feet, for at these get I grace.[7]

Anon our Lady gave leave to her and all those that were there about to do what worship and reverence they would to that precious body. And anon Mary Magdalene took our Lord's feet and our Lady's sisters took his

---

7. Mary asks to venerate the most humble aspect of the physical body of Jesus. She is traditionally pictured at the feet of Jesus, and later in chapter 85 (p. 152) Margery, for whom the Magdalene is a powerful example of love and piety, venerates Jesus' toes.

hands, the one sister one hand and the other sister another hand, and wept full sorely while kissing those hands and those precious feet.

And the said creature thought that she ran ever to and fro as if she had been a woman without reason, greatly desiring to have had the precious body by herself alone so that she might have wept enough in the presence of that precious body, for she thought that she would have died with weeping and mourning in his death for the love that she had of him.

And immediately she saw Saint John the Evangelist, Joseph of Arimethea, and other friends of our Lord come and would bury our Lord's body and prayed our Lady that she would suffer them to bury that precious body. Our doleful Lady said to them, "Sirs, would you take away from me my Son's body? I might never look upon him enough while he live; I pray you, let me have him now he is dead, and part not my son and me asunder. And, if you will bury him anyway, I pray you bury me with him, for I may not live without him."

And the creature thought that they prayed our Lady so fair, till at the last our Lady let them bury her dear son with great worship and with great reverence as it belonged to them to do.

81. When our Lord was buried, our Lady fell down swooning as she would have come from the grave, and Saint John took her up in his arms and Mary Magdalene went on the other side to support and comfort our Lady in as much as they could or might. Then the said creature, desiring to abide still by the grave of our Lord, mourned, wept, and sorrowed with loud crying for the tenderness and compassion that she had of our Lord's death and many a lamentable desire that God put in her mind for the time. Wherefore the people wondered upon her, having great marvel what ailed her, for they knew full little the cause. She thought she would never have parted thence but desired to have died there and be buried with our Lord.

Afterward the creature thought she saw our Lady go homeward again. And, as she went, there came many good women toward her and said, "Lady, woe is us that your son is dead and that our people have done him so much despite."

And then our Lady, bowing down her head, thanked them full meekly with manner and with countenance, for she might not speak, her heart was so full of heaviness. Then the creature thought, when our Lady was come home and was laid down on a bed, that she made for our Lady a good hot drink[8] and brought it to her to comfort her, and then our Lady said unto her, "Do it away, daughter. Give me no food but my own child."

The creature said again, "A, blessed Lady, you must needs comfort yourself and cease from your sorrowing."

---

8. On this extrabiblical detail, see Gibson (1989), p. 51.

"A, daughter, where should I go or where should I dwell without sorrow? I tell you certain, there was never woman on earth had so great a cause to sorrow as I have, for there was never woman in this world bore a better child, nor a meeker to his mother, than my son was to me."

And she thought she heard our Lady cry anon with a lamentable voice and said, "John, where is my son Jesus Christ?"

And Saint John answered again and said, "Dear Lady, you know well that he is dead."

"A, John," she said, "that is to me a care-full counsel."

The creature heard as clearly this answer in the understanding of her soul as she would understand one man speak to another. And anon the creature heard Saint Peter knocking at the door, and Saint John asked who was there. Peter answered, "I, sinful Peter, who has forsaken my Lord Jesus Christ."

Saint John would have had him come in, and Peter would not till our Lady bade him come in. And then Peter said, "Lady, I am not worthy to come in to you," and was still without the door.

Then Saint John went to our Lady and told her that Peter was so abashed that he dared not come in. Our Lady bade Saint John go again quickly to Saint Peter and bid him come in to her. And then the creature in her ghostly sight beheld Saint Peter come before our Lady and fall down on his knees with great weeping and sobbing, and say, "Lady, I cry you mercy, for I have forsaken your worthy son and my sweet master who has loved me full well, and therefore, Lady, I am never worthy to look on him nor you either but by your great mercy."

"A, Peter," said our Lady, "dread you not, for though you have forsaken my sweet son, he forsook never you, Peter, and he shall come again and comfort us all right well, for he promised me, Peter, that he would come again on the third day and comfort me. A, Peter," said our Lady, "full long time shall I think it till that day comes that I may see his blessed face."

Then our Lady lay still on her bed and heard how the friends of Jesus made their complaint for the sorrow that they had. And ever our Lady lay still, mourning and weeping with heavy manner, and at the last Mary Magdalene and our Lady's sisters took their leave of our Lady to go buy ointment that they might anoint therewith our Lord's body. Then the creature was left still with our Lady and thought it a thousand years till the third day came, and that day she was with our Lady in a chapel where our Lord Jesus Christ appeared unto her and said, "Salve sancta parens[9] And then the creature thought in her soul that our Lady said, "Are you my sweet son, Jesus?"

And he said, "Yes, my blessed Mother, I am your own son, Jesus." Then he took up his blessed mother and kissed her full sweetly. And then the

9. "Greetings, blessed parent." The greeting is used as part of the Mass of the Blessed Mary. See also *Meditations*, p. 199.

creature thought that she saw our Lady feel and examine our Lord's body all about, and his hands and his feet, if there were any soreness or any pain. And she heard our Lord say to his mother, "Dear Mother, my pain is all gone, and now shall I live for evermore. And, mother, so shall your pain and your sorrow be turned into full great joy. Mother, ask what you will I shall tell you."

And when he had suffered his mother to ask what she would and had answered her questions, then he said, "Mother, by your leave I must go speak with Mary Magdalene."

Our Lady said, "It is well done, for, son, she has full much sorrow for your absence. And, I pray you, be not long from me."

These ghostly sights and understandings caused the creature to weep, to sob, and to cry full loudly so that she might not measure herself nor restrain herself from it on Easter Day and other days when our Lord would visit her with his grace, blessed and worshipped may he be. And anon after the creature was in her contemplation with Mary Magdalene, mourning and seeking our Lord at the grave, and heard and saw how our Lord Jesus Christ appeared to her in likeness of a gardener, saying, "Woman, why weep you?"[1]

Mary, not knowing what he was, all inflamed with the fire of love, said to him again, "Sir, if you have taken away my Lord, tell me, and I shall take him again."

Then our merciful Lord, having pity and compassion for her, said, "Mary."

And with that word she, knowing our Lord, fell down at his feet and would have kissed his feet, saying, "Master."

Our Lord said to her, "Touch me not."

Then the creature thought that Mary Magdalene said to our Lord, "A, Lord, I see well you will not that I be so homely with you as I have been before," and made a heavy countenance.

"Yes, Mary," said our Lord, "I shall never forsake you, but I shall ever be with you without end."

And then our Lord said to Mary Magdalene, "Go tell my brothers and Peter that I am up risen."

And then the creature thought that Mary went forth with great joy, and that was a great marvel to her that Mary rejoiced, for, if our Lord had said to her as he did to Mary, she thought she could never have been merry. That was when she would have kissed his feet, and he said, "Touch me not." The creature had such great sorrow and heaviness in that word that ever when she heard it in any sermon, as she did many times, she wept, sorrowed, and cried as if she would have died of the love and desire that she had to be with our Lord.

---

1. For this encounter, see John 20.1–81.

82. On Purification Day or else Candlemas Day,[2] when the said creature beheld the people with their candles in church, her mind was ravished into a beholding of our Lady offering her blissful son, our Savior, to the priest Simeon in the temple, as verily to her ghostly understanding as if she had been there in her bodily presence to have offered with our Lady's own person. Then was she so comforted by the contemplation in her soul that she had in the beholding of our Lord Jesus Christ and of his blessed Mother, of Simeon the priest, of Joseph, and of other persons who there were when our Lady was purified, and of the heavenly songs that she thought she heard when our blissful Lord was offered up to Simeon that she might hardly bear up her own candle to the priest, as other folk did at the time of offering, but went wavering on each side as if she had been a drunken woman, weeping and sobbing so sorely that scarcely she might stand on her feet for the fervor of love and devotion that God put in her soul through high contemplation.

And sometimes she might not stand but fell down among the people and cried full loudly, so that many men wondered on her and marveled what ailed her, for the fervor of the spirit was so much that the body failed and might not endure it. She had such holy thoughts and meditations many times when she saw women be purified of their children. She thought in her soul that she saw our Lady be purified and had high contemplation in beholding the women who came to offer with the women who were purified. Her mind was all drawn from the earthly thoughts and earthly sights and set altogether on ghostly sights, which were so delectable and so devout that she might not in the time of fervor withstand her weeping, her sobbing, nor her crying, and therefore suffered she full much wondering, many a jibe and many a scorn.

Also when she saw weddings, men and women being joined together after the law of the church, anon she had in meditation how our Lady was joined to Joseph and of the ghostly joining of man's soul to Jesus Christ, praying to our Lord that her love and her affection might be joined to him only without end, and that she might have grace to obey him, love and dread him, worship and praise him, and no thing to love but what he loved, or no thing to will but what he would, and ever to be ready to fulfill his will both night and day without grudging or heaviness, with all gladness of spirit, and many more holy thoughts than she ever could repeat, for she had them not of her own study nor of her own wit, but of his gift whose wisdom is incomprehensible to all creatures, save only to those whom he chooses and illumines more or less as he himself wills, for his will may not be constrained, it is in his own free disposition.

2. February 2 is the Feast of the Purification; it was marked by an elaborate procession in which each parishioner carried a candle. See Duffy (1992), pp. 15ff. The Feast commemorates Mary's purification after childbirth and her presentation of the baby Jesus in the Temple. See Luke 2.22–38 for the Gospel account of the scene Margery "sees."

She had these thoughts and these desires with profound tears, sighings, and sobbings, and sometimes with great violent cryings as God would send it, and sometimes soft tears and secret, without any violence. She might neither weep loud nor still but when God would send it her, for she was sometimes so barren of tears a day or sometimes half a day and had such great pain for the desire that she had for them that she would have given all this world, if it had been hers, for a few tears, or have suffered right great bodily pain to have gotten them with. And then, when she was so barren, she could find no joy nor any comfort in food or drink or dalliance but ever was heavy in manner and in countenance till God would send them to her again, and then was she merry enough. And, although it was that our Lord withdrew from her sometimes the abundance of tears, yet he withdrew not from her holy thoughts or desires for years together, for ever her mind and her desire was toward our Lord. But she thought there was no savor nor sweetness but when she might weep, for then she thought that she could pray.

83. Two priests who had great trust in her manner of crying and weeping were nevertheless sometimes in great doubt whether it was deceptive or not. Forasmuch as she cried and wept in the sight of the people, they had a private conceit, she unknowing, that they would prove whether she cried because the people should hear her or not.

And on a day the priests came to her and asked if she would go two miles from where she dwelled, on pilgrimage to a church that stood in the field, a good distance from any other house, which was dedicated in honor of God and Saint Michael the Archangel. And she said she would go with them with good will. They took with them a child or two and went to the said place all together. When they had for a while made their prayers, the said creature had so much sweetness and devotion that she might not keep it privy but burst out in violent weeping and sobbing and cried as loud, or else louder, than she did when she was among the people at home, and she could not restrain herself therefrom, no persons being there present other than the two priests and a child or two with them. And then, as they came homeward again, they met women with children in their arms, and the foresaid creature asked if there were any man child among them, and the women said, "No." Then was her mind so ravished into the childhood of Christ for the desire that she had to see him that she might not bear it but fell down and wept and cried so sorely that it was a marvel to hear it. Then the priests had the more trust that it was right well with her when they heard her cry in a privy place as well as in an open place and in the field as in the town.

Also there were nuns who desired to have knowledge of the creature so that they should the more be stirred to devotion. She was in their church at midnight to hear their matins, and our Lord sent her such high devotion and such high meditation and such ghostly comforts that she was all inflamed with the fire of love, which increased so sorely that it burst out with loud voice and great crying, so that our Lord's name was the more magnified among his servants, those who were good, meek, and simple souls and would believe the goodness of our Lord Jesus Christ, who gives his grace to whom he will. And specially to those who doubt not or mistrust not in their asking, her crying greatly profited to the increase of merit and of virtue. To those who little trusted and little believed, perhaps there was little increase of virtue and of merit. But whether the people believed in her crying or not, her grace was never the less but ever increased.

And as well and as goodly our Lord visited her in night as in day, when he would, and how he would, and where he would, for she lacked no grace but when she doubted or mistrusted the goodness of God, supposing or dreading that it was the wile of her ghostly enemy to inform her or teach her otherwise than was to her ghostly health. When she supposed thus or consented to any such thoughts through the stirring of any man or through any evil spirit in her mind that would many a time have had her leave off her good purpose, had the mighty hand of our Lord's mercy not withstood his great malice, then lacked she grace and devotion and all good thoughts and all good minds, till she was, through the mercy of our Lord Jesus Christ, compelled to believe steadfastly, without any doubting, that it was God who spoke in her and would be magnified in her for his own goodness and her profit and for the profit of many others.

And, when she believed that it was God and no evil spirit that gave her so much grace of devotion, contrition, and holy contemplation, then had she so many holy thoughts, holy speeches, and dalliance in her soul teaching her how she should love God, how she should worship him and serve him, that she could never relate but a few of them. They were so holy and so high that she was abashed to tell them to any creature, and also they were so high above her bodily wits that she might never express them with her bodily tongue just as she felt them. She understood them better in her soul than she could utter them. If one of her confessors came to her when she rose up newly from her contemplation, or else from her meditation, she could have told him many things about the dalliance that our Lord dallied to her soul, and in a short time after she had forgotten the most part thereof and nearly everything.

84. The Abbess of Denney,[3] a house of nuns, oftentimes sent for the said creature in order that she should come to speak with her and with her sisters. The creature thought she would not go till another year, for she might badly endure the labor. Then, as she was in her meditation and had great sweetness and devotion, our Lord commanded her to go to Denney and comfort the ladies who desired to common with her, saying

---

3. Denney was a house of Franciscan Minoresses in Cambridgeshire.

in this manner to her soul, "Daughter, go forth to the house of Denney in the name of Jesus, for I will that you comfort them."

She was loath to go, for it was pestilence time,[4] and she thought that she would for no good have died there. Our Lord said to her mind again, "Daughter, you shall go safe and come safe again."

She went then to a worshipful burgess's wife, who loved her and trusted her right much, whose husband lay in great sickness, and told the worshipful wife that she would go to Denney. The worthy woman would that she should not have gone and said, "I would not for forty shillings," she said, "that my husband died while you were out."

And she said again, "If you would give me a hundred pounds, I would not abide at home."

For when she was bidden in her soul to go, she would in no way withstand it, but for anything she would go forth, whatever befell. And, when she was bidden be at home, she would for no thing go out. And then our Lord told her that the foresaid burgess should not die. Then went she again to the worthy wife and bade her be of good comfort, for her husband should live and fare right well, and he should not die yet. The good wife was right glad and said again to her, "Now gospel may it be in your mouth."

Afterward the creature would have sped herself forth as she was commanded, and, when she came to the water's side, all the boats were away toward Cambridge before she came. Then had she much heaviness how she should fulfill our Lord's bidding. And anon she was bidden in her soul that she should not be sorry nor heavy, for she would be provided for well enough and she should go safe and come safe again. And it befell so indeed.

Then our Lord made a manner of thanking to her, forasmuch as she in contemplation and in meditation had been his mother's maiden and helped to keep him in his childhood and so forth unto the time of his death, and said unto her, "Daughter, you shall have as great meed and as great reward with me in heaven for your good service and the good deeds that you have done in your mind and meditation as if you had done those same deeds with your bodily wits outwardly. And also, daughter, when you do any service to yourself and to your husband in food or drink or any other thing that is needful to you, to your ghostly fathers, or to any other that you receive in my name, you shall have the same meed in heaven as though you did it to my own person or to my blessed mother, and I shall thank you therefore.

"Daughter, you say that it is to me a good name to be called all good, and you shall find that name is all good to you. And also, daughter, you say it is well worthy that I be called all love, and you shall well find that I am all love to you, for I know every thought of your heart. And I know

---

4. In other words, a period of plague.

well, daughter, that you have many times thought, if you had had many churches full of nobles, you would have given them in my name. And also you have thought that you would, if you had had good enough, have made many abbeys for my love for religious men and women to dwell in and would have given each of them a hundred pounds a year in order to be my servants. And you have also in your mind desired to have many priests in the town of Lynn who might sing and read night and day to serve me, worship me, and praise and thank me for the goodness that I have done to you on earth. And therefore, daughter, I promise you you shall have the same meed and reward in heaven for these good wills and these good desires as if you had done them in deed.

"Daughter, I know all the thoughts of your heart that you have to all manner of men and women, to all lepers, and to all prisoners, and as much good as you would give them a year to serve me with I take it as if it were done in deed. And, daughter, I thank you for the charity that you have toward all lecherous men and women, for you pray for them and weep many a tear for them, desiring that I should deliver them out of sin and be as gracious to them as I was to Mary Magdalene and that they might have as great love toward me as Mary Magdalene had. And with this condition you would that every one of them should have twenty pounds a year to love me and praise me. And, daughter, this great charity that you have toward them in your prayer pleases me right well. And also, daughter, I thank you for the charity that you have in your prayer when you pray for all Jews and Saracens and all heathen people, that they should come to Christian faith so that my name might be magnified in them, and for the holy tears and weepings that you have wept for them, praying and desiring that if any prayer might bring them to grace or to Christendom that I should hear your prayer for them if it were my will. Furthermore, daughter, I thank you for the general charity that you have toward all the people who are now in this world living and toward all those who are to come, until this world's end, that you would be hacked as small as meat for the pot for their love, so that I would, by your death, save them all from damnation if it pleased me, for you say often in your thought that there are enough in hell and you would that never more should men deserve to come therein. And therefore, daughter, for all these good wills and desires you shall have full high meed and reward in heaven.

"Believe it right well, and doubt it never a bit, for all these graces are my graces, and I work them in you myself so you should have the more meed in heaven. And I tell you truly, daughter, every good thought and every good desire that you have in your soul is the speech of God, even if it be so that you hear me not speak to you sometimes as I do sometimes to your clear understanding. And therefore, daughter, I am as a hidden God in your soul, and I withdraw sometimes your tears and your devotion so that you should think in yourself that you have no goodness of yourself but all goodness comes of me, and also you should verily know what pain it is to forbear me, and how sweet it is to feel me, so that you should be the more busy to seek me again, also, daughter, because you should know what pain other men have who would feel me and may not. For there is many a man on earth that, if he had but one day in all his lifetime of such as you have many days, he would ever love me the better and thank me for that one day. And you may not, daughter, forebear me one day without great pain. Therefore, daughter, you have great cause to love me right well, for it is for no wrath, daughter, that I withdraw sometimes from you the feeling of grace and the fervor of devotion, but so that you should know right well that you may be no hypocrite for any weeping, for any crying, for any sweetness, for any devotion, for any mind of my passion, nor for any other ghostly grace that I give or send to you.

"For these are not the devil's gifts, but they are my graces and my gifts, and these are my own special gifts that I give to my own chosen souls, which I knew without beginning should come to grace and dwell with me without ending. For in all other things you may be a hypocrite if you will, that is to say, in understanding, in bidding many beads, in great fasting, in doing great penance outwardly so that men may see it, or in doing great alms deeds with your hands, or in speaking good words with your mouth. In all these, daughter, you may be a hypocrite if you will, and you may also do them well and holily if you yourself will. Lo, daughter, I have given you such a love that you shall no hypocrite be therein. And, daughter, you shall never lose time while you are occupied therein, for who so thinks well, he may not sin for the time. And the devil knows not the holy thoughts that I give you, nor any man on earth knows how well and holily you are occupied with me, nor you yourself can tell the great grace and goodness that you feel in me. And therefore, daughter, you beguile both the devil and the world with your holy thoughts, and it is right great folly to the people of the world to judge your heart that no man may know but God alone.

"And therefore, daughter, I tell you truly you have as great cause to enjoy and be merry in your soul as any lady or maiden in this world. My love is so much toward you that I may not draw it from you, for, daughter, no heart may think nor tongue tell the great love that I have toward you, and of that I take witness of my blessed mother, of my holy angels, and of all the saints in heaven, for they all worship me for your love in heaven. And so shall I be worshipped on earth for your love, daughter, for I will have the grace that I have showed to you on earth known to the world, so that the people may wonder on my goodness and marvel at my great goodness that I have showed to you who has been sinful, and, because I have been so gracious and merciful to you, those who are in the world shall not despair, be they never so sinful, for they may have mercy and grace if they themselves will."

85. On a time, as the said creature was kneeling before an altar of the cross and saying a prayer, her eyes were ever together as though she should have slept. And at the last she might not choose; she fell into a little slumbering, and anon appeared verily to her sight an angel all clothed in white, as much as it had been a little child, bearing a huge book before him. Then said the creature to the child, or else to the angel, "A," she said, "This is the book of life."

And she saw in the book the Trinity, and all in gold. Then said she to the child, "Where is my name?"

The child answered and said, "Here is your name, written at the Trinity's foot," and therewith he was gone, she knew not how.

And anon after our Lord Jesus Christ spoke unto her and said, "Daughter, look that you be now true and steadfast and have a good faith, for your name is written in heaven in the book of life, and this was an angel that gave you comfort. And therefore, daughter, you must be right merry, for I am right busy both forenoon and afternoon to draw your heart into my heart, for you should keep your mind altogether on me, and that shall most increase your love toward God. For, daughter, if you will draw after God's counsel, you may not do amiss, for God's counsel is to be meek, patient in charity and in chastity.

Another time, as the creature lay in her contemplation in a chapel of our Lady, her mind was occupied in the Passion of our Lord Jesus Christ, and she thought verily that she saw our Lord appear to her ghostly sight in his manhood, with his wounds bleeding as fresh as though he had been scourged before her. And then she wept and cried with all the mights of her body, for, if her sorrow was great before this ghostly sight, yet it was well greater afterward than it was before, and her love was more increased toward our Lord. And then had she great wonder that our Lord would become man and suffer such grievous pains for her, who was so unkind a creature to him.

Another time, as she was in a church of Saint Margaret, in the choir, being in great sweetness and devotion, with great plenty of tears, she asked our Lord Jesus Christ how she might best please him. And he answered to her soul, saying, "Daughter, have mind of your wickedness and think on my goodness."

Then she prayed many times and often these words, "Lord, for your great goodness have mercy on all my wickedness as surely as I was never so wicked as you are good, nor ever may be, though I would, for you are so good that you may no better be. And therefore it is great wonder that ever any man should be parted from you without end."

Then, as she lay still in the choir, weeping and mourning for her sins, suddenly she was in a manner of sleep. And anon she saw with her ghostly eye our Lord's body lying before her, and his head, as she thought, fast by her with his blessed face upward, the seemliest man that ever might be seen or thought of. And then to her sight came one with a dagger and cut that precious body all along the breast. And anon she wept wonder sore, having more mind, pity, and compassion of the passion of our Lord Jesus Christ than she had before. And so every day increased her mind and her love toward our Lord, blessed may he be, and the more that her love increased, the more was her sorrow for the sin of the people.

Another time, the said creature being in a chapel of our Lady sorely weeping in the mind of our Lord's passion and such other graces and goodness as our Lord ministered to her mind, and suddenly, she knew not how soon, she was in a manner of sleep. And anon in the sight of her soul she saw our Lord standing right up over her, so near that she thought she took his toes in her hand and felt them, and to her feeling they were as they had been very flesh and bone. And then she thanked God for all, for through these ghostly sights her affection was all drawn into the manhood of Christ and into the mind of his passion until that time that it pleased our Lord to give her understanding of his inunderstandable Godhead.

As is written before, this manner of visions and feelings she had soon after her conversion, when she was fully set and purposed to serve God with all her heart, unto her power, and had fully left the world, and kept the church both forenoon and afternoon, and most specially in Lenttime, when she with great insistence and much prayer had leave of her husband to live chaste and clean and did great bodily penance before she went to Jerusalem. But afterward, when she and her husband with one assent had made a vow of chastity, as is before written, and she had been at Rome and Jerusalem and suffered much despite and reproof for her weeping and her crying, our Lord of his high mercy drew her affection into his Godhead, and that was more fervent in love and desire and more subtle in understanding than was the manhood. And nevertheless the fire of love increased in her, and her understanding was more illumined and her devotion more fervent than it was before, while she had her meditation and her contemplation only in his manhood; yet had she not that manner of working in crying as she had before, but it was more subtle and more soft and more easy for her spirit to bear and plenteous in tears as ever it was before.

Another time, as this creature was in a house of the Friar Preachers within a chapel of our Lady, standing in her prayers, her eyelids went a little together with a manner of sleep, and suddenly she saw, she thought, our Lady in the fairest sight that ever she saw, holding a fair white kerchief in her hand and saying to her, "Daughter, will you see my son?"

And anon forthwith she saw our Lady have her blessed son in her hand and swathe him full lightly in the white kerchief so that she might well behold how she did it. The creature had then a new ghostly joy and a new ghostly comfort, which was so marvelous that she could never tell it as she felt it.

86. On a time our Lord spoke to the said creature when it pleased him, saying to her ghostly understanding, "Daughter, for as many times as you have received the blessed sacrament of the altar with many holy thoughts, more than you can repeat, for so many times shall you be rewarded in heaven with new joys and new comforts. And, daughter, in heaven shall it be known to you how many days you have had of high contemplation through my gift on earth. And of all it is so that they are my gifts and my graces which I have given you; yet shall you have the same grace and reward in heaven as if they were of your own merits, for freely I have given them to you. But highly I thank you, daughter, that you have suffered me to work my will in you and that you would let me be so homely with you. For in anything, daughter, that you might do on earth you might no better please me than to suffer me to speak to you in your soul, for at that time you understand my will, and I understand your will.

"And also, daughter, you call my mother to come into your soul and take me in her arms and lay me to her breasts and give me suck. Also, daughter, I know the holy thoughts and the good desires that you have when you receive me and the good charity that you have toward me in the time that you receive my precious body into your soul, and also how you call Mary Magdalene into your soul to welcome me, for, daughter, I know well enough what you think. You think that she is worthiest in your soul, and most you trust in her prayers, next to my mother's, and so you may right well, daughter, for she is a right great mean to me for you in the bliss of heaven. And sometimes, daughter, you think your soul so large and so wide that you call all the court of heaven into your soul to welcome me. I know right well, daughter, what you say, 'Come all twelve apostles who were so well beloved of God on earth and receive your Lord in my soul.' Also you pray Katherine, Margaret, and all holy virgins to welcome me in your soul. And then you pray my blessed mother, Mary Magdalene, all apostles, martyrs, confessors,[5] Katherine, Margaret, and all holy virgins that they should array the chamber of your soul with many fair flowers and with many sweet spices that I might rest therein.

"Furthermore you think sometimes, daughter, as though you had a cushion of gold, another of red velvet, the third of white silk in your soul. And you think that my Father sits on the cushion of gold, for to him is appropriated might and power. And you think that I, the Second Person, your love and your joy, sit on the red cushion of velvet, for upon me is all your thought because I bought you so dear, and you think that you can never acquit me the love that I have showed you though you were slain a thousand times a day, if it were possible, for my love. Thus you think, daughter, in your soul, that I am worthy to sit on a red cushion in remembrance of the red blood that I shed for you. Moreover you think that the Holy Ghost sits on a white cushion, for you think that he is full of love

---

5. Those who have heroically confessed their faith.

and cleanness, and therefore it beseems him to sit on a white cushion, for he is giver of all holy thoughts and chastity. And yet I know well enough, daughter, that you think you may not worship the Father unless you worship the Son, and that you may not worship the Son unless you worship the Holy Ghost.

"And also you think sometimes, daughter, that the Father is all mighty and all knowing and all grace and goodness, and you think the same of the Son, that he is all mighty and all knowing and all grace and goodness. And you think that the Holy Ghost has the same properties equal with the Father and the Son, proceeding from them both. Also you think that each of the three persons in Trinity has what the others have in their Godhead, and so you believe verily, daughter, in your soul, that there are three divers persons and one God in substance, and that each knows what the others know, and each may what the others may, and each wills what the others will. And, daughter, this a very faith and a right faith, and this faith have you only of my gift.

And therefore, daughter, if you will bethink you well, you have great cause to love me right well and to give me all wholly your heart so that I may fully rest therein as I myself will; for, if you suffer me, daughter, to rest in your soul on earth, believe it right well that you shall rest with me in heaven without end. And therefore, daughter, have you no wonder though you weep sorely when you are houseled and receive my blessed body in the form of bread, for you pray to me before you are houseled, saying to me in your mind, 'As surely, Lord, as you love me, make me clean from all sin and give me grace to receive your precious body worthily with all manner of worship and reverence.' And, daughter, know you well I hear your prayer, for a better word may you not say to my liking than 'as surely as I love you,' for then I fulfill my grace in you and give you many a holy thought; it is impossible to tell them all. And because of the great homeliness that I show toward you at times, you are much the bolder to ask me grace for yourself, for your husband, and for your children, and you make every Christian man and woman your child in your soul for the time and would have as much grace for them as for your own children. Also you ask mercy for your husband, and you think that you are much beholden to me, that I have given you such a man who would suffer you to live chaste, he being alive and in good health of body.

"Forsooth, daughter, you think full true, and therefore have you great cause to love me right well. Daughter, if you knew how many wives there are in this world who would love me and serve me right well and duly, if they might be as freely from their husbands as you are from yours, you would say that you were right much beholden unto me. And yet are they put from their wills and suffer full great pain, and therefore shall they have right great reward in heaven, for I receive every good will as for deed.

Sometimes, daughter, I make you to have great sorrow for your ghostly father's sins in special, so that he should have as full forgiveness for his sins as you would have for yours. And, sometimes when you receive the precious sacrament, I make you to pray for your ghostly father in this way: that as many men and women might be turned by his preaching as you would that were turned by the tears of your eyes and that my holy words might settle as sorely in their hearts as you would that they should settle in your heart. And also you ask the same grace for all good men who preach my word on earth, that they might be a profit to all reasonable creatures. And oftentimes, that day that you receive my precious body you ask grace and mercy for all your friends and for all your enemies that ever did you shame or reproof, either scorned you or jibed at you, for the grace that I work in you and for all this world, both young and old, with many tears, sore weeping and sobbing. You have suffered much shame and much reproof, and therefore shall you have full much bliss in heaven.

"Daughter, be not ashamed to receive my grace when I will give it to you, for I shall not be ashamed of you so that you shall be received into the bliss of heaven, there to be rewarded for every good thought, for every good word, and for every good deed, and for every day of contemplation, and for all good desires that you have had here in this world with me everlastingly as my worthy darling, as my blessed spouse, and as my holy wife. And therefore dread you not, daughter, though the people wonder why you weep so sorely when you receive me, for, if they knew what grace I put in you at that time, they would rather wonder that your heart burst not asunder. And so it should if I measured not that grace myself, but you yourself see well, daughter, that, when you have received me into your soul, you are in peace and in quiet and sob no longer.

"And thereof the people have great wonder, but it need no wonder be to you, for you know well that I fare like a husband who should wed a wife. At that time that he weds her, he thinks that he is sure enough of her and that no man shall part them asunder, for then, daughter, may they go to bed together without any shame or dread of the people and sleep in rest and peace if they will. And thus, daughter, it fares between me and you, for you have every week, specially on Sunday, great fear and dread in your soul about how you may best be sure of my love, and, with great reverence and holy dread, how you may best receive me to the salvation of your soul with all manner of meekness, lowness, and charity, as any lady in this world is busy to receive her husband when he comes home and has been long from her.

"My worthy daughter, I thank you highly for all men you have cared for in my name who have been sick and for all the goodness and service that you have done for them in any degree, for you shall have the same meed with me in heaven as though you had kept my own self while I was here on earth. Also, daughter, I thank you for as many times as you have bathed me in your soul at home in your chamber as though I had been there present in my manhood, for I know well, daughter, all the holy thoughts that you have showed to me in your mind. And also, daughter,

I thank you for all the times that you have harbored me and my blessed mother in your bed. For these and for all other good thoughts and good deeds that you have thought in my name and wrought for my love you shall have with me and with my mother, with my holy angels, with my apostles, with my martyrs, confessors and virgins, and with all my holy saints all manner of joy and bliss lasting without end."

87. The said creature lay full still in the church, hearing and understanding this sweet dalliance in her soul as clearly as one friend should speak to another. And, when she heard the great promises that our Lord Jesus Christ promised her, then she thanked him with great weepings and sobbings and with many holy and reverent thoughts, saying in her mind, "Lord Jesus, blessed may you be, for this deserved I never of you, but I would I were in that place where I should never displease you from this time forward."

With such manner of thoughts and many more than I could ever write she worshipped and magnified our Lord Jesus Christ for his holy visitation and his comfort. And in such manner visitations and holy contemplations as are before written, much more subtle and more high without comparison than are written, the said creature had continued her life through the preserving of our Savior Christ Jesus more than twenty-five years when this treatise was written, week by week and day by day, unless she were occupied with sick folk or else were hindered by other needful occupation that was necessary unto her or to her fellow Christians. Then it was withdrawn sometimes, for it will be had but in great quiet of soul through long exercise. By this manner of speech and dalliance she was made mighty and strong in the love of our Lord and greatly stabled in her faith and increased in meekness and charity with other good virtues. And she stably and steadfastly believed that it was God that spoke in her soul and no evil spirit, for in his speech she had the most strength and the most comfort and the most increase of virtue, blessed be God.

Divers times, when the creature was so sick that she thought to have been dead and other folk thought the same, it was answered in her soul that she should not die but she should live and fare well, and so she did. Sometimes our Lady spoke to her and comforted her in her sickness. Sometimes Saint Peter, or Saint Paul, sometimes Saint Mary Magdalene, Saint Katherine, Saint Margaret, or whatever saint in heaven that she could think on through the will and sufferance of God. They spoke to the understanding of her soul, and informed her how she should love God and how she should best please him, and answered to whatever she would ask of them, and she could understand by their manner of dalliance which of them it was who spoke unto her and comforted her. Our Lord of his high mercy visited her so much and so plenteously with his holy speeches and his holy dalliance that many times she knew not how the day went. She supposed sometimes of five hours or six hours it had not been the space of an hour. It was so sweet and so devout that it fared as if she had been in heaven. She thought it never long thereof, nor was she was ever irked thereof; the time went away she knew not how. She had rather have served God, if she might have lived so long, a hundred years in this manner of life than one day as she first began. And oftentimes she said to our Lord Jesus, "A, Lord Jesus, since it is so sweet to weep for your love on earth, I know well it shall be right joyful to be with you in heaven. Therefore, Lord, I pray you, let me never have another joy on earth but mourning and weeping for your love. For I think, Lord, though I were in hell, if I might weep there and mourn for your love as I do here, hell should not annoy me, but it should be a manner of heaven, for your love puts away all manner of dread of our ghostly enemy, for I had rather be there as long as you would and please you than be in this world and displease you. Therefore, Lord, as you will, so may it be."

88. When this book was first in writing, the said creature was more at home in her chamber with her writer and, for the speed of the writing, said fewer beads than she had done for years before. And, when she came to church and would hear mass, purposing to say her matins and such other devotions as she had used before that time, her heart was drawn away from the saying and set greatly on meditation. She being afraid of displeasing our Lord, he said to her soul, "Dread you not, daughter, for as many prayers as you would say I accept them as though you said them, and both your study, that you study in order to have written the grace that I have showed to you, and he who writes pleases me right much. For, though you were in the church and wept both together as sorely as ever you did, yet should you not please me more than you do with your writing, for daughter, by this book many a man shall be turned to me and believe therein.

"Daughter, where is a better prayer by your own reason than to pray to me with your heart or your thought? Daughter, when you pray by thought, you yourself understand what you ask of me, and you understand also what I say to you, and you understand what I promise you for you and for yours and for all your ghostly fathers. And, as for Master Robert, your confessor, I have granted you what you have desired, and he shall have half your tears and half the good works that I have wrought in you. Therefore he shall truly be rewarded for your weeping as though he had wept himself. And believe well, daughter, that you shall be full merry in heaven together at the last and shall bless the time that ever one of you knew the other. And, daughter, you shall bless me without end that ever I gave you so true a ghostly father; for, though he has been sharp to you sometimes, it has been greatly to your profit, for you would else have had too great an affection for his person. And, when he was sharp to you, then you ran with all your mind to me, saying, 'Lord, there is no trust but in you alone.' And then you cried to me with all your heart, 'Lord, for thi wowndys smarte drawe alle my lofe into thyn hert.'⁶ And, daughter, so have I done.

"You think oftentimes that I have done right much for you, and you think that it is a great miracle that I have drawn all your affection toward me, for sometimes you were so affected toward some singular person that you thought at that time it would have been in a manner impossible to have withdrawn your affection from him. And afterward you have desired, if it had pleased me, that the same person should have forsaken you for my love, for, if he had not supported you, few men would have set any price by you, as it seemed to you. And you thought, if he had forsaken you, it had been the greatest reproof that ever came to you before the people, and therefore you would have suffered that reproof with good will for my love if it had pleased me. And thus with such doleful thoughts you increased your love toward me, and therefore, daughter, I receive your desires as if they were done in deed. And I know right well that you have right true love toward that same person, and I have often said to you that he should be right fain to love you and that he should believe it is God who speaks in you and no devil. Also, daughter, that person has pleased me right well, for he has often in his sermons excused your weeping and your crying, and so has Master Alan also done, and therefore they shall have full great meed in heaven. Daughter, I have told you many times that I would maintain your weeping and your crying by sermons and preaching.

"Also, daughter, I tell you that Master Robert, your ghostly father, pleases me full much when he bids you believe that I love you. And I know well that you have great faith in his words, and so you may right well, for he will not flatter you. And also, daughter, I am highly pleased with him, for he bids you that you should sit still and give your heart to meditation and think such holy thoughts as God will put in your mind. And I have often times bid you so myself, and yet you will not act thereafter without much grudging. And yet I am not displeased with you, for, daughter, I have often said unto you that whether you pray with your mouth or think with your heart, whether you read or hear reading, I will be pleased with you. And yet, daughter, I tell you, if you would love me, that thinking is the best for you and shall most increase your love toward me; and the more homely that you suffer me to be in your soul on earth, it is worthy and rightful that I be the more homely with your soul in heaven. And therefore, daughter, if you will not act after my counsel, act after the counsel of your ghostly father, for he bids you do the same that I bid you do.

"Daughter, when your ghostly father says to you you displease God, you believe him right well, and then take you much sorrow and great

---

6. "Lord, for your wounds' smart, draw all my love into your heart." See chapter 65 (p. 118) for another version of this couplet.

heaviness and weep full fast till you have gotten grace again. And then I come oftentimes to you myself and comfort you, for, daughter, I may not suffer you to have pain any while but that I must make a remedy. And therefore, daughter, I come to you and make you sure of my love and tell you with my own mouth that you are as sure of my love as God is God and that no thing is so sure to you on earth that you may see with your bodily eye. And therefore, blessed daughter, love him who loves you and forget me not, daughter, for I forget not you, for my merciful eye is ever upon you. And that knows my merciful mother full well, daughter, for she has oftentimes told you so, and many other saints also. And therefore, daughter, you have great cause to love me right well and to give me all your whole heart with all your affections, for that I desire and nothing else of you. And I shall give you there again all my heart. And, if you will be buxom to my will, I shall be buxom to your will, daughter, believe it right well.

89. Also, while the foresaid creature was occupied about the writing of this treatise, she had many holy tears and weepings, and oftentimes there came a flame of fire about her breast, full hot and delectable, and also he who was her writer could not sometimes keep himself from weeping. And often in the meantime, when the creature was in church, our Lord Jesus Christ with his glorious Mother and many saints also came into her soul and thanked her, saying that they were well pleased with the writing of this book. And also she heard many times a voice of a sweet bird singing in her ear, and oftentimes she heard sweet sounds and melodies that passed her wit to tell them. And she was many times sick while this treatise was in writing, and, as soon as she would go about the writing of this treatise, she was suddenly in a manner hale and whole.

And often she was commanded to make herself ready in all haste. And on a time, as she lay in her prayers in the church at the time of Advent[7] before Christmas, she thought in her heart she would that God of his goodness would make Master Allen to say a sermon as well as he could. And, as quickly as she had thought thus, she heard our Sovereign Lord Christ Jesus say in her soul, "Daughter, I know right well what you think now of Master Allen, and I tell you truly that he shall say a right holy sermon. And look that you believe steadfastly the words that he shall preach as though I preached them myself, for they shall be words of great solace and comfort to you, for I shall speak in him."

When she had heard this answer, she went and told it to her confessor and two other priests in whom she trusted much. And, when she had told them her feeling, she was full sorry for dread whether he should say as well as she had felt or not, for revelations are hard sometimes to understand. And sometimes those that men think are revelations, they are de-

---

7. Advent is the penitential period that precedes Christmas.

ceits and illusions, and therefore it is not expedient readily to give credence to every stirring but soberly abide and prove if they are sent of God. Nevertheless, as to this feeling of this creature, it was very truth showed in experience, and her dread and her heaviness turned into great ghostly comfort and gladness.

Sometimes she was in great heaviness for many days together for her feelings, when she knew not how they should be understood, for the dread that she had of deceits and illusions, so that she thought she would that her head had been smitten from the body till God of his goodness declared them to her mind. For sometimes what she understood as bodily was to be understood as ghostly, and the dread that she had of her feelings was the greatest scourge that she had on earth and specially when she had her first feelings, and that dread made her full meek, for she had no joy in the feeling till she knew by experience whether it was true or not. But ever blessed may God be, for he made her always more mighty and more strong in his love and in his dread and gave her increase of virtue with perseverance.

Here ends this treatise, for God took him to his mercy who wrote the copy of this book, and, though he wrote not clearly nor openly to our manner of speaking, he in his manner of writing and spelling made true sentence, the which, through the help of God and of her who had all this treatise in feeling and working, is truly drawn out of the copy into this little book.

Book Two

1. After our Sovereign Savior had taken the person who wrote first the treatise before said to his manifold mercy, and the priest of whom is before written had copied the same treatise after his simple cunning, he held it expedient to the honor of the blissful Trinity that God's holy works should be notified and declared to the people, when it pleased him, to the worship of his holy name. And then he began to write in the year of our Lord 1438, on the feast of Saint Vital Martyr[1] such grace as our Lord wrought in his simple creature the years that she lived after, not all but some of them, after her own tongue.

And first here is a notable matter, which is not written in the foresaid treatise. It befell soon after the creature, before written, had forsaken the occupation of the world and was joined in her mind to God as much as frailty would suffer. The said creature had a son, a tall young man, dwelling with a worshipful burgess in Lynn, using merchandise[2] and sailing over the sea, whom she desired to have drawn out of the perils of this wretched and unstable world if her power might have attained thereto. Nevertheless she did as much as was in her, and, when she might meet with him at leisure, many times she counseled him to leave the world and follow Christ, insomuch that he fled her company and would not gladly meet with her.

So on a time it happened that the mother met with her son though it was against his will and his intent at that time. And, as she had done before time, so now she spoke to him again that he should flee the perils of this world and not set his study nor his business so much thereupon as he did. He, not consenting but sharply answering again, she, somewhat moved with sharpness of spirit, said, "Now since you will not leave the world at my counsel, I charge you, at my blessing, keep your body clean at the least from woman's fellowship till you take a wife after the law of the Church. And, if you do not, I pray God chastise you and punish you therefore."

They parted asunder, and soon after the same young man passed over the sea in the way of merchandise, and then, what through the evil enticing of other persons and the folly of his own governance, he fell into the sin of lechery. Soon after, his color changed, his face waxed full of whelks and splotches as if it had been a leper's. Then he came home

---

1. April 28.
2. Using in the sense of being employed in.

again into Lynn to his master with whom he had been dwelling before-time. His master put him out of his service for no default he found with him, but perhaps supposing he had been a leper, as it showed by his visage. The young man told where he liked how his mother had banned him, wherethrough, as he supposed, God so grievously punished him. Some persons, having knowledge of his complaint and compassion for his disease, came to his mother, saying she had done right evil, for through her prayer God had taken vengeance on her own child. She, taking little heed of their words, let it pass forth, since she would take no heed till he would come and pray for grace himself.

So at the last, when he saw no other remedy, he came to his mother, telling her of his misgovernance, promising he should be obedient to God and to her and to amend his default through the help of God, avoiding all misgovernance from that time forward, upon his power. He prayed his mother for her blessing, and specially he prayed her to pray for him, that our Lord of his high mercy would forgive him that he had trespassed and take away that great sickness for which men fled his company and his fellowship as they would a leper's. For he supposed by her prayers our Lord sent him that punishing, and therefore he trusted by her prayers to be delivered thereof if she would of her charity pray for him.

Then she, having trust of his amending and compassion of his infirmity, with sharp words of correction, promised to fulfill his intent if God would grant it. When she came to her meditation, not forgetting the fruit of her womb, she asked forgiveness for his sin and release from the sickness that our Lord had given him, if it were His pleasure and profit to his soul. So long she prayed that he was clean delivered of the sickness and lived many years after and had a wife and a child, blessed may God be, for he wedded his wife in Prussia in Germany. When tidings came to his mother from over the sea that her son had wedded, she was right glad and thanked God with all her heart, supposing and trusting he should live clean and chaste as the law of matrimony asks. Afterward, when God would, his wife had a child, a fair maid child.

Then he sent tidings to his mother into England how graciously God had visited him and his wife. His mother, being in a chapel of our Lady thanking God for the grace and goodness that he showed to her son and having the desire to see them if she might, immediately it was answered to her mind that she should see them all before she died. She had wonder of this feeling, how it should be so as she felt, inasmuch as they were beyond the sea and she on this half of the sea, never purposing to pass the sea while she lived. Nevertheless she knew well to God was nothing impossible. Therefore she trusted it should be so when God would, as she had feeling.

2. In a few years after this young man had wedded, he came home to England, to his father and his mother, all changed in his array and his

conditions. For before his clothes were all dagged[3] and his language all vanity; now he wore no slashes, and his dalliance was full of virtue. His mother, having great marvel of this sudden change, said unto him, "Benedicite, son, how is it with you that you are so changed?"

"Mother," he said, "I hope that through your prayers our Lord has drawn me, and I purpose by the grace of God to follow your counsel more than I have done before."

Then his mother, seeing this marvelous draught of our Lord, thanked God as she could, taking good heed of his governance for dread of simulation. The longer that she beheld his governance, the more sober she thought he was and the more reverent toward our Lord. When she knew it was the draught of our Lord's mercy, then she was full joyful, thanking God full many times for his grace and his goodness. Afterward, so he would be the more diligent and the more busy to follow our Lord's drawing, she opened her heart to him, showing him and informing how our Lord had drawn her through his mercy and by what means, also how much grace he had showed for her, the which he said he was unworthy to hear.

Then he went on many pilgrimages to Rome and to many other places to purchase himself pardon, resorting again to his wife and his child as he was bound to do. He informed his wife of his mother, insomuch that she would leave her father and her mother and her own country to come into England and see his mother. He was full glad thereof and sent word into England to his mother to notify her of his wife's desire and to learn whether his mother would counsel him to come by land or by water, for he trusted much in his mother's counsel, believing it was of the Holy Ghost.

His mother, when she had the letter from him and knew his desire, went to her prayer to know our Lord's counsel and our Lord's will. And, as she prayed for the said matter, it was answered to her soul that, whether her son come by land or by water, he should come in safekeeping. Then wrote she letters to him, saying that whether he came by land or by water he should come in safety by the grace of God.

When he was notified of his mother's counsel, he asked when ships should come into England and hired a ship, or else a part of a ship, in which he put his goods, his wife, his child, and his own self, purposing all to come into England together. When they were in the ship, there rose such tempests that they dared not take the sea, and so they came on land again, both him, his wife, and their child.

Then they left their child in Prussia with their friends, and he and his wife came into England by the land way to his father and to his mother. When they were come thither, his mother full much delighted in our Lord that her feeling was true, for she had feeling in her soul, as is writ-

3. Slashed and pointed along the hems; see chapter 2 (p. 8).

ten before, that, whether they came by land or by water, they should come in safety. And so it was indeed, blessed may God be.

They came home on Saturday in good health, and on the next day, that was Sunday, while they were at the meal at noon with other friends, he fell in great sickness so that he rose from the table and laid himself on a bed, which sickness and infirmity occupied him about a month, and then in good life and right belief he passed to the mercy of our Lord. So ghostly and bodily it might well be verified he shall come home in safety, not only into this deadly land but also into the land of living men, where death shall never appear. In a short time after, the father of the said person followed the son the way which every man must go.

Then lived still the mother of the said person, of whom this treatise specially makes mention, and she who was his wife, a German woman, dwelling with his mother for a year and a half, until the time that her friends who were in Germany, desiring to have her home, wrote letters to her and stirred her to resort to her own country. And so she, desiring the benevolence of her friends, uttered her conceit to her mother-in-law, declaring to her the desire of her friends, praying her for good love and leave that she might resort to her own country.

And so through her mother-in-law's consent she prepared herself to go as soon as any ships went into that land. So they inquired about a ship of that same land in which her own countrymen should sail thither, since they thought it was better that she should rather sail with them in their ship than with other men. Then she went to her confessor to be shriven, and, while she was being shriven, the said creature, her mother-in-law, went up and down in the choir, thinking in her mind, "Lord, if it were your will, I would take leave of my confessor and go with her over the sea."

Our Lord answered to her thought, saying, "Daughter, I know well, if I bid you go, you would go all ready. Therefore I will that you speak no word to him of this matter."

Then was she right glad and merry, trusting she should not go over the sea, for she had been in great peril on the sea before and purposed never to come thereon anymore by her own will. When her daughter-in-law was shriven, the good man who was confessor to them both at that time came to her and said, "Who shall go with your daughter to the sea side till she comes to her ship? It is not goodly that she should go so far with a young man alone in a strange country where neither is known," for a strange man was come for her and both were but little known in this country, wherefore her confessor had the more compassion for her.

Then the said creature said again, "Sir, if you will bid me, I shall go with her myself till she comes to Ipswich; there lies the ship and her own countrymen who shall lead her over the sea."

Her confessor said, "How should you go with her? You hurt your foot but lately, and you are not yet all whole, and also you are an old woman. You may not go."

"Sir," she said, "God, as I trust, shall help me right well."

Then he asked who should go with her and bring her home again.

And she said, "Sir, there is belonging to this church a hermit, a young man. I hope he will for our Lord's love go and come with me, if you will give me leave."

So she had leave to bring her daughter to Ipswich and then come again to Lynn. Thus they passed forth on their journey in the time of Lent, and, when they were five or six miles from Lynn, they came by a church, and so they turned in to hear mass. And, as they were in the church, the foresaid creature, desiring tears of devotion, none might purchase at that time, but ever was commanded in her heart to go over the sea with her daughter. She would have put it out of her mind, and ever it came again so fast that she might not have rest or quiet in her mind but ever was labored and commanded to go over the sea. She thought it was heavy for her to take such labor upon herself and excused herself to our Lord in her mind, saying, "Lord, you know well I have no leave of my ghostly father, and I am bound to obedience. Therefore I may not do thus without his will and his consent."

It was answered again to her thought, "I bid you go in my name, Jesus, for I am above your ghostly father, and I shall excuse you and lead you and bring you again in safety."

She would yet excuse herself if she might in any way, and therefore she said, "I am not provided sufficiently with gold or silver to go with as I ought to be, and, if I were and would go, I know well my daughter had rather I were at home, and perhaps the shipmasters should not receive me into their vessel in order to go with them."

Our Lord said again, "If I be with you, who shall be against you? I shall provide for you and get you friends to help you. Do as I bid you, and there shall no man of the ship say nay unto you."

The creature saw there was no other help but forth she must at the commanding of God. She thought that she would first go to Walsingham[4] and offer in worship of our Lady, and, as she was on the way thitherward, she heard tell that a friar should say a sermon in a little village a little out of her way. She turned into the church where the friar said the sermon, a famous man, and a great audience was had at his sermon. And many times he said these words, "If God be with us, who shall be against us?" through which words she was the more stirred to obey the will of God and performed her intent.

So she went forth to Walsingham, and afterward to Norwich with her daughter-in-law, and the hermit with them. When they came to Norwich, she met a Gray Friar, a worshipful clerk, a doctor of divinity who had heard before that time of her living and her feelings. The doctor showed

_____

4. Walsingham, just northeast of King's Lynn, was one of the most important pilgrimage sites in medieval England, containing images and relics devoted to the Virgin Mary and holy wells in which pilgrims bathed.

her great welcome and dallied with her as he had done before that time. She, many times sighing, was heavy in cheer and in countenance. The doctor asked what ailed her.

"Sir," she said, "when I came out of Lynn with the leave of my confessor, I purposed to lead my daughter to Ipswich, where is a ship in which she, by the grace of God, shall sail to Germany, and I then to turn home again to Lynn as soon as I might goodly, with a hermit who came with me for the same intent, to lead me home again. And he knew fully that I should do so. And, sir, when I was about six miles out of Lynn, in a church to make my prayers, I was commanded in my soul that I should go over the sea with my daughter, and I know well she would I were at home, and so would I if I dared. Thus was I moved in my soul and no rest might have in my spirit nor devotion till I consented to do as I was moved in my spirit, and this is to me great dread and heaviness."

The worshipful clerk said unto her, "You shall obey the will of God, for I believe it is the Holy Ghost that speaks in you, and therefore follow the moving of your spirit in the name of Jesus."

She was much comforted with his words and took her leave, going forth to the seaside with her fellowship. When they were come thither, the ship was ready to sail. Then she prayed the master that she might sail with them into Germany, and he goodly received her, and they who were in the ship said not once nay.

There was no one so much against her as was her daughter, who ought most to have been with her. Then she took her leave of the hermit who was come thither with her, rewarding him somewhat for his labor and praying him to excuse her to her confessor and to her other friends when he came home to Lynn, for it was not her knowing nor her intent when she parted from them to have passed the sea ever while she lived, "but," she said, "I must obey the will of God."

The hermit parted from her with heavy manner and came home again to Lynn, excusing her to her confessor and to other friends, telling them of their sudden and wonderful parting and how it was not his knowledge that they should have parted so suddenly asunder. The people that heard thereof had great wonder and said as they would. Some said it was a woman's wit and a great folly for the love of her daughter-in-law to put herself, a woman in great age, to perils of the sea and to go into a strange country where she had not been before nor knew how she should come again. Some held it was a deed of great charity, forasmuch as her daughter had before that time left her friends and her country and come with her husband to visit her in this country, so that she would now help her daughter home again into the country that she came from. Others, who knew more of the creature's living, supposed and trusted that it was the will and the working of almighty God to the magnifying of his own name.

3. The said creature and her fellowship entered their ship on the Thursday in Passion Week,[5] and God sent them fair wind and weather that day and the Friday, but on the Saturday our Lord, turning his hand as he liked, and the Palm Sunday also, proving their faith and their patience with the two nights, sent them such storms and tempests that they thought all to have perished. The tempests were so grievous and hideous that they might not rule or govern their ship. They knew no better exchange[6] than to commend themselves and their ship to the governance of our Lord; they left their craft and their cunning and let our Lord drive them where he would.

The said creature had sorrow and care enough; she thought she had never so much before. She cried to our Lord for mercy and the preserving of her and all her fellowship. She thought in her mind, "A, Lord, for your love came I hither, and you have oftentimes promised me that I should never perish either on land or on water or with any tempest. The people have many times banned me, cursed me, and reviled me for the grace that you have wrought in me, desiring that I should die in misfortune and great trouble, and now, Lord, it is likely that their banning comes to effect, and I, unworthy wretch, am deceived and defrauded of the promise that you have made many times unto me, who has ever trusted in your mercy and your goodness, unless you soon withdraw these tempests and show us mercy. Now may my enemies delight, and I may sorrow if they have their intent and I am deceived.

"Now, blissful Jesus, have mind of your manifold mercy and fulfill your promises that you have promised me. Show you are truly God and no evil spirit that has brought me hither into the perils of the sea, whose counsel I have trusted and followed for many years and shall do through your mercy if you deliver us out of these grievous perils. Help us and succor us, Lord, before we perish or despair, for we may not long endure this sorrow that we are in without your mercy and your succor."

Our merciful Lord, speaking in her mind, blamed her for her fearfulness, saying, "Why dread you? Why are you so afraid? I am as mighty here in the sea as on the land. Why will you mistrust me? All that I have promised you I shall truly fulfill, and I shall never deceive you. Suffer patiently a while and have trust in my mercy. Waver not in your faith, for without faith you may not please me. If you would verily trust in me and nothing doubt, you may have great comfort in yourself and might comfort all your fellowship, where you are now all in great dread and heaviness."

With such manner of dalliance, and much more high and holy than ever I could write, our Lord comforted his creature, blessed may he be.

---

5. Passion Week is the week before Holy Week, or the week that ends in Palm Sunday.
6. The word Kempe uses here is *chefsyawns,* a word of barter designating the exchange of goods or the changing of money or the business of borrowing money.

Holy saints that she prayed unto dallied unto her soul by the sufferance of our Lord, giving her words of great comfort. At the last came our Lady and said, "Daughter, be of a good comfort. You have ever found my tidings true, and therefore be no longer afraid, for I tell you truly these winds and tempests shall soon cease and you shall have right fair weather."

And so, blessed may God be, it was in short time after that their ship was driven into the Norway coast, and there they landed on Good Friday and abode there Easter Eve, and Easter Day, and the Monday after Easter. And on that Monday they were houseled within the ship, all that belonged to the ship. On Easter Day the master of the ship and the said creature and others, the greatest part of the group, went on land and heard their service at the church. After the use of the country the cross was raised on Easter Day about noon time, and she had her meditation and her devotion with weeping and sobbing, as well as if she had been at home. God drew not his grace from her, neither in church, nor on ship, nor on the sea, nor in any place that she came to, for ever she had him in her soul.

When they had received the sacrament on Easter Monday, as is written before, our Lord sent them a fair wind that brought them out of that country and drove them home into Germany as they desired. The foresaid creature found such grace in the master of the ship, so that he ordained for her meat and drink and all that was necessary unto her, as long as she was within the ship, and was as tender to her as if she had been his mother. He covered her in the ship with his own clothes, else she might have died for cold; she was not provided for as others were. She went at the bidding of our Lord, and therefore her master who bade her go provided for her so that she fared as well as any of her fellowship, worship and praising be to our Lord therefore.

4. The said creature abode in Danzig in Germany about five or six weeks and had right good welcome of many people for our Lord's love. There was no one so much against her as was her daughter-in-law, who was most bound and beholden to have comforted her if she had been natural.

Then the creature delighted in our Lord that she had so great welcome for his love and purposed to abide there the longer time. Our Lord, speaking to her thought, admonished her to go out of the country. She was then in great heaviness and doubt how she should do the bidding of God, which she would in no way withstand, and had neither man nor woman to go with her in fellowship. By the water would she not go as nigh as she might, for she was so afraid on the sea as she came thitherward; and by the land-way she might not go easily, for there was war in the country that she should pass by.[7]

---

7. The route from Danzig to Calais lay through the territory claimed by the Teutonic Order, at that time under imminent attack from Poland.

So what through one cause and another she was in great heaviness, not knowing how she should be relieved. She went into a church and made her prayers that our Lord, just as he commanded her to go, he should send her help and fellowship with which she might go. And suddenly a man, coming to her, asked if she would go on pilgrimage to a far country from thence, to a place called Wilsnack[8] where is worshipped the Precious Blood of our Lord Jesus Christ, which by miracle came from three hosts, the sacrament of the altar, which three hosts and precious blood be there unto this day, had in great worship and reverence and sought from many a country. She with glad countenance said that she would go thither if she had good fellowship and if she knew of any honest man who might afterward bring her into England.

And he promised her that he would go on pilgrimage with her to the foresaid place on his own cost, and afterward, if she would repay his cost into England, he should come with her till she was on the coasts of England, where she might have good fellowship from her nation. He provided a small vessel, a little ship, in which they should sail toward the holy place, and then might she have no leave to go out of that land, for she was an English woman, and so had she great vexation and much hindrance before she might get leave of one of the Teutonic Knights to go thence.[9] At the last, through the stirring of our Lord, there was a merchant of Lynn who heard tell thereof, and he came to her and comforted her, promising her that he should help her from thence, either privately or openly. And this good man through great labor got her leave to go wherever she would.

Then she, with the man who had provided for her, took their vessel, and God sent them calm wind, which wind pleased her right well, for there rose no wave on the water. Her fellowship thought they sped no way and were heavy and grudging. She prayed to our Lord, and he sent them wind enough so that they sailed a great course and the waves rose sorely. Her fellowship was glad and merry, and she was heavy and sorry for dread of the waves. When she looked upon them, she was ever afraid. Our Lord, speaking to her spirit, bade her lay down her head so that she should not see the waves, and she did so. But ever she was afraid, and therefore was she often times blamed.

And so they sailed forth to a place which is called Stralsund.[1] (If the names of the places be not right written, let no man marvel, for she studied more about contemplation than the names of the places, and he who wrote them had never seen them, and therefore have him excused.)

---

8. Wilsnack, in Brandenburg, Germany, contained a pilgrimage site devoted to three hosts, which had miraculously been left whole after the church and the village were burned.
9. In 1433 the uneasy trade relations between England and Prussia made traveling between the two countries difficult.
1. In Pomerania, Germany.

5. When they were come to Stralsund, they took the land, and so the said creature with the foresaid man went toward Wilsnack in great dread and passed many perils. The man who was her guide was ever afraid and would ever have forsaken her company. Many times she spoke as fair to him as she could so that he should not forsake her in those strange countries and in the midst of her enemies, for there was open war between the English and those countries.

Therefore her dread was much the more, and ever in it our Lord spoke to her mind, "Why do you dread? No man shall do any harm to you, nor to any you go with. Therefore comfort your man and tell him no man shall hurt him nor harm him while he is in your company. Daughter, you know well that a woman who has a fair man and a seemly for her husband, if she loves him, she will go with him wherever he will. And, daughter, there is none so fair and so seemly nor so good as I. Therefore, if you love me, you shall not dread to go with me wherever I will have you. Daughter, I brought you hither, and I shall bring you home again into England in safety. Doubt it not, but believe it right well."

Such holy dalliance and speeches in her soul caused her to sob right violently and weep full plenteously. The more she wept, the more irked was her man of her company and the more he busied himself to go from her and leave her alone. He went so fast that she might not follow without great labor and great trouble. He said that he was afraid that enemies and thieves should take her away from him perhaps and beat him and rob him also. She comforted him as well as she could and said she dared undertake that no man should either beat them or rob them nor say any evil word to them.

And soon after their dalliance there came a man out of a wood a tall man with a good weapon and who seemed well arrayed to fight. Then her man, being in great dread, said to her, "Lo, what say you now?"

She said, "Trust in our Lord God and dread no man."

The man came by them and said no evil word to them, so they passed forth toward Wilsnack with great labor. She might not endure such great journeys as the man might, and he had no compassion for her nor would wait for her. And therefore she labored as long as she might till she fell into sickness and might go no farther. It was a great marvel and miracle that a woman unused to going and also about three score years of age should daily endure to keep up her journey and her pace with a man vigorous and eager to go.

On Corpus Christi Eve[2] it happened they came to a little hostel far from any town, and there might they get no bedding but a little straw. And the said creature rested her thereupon that night and the next day till it was again evening. Our Lord sent lightning, thunder, and rain nearly all the time so that they dared not labor outward. She was full glad thereof,

---

2. The Feast of Corpus Christi occurs on the Thursday after Trinity Sunday.

for she was right sick, and she knew well, if it had been fair weather, the man who went with her would not abide for her; he would have gone from her. Therefore she thanked God who gave him the occasion for abiding though it was against his will.

And in the meantime, because of her sickness there was ordered a wagon, and so she was carried forth to the Holy Blood of Wilsnack with great penance and great trouble. The women in the country as they went, having compassion, said many times to the foresaid man that he was worthy of great blame because he labored her so sorely. He, desiring to be delivered of her, cared not what they said nor evermore spared her. Thus what with well and with woe through the help of our Lord she was brought to Wilsnack and saw that Precious Blood which by miracle came out of the blissful sacrament of the altar.

6. They bode not long in the said place, but in a short time they took their way toward Aachen, riding in wagons till they came to a river where there was a great concourse of people, some to Aachen and some to other places, among which was a monk, a full reckless man and evil governed, and in his company were young men, merchants. The monk and the merchants knew well the man who was guide to the said creature and called him by his name, showing him right glad welcome. When they had passed the river and went on the land, the monk with the merchants and the said creature with her man all in fellowship together in wagons, they, having great thirst, came by a house of Friar Minors. They bid then the said creature go into the friars and get them some wine.

She said, "Sirs, you shall have me excused, for if it were a house of nuns, I would readily go, but forasmuch they are men I shall not go by your leave."

So went one of the merchants and fetched them a vessel of wine. Then came friars to them and prayed them that they would come and see the blissful sacrament in their church, for it was within the octave of Corpus Christi,[3] and it stood open in a crystal so that men might see it if they would. The monk and the men went with the friars to see the precious sacrament. The said creature thought she would see it as well as they and followed after, though it was against her will. And, when she beheld the precious sacrament, our Lord gave her so much sweetness and devotion that she wept and sobbed wonder sore and might not restrain herself therefrom. The monk was angry and all her fellowship because she wept so sorely, and, when they were come again to their wagons, they chided her and rebuked her, calling her hypocrite and said many an evil word unto her. She, to excuse herself, laid scripture against them, verses of the

---

3. In other words, within eight days after the Feast of Corpus Christi.

Psalter, "Qui seminant in lacrimis" and cetera "euntes ibant and flebant" and cetera, and such other.[4]

Then were they even angrier, and said that she should no longer go in their company, and caused her man to forsake her. She meekly and benignly prayed them that they would for God's love suffer her to go forth in their company and not leave her alone, where she knew no man nor no man her whether she should go. With great prayer and urgency she went forth with them till they came in the octave of Corpus Christi to a good town. And there they said utterly for no thing should she any longer go with them. He who was her guide and had promised her to have brought her into England forsook her, delivering her gold and such thing as he had of hers in keeping, and offered to have lent her more gold if she had wished.

She said to him, "John, I desired not your gold; I had rather your fellowship in these strange countries than all the good you have, and I believe you should more please God to go with me, as you promised me at Danzig, than if you went to Rome on your feet."

Thus they put her out of their company and let her go where she would.

She said then to him who had been her guide, "John, you forsook me for no other cause but that I weep when I see the sacrament and when I think on our Lord's passion. And, since I am forsaken for God's cause, I believe that God shall provide for me and bring me forth as he would himself, for he deceived me never, blessed may he be."

So they went their way and left her there still. The night fell upon her, and she was right heavy, for she was alone. She knew not with whom she might rest on that night nor with whom she should go the next day. There came priests of that country to her where she was at hostel. They called her English "sterte"[5] and spoke many lewd words unto her, showing unclean manner and countenance, offering to lead her about if she wished. She had much dread for her chastity and was in great heaviness. Then went she to the good wife of the house, praying her to have some of her maidens who might lie with her that night. The good wife assigned two maidens, who were with her all that night, yet dared she not sleep for dread of being defiled. She woke and prayed nearly all that night that she might be preserved from all uncleanness and meet with some good fellowship that might help her forth to Aachen.

Suddenly she was commanded in her soul to go to church early on the next day, and there should she meet with fellowship. On the next day

---

4. The verses are drawn from Psalm 126.5–6: "They that sow in tears shall reap in joy. He that goeth forth and weepeth, bearing precious seed, shall doubtless come again with rejoicing, bringing his sheaves with him."

5. Tail. This is probably a reference to continental slurs against the English, who were described as having tails, though the term (*sterte*) may also be a lewd term for an Englishwoman.

early she paid for her lodging, asking of her hosts if they knew of any fellowship going to Aachen. They said, "No."

She, taking her leave of them, went to the church to feel out and prove if her feelings were true or not. When she came there, she saw a company of poor folk. Then went she to one of them, asking whither they were purposed to go. He said, "To Aachen."

She prayed him that he would suffer her to go in their company. "Why, dame," he said, "have you no man to go with you?"

"No," she said, "my man is gone from me."

So she was received into a company of poor folk, and, when they came to any town, she bought her food, and her fellowship went on begging. When they were outside the towns, her fellowship took off their clothes, and, sitting naked, picked themselves. Need compelled her to abide with them and prolong her journey and be at much more cost than she should else have been. This creature was embarrassed to put off her clothes as her fellows did, and therefore she through her commoning had part of their vermin and was bitten and stung badly both day and night till God sent her other fellowship. She kept their fellowship with great anguish and trouble and much hindrance unto the time that they came to Aachen.

7. When they were come to Aachen, the said creature met with a monk of England, who was going toward Rome. Then was she much comforted, inasmuch as she had a man whom she could understand. And so they abided there together ten or else eleven days to see our Lady's smock and other holy relics which were shown on Saint Margaret's Day.[6] And in the meantime that they abided there it happened that a worshipful woman came from London, a widow with a great household with her, to see and worship the holy relics. The said creature came to this worthy woman, complaining that she had no fellowship to go with her home into England. The worthy woman granted her all her desire, and had her eat and drink with her, and made her right good comfort. When Saint Margaret's Day was come and gone and they had seen the holy relics, the worshipful woman sped herself fast out of Aachen with all her household. The said creature, thinking to have gone with her and thus defrauded of her purpose, was in great heaviness. She took her leave of the monk who was going toward Rome, as is written before, and afterward got herself a wagon with other pilgrims and pursued after the foresaid worthy woman as fast as she might, to see if she could overtake her, but it would not be.

Then it happened that she met with two men of London going toward London. She prayed them to go in their company. They said, if she might endure to go as quickly as they, she should be welcome, but they might not have any great hindrance; nevertheless they would help her forth in her journey with a good will. So she followed after them with great labor till they came to a good town where they met pilgrims of England, come from the court of Rome and who should go home again into England. She prayed them that she might go with them, and they said shortly that they would not hinder their journey for her, for they were robbed and had but little money to bring them home, wherefore they must needs make the sharper journey. And therefore, if she might endure to go as quickly as they, she should be welcome, otherwise, not. She saw no other succor than to abide with them as long as she might, and so left those other two men and abode still with these men. Then they went to their meal and made merry. The said creature looked a little beside her and saw a man lying and resting himself on a bench's end. She inquired what man that was. They said it was a friar, one of their fellowship. "Why eats he not with you?"

"For we were robbed as well as he and therefore each man must help himself as well as he may."

"Well," said she, "he shall have part of such good as God sends me."

She trusted well that our Lord should provide for them both as was needful to them. She had him eat and drink and comforted him right much. Afterward they went all in company together. The said creature came soon behind; she was too aged and too weak to hold foot with them. She ran and leapt as fast as she might till her mights failed. Then she spoke with the poor friar, whom she had comforted before, offering to acquit his costs till he came to Calais, if he would abide with her and let her go with him till they came there, and yet to give him reward besides for his labor. He was well content and consented to her desire. So they let their fellowship go forth, and they two followed softly as they might endure.

The friar, being badly off for thirst, said to the creature, "I know these countries well enough, for I have often times gone thus toward Rome, and I know well there is a place of recreation a little hence: Let us go thither and drink."

She was well pleased and followed him. When they came there, the good wife of the house, having compassion for the creature's labor, counseled that she should take a wagon with other pilgrims and not go so with a man alone. She said that she was purposed and fully trusted to have gone with a worshipful woman of London, and she was deceived. By the time they had rested themselves a while and dallied with the good wife of the house, there came by a wagon with pilgrims. The good wife, having knowledge of the pilgrims in the wagon, when they were passed her house, she called them again, beseeching them that this creature might ride with them in their wagon for the more speed of her journey. They, kindly consenting, received her into their wagon, riding all together till they came to a good town where the said creature perceived the worshipful woman of London of whom is before said.

The she prayed the pilgrims that were in the wagon they should hold her excused and let her pay for the time that she had been with them as they liked, for she would go to a worshipful woman of her nation that she perceived was in the town, with whom she had made agreement when she was at Aachen to go home with her into England. She had good love and leave and parted from them. They rode forth, and she went to the worshipful woman, thinking to have been received with a right glad welcome. And it was even right contrary; she found a right short welcome and had right sharp language, the worshipful woman saying to her, "What think you to go with me? Nay, I do you well to know I will not meddle with you."

The creature was so rebuked that she knew not what to do. She knew no man there, and no man knew her. She knew not whither to go. She knew not where the friar was who should have been her guide, nor whether he should come that way or no. She was in great doubt and heaviness, the greatest, as she thought, that she had suffered since she was come out of England. Nevertheless she trusted in our Lord's promise and abode still in the town till God would send her some comfort. And, when it was near even, she saw the friar coming into the town. She hied her to speak with him, complaining how she was deceived and refused by the good woman that she trusted so much to. The friar said they should do as well as God would give them grace and comforted her within his power, but he said he would not abide in that town that night, for he knew well it was a perilous people. Then went they forth together out of the town again in the evening with great dread and heaviness, mourning by the way where they should have lodging that night. They happened to come under a wood's side, busily beholding if they might spy any place wherein they might rest. And, as our Lord would, they perceived a house or two, and in haste thither they drew where was dwelling a good man with his wife and two children. But kept they no hostel nor would they receive guests to their lodging. The said creature saw a heap of ferns in a house, and with great urgency she purchased grace to rest herself on the ferns that night. The friar with great prayer was laid in a barn, and they thought they were well eased that they had the house over them.

On the next day they made compensation for their lodging, taking the way to Calais, going weary ways and grievous in deep sands, hills, and valleys two days before they came thither, suffering great thirst and great penance, for there were few towns by the way that they went and full feeble lodgings.

And on nights had she most dread often times, and perhaps it was of her ghostly enemy, for she was ever afraid to have been ravished or defiled. She dared trust on no man; whether she had cause or no; she was ever afraid. She dared hardly sleep any night, for she thought men would have defiled her. Therefore she went to bed gladly no night, unless she had a woman or two with her. For that grace God sent her, whereso she

came, for the most part maidens would with good cheer lie by her, and
that was to her great comfort. She was so weary and so overcome with
labor going to Calais that she thought her spirit should have departed
from her body as she went in the way. Thus with great labors she came
to Calais and the good friar with her, who full kindly and honestly had
been governed toward her the time that they went together. And therefore she gave him reward as she was able, so that he was well pleased and
content and departed asunder.

8. In Calais this creature had good welcome of divers persons, both of
men and of women, who had never seen her before. There was a good
woman who had her home to her house, who washed her full cleanly and
had her put on a new smock and comforted her right much. Other good
persons had her to food and to drink.

While she was there abiding shipping three or four days, she met there
with divers persons who had known her before who spoke fairly to her and
gave her kindly language. Other thing they gave her none, the persons
abiding shipping as she did—she, desiring to sail with them to Dover,
naught they would help her nor let her know what ship they purposed to
sail in. She asked and spied as diligently as she could, and ever she had
knowledge of their intent one way or other till she was shipped with them,
and, when she had borne her things into the ship where they were, supposing they should have sailed in haste, she knew not how soon, they provided themselves another ship ready to sail. What the cause was she knew
never. Through grace, she, knowing of their purpose, how ready they
were to sail, left all her things in the vessel that she was in and went to the
ship where they were, and through our Lord's help she was received into
the ship. And there was the worshipful woman of London who had refused her as is before written. And so they sailed all together to Dover.

The said creature, perceiving through their manner and countenance
that they had little affection for her person, prayed to our Lord that he
would grant her grace to hold her head up and preserve her from voiding
of unclean matter in their presence, so that she should cause them no
abomination. Her desire was fulfilled so that, others in the ship voiding
and casting full violently and uncleanly, she, all marveling at her, might
help them and do what she would. And specially the woman of London
had most of that passion and that infirmity, whom this creature was most
busy to help and comfort for our Lord's love and for charity; other cause
had she none.

So they sailed forth till they came to Dover, and then each one of that
company got himself a fellowship to go with if he liked, save she only, for
she might get no fellow for her ease. Therefore she took her way toward
Canterbury by herself alone, sorry and heavy in manner that she had no
fellowship and that she knew not the way. She was up early in the morning and came to a poor man's house, knocking at the door. The good poor

man, hastily dressed in his clothes, unfastened and unbuttoned, came to the door to learn her will. She prayed him, if he had any horse, that he would help her to Canterbury, and she should acquit his labor. He, desiring to do her pleasure in our Lord's name, fulfilled her intent, leading her to Canterbury. She had great joy in our Lord, who sent her help and succor in every need, and thanked him with many a devout tear, with much sobbing and weeping, nearly in every place that she came in, so that all cannot be written, as well on the yon half of the sea as on this half, on the water as on the land, blessed may God be.

9. From thence she went to London, clad in a cloth of canvas, a garment of sack, as she had gone in beyond the sea. When she was come into London, many people knew her well enough. Inasmuch as she was not clad as she would have been, for lack of money, she, desiring to have gone unknown until the time that she might have borrowed money, bore a kerchief before her face. Notwithstanding she did so, some dissolute persons, supposing it was Mar. Kempe of Lynn,[7] said, so that she might easily hear, these words as a reproof: "A, you false flesh, you shall no good meat eat."

She, not answering, passed forth as if she had not heard. The foresaid words were never of her speaking, neither of God nor of good man, though so were they laid to her, and she, many times and in many places, had great reproof thereby.

They were devised by the devil, father of lies, favored, maintained, and born forth by his members, false envious people, having indignation at her virtuous living, not of power to hinder her but through their false tongues. There was never man or woman who ever might prove that she said such words, but ever they made other liars their authors, saying in excusing themselves that other men told them so. In this manner were these false words devised through the devil's suggestion. Some one person or else more persons, deceived by their ghostly enemy, contrived this tale not long after the conversion of the said creature, saying that she, sitting at the meal on a fish day at a good man's table, served with divers fishes such as red herring and good pike and such other, thus she was to have said, as they reported, "A, you false flesh, you would now eat red herring, but you shall not have your will." And therewith she set away the red herring and ate the good pike. And such other thus she was to have said, as they said, and thus it sprang into a manner of proverb against her that some said, "false flesh, you shall eat no herring."[8]

And some said the words which are before written, and all was false, but yet were they not forgotten; they were repeated in many a place where

---

7. Only here does Margery Kempe sign her book, or her life.
8. Red herring is the lesser fish, so choosing to eat it rather than pike would be construed as an act of humility. Margery is thus accused of pretending to avoid an act of public humility by choosing the more delectable of the fish.

she was never known. She went forth to a worshipful widow's house in London, where she was goodly received and had great welcome for our Lord's love, and in many places of London she was highly cherished in our Lord's name, God reward them all. There was one worshipful woman who specially showed her high charity, both in food and in drink and in giving other rewards, in whose place on a time, she was at a meal with other divers persons of divers conditions, she unknown unto them and they unto her, of whom some were of the cardinal's house (as she had by the relation of another); and they had a great feast and fared right well.

And, when they were in their mirths, some repeated the words before written or others like them, that is to say, "You false flesh, you shall not eat of this good meat." She was still and suffered a good while. Each of them gossiped to one another, having great game at the imperfection of the person whom these words were said of. When they had well sported themselves with these words, she asked them if they had any knowledge of the person who was to have said these words. They said, "Nay forsooth, but we have heard told that there is such a false feigned hypocrite in Lynn who says such words, and, leaving off great meats, she eats the most delicious and delectable meats that come on the table."

"Lo, sirs," she said, "you ought to say no worse than you know and yet not so evil as you know. Nevertheless here you say worse than you know, God forgive it you, for I am that same person to whom these words are imputed, who oftentimes suffers great shame and reproof and am not guilty in this matter, God I take to record."

When they beheld her not moved in this matter, reproving them for nothing, desiring through the spirit of charity their correction, they were rebuked by their own honesty, obeying themselves to making satisfaction.

She spoke boldly and mightily whereso she came in London against swearers, cursers, liars and such other vicious people, against the pompous array both of men and of women. She spared them not; she flattered them not, neither for their gifts, nor for their food, nor for their drink. Her speaking profited right much in many persons.

Therefore, when she came into church to her contemplation, our Lord sent her full high devotion, thanking her that she was not afraid to reprove sin in his name and because she suffered scorns and reproofs for his sake, promising her fully much grace in this life and after this life to have joy and bliss without end. She was so comforted in the sweet dalliance of our Lord that she might not measure herself nor govern her spirit after her own will nor after the discretion of other men, but according as our Lord would lead it and measure it himself, in sobbing full violently and weeping full plenteously, wherefore she suffered full much slander and reproof, specially from the curates and priests of the churches in London. They would not suffer her to abide in their churches, and therefore she went from one church to another so that she should not be tedious unto them. Many of the common people magnified God in her, having good trust that it was the goodness of God which wrought that high grace in her soul.

10. From London she went to Shene three days before Lammas Day[9] to purchase her pardon through the mercy of our Lord. And, when she was in the church at Shene, she had great devotion and full high contemplation. She had plenteous tears of compunction and of compassion in the remembrance of the bitter pains and passions which our merciful Lord Jesus Christ suffered in his blessed manhood. Those who saw her weep and heard her so violently sob were taken with great marvel and wonder at what was the occupation of her soul.

A young man who beheld her manner and her countenance, moved through the Holy Ghost, went to her, when he might goodly, by himself alone, with fervent desire to have understanding what might be the cause of her weeping, to whom he said, "Mother, if it pleases you, I pray you to show me the occasion of your weeping, for I have not seen a person so plenteous in tears as you are, and, specially, I have not heard before any person so violent in sobbing as you are. And, mother, though I am young, my desire is to please my Lord Jesus Christ and so to follow him as I can and may. And I purpose me by the grace of God to take the habit of this holy religion, and therefore I pray you be not strange unto me. Show motherly and kindly your conceit unto me as I trust in you."

She, benignly and meekly with gladness of spirit, as she thought it expedient, commended him in his intent and showed to him in part that the cause of her weeping and sobbing was her great unkindness[1] against her maker, wherethrough she had many times offended his goodness, and the great abomination that she had for her sins caused her to sob and weep. Also the great excellent charity of her redeemer, by which, through the virtue of his passion suffering and his precious blood shedding, she was redeemed from everlasting pain, trusting to be an heir of joy and bliss, moved her to sob and weep, as was no marvel. She told him many good words of ghostly comfort, through which he was stirred to great virtue, and afterward he ate and drank with her in the time that she was there and was full glad to be in her company.

On Lammas Day was the principal day of pardon, and, as the said creature went into the church at Shene, she had a sight of the hermit who led her out of Lynn when she went toward the sea with her daughter-in-law,

9. Lammas Day, August 1, is the date of the Feast of St. Peter in Chains (celebrating his deliverance from chains), the day on which quarter rents were collected, and a day associated with harvest thankfulness. The pope had also set the day aside for special pardons for those who honored St. Bridget by visiting her sites. Shene (later named Richmond) was the location for a Carthusian monastery founded by Henry V in 1415 and for a Briggitine House called Mount Sion. Sion was later moved a little lower down the Thames; it is to this house, incomplete at the time of her visit, that Margery comes. Margery's devotion to St. Bridget makes it a natural destination for her before she returns home to King's Lynn.
1. The word used here is *unkendnes*, meaning both unkind and unnatural.

as is written before. Anon, with great joy of spirit she offered herself to his presence, welcoming him with all the mights of her soul, saying unto him, "A, Reynald, you are welcome. I trust our Lord sent you hither, for now I hope, as you led me out of Lynn, you shall bring me home again to Lynn."

The hermit showed short welcome and heavy countenance, neither in will nor in purpose to bring her home to Lynn as she desired. He, answering full shortly, said, "I do you well to let you know your confessor has forsaken you because you went over the sea and would tell him no word thereof. You took leave to bring your daughter to the seaside; you asked no leave for any farther. There was no friend you had who knew of your counsel; therefore I suppose you shall find but little friendship when you come there. I pray you, get you fellowship where you can, for I was blamed for your default when I led you last; I will no more."

She spoke fair and prayed, for God's love, that he would not be displeased, for those who loved her for God before she went out, they would love her for God when she came home. She offered to acquit his costs by the way homeward. So at the last he, consenting, brought her again to London and afterward home to Lynn, to the high worship of God and to the great merit of both of their souls. When she was come home to Lynn, she obeyed herself to her confessor. He gave her full sharp words, for she was his obediencer[2] and had taken upon herself such a journey without his knowing. Therefore he was moved the more against her, but our Lord helped her so that she had as good love of him and of other friends afterward as she had before, worshipped be God. Amen.[3]

• • •

This creature, of whom is treated before, used for many years to begin her prayers in this manner. First when she came to church, kneeling before the sacrament in the worship of the blessed Trinity (Father, Son, and Holy Ghost, one God and three Persons), of that glorious Virgin, Queen of Mercy, our Lady Saint Mary, and of the twelve apostles, she said this holy hymn "Veni creator spiritus"[4] with all the verses belonging thereto, so that God should illumine her soul, as he did his apostles on Pentecost Day,[5] and endue her with the gifts of the Holy Ghost so that she might have grace to understand his will and perform it in working, and so that she might have grace to withstand the temptations of her ghostly enemies and eschew all manner of sin and wickedness.

2. Margery had vowed obedience to her confessor. The word could also be used to denote someone who had vowed obedience to a rule or office.
3. The second book of the *Book* ends only nine lines into a leaf. The remainder of the leaf is left blank. On the opposite side of the leaf begin the prayers. Therefore, the *Book* is set up as being composed of three distinct parts.
4. The hymn sung on the Feast of Pentecost, "Come Holy Spirit."
5. Pentecost is the seventh Sunday after Easter and celebrates the descent of the Holy Ghost.

When she had said "Veni creator spiritus" with the verses, she said in this manner, "The Holy Ghost I take to witness, our Lady, Saint Mary, the mother of God, all the holy court of heaven, and all my ghostly fathers here on earth, that, though it were possible that I might have all knowing and understanding of the secrets of God through the telling of any devil of hell, I would not. And as surely that I should not know, hear, see, feel, or understand in my soul in this life more than is the will of God that I should know, so surely God may help me in all my works, in all my thoughts, and in all my speeches, eating and drinking, sleeping and waking.

"As surely as it is not my will nor my intent to worship any false devil for my God, nor any false faith, nor have any false belief, so surely I defy the devil, and all his false counsel, and all that ever I have done, said, or thought, after the counsel of the devil, thinking it had been the counsel of God and inspiration of the Holy Ghost. If it has not been so, God, who is the in-seer and knower of the secrets of all men's hearts, have mercy on me therefore and grant me in this life a well of tears springing plenteously, with which I may wash away my sins through your mercy and your goodness.

"And, Lord, for your high mercy, all the tears that may increase my love for you and increase my merit in heaven, help and profit my fellow Christian souls, alive or dead, visit me with here on earth. Good Lord, spare no more the eyes in my head than you did the blood in your body which you shed plenteously for sinful man's soul, and grant me so much pain and sorrow in this world that I be not hindered from your bliss and from the beholding of your glorious face when I shall pass hence.

"As for my crying, my sobbing, and my weeping, Lord God almighty, as surely as you know what scorns, what shames, what despites, and what reproofs I have had for it, and, as surely as it is not in my power to weep either loud or still for any devotion nor for any sweetness but only through the gift of the Holy Ghost, so surely, Lord, excuse me before all this world, so that it knows and believes that it is your work and your gift for the magnifying of your name and for the increasing of other men's love for you, Jesus. And I pray you, sovereign Lord Christ Jesus, that as many men may be turned by my crying and my weeping as have scorned me for it or shall scorn me unto the world's end, and many more if it be your will. And, as regards any earthly man's love, as surely as I would no love have but God to love above all thing and all other creatures to love for God and in God, all so surely quench in me all fleshly lust and in all those in whom I have beheld your blissful body.

"And give us your holy dread in our hearts for your wounds' smart.[6] Lord, make my ghostly fathers dread you in me and love you in me, and make all the world have more sorrow for their own sins because of the sor-

---

6. This sentence echoes the devotional couplet that is repeated twice in the *Book*; see chapters 65 (p. 118) and 88 (p. 158).

row that you have given me for other men's sins. Good Jesus, make my will your will and your will my will so that I may no will have but your will only.

"Now, good Lord Christ Jesus, I cry you mercy for all the estates that are in Holy Church, for the Pope and all his cardinals, for all archbishops and bishops, and for all the order of priesthood, for all men and women of religion, and specially for those who are busy to save and defend the faith of Holy Church. Lord, for your mercy bless them and grant them the victory of all their enemies and speed them in all that they go about to your worship; for all who are in grace at this time God send them perseverance unto their lives' end. And make me worthy to share in their prayers and they mine and each of us of the others'.

"I cry you mercy, blissful Lord, for the King of England and for all Christian kings and for all lords and ladies who are in this world. God, set them in such governance so they may most please you and be lords and ladies in heaven without end. I cry you mercy, Lord, for the rich men in this world who have your goods in their wielding; give them grace to spend them to your pleasing. I cry you mercy, Lord, for Jews, and Saracens, and all heathen people. Good Lord, have mind that there is many a saint in heaven who sometime was a heathen on earth and that you have spread your mercy to those who are on earth.

"Lord, you say yourself there shall no man come to you without you, nor any man be drawn unless you draw him. And therefore, Lord, if there be any man undrawn, I pray you draw him after you. Me have you drawn, Lord, and I deserved never to be drawn, but after your great mercy you have drawn me. If all this world knew all my wickedness as you do, they would marvel and wonder at the great goodness that you have showed me. I would that all this world were worthy to thank you for me, and, as you have made of unworthy creatures worthy, so make all this world worthy to thank you and praise you.

"I cry you mercy, Lord, for all false heretics and for all misbelievers, for all false tithers, thieves, adulterers and all common women, and for all mischievous livers. Lord, for your mercy have mercy upon them, if it be your will, and bring them out of their misgovernance the sooner for my prayers. I cry you mercy, Lord, for all those who are tempted and vexed with their ghostly enemies, that you of your mercy give them grace to withstand their temptations and deliver them thereof when it is your greatest pleasure.

"I cry you mercy, Lord, for all my ghostly fathers, that you vouchsafe to spread as much grace in their souls as I would that you did in mine. I cry you mercy, Lord, for all my children, ghostly and bodily, and for all the people in this world, that you make their sins to me by very contrition as they were my own sins, and forgive them, as I would that you forgive me. I cry you mercy, Lord, for all my friends and for all my enemies, for all who are sick, specially for all lepers, for all bedridden men and women, for all who are in prison, and for all creatures who in this world have spoken of me either good or ill, or shall do unto the world's end. Have mercy upon them and be as gracious to their souls as I would that you were to mine.

"And those who have said any evil of me, for your high mercy, forgive it them; and those who have said well, I pray you, Lord, reward them, for that is through their charity and not through my merits, for, though you suffered all this world to avenge you on me and to hate me because I have displeased you, you did me no wrong.

"I cry you mercy, Lord, for all the souls that are in pains of purgatory, there abiding your mercy and the prayers of Holy Church as surely, Lord, as they are your own chosen souls. Be as gracious to them as I would that you were to mine if it were in the same pain that they are in.

"Lord Christ Jesus, I thank you for all health and all wealth, for all riches and all poverty, for sickness and all scorns, for all spites and all wrongs, and for all divers tribulations that have befallen or shall befall to me as long as I live. Highly I thank you that you would let me suffer anything in this world in remission of my sins, and for the increase of my merit in heaven as surely I have great cause to thank you. Hear my prayers, for, though I had as many hearts and souls closed in my soul as God knew without beginning how many should dwell in heaven without end, and as there are drops of water, fresh and salt, pebbles of gravel, stones small and great, grasses growing in all the earth, kernels of grain, fishes, fowls, beasts and leaves upon trees when there is greatest plenty, feathers of fowls or hair of beasts, seeds that grow in herb, or in weed, in flower, on land, or in water when most grow, and as many creatures as on earth have been and are or shall be and might be by your might, and as there are stars and angels in your sight or other kinds of good that grow upon earth, and each were a soul as holy as ever was our lady Saint Mary who bore Jesus our Savior, and, if it were possible that each could think and speak as great reverence and worship as ever did our lady Saint Mary here on earth and now does in heaven and shall do without end, I may right well think in my heart and speak it with my mouth at this time in worship of the Trinity and of all the court of heaven, to the great shame and disgrace of Satan that fell from God's face and of all his wicked spirits, that all these hearts and souls could never thank God nor fully praise him, fully bless him nor fully worship him, fully love him nor fully give laudation, praising, and reverence to him as he were worthy to have for the great mercy that he has showed to me on earth, that I cannot do nor may do.

"I pray my Lady, who is the only mother of God, the well of grace, flower and fairest of all women that ever God wrought on earth, the most worthy in his sight; the most dear, precious, and dearly esteemed, most worthy to be heard of God, and the highest that has deserved it in this life, benign lady, meek lady, charitable lady, with all the reverence that is in heaven and with all your holy saints, I pray you, Lady, offer thanks and praisings to the blissful Trinity for love of me, asking mercy and grace for me and for all my ghostly fathers and perseverance unto our lives' end in that life one may most please God in.

"I bless my God in my soul and you all that are in heaven. Blessed may God be in you all and you all in God. Blessed be you, Lord, for all your mercies that you have showed to all that are in heaven and in earth. And specially I bless you, Lord, for Mary Magdalene, for Mary of Egypt, for Saint Paul, and for Saint Augustine.[7] And, as you have there shown mercy to them, so show your mercy to me and to all that ask you mercy of heart. The peace and the rest that you have bequeathed to your disciples and to your lovers, the same peace and rest may you bequeath to me on earth and in heaven without end.

"Have mind, Lord, of the woman who was taken in adultery[8] and brought before you, and, as you drove away all her enemies from her and she stood alone by you, so verily may you drive away all my enemies from me, both bodily and ghostly, so that I may stand alone by you and make my soul dead to all the joys of this world and quick and greedy to high contemplation in God.

"Have mind, Lord, of Lazarus,[9] who lay four days dead in his grave, and, as I have been in that holy place where your body was quick and dead and crucified for man's sin and where Lazarus was raised from death to life, as surely, Lord, if any man or woman be dead in this hour by deadly sin, if any prayer may help them, hear my prayers for them and make them to live without end.

"Grant mercy, Lord, for all those sins that you have kept me from which I have not done, and grant mercy, Lord, for all the sorrow that you have given me for those that I have done, for these graces and for all other graces which are needful to me and to all the creatures in earth. And for all those that believe and trust or shall believe and trust in my prayers into the world's end, such grace as they desire, ghostly or bodily, to the profit of their souls, I pray you, Lord, grant them for the multitude of your mercy. Amen."

Jhesu mercy quod Salthows.[1]

---

7. St. Augustine of Hippo. St. Mary of Egypt was the third-century prostitute who, in grief for her sins, lived forty years as a desert saint.
8. See John 8.
9. Lazarus was the brother of Martha and Mary; Jesus raised him from the dead. See John 11.1–44.
1. The thanksgiving of Salthows, the man who copied the manuscript probably in the mid-fifteenth century, is centered and written on the bottom of the last leaf.

CONTEXTS

From The Constitutions of Thomas Arundel[†]

[Thomas Arundel, archbishop of Canterbury, published his *Constitutions* in 1409. They were especially formulated to establish the terms of religious orthodoxy and thus to combat the threat posed by heretical views of scripture, worship, and belief. The *Constitutions* retained their importance during the sixteenth century, when they were cited to describe the difficulties of pre-Reformation England. This translation of the *Constitutions* is by John Foxe (1516–1587), whose *Acts and Monuments* (1563) came to define the reformed English nation.]

Thomas, by the permission of God, archbishop of Canterbury, primate of all England, and legate of the see apostolic: to all and singular our reverend brethren, fellow bishops, and our suffragans; and to abbots, priors, deans of cathedral churches, archdeacons, provosts and canons; also to all parsons, vicars, chaplains, and clerks in parish churches, and to all laymen, whom and wheresoever dwelling within our province of Canterbury, greeting, and grace to stand firmly in the doctrine of the holy mother church. *Thirteen articles.*

It is a manifest and plain case, that he doth wrong and injury to the most reverend council, who so revolteth from the things being in the said council once discussed and decided; and whosoever dareth presume to dispute of the supreme or principal judgment here in earth, in so doing incurreth the pain of sacrilege, according to the authority of civil wisdom and manifold tradition of human law. Much more then, they, who, trusting to their own wits are so bold to violate, and with contrary doctrine to resist, and in word and deed to contemn, the precepts of laws and canons rightly made and proceeding from the keybearer and porter of eternal life and death, bearing the room and person not of pure man, but of true God here in earth; which also have been observed hitherto by the holy fathers, our predecessors, unto the glorious effusion of their blood, and voluntary sprinkling out of their brains, are worthy of greater punishment, deserving quickly to be cut off, as rotten members, from the body of the church militant. For such ought to consider what is in the Old Testament written, 'Moses and Aaron among his priests,' that is, were chief heads amongst them; and in the New Testament, among the apostles there was a certain difference: and though they were all apostles, yet was it granted of the Lord to Peter, that he should bear pre-eminence above the other apostles; and also the apostles themselves would the same, that he should be the chieftain over all the rest; and being called Cephas, that is, Head, should be as a prince over the apostles, unto whom it was said, 'Thou being once converted, confirm thy brethren.' As though he would say,

† From *The Acts and Monuments of John Foxe*, ed. George Townsend (1843–49); NY: AMS Press, 1965) 3: 242–48. Courtesy of AMS Press.

If there happen any doubt among them, or if any of them chance to err and stray out of the way of faith, of just living, or right conversation, do thou confirm and reduce him into the right way again, which thing, no doubt, the Lord would never have said unto him, if he had not so minded, that the rest should be obedient unto him. And yet, all this notwithstanding, we know and daily prove what we are sorry to speak, how the old sophister, the enemy of mankind (foreseeing and fearing lest the sound doctrine of the church, determined from ancient times by the holy forefathers, should withstand his malice, if it might keep the people of God in unity of faith under one head of the church), doth therefore endeavour, by all means possible, to extirpate the said doctrine, feigning vices to be virtues. And so, under false pretences of verity dissimuled, he soweth discord among catholic people, to the intent that some going one way, some another, he, in the mean time, may gather to himself a church of the malignant, differing wickedly from the universal mother, holy church: in which, Satan, transforming himself into an angel of light, bearing a lying and deceitful balance in his hand, pretendeth great righteousness, in contrarying the ancient doctrine of the holy mother church, and refusing the traditions of the same, determined and appointed by holy fathers; persuading men, by feigned forgeries, the same to be nought, and so inducing other new kinds of doctrine, leading to more goodness, as he by his lying persuasions pretendeth, although he in very truth neither willeth nor mindeth any goodness, but rather that he may sow schisms, whereby divers opinions, and contrary to themselves, being raised in the church, faith thereby may be diminished, and also the reverend holy mysteries, through the same contention of words, may be profaned by Pagans, Jews, and other infidels, and wicked miscreants. And so that figure in the Apocalypse, chap. vi. is well verified, speaking of him that sat on the black horse, bearing a pair of balances in his hand; by which heretics are understood, who, at the first appearance, like to weights or a balance, make as though they would set forth right and just things, to allure the hearts of the hearers; but afterwards appeareth the black horse, that is to say, their intention, full of cursed speaking. For they, under a diverse show and colour of a just balance, with the tail of a black horse sprinkling abroad heresies and errors, do strike; and, being poisoned themselves, under colour of good, raise up infinite slanders, and, by certain persons fit to do mischief, do publish abroad, as it were, the sugared taste of honey mixed with poison, thereby the sooner to be taken: working and causing, through their sleight and subtleties, that error should be taken for verity, wickedness for holiness and for the true will of Christ. Yea, and moreover, the foresaid persons thus picked out, do preach before they be sent, and presume to sow the seed, before the seed discreetly be separate from the chaff; who, not pondering the constitutions and decrees of the canons pro-

vided for the same purpose against such pestilent sowers, do prefer sacrifice diabolical (so to term it), before obedience to be given to the
holy church militant.

We, therefore, considering and weighing that error which is not resisted seemeth to be allowed, and that he openeth his bosom too wide,
who resisteth not the viper, thinking there to thrust out her venom; and
willing, moreover, to shake off the dust from our feet, and to see to the
honour of our holy mother church, whereby one uniform holy doctrine
may be sown and planted in the church of God, namely, in this our
province of Canterbury, so much as in us doth lie, to the increase of faith
and service of God, first rooting out the evil weeds and offendicles which,
by the means of perverse preaching and doctrine, have sprung up hitherto, and are likely more hereafter to grow; purposing by some convenient
way, with all diligence possible, to withstand them in time, and to provide for the peril of souls which we see to rise under pretence of the
premises; also, to remove all such obstacles, by which the said our purpose may be stopped, by the advice and assent of all our suffragans and
other prelates, being present in this our convocation of the clergy, as also
of the procurators of them that be absent, and at the instant petition of
the procurators of the whole clergy within this our province of Canterbury, for the more fortification of the common law in this part; adding
thereunto punishment and penalties condign, as be hereunder written.

We will and command, ordain and decree: That no manner of person, The first
secular or regular, being authorized to preach by the laws now prescribed, constitu-
or licensed by special privilege, shall take upon him the office of preach- tion.
ing the word of God, or by any means preach unto the clergy or laity,
whether within the church or without, in English, except he first present
himself, and be examined by the ordinary of the place, where he preacheth: and so being found a fit person, as well in manners as knowledge,
he shall be sent by the said ordinary to some one church or more, as shall
be thought expedient by the said ordinary, according to the quality of the
person. Nor any person aforesaid shall presume to preach, except first he
give faithful signification, in due form, of his sending and authority; that
is, that he that is authorized, do come in form appointed him in that behalf, and that those that affirm they come by special privilege, do show
their privilege unto the parson or vicar of the place where they preach.
And those that pretend themselves to be sent by the ordinary of the place,
shall likewise show the ordinary's letters made unto him for that purpose,
under his great seal. Let us always understand, the curate (having the per-
petuity) to be sent of right unto the people of his own cure: but if any person aforesaid shall be forbidden by the ordinary of the place, or any other
superior, to preach, by reason of his errors or heresies which before, per-
adventure, he hath preached and taught; that then, and from thenceforth, he abstain from preaching within our province, until he have
purged himself, and be lawfully admitted again to preach by the just ar-

bitrement of him that suspended and forbade him; and shall always, after that, carry with him, to all places wheresover he shall preach, the letters testimonial of him that restored him.

Moreover the parish priests or vicars temporal, not having perpetuities, nor being sent in form aforesaid, shall simply preach in the churches where they have charge, only those things which are expressly contained in the provincial constitution set forth by John, our predecessor, of good memory, to help the ignorance of the priests, which beginneth, 'Ignorantia Sacerdotum;' which book of constitutions we would should be had in every parish church in our province of Canterbury, within three months next after the publication of these presents, and (as therein is required) that it be effectually declared by the priests themselves yearly, and at the times appointed. And, lest this wholesome statute might be thought hurtful to some, by reason of payment of money, or some other difficulty, we therefore will and ordain, that the examinations of the persons aforesaid, and the making of their letters by the ordinary, be done gratis and freely, without any exaction of money at all by those to whom it shall appertain. And if any man shall willingly presume to violate this our statute grounded upon the old law, after the publication of the same, he shall incur the sentence of greater excommunication, 'ipso facto:' whose absolution we specially reserve, by tenor of these presents, to us and our successors. But, if any such preacher, despising this wholesome statute, and not weighing the sentence of greater excommunication, do, the second time, take upon him to preach, saying and alleging, and stoutly affirming, that the sentence of greater excommunication aforesaid cannot be appointed by the church in the persons of the prelates of the same, that then the superiors of the place do worthily rebuke him, and forbid him from the communion of all faithful Christians.

And that the said person hereupon lawfully convicted (except he recant and abjure after the manner of the church) be pronounced a heretic by the ordinary of the place. And that from thenceforth he be reputed and taken for a heretic and schismatic, and that he incur 'ipso facto' the penalties of heresy and schismacy, expressed in the law; and, chiefly, that his goods be adjudged confiscate by the law, and apprehended, and kept by them to whom it shall appertain. And that his fautors, receivers, and defenders, being convicted, in all cases be likewise punished, if they cease not off within one month, being lawfully warned thereof by their superiors.

The second constitution.
Furthermore, no clergyman, or parochians[1] of any parish or place within our province of Canterbury, shall admit any man to preach within their churches, church-yards, or other places whatsoever, except first there be manifest knowledge had of his authority, privilege, or sending thither, according to the order aforesaid: otherwise the church, church-yard, or what place soever, in which it was so preached, shall 'ipso facto'

---

1. Parishioners, laymen.

receive the ecclesiastical interdict, and so shall remain interdicted, until A.D.
they that so admitted and suffered him to preach, have reformed them- 1409.
selves, and obtained the place so interdicted to be released in due form
of law, either from the ordinary of the place, or else his superior.

Moreover, like as a good householder casteth wheat into the ground, The third
well ordered for that purpose, thereby to get the more increase, even constitu-
so we will and command, that the preacher of God's word, coming in tion.
form aforesaid, preaching either unto the clergy or laity, according to
his matter proposed, shall be of good behaviour, sowing such seed as
shall be convenient for his auditory: and chiefly preaching to the clergy, he shall touch the vices, commonly used amongst them; and to the
laity, he shall declare the vices commonly used amongst them; and not
otherwise. But if he preach contrary to this order, then shall he be
sharply punished by the ordinary of that place, according to the quality of that offence.

Item, Forasmuch as the part is vile, that agreeth not with the whole, The fourth
we do decree and ordain, that no preacher aforesaid, or any other per- constitu-
son whatsoever, shall otherwise teach or preach concerning the sacra tion.
ment of the altar, matrimony, confession of sins, or any other sacrament of the church, or article of the faith, than what already is discussed by the holy mother church; nor shall bring any thing in doubt
that is determined by the church, nor shall, to his knowledge, privily
or apertly pronounce blasphemous words concerning the same; nor
shall teach, preach, or observe any sect, or kind of heresy whatsoever,
contrary to the wholesome doctrine of the church. He that shall wittingly and obstinately attempt the contrary after the publication of
these presents, shal incur the sentence of excommunication 'ipso
facto:' from which, except in point of death, he shall not be absolved,
until he have reformed himself by abjuration of his heresy, at the discretion of the ordinary in whose territory he so offended, and have
received wholesome penitence for his offences. But if the second time
he shall so offend, being lawfully convicted, he shall be pronounced a
heretic, and his goods shall be confiscated, and apprehended, and kept
by them to whom it shall appertain. The penance before-mentioned,
shall be after this manner: if any man, contrary to the determination
of the church, that is, in the decrees, decretals, or our constitutions
provincial, do openly or privily teach or preach any kind of heresy or
sect, he shall, in the parish church of the same place where he so
preached, upon one Sunday or other solemn day, or more, at the discretion of the ordinary, and as his offence is more or less, expressly
revoke what he so preached, taught, or affirmed, even at the time of
the solemnity of the mass, when the people are most assembled; and
there shall he effectually, and without fraud, preach and teach the very
truth determined by the church; and, further, shall be punished after

A.D.
1409.

the quality of his offence, as shall be thought expedient, at the discretion of the ordinary.

The fifth constitution.

Item, Forasmuch as a new vessel, being long used, savoureth after the head, we decree and ordain, that no schoolmasters and teachers whatsoever, that instruct children in grammar, or others whosoever, in primitive sciences, shall, in teaching them, intermingle any thing concerning the catholic faith, the sacrament of the altar, or other sacraments of the church, contrary to the determination of the church; nor shall suffer their scholars to expound the holy Scriptures (except the text, as hath been used in ancient time); nor shall permit them to dispute openly or privily concerning the catholic faith, or sacraments of the church. Contrariwise, the offender herein shall be grievously punished by the ordinary of the place, as a favourer of errors and schisms.

The sixth constitution.

Item, For that a new way doth more frequently lead astray, than an old way, we will and command, that no book or treatise made by John Wickliff, or others whomsoever, about that time, or since, or hereafter to be made, be from henceforth read in schools, halls, hospitals, or other places whatsoever, within our province of Canterbury aforesaid, except the same be first examined by the university of Oxford or Cambridge; or, at least, by twelve persons, whom the said universities, or one of them, shall appoint to be chosen at our discretion, or the laudable discretion of our successors; and the same being examined as aforesaid, to be expressly approved and allowed by us or our successors, and in the name and authority of the university, to be delivered unto the stationers to be copied out, and the same to be sold at a reasonable price, the original thereof always after to remain in some chest of the university. But if any man shall read any such kind of book in schools or otherwise, as aforesaid, he shall be punished as a sower of schism, and a favourer of heresy, as the quality of the fault shall require.

The seventh constitution.

Item, It is a dangerous thing, as witnesseth blessed St. Jerome, to translate the text of the holy Scripture out of the tongue into another; for in the translation the same sense is not always easily kept, as the same St. Jerome confesseth, that although he were inspired, yet oftentimes in this he erred: we therefore decree and ordain, that no man, hereafter, by his own authority translate any text of the Scripture into English or any other tongue, by way of a book, libel, or treatise; and that no man read any such book, libel or treatise, now lately set forth in the time of John Wickliff, or since, or hereafter to be set forth, in part or in whole, privily or apertly, upon pain of greater excommunication, until the said translation be allowed by the ordinary of the place, or, if the case so require, by the council provincial. He that shall do contrary to this, shall likewise be punished as a favourer of error and heresy.

The eighth constitution.

Item, For that Almighty God cannot be expressed by any philosophical terms, or otherwise invented of man: and St. Augustine saith, that he hath oftentimes revoked such conclusions as have been most true, because

they have been offensive to the ears of the religious; we do ordain and spe- A.D.
cially forbid, that any manner of person, of what state, degree, or condi- 1409.
tion soever he be, do allege or propone any conclusions or propositions in
the catholic faith, or repugnant to good manners (except necessary doctrine pertaining to their faculty of teaching or disputing in their schools or
otherwise), although they defend the same with ever such curious terms
and words. For, as saith blessed St. Hugh of the sacraments, 'That which
oftentimes is well spoken, is not well understood.' If any man, therefore,
after the publication of these presents, shall be convicted wittingly to have
proponed such conclusions or propositions, except (being monished)he
reform himself in one month, by virtue of this present constitution, he
shall incur the sentence of greater excommunication 'ipso facto,' and
shall be openly pronounced an excommunicate, until he hath confessed
his fault openly in the same place where he offended, and hath preached
the true meaning of the said conclusion or proposition in one church or
more, as shall be thought expedient to the ordinary.

Item, No manner of person shall presume to dispute upon the articles The ninth
determined by the church, that are contained in the decrees, decretals, constitu-
or constitutions provincial, or in the general councils; but only to seek out tion.
the true meaning thereof, and that expressly, whether it be openly or in
secret; and none shall call in doubt the authority of the said decretals or
constitutions, or the authority of him that made them; or teach any thing
contrary to the determination thereof: and, chiefly, concerning the adoration of the holy cross, the worshipping of images, of saints, going on pril-
grimage to certain places, or to the relics of saints, or against the oaths, in
cases accustomed to be given in both common places, that is to say, spiritual and temporal. But by all it shall be commonly taught and preached,
that the cross and image of the crucifix, and other images of saints, in honour of them whom they represent, are to be worshipped with procession,
bowing of knees, offering of frankincense, kissings, oblations, lighting of
candles, and pilgrimages, and with all other kind of ceremonies and manners that have been used in the time of our predecessors; and that giving
of oaths in cases expressed in the law, and used of all men to whom it be-
longeth, in both common places, ought to be done upon the book of the
gospel of Christ. Contrary unto this whosoever doth preach, teach, or obstinately affirm, except he recant in manner and form aforesaid, shall
forthwith incur the penalty of heresy, and shall be pronounced a heretic,
in all effect of law.

Item, We do decree and ordain, that no chaplain be admitted to cele- The tenth
brate in any diocese within our province of Canterbury, where he was not constitu-
born, or received not orders; except he bring with him his letters of or- tion.
ders, and letters commendatory from his ordinary, and also from other
bishops in whose diocese of a long time he hath been conversant,
whereby his conversation and manners may appear; so that it may be
known, whether he hath been defamed with any new opinions touching

the catholic faith, or whether he be free from the same: otherwise, as well he that celebrateth, as he that suffereth him to celebrate, shall be sharply punished at the discretion of the ordinary.

Finally, Because those things which newly and unaccustomably creep up, stand in need of new and speedy help, and where more danger is, there ought to be more wary circumspection and stronger resistance; and not without good cause, the less noble ought discreetly to be cut away, that the more noble may the more perfectly be nourished: considering, therefore, and in lamentable wise showing unto you, how the ancient university of Oxford, which as a fruitful vine was wont to extend forth her fruitful branches to the honour of God, the great perfection and defence of the church, now partly being become wild, bringeth forth bitter grapes, which being indiscreetly eaten of ancient fathers, that thought themselves skilful in the law of God, hath set on edge the teeth of their children: and our province being infected with divers and unfruitful doctrines, and defiled with a new and damnable name of Lollardy, to the great reproof and offence of the said university, being known in foreign countries, and to the great irksomeness of the students there, and to the great damage and loss of the church of England, which in times past by her virtue, as with a strong wall, was wont to be defended, and now is like to run into ruin not to be recovered: at the supplication, therefore, of the whole clergy of our province of Canterbury, and by the consent and assent of all our brethren and suffragans, and other the prelates in this convocation assembled, and the proctors of them that are absent, lest the river being cleansed, the fountain should remain corrupt, and so the water coming from thence should not be pure, intending most wholesomely to provide for the honour and utility of our holy mother the church and the university aforesaid: we do ordain and decree, that every warden, provost, or master of every college, or principal of every hall within the university aforesaid, shall, once every month at the least, diligently inquire in the said college, hall, or other place where he hath authority, whether any scholar or inhabitant of such college or hall, etc. have holden, alleged, or defended, or by any means proponed, any conclusion, proposition, or opinion, concerning the catholic faith, or sounding contrary to good manners, or contrary to the determination of the church, otherwise than appertaineth to necessary doctrine; and if he shall find any suspected or defamed herein, he shall, according to his office, admonish him to desist. And if, after such monition given, the said party offend again in the same or such like, he shall incur 'ipso facto' (besides the penalties aforesaid) the sentence of greater excommunication. And nevertheless, if it be a scholar that so offendeth the second time, whatsoever he shall afterwards do in the said university shall not stand in effect. And if he be a doctor, a master, or bachelor, he shall forthwith be suspended from every scholar's act, and in both cases shall lose the

right that he hath in the said college or hall, whereof he is, 'ipso facto;' A.D.
and by the warden, provost, master, principal, or other to whom it 1409.
appertaineth, he shall be expelled, and a catholic, by lawful means,
forthwith placed in his place. And if the said wardens, provosts, or masters of colleges, or principals of halls, shall be negligent concerning the
inquisition and execution of such persons suspected and defamed, by
the space of ten days from the time of the true or supposed knowledge
of the publication of these presents, that then they shall incur the sentence of greater excommunication, and nevertheless shall be deprived
'ipso facto' of all the right which they pretend to have in the colleges,
halls, etc., and the said colleges and halls, to be effectually vacant: and
after lawful declaration hereof made by them to whom it shall appertain, new wardens, provosts, masters, or principals, shall be placed in
their places, as hath been accustomed in colleges and halls being
vacant in the said university. But if the wardens themselves, provosts,
masters, or principals aforesaid, be suspected and defamed of and concerning the said conclusions or propositions, or be favourers and
defenders of such as do therein offend, and do not cease, being there
of warned by us, or by our authority, or by the ordinary of the place:
that then by law they be deprived, as well of all privilege scholastical,
within the university aforesaid, as also of their right and authority in
such college, hall, etc., besides other penalties beforementioned, and
that they incur the said sentence of greater excommunication.

But if any man, in any case of this present constitution, or any above The
expressed, do rashly and wilfully presume to violate there our statutes in twelfth
any part thereof, although there be another penalty expressly there lim- constitu-
ited, yet shall he be made altogether unable and unworthy by the space tion.
of three years after, without hope of pardon, to obtain any ecclesiastical
benefice within our province of Canterbury: and nevertheless, according
to all his demerits and the quality of his excess, at the discretion of his superior, he shall be lawfully punished.

And further, that the manner of proceeding herein be not thought The thir-
uncertain, considering with ourselves, that although there be a kind of teenth
equality in the crimes of heresy and offending the prince, as is constitu-
avouched in divers laws, yet the fault is much unlike, and that to offend tion.
the divine Majesty requireth greater punishment than to offend the
prince's majesty: and where it is sufficient, for fear of danger that might
ensue by delays, to convince by judgment the offender of the prince's
majesty, proceeding against him fully and wholly, with a citation sent
by messenger, by letters, or edict not admitting proof by witnesses, and
sentence definitive to be: we do ordain, will, and declare, for the easier punishment of the offenders in the premises, and for the better
reformation of the church divided and hurt, that all such as are
defamed, openly known, or vehemently suspected, in any of the cases
aforesaid, or, in article of the catholic faith, sounding contrary to good

A.D.
1409.
manners, by the authority of the ordinary of the place or other superior, be cited personally to appear, either by letters, public messenger being sworn, or by edict openly set at that place where the said offender commonly remaineth, or in his parish church, if he have any certain dwelling house; otherwise, in the cathedral church of the place where he was born, and in the parish church of the same place where he so preached and taught: and afterwards, certificate being given that the citation was formerly executed against the party cited being absent and neglecting his appearance, it shall be proceeded against him fully and plainly, without sound or show of judgment, and without admitting proof by witnesses and other canonical probations. And also, after lawful information had, the said ordinary (all delays (set apart) shall signify, declare, and punish the said offender, according to the quality of his offense, and in form aforesaid; and further, shall do according to justice, the absence of the offender notwithstanding.

Given at Oxford.

From Meditations on the Life of Christ[†]

[The *Meditations on the Life of Christ*, falsely attributed to St. Bonaventure, is a late-thirteenth-century account of the story of Christ. Though the narrative is drawn from scripture, it contains details and scenes not described in the Bible, along with directives to the reader and short homilies. It was widely available and very popular throughout the Middle Ages, translated and adapted into many languages, including English. The Middle English translation by Nicholas Love, made at the behest of Archbishop Thomas Arundel, was a key text of late-medieval English orthodoxy. The semifictional picture the *Meditations* provided of the life of Christ is important to Kempe's handling of her own version of the Passion narrative.]

Here Begins the Prologue to the Meditations
on the Life of Our Lord Jesus Christ

Among the noteworthy virtues and excellences of the most holy Saint Cecilia, we read that she always carried the Gospel of Christ hidden in her bosom, which I think means that she had chosen the most pious facts of the life of Jesus, as shown in the Gospel, on which to meditate day and night with pure and undivided heart and single-minded and fervent intent. And when she had finished the text she began again with sweet and pleasant enjoyment to ponder on these things, cultivating them in the secret of her heart with prudent consideration. I wish to en-

† From *Meditations on the Life of Christ*, trans. and ed. Isa Ragusa and Rosalie B. Green (Princeton: Princeton UP 1961) 1–2; 359–64. Copyright © 1961, renewed 1989 by Princeton University Press. Reprinted by permission of Princeton University Press.

courage you to do likewise because, above all the studies of spiritual exercise, I believe that this one is the most necessary and the most fruitful and the one that may lead to the highest level. You will never find better instruction against vain and fleeting blandishments, against tribulation and adversity, against the temptations of enemies and vices, than in the life of Christ, which was without blemish and most perfect. Through frequent and continued meditation on His life the soul attains so much familiarity, confidence, and love that it will disdain and disregard other things and be exercised and trained as to what to do and what to avoid.

I say first that the continuous contemplation of the life of Jesus Christ fortifies and steadies the intellect against trivial and transient things, as is disclosed in the example of the Blessed Cecilia, whose heart was so permeated with the life of Christ that trivial things could not enter. Thus during the pomp of the wedding, when there was so much vanity, with the organs singing, and dishonest hearts, she attended only to God, saying, "O Lord, may my heart and my body become pure, that I may be untroubled."

In the second place it fortifies against trials and adversity, as is shown by the holy martyrs about whom Bernard in his 61st sermon on the Canticles said, "In this way martyrdom is endured, that you consider the wounds of Christ in all devotion and dwell in continued contemplation. In this will the martyr remain happy though his whole body be lacerated and iron torture his sides. Thus where is the soul of the martyr? Surely in the wounds of Christ, since the wounds are clearly an entrance. If it were inside himself, he would feel the iron searching him; he could not bear the pain but would feel it and recant."

* * *

LXXV. Meditation on the Lord Jesus Descending into Hell on the Sabbath Day

Father, may all tongues give thanks to you for the abundance of your goodness, which did not spare the only Son of your heart but gave Him up to death for us that we may have Him as such a faithful advocate before you in heaven." The same, "And to you, Lord Jesus, strongest of zealots, what thanks may I give, what return worthy of you—I, a man, dust and ashes, a vile figment? What could you have done for my salvation that you did not do? From the sole of your foot to the crown of your head you plunged wholly into the waters of the Passion, in order to draw me out of them, and the waters entered your very soul; for you lost your soul in death to restore my lost one to me. Behold, you bind me with a double debt; for that which you gave and for that which you lost for my sake, I am your debtor; and I do not have anything better that I can give you than this life of mine, which you gave me twice, once in the creation, again in the redemption. For your precious soul, so troubled, I do not find anything worthy for a man to offer in return. For if I could repay you for it with heaven and earth and all their beauty, surely I would not reach the measure of my debt at all. That I give back what I owe and what I can pay of my debt to you, O Lord, is by your favor. You should be loved by me with my whole heart, whole mind, whole soul, whole strength, and your footsteps should be followed by me, for you deigned to die for me; but how can this be done in me except by you? My soul stays close to you, for all its strength depends on you." Thus Bernard. There you have, then, the Blessed Bernard in his mellifluous way talking of the mellifluous and most beautiful Passion of the Lord. See that you do not receive it in vain. But with your whole heart and whole mind turn toward the Passion of the Lord, through the passages cited, for this meditation stands out above all others in His life. Let us now approach the Resurrection of the Lord Jesus.

LXXXVI. Of the Resurrection of the Lord and How He First Appeared to His Mother on the Sunday

On Sunday, very early in the morning, the Lord Jesus came to the tomb with an honorable multitude of angels, and reassuming His most sacred body, by His own strength He rose and came forth, the tomb being shut close. At the same hour, that is, very early in the morning, Mary Magdalen and Jacobi and Salome, after asking permission from the Lady, set out to go to the tomb with their ointments. The Lady, however, stayed in the house and prayed, saying, "Most clement Father, most merciful Father, you know that my Son is dead. He was nailed to the cross between two thieves, and I buried Him with my own hands; but you are powerful, Lord, and can restore Him to me uninjured. I beg your Majesty to send Him back to me. Why is He so long in coming to me? Send Him back to me, I pray, for my soul will not rest unless I see Him. O my sweetest Son, how are you? What are you doing? What causes your delay? I beg you not to wait any longer to come to me, for you said, 'On the third day I will rise again' (Matt. xxvii, 63). Is not today the third day, my Son? Not yesterday but the day preceding, that is, the day before yesterday, was the great but exceedingly bitter day, the day of calamity and death, of shadows and blackness, of separation and your death. Therefore, my Son, today is the third day. Rise up then, my glory and all my good, and return. More than anything else I long to see you. Let your return console me, as your departure so saddened me. Come back then, my Beloved; come, Lord Jesus; come, my only hope; come to me, my Son." While she was praying thus, and gently shedding tears, behold suddenly the Lord Jesus came, in the whitest garments, with serene face, beautiful, glorious, and rejoicing, and said to her, as if beside her, "Hail, saintly parent." She immediately turned around. "Are you," she said, "my Son Jesus?" And she knelt, adoring Him. Her Son said, "My sweetest mother, it is I. I have risen and am with you." Then, rising, she embraced Him with tears of joy and, placing her cheek to His, drew Him close, resting wholly against Him; and He supported her willingly. Afterwards, when they were sitting down together, she looked intently and earnestly at His face and at the scars on His hands and asked whether all the pain had gone. He said, "Reverend mother, all pain has gone from me, and I have overcome death, and sorrow, and all hardships, nor could I feel anything of that kind now." And she said, "Blessed be your Father, who gave you back to me: may His name be praised and exalted and magnified forevermore." Thus they stayed and conversed together, mutually rejoicing and keeping the Pasch delightfully and lovingly. And the Lord Jesus told her how He had liberated His people from Hell and all that He had done in those three days. Now, therefore, behold a great Pasch!

LXXXVII. How the Magdalen and the Other Two Marys Came to the Tomb and of the Running of Peter and John

The Magdalen and the other two Marys, as I said, went to the tomb with the ointments. While they were outside the gates of the city, they recalled to memory the afflictions and pains of their Master, and in all the places where something notable had been done to Him, or had been done by Him, they halted for a little while and knelt, kissing the ground, uttering groans and sighs, and saying, "Here we met Him with the cross on His shoulders, when His mother was half dead; here He turned to the women; here, wearied, He laid down the cross and leaned for a little while on this stone; here they struck Him so cruelly and harshly to make Him walk faster, and forced Him almost to run; here they stripped Him and left Him totally naked; here they fastened Him to the cross." And then with great cries and floods of tears, prostrate on their faces, they adored and kissed the cross, still red with the precious blood of the Lord. Then, rising and going toward the sepulcher, they said, "Who will roll the stone from the entrance of the tomb for us?" And looking, they see the stone rolled away, and sitting on it the angel of the Lord, who says to them, "Do not be afraid" etc., as is related in the Gospel (Matt. xxviii, 5). However, disappointed in their hopes, for they counted on finding the body of the Lord, not listening to the word of the angel, they go back in great fright to the disciples, announcing the body of the Lord to have been taken away. Then Peter and John run together to the tomb. Look at them well: they run, the Magdalen and her companions run after them, they all run seeking their Lord, their heart and their soul; they run very faithfully, and very fervently, and very anxiously. When they come to the tomb, looking in they do not see the body, but they see the linen cloths and the sudarium, and they withdraw. Feel for them, for they are in great affliction. They seek their Lord and do not find Him, and they do not know where else they ought to look: therefore, grieving and lamenting, they go away.

LXXXVIII. How the Lord Appeared to the Three Marys

But the Marys stay in the same place and, looking into the tomb, see two angels dressed in white, who say to them, "Whom do you seek, the living with the dead?" (Luke xxiv, 5). However, the women neither attend to their words nor accept any consolation from the angelic vision, for they are seeking not angels but the Lord of angels. The two Marys, in great fright, as if absorbed, went a little distance away and sat grieving. But the Magdalen, not knowing what else she should do, because she could not live without her Master and did not find Him there and did not know where to look for Him, stayed weeping outside of the tomb. Once more looking into the tomb, therefore, always hoping to see Him again there where she had buried Him, she saw the two seated angels, who said to her, "Woman, why do you weep? Whom do you seek?" And she said, "They have taken my Lord away, and I do not know where they have laid Him." See the wonderful workings of love: a little while before she had heard from one angel that He was risen, and afterwards from the two that He was alive, and she did not remember, but said, "I do not know." Love made this happen, for, as Origen says, her soul was not here, where she was, but there, where her Master was. She did not know how to think, speak, or hear anything except of Him. When she cried and paid no attention to the angels, her Master for love could not hold back any longer. Therefore the Lord Jesus turned to His mother and said that He wished to go to console her. She approved very much and said, "My blessed Son, go in peace and console her, for she loves you very much and grieves very much at your death; and remember to come back to me," and, embracing Him, she let Him go. He went to the tomb in the garden where the Magdalen was and said to her, "Woman, whom do you seek? Why do you weep?" And she, like an inebriate, not yet recognizing Him, said, "Lord, if you carried Him off, tell me where you have laid Him, and I will take Him away." Look at her well, how with tearstained face she entreats Him humbly and devoutly to lead her to Him whom she seeks; for she always hoped to hear something new about her Beloved. Then the Lord said to her, "Mary." It was truly as if she came back to life, and, recognizing Him by His voice, she said with indescribable joy, "Rabbi," that is, Master, "you are the Lord whom I sought: why did you hide from me so long?" And she ran towards His feet, wishing to kiss them. But the Lord, wishing to elevate her soul to the things of heaven, so that she should not seek

Him from then on on earth, said, "Do not touch me, for I have not yet ascended to my Father. But tell my brothers: 'I ascend to my Father and your Father'" etc. And He added, "Did I not predict to you that on the third day I would rise? Why then did you seek me in the sepulcher?" And she said, "I tell you, Master, that so much grief from the harshness of your Passion and death filled my heart that everything was obliterated. I could remember nothing except your dead body and the place where I buried it, and on that account I brought the ointment this morning. Blessed be your magnificence, that deigned to rise and come back to us!" Thereupon they stayed together lovingly with great joy and gladness. She looked at Him closely and asked about each thing, and He answered willingly. Now this is then a great Pasch! Although it seemed at first that the Lord held back from her, I can hardly believe that she did not touch Him familiarly before He departed, kissing His feet and His hands. But He acted thus, as His words at the beginning show, either because in this way He exposed Himself as He was in her heart, according to common exposition, or, as I said, because He wished to elevate her soul to the things of heaven, as Bernard seems to indicate. One can piously believe that He visited her thus lovingly and singularly, before all the others that are referred to in writing, for her pleasure, and not to distress her. Mysteriously, therefore, not pertinaciously, He spoke those words; for the most benign Lord is not pertinacious or harsh, especially not to those who love Him. After a little time the Lord departed, saying that He must visit the others. Then the Magdalen, as if changed, though just as unwilling ever to part from Him, says, "Lord, as I see, your relationship with us will not be as it used to be. I beg you not to forget me. Remember, Lord, the good things that you gave me, and the intimacy and love that you granted me, and remember me, O Lord my God." And the Lord says to her, "Do not be afraid: be confident and constant, for I shall always be with you." Then she receives a benediction from Him and, leaving Christ, joins her companions and tells this to them. Rejoicing in the Resurrection of the Lord, but saddened at not seeing Him, they depart with her. While the three Marys are going along together, before they reach the city, the Lord Jesus appears to them, saying, "Hail." They are happier than I can say and, prostrating themselves, embrace His feet. Similarly questioning Him and gazing at Him, and receiving cheerful responses, they make a great Pasch. Then the Lord Jesus says to them, "Tell my brothers to come into Galilee: there they shall see me (Matt. xxviii, 10), as I predicted." You see that the Master of humility calls the disciples His brothers: does He ever abandon this virtue? And you, if you desire the understanding and consolation of these things, remember what I said to you before, that your soul should be in all places and deeds just as if you were present there in body. And the same applies to what is said below.

From The Shewings of Julian of Norwich[†]

[Julian of Norwich, who lived as a recluse in Norwich during the late four-teenth and early fifteenth centuries, is one of the finest late-medieval writers of English prose. Her *Shewings* exist in two versions, a Short Text and a Long Text. Julian's profound account of a religious experience she had in May 1373 is centered by her very personal picture of a merciful and gracious God that she describes herself as compelled to explain and transmit. In Book 1, chapter 18, Kempe describes herself as visiting Julian of Norwich.]

II. The second chapter. Of the tyme of these revelations, and how shee asked three petitions.

These Revelations were shewed to a simple creature that cowde no letter[1] the yeere of our Lord 1373, the eighth day of May, which creature desired afore three gifts of God. The first was mende of[2] His passion. The second was bodily sekenesse[3] in youth at thirty yeeres of age. The third was to have of Gods gift three wounds. As in the first methought[4] I had sume feleing in the passion of Christe, but yet I desired more be[5] the grace of God. Methought I would have beene that time with Mary Magdalen and with other that were Crists lovers, and therefore I desired a bodily sight wherein I might have more knowledge of the bodily peynes of our Saviour, and of the compassion our Lady and of all His trew lovers that seene[6] that time His peynes, for I would be one of them and suffer with Him. Other sight ner[7] sheweing of God desired I never none till the soule was departid fro[8] the body. The cause of this petition was that after the sheweing I should have the more trew minde in[9] the passion of Christe.

    The second came to my mynde with contrition frely desireing that sekenesse so herde as to deth[1] that I might in that sekeness underfongyn[2] alle my rites of Holy Church, myselfe weneing[3] that I should dye, and that all creatures might suppose the same that seyen[4] me, for I would have no manner comfort of eardtly life. In this sekenesse I desired to have all manier peynes bodily and ghostly[5] that I should have if I should dye, with

---

† From *The Shewings of Julian of Norwich*, ed. Georgia Ronan Crampton, TEAMS (Kalamazoo, MI: Medieval Institute Publications, 1996), chapters 2, 3, 4, 5. Reprinted by permission of the Board of the Medieval Institute and the editor.

1. **cowde no letter,** knew no letters, could not read; or possibly, did not know Latin.
2. **mende of,** attention to, understanding, realization.
3. **sekenesse,** sickness.
4. **methought,** it seemed to me; **sume feleing in,** some feeling of.
5. **be,** by.
6. **seene,** saw; **peynes,** pains.
7. **ner,** nor.
8. **fro,** from.
9. **trew minde in,** true understanding of.
1. **sekenesse so herde as to deth,** a deathly sickness.
2. **underfongyn,** receive.
3. **weneing,** supposing.
4. **seyen,** saw; **eardtly,** earthly.
5. **ghostly,** spiritual.

all the dreds and tempests of the fends,[6] except the outpassing of the soule. And this I ment for I would be purged be the mercy of God and after lyven[7] to the worshippe of God because of that sekenesse; and that for the more speede in my deth, for I desired to be soone with my God.

These two desires of the passion and the sekenesse I desired with a condition, seying thus: "Lord, thou wotith[8] what I would, if it be Thy will that I have it, and if it be not Thy will, good Lord, be not displeased, for I will nought, but as Thou wilt." For the third, by the grace of God and teachyng of Holy Church, I conceived a mighty desire to receive three wounds in my life; that is to sey, the wound of very[9] contrition, the wound of kinde compassion, and the wound of willfull longing to God. And all this last petition I asked without any condition. These two desires foresaid passid fro[1] my minde, and the third dwelled with me continually.

III. Of the sekenese opteyned of God be petition. Third chapter.

And when I was thirty yers[2] old and halfe, God sent me a bodely sekeness in which I lay three dayes and three nights, and on the fourth night I tooke all my rites of Holy Church and wened not a levyd[3] till day; and after this I langorid forth two dayes and two nights. And on the third night I wened[4] oftentimes to have passyd, and so wened they that were with mee; and, in youngith[5] yet, I thought great sweeme[6] to dye; but for nothing that was in earth that me lekid to levin for,[7] ne for no peyne that I was aferd[8] of, for I trusted in God of His mercy. But it was to have lyved that I might have loved God better and longer tyme, that I might have the more knoweing and lovyng of God in blisse of Hevyn. For methought[9] all the time that I had lived here so little and so short, in reward of that endlesse blisse, I thought, nothing. Wherefore I thought, "Good Lord, may my living no longer be to Thy worshippe?" And I understood by my reason and be my feleing[1] of my peynes that I should dye, and I assented fully with all—with all the will of my herte to be at God will.[2] Thus I durid till day, and be than my body was dede[3] fro the middis downewards as to my feleing. Then was I stered to be sett upright, underlenand[4] with helpe, for

6. **fends,** fiends.
7. **lyven,** live; **worshippe,** honor.
8. **wotith,** know.
9. **very,** true, genuine.
1. **fro,** from.
2. **yers,** years.
3. **wened not a levyd,** believed I would not live; **langorid,** languished.
4. **wened,** thought, supposed.
5. **youngith,** youth.
6. **sweeme,** a pity, regret.
7. **me lekid to levin for,** it gave me pleasure to live for.
8. **ne,** nor; **aferd,** afraid.
9. **methought,** it seemed to me; **in reward of,** in comparison with.
1. **feleing,** feeling.
2. **God will,** God's will, i.e., at God's disposal; **durid,** endured.
3. **dede fro,** dead from; **middis,** middle; **stered,** prompted, took a notion.
4. **underlenand,** leaning with support from beneath.

to have more fredam of my herte to be at Gods will, and thinkeing on God while my life would lest.

My curate was sent for to be at my endeing, and by than[5] he cam I had sett my eyen[6] and might not speke. He sett[7] the cross before my face and seid, "I have browte[8] thee the image of thy maker and Saviour. Louke thereupon and comfort thee therewith." Methought[9] I was wele for my eyen were sett up rightward into Hevyn[1] where I trusted to come be the mercy of God, but nevertheless I assented to sett my eyen in the face of the Crucifix, if I might; and so I dede.[2] For methought I might longer duren to loke[3] even forth than right up. After this my sight began to failen and it was all derke[4] about me in the chamber as it had be night, save in the image of the Cross wherein I beheld a comon light, and I wiste[5] not how. All that was beside the Cross was uggely to me as if it had be mekil[6] occupyed with the fends.[7] After this the other party of my body began to dyen so ferforth that onethys[8] I had ony feleing, with shortnesse of onde; and than I went sothly[9] to have passid.[1]

And in this, sodenly all my peyne was taken fro me, and I was as hele,[2] and namely in the other party[3] of my body, as ever I was aforn. I mervalid at this soden change, for methought it was a privy[4] workeing of God and not of kinde, and yet by the feleing of this ease I trusted never the more to levyn.[5] Ne the feleing of this ease was no full ease to me, for methought I had lever a be[6] deliveryd of this world. Than came suddenly to my minde,[7] that I should desyre the second wounde of our Lords gracious gift, that my body might be fulfilled with minde and felyng of His blissid passion, for I would that His peynes were my peynes, with compassion, and, afterward, longeing[8] to God. But in this I desired never bodily sight nor sheweing of God, but compassion as a kinde[9] soule might have with

---

5. **by than,** by the time that.
6. **I had sett my eyen,** my eyes were fixed in the death stare.
7. **sett,** placed.
8. **browte,** brought; **Louke,** look.
9. **Methought,** It seemed to me; **eyen,** eyes; **sett,** fixed.
1. **Hevyn,** Heaven.
2. **dede,** did.
3. **duren to loke,** be able to look; **forth than,** straight ahead rather than.
4. **derke,** dark.
5. **wiste,** knew.
6. **mekil,** much.
7. **fends,** fiends; **party,** part.
8. **onethys,** scarcely; **ony feleing,** any feeling; **onde,** breath.
9. **went sothly,** truly thought.
1. **passid,** died.
2. **hele,** well.
3. **party,** part; **aforn,** before.
4. **privy,** mysterious; **kinde,** nature.
5. **levyn,** live.
6. **lever a be,** rather have been.
7. **minde** understanding, realization.
8. **longeing,** longing (possibly belonging).
9. **kinde,** natural, kindly.

our Lord Jesus that for love would beene a dedely man,[1] and therefore I desired to suffer with Him.

IV. Here begynnith the first revelation of the pretious crownyng of Criste etc. in the first chapter, and how God fullfilleth the herrte with most joy, and of His greate meekenesse; and how the syght of the passion of Criste is sufficient strength ageyn all temptations of the fends, and of the great excellency and mekenesse of the blissid Virgin Mary. The fourth chapter.

In this sodenly I saw the rede blode trekelyn[2] downe fro under the garlande hote and freisly[3] and ryth plenteously, as it were in the time of His passion that the garlande of thornys[4] was pressid on His blissid hede. Ryte so, both God and man, the same that sufferd thus for me, I conceived treuly and mightily that it was Himselfe shewed it me without ony mene.[5]

And in the same sheweing sodenly the Trinite fullfilled the herte[6] most of joy; and so, I understood, it shall be in Hevyn withoute end to all that shall come there. For the Trinite is God, God is the Trinite. The Trinite is our maker and keeper, the Trinite is our everlasting lover, everlasting joy and blisse, be our Lord Jesus Christ; and this was shewed in the first and in all, for where Jesus appereith[7] the blissid Trinite is understond, as to my sight. And I said, "Benedicite, Domine."[8] This I said for reverence in my meneing[9] with a mighty voice, and full gretly was astonyed[1] for wonder and mervel that I had, that He that is so reverend and dredfull[2] will be so homley with a synfull creture liveing in wretched flesh. This I tooke for the time of my temptation, for methowte by the sufferance of God I should be tempted of fends or I dyed.[3] With this sight of the blissid passion, with the Godhede that I saw in myne understonding, I knew wele that it was strength enow[4] to me, ya, and to all creturers leving,[5] ageyn all the fends of Hell and ghostly temptation.

In this He browght our blissid Lady to my understondyng.[6] I saw hir ghostly in bodily likeness, a simple mayde and a meke, young of age and little waxen[7] above a child, in the stature that she was wan[8] she

1. **would beene a dedely man**, was willing to be a mortal person.
2. **rede blode trekelyn**, red blood trickling.
3. **freisly**, afresh; **ryth**, right; **that**, when.
4. **thornys**, thorns.
5. **ony mene**, any intermediary.
6. **herte**, heart.
7. **appereith**, appears.
8. **Benedicite, Domine**, Blessed be Thou, Lord.
9. **meneing**, intention.
1. **astonyed**, astonished.
2. **reverend and dredfull**, revered and awe inspiring; **homley**, intimate, familiar; **synfull creture liveing**, sinful creature living.
3. **of fends or I dyed**, by fiends before I died.
4. **enow**, enough; **ya**, yeah, indeed.
5. **leving**, living; **ageyn**, against.
6. **understondyng**, mind.
7. **waxen**, grown.
8. **wan**, when.

conceived with child. Also God shewid in party[9] the wisedam and the trueth of his soule, wherein I understood the reverend beholding that she beheld hir God and maker mervelyng with greate reverence that He would be borne of hir that was a simple creature of His makeyng. And this wisdam and trueth, knowyng the greteness of hir maker and the littlehede of hirselfe, that is made, caused hir sey full mekely to Gabriel, "Lo, me, Gods handmayd." In this sight I understoode soth-ly[1] that she is mare than all that God made beneath hir in worthyness and grace. For aboven hir is nothing that is made but the blissid manhood of Criste, as to my sight.

V. How God is to us everything that is gode, tenderly wrappand us; and all thing that is made, in regard to Almighty God, it is nothing; and how man hath no rest till he nowteth himselfe and all thing for the love of God. The fifth chapter.

In this same time our Lord shewed to me a ghostly sight of His homely[2] loveing. I saw that He is to us everything that is good and comfortable for us. He is oure clotheing, that for love wrappeth us, halsyth us, and all becloseth us[3] for tender love, that He may never leeve us, being to us althing that is gode as to myne understondyng. Also in this He shewed a littil thing the quantitype of an hesil nutt[4] in the palme of my hand, and it was as round as a balle. I lokid there upon with eye of my understondyng and thowte, What may this be? And it was generally answered thus: *It is all that is made*. I mervellid how it might lesten,[5] for methowte it might suddenly have fallen to nowte for littil. And I was answered in my understondyng, *It lesteth and ever shall, for God loveth it; and so all thing hath the being*[6] *be the love of God*.

In this littil thing I saw three properties: the first is that God made it, the second is that God loveth it, the third, that God kepith it. But what is to me sothly the maker, the keper, and the lover I canot tell, for till I am substantially onyd[7] to Him I may never have full rest ne very[8] blisse; that is to sey, that I be so festined to Him, that there is right nowte that is made betwix my God and me. It needyth us to have knoweing of the littlehede[9] of creatures and to nowtyn allthing that is made[1] for to love and howe[2] God that is unmade. For this is the cause why we be not all in ease of

9. **party**, part.
1. **sothly**, truly; **mare**, more.
2. **homely**, intimate.
3. **wrappeth . . . becloseth us**, winds about us, embraces us, and entirely encloses us.
4. **hesil nutt**, hazel nut.
5. **lesten**, last.
6. **the being**, existence.
7. **substantially onyd**, integrally joined.
8. **ne very**, nor true.
9. **littlehede**, smallness.
1. **to nowtyn . . . made**, value as nothing everything created.
2. **howe**, have; **unmade**, without creator.

herete[3] and soule, for we sekyn here rest in those things that is so littil, wherin is no rest, and know not our God that is al mighty, al wise, all gode; for He is the very rest. God will be knowen, and Him liketh[4] that we rest in Him. For all that is beneth Him sufficeth not us. And this is the cause why that no soule is restid till it is nowted[5] of all things that is made. Whan[6] he is willfully nowtid for love, to have Him that is all, then is he abyl to receive ghostly rest.

Also our Lord God shewed that it is full gret plesance to Him that a sily[7] soule come to Him nakidly and pleynly and homely. For this is the kinde yernings[8] of the soule by the touching of the Holy Ghost, as be the understondyng that I have in this sheweing: "God of Thy goodnesse, give me Thyselfe, for Thou art enow[9] to me, and I may nothing aske that is less that may be full worshippe to Thee. And if I aske anything that is lesse, ever me wantith; but only in Thee I have all." And these words arn[1] full lovesome to the soule, and full nere, touchen the will of God and His goodness. For His goodness comprehendith all His creatures and all His blissid works and overpassith without end. For He is the endleshede, and He hath made us only to Himselfe and restorid us be His blissid passion, and kepith us in His blissid love; and all this is of His goodness.

From The Book of Saint Bride[†]

[St. Bridget of Sweden (1303–1373) was a visionary, pilgrim, spokeswoman for international peace, prophet, and founder of the Brigittine Order, to which Syon Abbey, where Margery ends her journey described in Book 2, belonged. Her life—she was married, had many children, and lived much of her life in Rome, away from her home in Sweden—serves as another important model for Kempe's description of Margery. When Margery visits Rome (Book 1, chapters 32–41), St. Bridget is especially present to her.]

Our Lord Jesus Christ tells Saint Bride why he chose her to be his spouse, and how as a bride she ought to array herself and be ready for him. [Book 1, chapter 2]

"I am the Creator of Heaven and earth and sea and of all the things that are in them. I am one with the Father and the holy Spirit, not as gods of stone or gold, as was sometimes proclaimed, nor as many gods, as used

3. **herete**, heart; **sekyn**, seek.
4. **Him liketh**, it pleases Him.
5. **nowted**, stripped.
6. **Whan**, When.
7. **sily**, innocent, simple.
8. **kinde yernings**, natural yearning.
9. **enow**, enough.
1. **arn**, are.
† From *Saint Bride and Her Book*, trans. Julia Bolton Holloway, Focus Library of Medieval Women (Newburyport, MA: Focus Texts, 1992) 33–35, 40–50. Reprinted by permission of Boydell & Brewer Ltd.

to be the custom; but one God, Father and Son and holy Spirit, three Persons and one in substance, Creator of all things and made of none, unchangeable and almighty, enduring without beginning and without end. I am he who was born of the Virgin, not leaving the God head but knitting it to the manhood, so that I should be in one person the very Son of God and the Son of the Virgin. I am he who hung upon the cross and died and was buried, the Godhead remaining unhurt. For though the manhood and body which I, the Son, alone took upon myself, was dead, yet in the Godhead, in which I was one God with the Father and the holy Spirit, I lived eternally. I am also the same who rose from death and ascended into heaven who now speaks with you through my Spirit. I have chosen and taken you to myself to be my bride to reveal to you my secret counsels, for this so pleases me. And also you are mine by all manner of right, when in the death of your husband you gave your will into my hands, and also after his death, when you thought and prayed how you might become poor for me and for me abandon all things.[1] And therefore by right you are mine and for so much charity it is right for me to prepare for you; therefore I take you as my Bride and for my own proper delight, such as seems good to have with a chaste soul.[2]

"To the Bride therefore it is right to be ready when her husband will make his wedding, that she be beautifully arrayed and clean. Then are you well cleansed, if your thought is always about your sins; how I cleansed you from the sin of Adam in your baptism and how often I have permitted you and supported you when you have fallen into sin. The Bride also ought to have tokens of her husband on her breast; that is, to take heed of the benefits and works which I have done for you; that is to say, how nobly I made you, giving you a body and a soul, and how nobly I have endowed you, giving you health and temporal goods, and how sweetly I redeemed you when I died for you and restored you to your heritage, if you would have it. The Bride ought also to do the will of her husband. What is my will, but that you will love me above all things and to desire no other thing but me? I have made all things for man, and all of them subject to him; but he loves all things except me, and truly hates nothing but me. I redeemed for him his heritage which he had lost. But he is so alienated and turned away from reason that he prefers this transitory praise that is but like sea spume, which suddenly rises up like a mountain and as soon falls down to nothing, than everlasting worship in which there is endless good.

"But you, my Bride, if you desire nothing but me, if you despise all things for me, not only your children and kindred, but also respect and riches, I shall give you the most precious and sweetest reward, not gold

---

1. See Edward Cutts, "Consecrated Widows of the Middle Ages," *Scenes and Characters of the Middle Ages* (London: Vertue, 1902), pp. 152–156; Elizabeth M. Makowski, "Canon Law and Medieval Conjugal Rights," *Journal of Medieval History* 3 (1977) 99–114.
2. Bridget is influenced by Bernard on the Song of Songs of Solomon.

and silver, but myself, to be your husband and endless reward, who am the king of bliss. And if you are ashamed of being poor and despised, see that I, your God, go before you, whom servants and friends abandoned on earth; for I looked not for earthly friends, but heavenly ones. And if you fear and dread the burden of labor and sickness, consider how grievous it is to burn in the fire which you would have deserved, if you had offended a temporal lord as you have offended me. For though I love you with all my heart, yet I shall not go against justice in the least point, but according to how you have transgressed in all your members unless in all that you have performed satisfaction. Nevertheless, if you have a good will and purpose to amend, I change justice into mercy, forgiving grievous torments for a little amending. Therefore, take upon yourself gladly a little labor, so that you may the sooner be made clean and come to a great reward. For it is right for the bride to work with her husband until she is weary, so that she afterwards may more surely and trustingly take her rest with him."

Our Lord Jesus Christ stirs Saint Bride not to be afraid of his speaking with her, teaching her the difference between the good Spirit and the evil one. [I.4]

"I am Creator of all things and Redeemer: why do you dread my words and why did you think of what Spirit they were, whether of the good or the evil? Tell me what you found in my words that your own conscience told you not to do? Or ordered you anything against reason?"

The spouse, Saint Bride, answered: "Nothing, Lord, but all that you said is true and I erred sinfully."

Then said our Lord: "I told you of three things by which you may know a good Spirit. First, I told you to worship your God who made you and gave you all that you have, and this your own reason teaches you, to worship him above all things. Second, I told you to keep and hold the right faith; that is, to believe that nothing is done nor may be done without God. The third, I told you to love all things with reasonable temperance and continence; for the world is made for man and he should use it according to his need.

"So also are there three things contrary to these. You may know the unclean spirit because he stirs you to seek your own worship and praise and to be proud of the gifts that God gave you; and he stirs you to intemperance in all your members and of all other things, and to these he inflames your heart. He deceives also sometimes under the appearance of what is good; and therefore I have asked you to examine your conscience and open it to spiritual wise men. Therefore do not doubt that the good Spirit of God is then with you when you desire nothing but God, and of him you are all inflamed. For that I alone may do and it is impossible for the fiend to come near to you. Nor may he come near to any evil man, un-

less he is permitted by me, other than because of his sins or for some secret judgment known to me.

✳   ✳   ✳

**Our Lord Jesus Christ teaches Saint Bride how active life and con-
templative ought to be kept through the example of Mary and Martha;
and first, of contemplative life. [VI.65]**

The Son of God says: "Bride, there are two lives which are compared to Mary and Martha; which lives, if a man or a woman would
follow he must first make clean confession of all his sins, being himself truly sorry for them, having the desire never to sin again.[3] The first
life, as the Lord bears witness, Mary chose; and it leads to the contemplation of heavenly things; and this is the best part and day's journey to everlasting health. Therefore every man and woman who desires
to take and hold to the life of Mary, it is enough for him to have two
things that are necessary to the body; that is, clothing without vanity
or showing of pride, and food and drink in scarceness and not in super-
fluity. He must also have charity without any evil delight, and reasonable fasting after the rules of holy Church. And in his fasting he must
take heed that he not become ill from unreasonable abstinence, unless
by such sickness his prayers or preaching or other good deeds thereby
are lessened, by which he might profit both his neighbor and himself.
He must also carefully examine himself, that by his fasting he is neither made dull nor hasty to the rigor of justice or slow to the works of
pity, to punish those who are rebellious, and to make unfaithful men
subject to the yoke of faith, It is necessary to have bodily strength as
well as spiritual. Therefore anyone who is sick or feeble, who would
rather fast to my praise than eat, he shall have as great reward for his
good will as does he who fasts reasonably for charity. And in the same
way he who eats out of holy obedience, willing rather to fast than to
eat, shall have the same reward as he who fasts.

"Second, Mary ought not to delight in the praise of the world nor of its
prosperity; nor ought he to sorrow at its adversity, except in that he ought
to delight when wicked men are made devout and that lovers of the world
are made lovers of God, and when good men profit in goodness and, by
laboring in the service of God, are made more devout. Of this also ought
he who is Mary to sorrow; that sinners fall into worse sin, and that God is
not loved by his creature, and that God's commandments are despised
and not kept.

---

3. The androgynous Middle English grammar of this section is powerful, where the female Mary
Magdalen and Martha are to be enacted by the male, as well as female, readers of Saint Bride's
text, and referred to as "he" and "him." In Latin this effect does not occur, though it would have
in the original Swedish. Bride visited the Sainte Baume, the region legendarily associated with
Mary Magdalen, and had named one of her daughters Martha. Mary Magdalen was considered
by the medieval world to be the first monk.

"Third, Mary ought not to be idle any more than is Martha; but after he takes his necessary sleep, he ought to rise, and with inward attentiveness of heart thank God who of his charity and love made everything from nothing; and of that same charity, taking the body of man, he made all things again; showing by his Passion and death his love for man, more than you who might not be. Mary must also thank God for all those who are saved; and for all who are in Purgatory, and for them who are in the world, praying God humbly that he suffered them not to be tempted beyond their strength. Mary must also be discreet in prayer, and orderly in the praising of God, for if he has the necessities of life without business, he ought to make longer prayers. And if he grows bored with praying, and temptations grow upon him, then he may labor with his hands at some honest and profitable work, either to his own profit if he have need, or else to the profit of others. And if he is weary and bored both in prayer and in labor, then he may have some honest occupation, or hear words of others' edification with all seriousness, and without dissolution and vanity, until the body and soul be made more able and quick to the service of God. If he who is Mary be such that he has not bodily sustenance but of his own labor, then he must make his prayer shorter for such needful work; and that same labor shall be profiting and increasing of prayer. If Mary can not work, or may not, then be not too ashamed or despairing about begging, but rather joyful; for then he follows me, the Son of God; for I made myself poor than man should become rich.[4] And if he who is Mary be subject to obedience, he should live in obedience to his prelate, and the crown of reward shall be double the more than he was at his own liberty.

"Fourth, Mary ought not to be covetous, no more than was Martha. But he ought to be truly generous; for Martha gives temporal goods for God, so ought Mary to give spiritual goods. And therefore, if Mary has loved God entirely in his heart, he should be careful of that word that many have in their mouths, saying: 'It is nothing to me, if I may help my own soul, What do I care about the works of my neighbors?' Or this: 'I am good: why should I care about how other men live?' O daughter, they who say and think such words, if they see their friend troubled or dishonestly treated, they should risk their deaths to deliver their friend from tribulation. So must Mary do; he ought to sorrow that his God is offended, and that his brother, or his neighbor, is hurt; or if any fall into sin, Mary ought to labor as much as he may that he be delivered—nevertheless, with discretion. And if for that Mary is persecuted, he must seek another more secure place. For I myself who am God have said so: 'Si vos persecuti fuerint in una civitate fugite in aliam'; that is, if they persecute you in one city, flee to another. And

---

4. Saint Bride herself, when in Rome, during which time this portion of the Revelations was being written, was forced to beg for her sustenance.

so did Paul, for it became necessary at one time; and therefore he was let down over the wall in a basket.

"Therefore, that Mary be generous and merciful, five things are necessary to her: first, a house in which guests can sleep; second, clothes to cloth the naked; third, food to feed the hungry; fourth, fire to make the cold hot and warm; fifth, medicine for the sick.

"The house of Mary is his heart, whose wicked guests are all the things that come to him and trouble his heart, such as anger, despair, sloth, greed, pride, and many others, which enter in by the five senses. Therefore all these vices, when they come, ought to lie as guests who sleep at rest. For as an innkeeper receives guests both good and bad with patience, so ought Mary to suffer all things for God by the virtue of patience, and not consent to sin nor delight in it, but remove it from his heart as much as he may little by little with the help of God's grace; and if he may not remove them and put them away, let him endure them patiently against his will, as guests knowing certainly that they will reap him more rewards, and in no ways to damnation.

"Second, Mary ought to have clothes to clothe his guests, that is, humility, inward and outward, and compassion of heart for the disease of one's fellow Christian.[5] And if Mary is despised by men, then he should think how I, God, was despised, taunted and suffered it patiently: how I was judged and spoke not; how I was scourged and crowned with thorns, and did not complain. Mary must also take heed that he show no tokens of wrath or impatience to them who taunt him or despise him; but he ought to bless them who persecute him, so that they who see it may bless God, whom Mary follows; and God himself shall return blessings for curses. Mary also must beware that he neither backbite nor criticize those who burden him or trouble him. For it is damnable to backbite and to hear a backbiter and to criticize his neighbour impatiently; and therefore, that Mary may have the gift of meekness perfectly, he must study to admonish and to warn them of the perils for backbiting others, exhorting them with charity by speech and example to true humility. Also the cloth of Mary ought to be compassion; for if he sees his fellow Christian sin, he ought to have compassion on him, and to pray to God to have mercy on him. And if he sees his neighbor suffer wrong or harm or be taunted, he ought to be sorry for that, and to help him with his prayers and other help and actions. Yes, against the great men of the word; for true compassion seeks not what he wants for himself, but for his fellow Christian. But if Mary is such who is not heard amongst princes and great men and at leaving his cell gains nothing, then he should pray to God carefully for those who are in pain; and God, beholder of the heart, shall for the charity

---

5. The Middle English, in this text and in others, is one's *"eyn cristen,"* one's "even Christian," one's "equal Christian," which has no equivalent democratic term in modern English usage.

of him who prays turn the hearts of men to peace which are diseased. And either he shall be delivered of his tribulation, or else God shall give him patience, so that his reward in heaven shall be doubled. Therefore such a cloth of humility or of compassion ought to be in Mary's heart. For there is nothing which draws God so into a soul as humility and compassion for his fellow Christian.

"Third, Mary must have food and drink for guests. For grievous guests are lodged in Mary's heart, when the heart is ravished out of itself and desires to see delectable things in this world and to have temporal possessions; when his ear desires to hear his own praises; when the flesh seeks to delight in fleshly things; when the spirit pretends to be frail and excuses sin; when there is tardiness to do good and forgetfulness of things that are to come; when good deeds are considered to be many and the evil thought to be few and forgotten. Against such guests Mary has need of counsel, that he dissemble not nor fall asleep. Therefore Mary, heartened with faith, must rise firmly and answer thus to these guests: 'I will not have any temporal things, except those which are necessary to sustain the body. I will not spend the best hour or time, except to praise God. Nor will I take heed of fair or foul, nor what is profitable or unprofitable to the flesh, nor what is savory or unsavory to the taste, except only the pleasure of God and profitable to the soul; for I do not wish to live hour by hour, except to praise God.' Such a will is food to guests who may come, and such an answer quenches inordinate delights.

"Fourth, Mary must have a fire to make her guests warm, and to give them light. This fire is the heat of the holy Spirit; for it is impossible for any man to forsake his own will or the carnal affection of his friends or the love of riches, but by the working inspiration and heat of the holy Spirit. Neither may Mary himself, be he never so perfect, begin nor continue any good life without sweetness and information of the same holy Spirit. Therefore, that Mary illumines and lights the guests that come first, he must think thus: 'God made me for that skill that I should praise him, love him and dread him above all things; and he was born of a Virgin to teach the way to heaven, which I should follow with humility. And after, with his death, he opened heaven, that by desiring and advancing I should haste there.' Mary must also examine all his works and thoughts and desires, and how he has offended God, and how patiently God suffered man, and how in many ways God calls man to him. For such thoughts and others like them are the guests of Mary, which are all in darkness; but if they are lightened with the fire of the holy Spirit, which fire comes to the heart when Mary thinks it is reasonable to serve God, and when he would rather suffer all pain than wittingly provoke God to anger, by whose goodness his soul is made and bought again with his blessed blood. The heart also is lit by this good fire, when reason thinks and discerns by what intent each guest, that is, each thought, comes, when the heart examines if the thought goes to everlasting joy or to transitory joy; if it leave no thought undiscussed, none unpunished, none without dread. Therefore, that this fire may be got, and kept when it is obtained, it is necessary for Mary to gather together dry wood, by which this fire is fed; that is, that he be concerned about the stirrings of the flesh, that the flesh begin not to be wanton; and that he put to all diligence, that the works of pity and devout prayer be enlarged and increased, in which the holy Spirit delights. But above all it is to know and see that where fire is kindled in a close vessel and has no ash, the fire is soon quenched and the container becomes cold. And so is it with Mary; for if Mary desires to live only to praise God, then it is necessary for him that his mouth be opened and the fame of his charity to go out. Then is the mouth opened, when by speaking in fervent charity he gets spiritual sons for God.

"But Mary must be very careful that he open the mouth of his preaching when they who are good may be made more fervent, and they who are wicked may be amended, where righteousness may be increased and evil habits removed. For my Apostle Paul would sometimes have spoken; but he was forbidden by my Spirit, and therefore at the right time he was still, and at the convenient time he spoke; and sometimes he used soft words, and sometimes sharp; and all his words and deeds were to the praise of God and to strengthen faith. But if Mary may not preach,[6] and has the desire and the knowledge how to preach, he must do so as a fox that goes about seeking many places with his feet; and when he finds the best and most suitable places, there he makes a den to rest in. So Mary must with words, examples, and prayers try the hearts of many; and when he finds hearts more able to receive the word of God, there must he stay and rest, admonishing and stirring whom he may. Mary must also work that a fitting show be given to his flame of fire: for the greater the flame is, the more people are illumined and enflamed by it. The flame has then a fitting show, where Mary neither dreads criticism nor shame, nor seeks his own praise, when he dreads neither contrarious things, nor delights in wealth and prosperity. And then it is more acceptable to God that Mary do his good deeds in the open rather than in private, to that extent that they who see them may praise and worship God.

"Also, Mary ought to give out two flames, one in private, another openly: that is, to have double humility; the first in the heart, inwardly, the other outwardly. The first is that Mary thinks himself unworthy and unprofitable in all goodness, and that he prefers not nor exhalts himself in his own conceit above any person; and that he does not desire to be seen and praised, but that he flees from all pride and haughtiness, desiring God above all things and following his words. If Mary send out such a flame in his deeds, then shall his heart be lit with charity, and all con-

---

6. Bride is remembering that Paul forbade women to preach, I Corinthians 7.3–6.

trary things that come to him shall be overcome and easily endured. The second flame must be in the open; for if true humility is in the heart, it ought to appear in clothing and to be heard in the mouth and to be fulfilled in deeds. True humility is in the clothing when Mary chooses cloth of less price, from which he may gain warmth and profit, rather than cloth of more value, of which he might be proud and show off. For cloth which is cheap and is called by men vile and abject is truly fair to God because it provokes humility. But that cloth which is bought with great price and is called fair is foul to God; for it takes away the fairness of angels, which is humility. Nevertheless, if Mary is compelled by any reasonable cause to have better clothing than he would want, be not troubled therefore; for by that shall his reward be greater.

"Also Mary ought to be meek in mouth, speaking humble words; fleeing from vain words and such as cause laughter; being careful of much speech; not using subtle nor pretty words; nor professing his own will or words before the comprehension and feeling of those who are better. And if Mary is praised for any good deed, he should not be exalted thereby with pride, but should answer thus: 'Laus sit deo qui dedit omnia,' that is, praising God who gave all goodness. For what am I but dust before the face of the wind; or what good comes of me, earth without water? And if he is criticized, he should not be downcast but answer thus: 'It is appropriate; for I have so often offended in the sight of God and not done penance for which I should earn greater torment. Therefore pray for me that by enduring temporal reprimands, I may escape everlasting ones.' If Mary is provoked by wrath to any misjudgment of his fellow Christian, he must be prudently careful of any indiscreet answer; for pride is often associated with wrath, and therefore it is wholesome advice that when wrath and pride come about, that he hold his lips tightly together until he can ask for help from God for endurance and patience; and until he may be advised what and how to answer; or until he may overcome himself. For then wrath is quenched in the heart and men may answer wisely to those who are unwise.

"You know also that the devil is greatly envious of Mary; and therefore if he may not stop him by breaking God's commandments, then he stirs him to be easily moved with great wrath, or else to the dissoluteness of vain mirth, or else to dissolute and playful words. Therefore Mary must ask for help from God that all his words and deeds may be governed by God and addressed to God. Also Mary must have meekness in his actions, that he does the right not because of earthly praise; that he attempt nothing new, that he be not ashamed of being humble; that he flee singularity in his works, that he respect all; and that in all things he consider himself unworthy. Also Mary ought rather to sit with the poor than with the rich; rather he should obey than be obeyed; rather to be silent than to speak; rather to be alone solitary than be constantly amongst the great of the world and among his worldly friends. Mary must hate his own will and think always on his death. Mary ought not to be idle, nor complain, nor be forgetful of the justice of God and of his own affections. Mary must be fervent in confession, careful concerning temptations, desiring to live for the right and for nothing else but the praise of God and that the health of souls be increased and enlarged.

"Therefore, if Mary, who is thus disposed as I have now said, be chosen by Martha, and obeying, for the love of God takes the rule of many souls, there shall be given to him a double crown of reward, as I show you in a parable. There was a certain lord of great power who had a ship filled with precious merchandise, and said to his servants: 'Go to such a harbor, and you shall gain much for me, and glorious fruit. If the wind rises against you, work hard and do not become weary; for your reward shall be great.' Then the servants sailed away. And the wind became strong, and tempests arose, and the ship was grievously battered. Because of this the ship's captain was exhausted and all despaired of their lives. And then they agreed to come to any harbor that the wind could blow them to, and not to the haven that the lord had assigned to them. When one of the servants who was more loyal than the others heard this, he wailed and out of fervent love and zeal that he had for his lord, he violently seized hold of the steering board of the ship and with great strength he brought the ship to the harbor the lord desired. Therefore this man who thus manfully brought the ship to the harbor is to be rewarded with more singular rewards than any other.

"It is the same with a good priest who for love of God and salvation of souls takes charge of the steering, not paying heed to fame, for he shall be doubly rewarded: first, because he shall be partner of all the good deeds of those whom he has brought to the haven; second, because his joy and bliss shall be increased without end. And so shall it be against those who desire fame and responsibility; for they shall be partner to all the pains and sins of those that they have chosen to govern. Second, for their confusion shall be without end. For the priests who desire fame are more like whores than priests. For they deceive souls with their evil words and examples; and they are unworthy to be called either Mary or Martha, unless they make amends with penance. Fifth, Mary ought to give his guests medicine; that is, delight and comfort them with God's words. For to all things that ever happen to him, whether they be joyful or burdensome, he ought to say: 'I will this; whatever God wills, I will do; and to his will I am readily obedient; though I should go to Hell." For such a will is medicine against evil things that occur to the heart, and this will is delight in tribulation and a good restraint in prosperity. But because Mary has many enemies he must therefore make his confession frequently. For as long as he remains in a state of sin and could have confessed and is negligent and takes no heed, then is he rather to be called an apostate before God than Mary."

Of the deeds of the active life which are understood by Martha. Chapter 11. [VI.65 continued]

"You must know also that though the part of Mary is best, yet the part of Martha is not evil, but praiseworthy and very pleasing to God. Therefore I shall tell you how Martha ought to be governed. For he ought to have five good things as well as Mary. First, the right faith regarding God's Church. Second, to know the commandments of the Godhead and the counsels of the truth of the Gospel; and these he ought perfectly to keep in thought and deed. Third, he ought to keep his tongue from evil words that are against God and his neighbor, and his hand from all dishonest and unlawful actions, and his heart from too much greed and pleasure. He ought also to be content with the goods God has given him, and not to desire superfluous things. Fourth, he ought to fulfill the deeds of mercy reasonably and modestly, that in doing those deeds he offends in no way. Fifth, he ought to love God above all things and more than himself. So did Martha, for he gave joyfully of himself, following my words and deeds; and after she gave all her goods for my love. And therefore she loathed temporal things, and sought heavenly things, and suffered heavenly things patiently, and took heed and care of others as of herself. And therefore she thought always on my charity and Passion; and she was glad in tribulation and loved all as a mother. The same Martha also followed me every day, desiring nothing but to hear words of life. She had compassion on those who were grieving; she comforted the sick; she neither cursed nor said evil to any. But she did not imitate the pushiness of her neighbor and prayed for all. Therefore every man who desires charity actively ought to follow Martha in loving his neighbor, to bring him to heaven, but not in favoring and nourishing his vices and sins. He ought also to flee his own vanity, pride and doubleness. Also he ought not to use wrath or envy.

But mark well that Martha, praying for her brother Lazarus when he was dead, came first to me. But her brother was not yet raised until Mary came after, when she was called. And then for both sisters their brother was raised from the dead to life.[7] So in spiritual life he who perfectly desires to be Mary must first be Martha, laboring physically to my praise. And he ought first to learn how to withstand the desires of the flesh and the temptation of the fiend and afterwards he may with deliberation ascend up the height of Mary. For he who is unproved and tempted, and he who has not overcome the lusts of his flesh, how may he continually heed and choose heavenly things? Who is the dead brother of Mary and Martha, but an unperfect work? For often a good work is done with an indiscreet intent and with an ill advised heart, and therefore it is done dully and slowly. But for the working of good deeds to be acceptable to me, it

7. John 11.1–24.

must be raised and quickened by Martha and Mary; that is, when the neighbor is clearly loved for God and to God, and God alone is desired above all things. And then every good work of man is pleasing to God. Therefore I said in the Gospel that Mary chose the better part; for then the part of Martha is also good, when he grieves for the sins of his fellow Christians; and then is the part of Martha better, when he labors that men may continue in the good life wisely and honestly, and that only for the love of God.

"But the part of Mary is best when he beholds only heavenly things and the profit of souls. And the Lord enters into the house of Martha and Mary when the heart is fulfilled with good affections; and at peace away from the noise of worldly things; and thinking of God as always present; and not only contemplating and meditating on his love, but laboring in that day and night.

From The Life of Marie d'Oignies by Jacques de Vitry[†]

[*The Life of Marie d'Oignies* is one of the texts that the *Book* describes as being read to Margery. Noted for her piety, her service to others, her married chastity, her devotions, and her tears, Marie d'Oignies served as a powerful model for female sanctity during the late Middle Ages.]

Book I

IIA. Her Childhood

There was in the diocese of Liège in a town called Nivelles a certain young woman whose name was Marie, as gracious in life as in name. Her parents were not of common stock but even though they abounded in riches and many temporal goods yet, even from her early childhood, her inclination was never attracted by transitory goods. Cast in this way upon the Lord (cf. I Pt 5:7) almost from the womb, she never or rarely mixed with those who were playing as is the custom of small girls nor "did she make herself partaker with them that walked in lightness" (Tb 3: 17). Rather, she kept her soul from the concupiscence and vanity of them all and foreshadowed in her youth what, through a divine sign, she would be in the future in her old age.[1] Wherefore when she was still young, she would frequently kneel before her bed at night and offer up certain prayers which she had learned to the Lord as the first fruits of her life (cf. Ex 22: 29).

---

† From *The Life of Marie d'Oignies by Jacques de Vitry*, trans. Margot H. King (Saskatoon, Saskatchewan: Peregrina Publishing Co., 1986), Book 1, chapters IIA, 12, 13, 16, 17, 19. Reprinted by permission of the publisher.

1. This is merely a rhetorical device for, in fact, Marie died at the age of thirty-six.

Thus mercy and righteousness grew in her from her infancy and she loved[2] the ascetic life[3] as if with a natural affection.[4] For example, it once happened that when some Cistercian brothers were passing in front of her father's house, she glanced up at them and she so admired their religious habit that she followed them stealthily. And when she could do no more, she put her own feet in the footprints of those lay brothers or monks from her great desire.

And when her parents, as is the custom of worldly people, wished to adorn her in delicate and refined clothing, she was saddened and rejected them as if what she had read had impressed itself naturally in her spiritual consciousness,[5] that is to say, those things which Peter the Apostle had said concerning women: "Do not dress up for show: doing up your hair, wearing gold bracelets and fine clothes" (I Pt 3: 3), and what Paul the apostle had said: "Without braided hair or gold and jewellery or expensive clothes" (I Tm 2: 9). When her parents saw this kind of behaviour, they mocked their little girl and said, "What kind of person is our daughter going to be?"

12. Her Marriage

Her parents were indignant when they saw these auspicious deeds and when she was fourteen years old they joined her in marriage to a certain youth.[6] Living apart from her parents, she was now set on fire with such an ecstasy of ardour and punished her body with such warfare that she enslaved it to such a degree that it frequently happened that after she had toiled for a large part of the night with her own hands,[7] she would pray for a lengthy period after she had finished her work. As often as was licit for her, she passed a very short part of the night in sleep on planks which she had concealed at the foot of her bed. And because she clearly did not have power over her own body, she secretly wore a very rough cord under her clothing which she bound with great force.

I do not say these things to commend the excess but so that I might show her fervour. In these and in many other things wherein the privi-

---

2. "diligebat": in these lives, *diligo* usually means to love in the natural order, as distinct from divine love. Here, Jacques adds the rider, *quasi naturali affectione*.
3. "religionem": religious life or, better, the ascetic life.
4. "naturali affectione": here not affectivity but the more obvious "affection."
5. "acsi naturaliter ejus animo impressum legeretur": While this indicates that, unlike many mediæval women, Marie was literate, it also refers to the memory which, according to Mary Carruthers, was conceived of as "a mental picture" or phantasm which is impressed like a seal in wax upon the brain and reading primarily a visual act whereby "whatever enters the mind changes into a 'see-able' form for storing in memory": *The Book of Memory: A Study of Memory in Medieval Culture* (Cambridge: Cambridge University Press, 1996) 17–18.
6. This young man whose name was John was the brother of Master Giles, chaplain of the church of Willambroux.
7. Jacques devotes Chapter 38 to Marie's work with her hands. Although manual labour had been an integral part of the way of life of the desert fathers and mothers and in the Rule of St. Benedict, by the late Middle Ages it was little regarded by worldly monastics and was one of the characteristics emphasised by those who wished to restore an apostolic and desert fervour to their lives.

lege of grace operated, let the discreet reader pay attention that what is a privilege for a few does not make a common law. Let us imitate her virtues but we cannot imitate the works of her virtues without individual privilege. Although the body be forced to serve the spirit (cf. Rm 7: 25) and although we ought "to carry the wounds of the Lord Jesus Christ in our body" (Gal 6: 17), yet we know that "the honour of the King loves justice" (Ps 98: 4) and sacrifice from the robbery of the poor is not pleasing to the Lord (cf. Is 61: 8). Necessary things are not to be taken from the poverty of the flesh, although vices are to be checked. Therefore, admire rather than imitate what we have read about the things certain saints have done through the familiar counsel of the Holy Spirit.

13. The Conversion of her Husband and their Chaste Life

And after she had lived in marriage with her husband, John, in this fashion for a short time, the Lord looked on the humility of his handmaid and hearkened to the tears of the suppliant, and John, who previously had had Marie as a wife, was inspired to entrust her to the protection of God. The Lord entrusted a chaste woman to a chaste man; he left her a faithful provider so that she might be comforted by the presence of a protector and thereby serve the Lord more freely. And John, who formerly had acted with a certain natural sweetness of spirit, did not oppose the holy plan of his wife (as is the custom of other men), but he suffered with her and bore with her labours good-naturedly enough. He was visited by the Lord and he not only promised to live a celibate and truly angelic life in continence, but also promised to imitate his companion in her holy plan and in her holy ascetic life by giving up everything to the poor for Christ.

16.

Your Cross and your passion marked the beginning of her conversion to you, the first fruits of love.[8] She "heard you hearing and was afraid" (Hb 3: 2); she "considered your works" (Eccl 7: 14) and feared.[9] One day, already chosen by you, she was visited by you and she considered the benefits which you had generously shown forth in the flesh to humanity. She found such grace of compunction therein that a great abundance of tears[1] was pressed out by the wine-press of your Cross in the passion and her tears flowed so copiously on the floor that the ground in the church became muddy with her footprints. Wherefore for a long time after this vis-

---

8. "dilectionis": her human love.
9. The beginning of Marie's conversion was the fear which arose from her meditation upon the Passion.
1. Overcome with grief over Christ's degradation on the Cross, Marie was filled with compunction and wept. Within the monastic tradition, compunction was highly esteemed. Its roots go back to the Egyptian and Syrian deserts and it was considered to be an infused gift of God. True compunction is an interior grace occasioned by an awareness of one's unworthiness before God and remembrance of sin, accompanied by tears. Sandra McEntire, *The Doctrine of Compunction in Medieval England: Holy Tears* (Lewiston NY: Edwin Mellen Press, 1990).

itation she could neither gaze at an image of the Cross, nor speak, nor hear other people speaking about the passion of Christ, without falling into ecstasy through a defect of the heart. Therefore she sometimes moderated her sorrow and restrained the flood of her tears and, disregarding Christ's humanity, would raise her consciousness to his divinity and majesty so that she might therein find consolation in his impassibility. But when she tried to restrain the intensity of the flowing river, then a greater intensity wondrously sprang forth. When she directed her attention to how great he was who had endured such degradation for us, her sorrow was renewed and new tears were revived in her soul through her sweet compunction.

17.

One day, just before Good Friday, when the Passion of Christ was approaching, she began to offer herself as a sacrifice with the Lord in even greater showers of tears and with sighs and gasps. One of the priests of the church softly but firmly exhorted her to pray in silence and to restrain her tears. She was always timid and, with the simplicity of a dove, tried to obey in all things but, conscious of the impossibility of this thing, she slipped out of the church unknown to him and hid herself in a secret place which was removed from everyone. There she tearfully implored the Lord that he show this priest that it is not in man's power to restrain the intensity of tears when the waters flow with the vehemence of the blowing spirit (cf. Ps 147: 18; Ex 14: 21).

Once when the priest celebrated Mass, "the Lord opened and none shut" (Is 22: 22) and "he sent forth waters and they overturned the earth" (Jb 12: 15). His spirit was drowned in such a flood of tears that he almost suffocated, and as much as he tried to repress its intensity, by that much the more was he drenched with his tears and the book and the altar cloths were dripping as well. What could he do, he who had been so thoughtless, he who had rebuked the handmaid of Christ? To his chagrin, he learned through experience what he previously had not wanted to know because of [a lack of] humility and compassion. After much sobbing and stammering in a faltering and disordered fashion, he barely escaped disaster. Someone who saw this and who knew the priest personally has borne witness to this. Long after Mass had ended, the handmaid of Christ returned and, speaking in a wondrous manner as if she had been present, reproachfully told the priest what had happened. "Now," she said, "you have learned from experience that it is not in man's power to restrain the intensity of the spirit when the south wind blows."

19. Her Confession

Now, after her compunction, let us look briefly at her confession. I call God as my witness that I was never able to perceive a single mortal sin in all her life or in anything that she said. If sometimes it seemed to her that she had committed a little venial sin, she would present herself to the priest with such sorrow of heart, with such timidity and shame, and with such contrition that she was often compelled to shout aloud from her intense anxiety of heart, like a woman in the throes of childbirth. Although she guarded herself against small and venial sins, it often happened that after a fortnight she could not detect even one disordered thought in her heart.[2] Since it is a habit of good minds to recognise a sin where there is none, she often flew to the feet of priests and made her confession and never stopped accusing herself. We could barely restrain from smiling when she remembered something she had idly said in her youth, for example, some words she had uttered in her childhood.

---

2. For the mediævals, thought (or memory) was located in the heart. See Carruthers, *The Book of Memory* 48–9.

CRITICISM

CLARISSA W. ATKINSON

Female Sanctity in the Late Middle Ages[†]

* * *

Whether or not piety can be "masculine" or "feminine," ways of living certainly are dictated by gender. As a woman, Margery was not eligible to become a priest or a monk or a friar. She might have become a nun, but apparently she had no vocation in youth to the religious life, and she followed the conventional program of the middle-class girl: marriage and motherhood. After her conversion she might still have entered a convent or cell with her husband's permission; late vocations were likely to cause problems, but they occurred fairly frequently throughout the Middle Ages.

Margery did not, however, choose to retire to a convent or a cell. On the contrary, she traveled widely after her conversion, and she ceased to live with her husband or to keep the needs of her household at the center of her attention. Such behavior (unlike her meditative practices) was neither prescribed nor suggested by the affective writers whose modes of prayer she followed. Her way of life was not dictated by any ecclesiastical authority, neither did she find models among the middle-class families of Lynn. Margery was well acquainted with housewives and mothers, business- and tradeswomen, nuns and anchoresses, but it is improbable that she knew anyone like herself.

However, there were other women whose lives were somewhat like Margery's, and it is certain that their existence helped to shape her vocation and her book. Indeed, by the fifteenth century, the lives and works of a great number of holy women had become part of the Christian story. David Knowles has pointed out that the century 1325–1425 produced many such women saints, "several of whom were, or had been, married women, all of whom led lives of external movement in which the visionary and abnormal elements were strongly in evidence, and most of whom wrote accounts of their experiences.[1] As far as we know, the only "holy woman" known personally to Margery was Julian of Norwich, and she may have known that Julian had written a book, although she did not speak of it. The other medieval (as opposed to biblical or legendary) women she mentioned were Birgitta of Sweden, Marie d'Oignies, and Elizabeth of Hungary; she certainly knew "Bride's book" and the biogra-

---

† From *Mystic and Pilgrim: The Book and the World of Margery Kempe* (Ithaca: Cornell UP, 1983) 159–61, 168–79, 190–94. Used by permission of the publisher, Cornell University Press. Citations from *The Book of Margery Kempe* refer to the EETS edition by Meech and Allen (1961). Bracketed page numbers refer to this Norton Critical Edition.
1. David Knowles, *The English Mystical Tradition*, p. 142.

phies of Marie and Elizabeth. But her acquaintance was not limited to the female figures who appear by name in her book.

Holy persons—saints and ecstatics and miracle workers—were the celebrities of the Middle Ages. In the merchant-trading communities of northeastern England, with their close ties to the Continent, reports of holy lives and miraculous happenings were circulated along with reports of storms at sea or political unrest abroad. Furthermore, the medieval Church was an international organization, and the friars especially belonged to international associations. They certainly knew about the women saints (particularly those connected to their own orders), and Margery would have heard from them about such lives. Just as important, the friars were not apt to be astounded or totally discouraging about Margery's unconventional way of life. The substantial sympathy and support she received from so many regular and secular churchmen reflects in part their awareness of the lives and reputations of the Continental women saints.

To understand the choices and decisions of any historical figure, we need to discover what varieties of roles and experience were available to her imagination. This is a special requirement of women's history, in which what is "available" is modified by the circumstances and restrictions of women's lives in particular times and places. Margery Kempe was troubled by instances of misunderstanding and persecution and very much afraid of demonic illusion, but she was not afraid that her way of life was wrong or "unnatural" even when others disapproved of it. She knew of the achievements of other visionary women and of the respectful attention accorded them, and that awareness helped her to discover and define as well as persist in her vocation.

* * *

Of all the Continental women saints, Birgitta of Sweden (1303–1373) exerted the most direct influence on the life and work of Margery Kempe. As we have seen, Margery was well aware of Birgitta and her *Revelations*, and she and her advisers were much affected by the furor over visionary women and their writings occasioned by the Swedish saint. The spheres in which Margery and Birgitta moved were very dissimilar, but the resemblances between the two women are nevertheless more striking than their differences.

Birgitta belonged to a noble family related to the ruling dynasty of Sweden. As with so many holy persons, her sanctity was obvious even in childhood; as a young girl she saw a vision of the crucified Christ.[2] At thirteen she was married to Ulf Gudmarsson, and she used the example of Saint Cecilia to persuade him that they should remain chaste until it was time

2. Johannes Jorgensen, *Saint Bridget of Sweden*, trans. Ingeborg Lund, 2 vols. (London, 1954) 1:47.

for them to conceive and raise children. They lived "as brother and sister" for two years, and (according to the testimony of their daughter Saint Catherine of Sweden) maintained strict sexual morality throughout their lives: "each time before they came together carnally they would always pray the same prayers to God, that He would not permit them to sin in the carnal act and that God would give them fruit who would always serve Him."[3] During the next twenty years, the couple had eight children.

Birgitta's first director-biographer was Canon Matthias of Linköping Cathedral, who shared with her not only his Swedish Bible and stories about pilgrimages in Europe and the Holy Land but his interest in the contemporary European mood of apocalyptic excitement. Birgitta took up an increasingly strict life, fasting, sleeping in straw on the floor, even burning herself with a wax candle on Fridays in memory of the Passion. She grew more and more dissatisfied with ordinary married life—with physical comfort and sexual pleasure—but remained at home until she left (in the late 1330s) to serve at the court of the king of Sweden and his French bride, where she was shocked at the prevalence of vice and corruption.

In 1341 Birgitta and her husband set out for Saint James, their first distant pilgrimage. Ulf became ill on the return journey, and Birgitta took the opportunity to secure his consent to a mutual vow of chastity. Ulf died in 1343, leaving Birgitta free to take up a vocation as a seer, reformer, pilgrim, and founder of a religious order. She began her new life with a long stay at the Cistercian monastery of Alvastra, where she found her second important director, Petrus Olai, who was ordered by God to write down Birgitta's revelations. When he hesitated, he was supernaturally knocked to the ground, after which he felt no further doubts. He remained with the saint until her death.

During her visit to Alvastra, Birgitta clarified her vocation, focusing her concern on the war raging in Europe, on the Babylonian Captivity of the pope, and on corruption in the ecclesiastical hierarchy. Both Christ and the Virgin came frequently to speak to her, and Jesus directed her to found a religious order. She went to the king in Stockholm, stopping along the way at Vadstena, where the mother house of the Birgittines would later be built. There she received detailed instructions and a Rule (the Rule of Saint Saviour) for an order of nuns to be dedicated to the glory of the Virgin. Although the foundations would include men, it was not a double order but a women's order ruled by an abbess. The women were to be served by monk-priests and lay brothers who would have their own buildings and chapel. Priests were necessary to celebrate the sacraments, and lay brothers for manual labor, but the Birgittine order existed for women and in honor of the Virgin, and its rule and organization were

---

3. *Acta et Processus Canonizacionis Beate Birgitte*, ed. Isak Collijn. Vol. 1 of *Samlingar utgivna au Svenska Fornskriftsällskapet* (Uppsala, 1924–31) p. 305.

designed to that end.[4] Whether through personal force, social standing, or a combination of these and other factors, Birgitta had no worries about the right and ability of women to lead. She had set the tone and conditions of her own marriage, and wherever she went she exerted personal, spiritual, and social authority—at home, at the Swedish court, or in Rome. Her visions tended to enhance her confidence, stressing the willing obedience and love of Christ toward his Mother.

In 1350, at the age of forty-seven, Birgitta left Sweden for Rome, where she remained until the end of her life. She felt some guilt and anxiety about her children, some of whom were still young and unsettled. However, she was constantly reassured by the Virgin, and warned that excessive love of her children (excessive if it kept her from God's work) came from the devil.[5] Like Saint Catherine, Birgitta became the "mother" of a *famiglia* devoted to her and committed to the reform of the Church and the return of the pope to Rome. She obeyed a divine command to study Latin, which was necessary for ecclesiastical correspondence and conversation, and was comforted by Saint Agnes when she complained that her lessons interfered with her prayers and that the study of Latin was a difficult and tedious task for an older person.

In 1371 Birgitta was ordered by Christ to visit the Holy Land; when she protested her age and infirmity, Christ said: "I will be with you and I will direct your road, and I will lead you thither and lead you back to Rome, and I will provide you more amply with what you need than ever before."[6] When Margery Kempe was sent to Germany at about sixty years of age, she complained that she had not money enough for the journey and that her daughter-in-law did not want her. Christ said: "I shall provide for thee, and get thee friends to help thee. Do as I bid thee, and no man of the ship shall say nay to thee" (p. 222) [165].

In an early vision (1347), Birgitta saw the kings of England and of

---

4. In *The History and Antiquities of Syon Monastery, the Parish of Islesworth, and the Chapelry of Hounslow* (London, 1840), George James Aungier reprints the Rule of Saint Saviour and discusses both the Birgittine order and the intentions of its founder.

5. Once when she was worried about her children's welfare, Birgitta had a vision: "And she saw in a vision a pot placed above a fire and a boy blowing on the coals so that the pot would catch fire. Blessed Birgitta said to him: 'Why do you try so hard to blow so that the pot will be set aflame?' The boy answered: 'So that the love of your children will be kindled and set on fire in you.' Blessed Birgitta asked: 'Who are you?' He said to her: 'I am the agent.' Then, realizing that an inordinate love for her children arose in her heart, she immediately corrected herself, so that nothing would interfere with the love of Christ" (*Den Heliga Birgittas Revelaciones Extravagantes* ed. Lennarr Hollman. Vol. 5 of *Samlingar ufgivna au Svenska Fornskriftsällskapet* (Uppsala, 1956), p. 218).

6. Translated and quoted in Jorgensen, *Bridget*, 2:238–239. Birgitta's pilgrimage was an important event in Christian art history; her visions of the Nativity and the Passion were extremely influential. In her revelation of the Nativity, the Virgin told Birgitta of the bloodless birth of the Child, from whom shone forth an extraordinary radiance—a light so bright that it obscured the candle Joseph brought into the stable. Immediately after Birgitta returned to Italy and reported her vision, artists began to depict the Nativity as revealed to the saint: the first such work was a Neapolitan fresco painted before 1380 (see Aron Andersson, *St. Birgitta and the Holy Land* [Stockholm, 1973], p. 112). At Calvary, Birgitta experienced a detailed, concrete revelation of Jesus's suffering and emaciated body on the Cross, and her description, which was widely circulated, contributed to the contemporary style of graphic, tortured crucifixes.

France as two wild beasts devouring France in their greed and hatred. Christ told the saint that peace would be achieved eventually through the issue of a royal marriage, but that the kings must first make peace in their hearts.[7] Perhaps it is not surprising that much later—after the marriage of Henry V and Catherine of Valois in 1420 and the birth of the infant Henry VI—the English Crown was counted among the most enthusiastic supporters of the cult of Saint Birgitta. The Lancastrian kings and their retainers, shadowed with the taint of the usurper, were anxious for heavenly legitimation and delighted with the wide dissemination of the saint's revelation.

Houses of the Birgittine order were gradually established throughout Europe during the century after the saint's death. The Birgittines came to England under the sponsorship of Henry V, who laid the first stone of Syon Abbey at Twickenham in 1415. Monks and nuns came from Sweden (by way of Lynn)[8] to instruct the English candidates. Their rule had not then been confirmed by the pope, and the Schism complicated the official establishment of the order in England, but the first nuns were professed in 1420. In 1431 the Abbey was moved to Islesworth, across the Thames from the Carthusian house at Sheen. On her return from Germany in 1434, Margery Kempe visited "Schene," glossed "syon" in the margin by the annotator of the manuscript: Syon Abbey was often named in contemporary records as "Mount Sion of Sheen." Margery went there, she said, "to purchase her pardon" (p. 245) [179], that is, the "Pardon of Syon," an indulgence made available to pilgrims by the pope.[9]

Syon was a center of mystical devotion, of Continental influence, and of "feminine" piety—meaning, in this instance, the piety of devout women living under female religious leadership.[1] Certainly it exempli-

---

7. "And if these two kings of France and England do indeed desire peace I will give everlasting peace," tr. and quoted in Jorgensen, *Bridget*, 1: 197.
8. Princess Philippa, sister of Henry V, was married to King Eric of Denmark and Sweden in 1406; she passed through Lynn on the way to her wedding: see *The Incendium Amoris of Richard Rolle of Hampole*, ed. Margaret Deanesly (Manchester, 1957) p. 99. A member of the princess's retinue visited Vadstena and announced that he intended to give land in England for a Birgittine convent: he never did so, but the king took up the project. Swedish Birgittine monks and nuns also traveled through Lynn on their visits to Syon Abbey: see *Incendium*, p. 107, and Aungier, *Antiquities*, p. 46. The royal wedding and the building of Syon took place while Margery was living in Lynn; she would have been aware of the excitement over the new order. The most complete account of the establishment of Syon Abbey is given in *Incendium*, pp. 91–130; it is summarized in David Knowles, *The Religious Orders in England* (Cambridge, 1957), 2:175–181.
9. The "Pardon of Syon" was celebrated in John Audelay's poem "A Salutation to St. Brigitte," written in the 1420s. It praised Pope Urban's grant of an indulgence for pilgrims to the abbey and said that Jesus himself would have granted the pardon if the pope had not done so. The pardon was available at Lammas time, which was the season of Margery's visit in 1434. Audelay's poem is reprinted in *The Revelations of Saint Birgitta*, ed. William Patterson Cumming (London, 1929), pp. xxxiii–xxxv.
1. The central purpose of the Birgittine order, as dictated by Christ, was the worship of the Virgin. See A. J. Collins, *The Bridgettine Breviary of Syon Abbey* (Worcester, 1963). *The Myroure of Oure Ladye*, an explanation and translation into English of the Hours and masses of the Virgin used at Syon, exemplifies the devotion to Mary which dominated Birgittine piety.

Hope Allen called Syon "a great centre of mystical piety in England, a bulwark of faith in indulgences and pilgrimages. . . . The early Bridgettines of Syon would seem to have been par-

fied a contemporary mood in which the spirituality of women was highly valued. The model for Birgittine convents might have been the founder's vision of the Nativity, in which Mary—the numinous figure—was attended by Joseph, who served God through serving the Virgin. English churchmen were prominent in the struggle for the Birgittine rule and order, which was carried on in Rome in the 1420s. They encountered some very powerful opposition, not only to the acceptance of Birgitta's *Revelations* but to the existence of religious houses for both women and men. Double monasteries were out of favor by the fifteenth century for a number of reasons, including the decline of some of the older orders and the chronic suspicion of cohabitation.[2] Also, Birgitta's emphasis on the abbess as superior was unpopular and perceived to be in conflict with the traditional understanding of 1 Timothy 2:12 ("I permit no woman to teach or to have authority over men; she is to keep silent"). Supporters of the Birgittines held that Paul's words applied within marriage, but that women might hold positions of authority outside of the marriage bond.

The cult of Saint Birgitta in fifteenth-century England was widespread and influential.[3] The large number of surviving manuscripts and early printed copies of *Lives* of the saint and of fragments of her *Revelations* testifies to the enthusiasm for Birgitta, and many of the manuscripts of English versions of the *Revelations* were owned by aristocratic women. Syon Abbey was popular and prosperous right up until the Dissolution; rich (often royal) patrons endowed it with money and land and gave books to the monastery library—usually, of course, to the brothers' library. Whatever Saint Birgitta's views of female leadership, and despite her own struggles, the nuns were not expected to read Latin. Syon was an important religious center, but the real heart of the cult of Birgitta in England was not there but at Oxford, where the chancellor of the university, Thomas Gascoigne, dedicated himself and his pen to her cause. Syon Abbey had an important place in contemporary mystical piety, but both the abbey and the *Revelations* may have had more influence on bookish men than on "ordinary" women.[4] It is interesting to find Margery Kempe visiting Syon, but it is also clear that the model of Saint Birgitta's life was more important in Margery's career than were the *Revelations* or the order.

Margery knew a great deal about Saint Birgitta and may have been aware of their common experience of conflict and distress over sexuality and family life. Birgitta's aristocratic birth and family tradition of sanctity

---

ticularly extreme feminists, a fact which will have been influential for English feminine piety at the time" (Meech and Allen, *Margery Kempe*, p. 349, n. 245–31). Allen refers to the controversy over the authority of the abbess, outlined in *Incendium*, pp. 91–130, and in Knowles, *Religious Orders*, 2:175–181. Syon was a center of mystical piety and of admired religious women, but the phrase "extreme feminists" is misleading in this context.

2. A full account of this struggle is given in Hans Cnattingius, *Studies in the Order of St. Bridget of Sweden*, 1:138–146 and *passim*.

3. The most complete account is F. R. Johnston, "The Cult of St. Bridget of Sweden in Fifteenth-Century England," Master's thesis (Manchester, 1947).

4. *Ibid.*, pp. 133, 147.

made her much less vulnerable than Margery Kempe, and the Swedish saint apparently was not criticized for her way of life. But like all Christian women, Birgitta had to confront within herself the conflict of sanctity with sexuality, marriage, and motherhood—perhaps even with women's "nature" as defined and understood in the Christian tradition. In childhood, Birgitta hated to give up singularity and holiness for the ordinariness of marriage. She obeyed her family by marrying, but attempted to preserve continence within marriage, first by a vow of chastity, then by separating "lust" from the duty of procreation. At the first opportunity she returned to continence. The incompatibility of sexual activity and sacred power constituted an obvious and obdurate dilemma: Christ himself addressed the subject in several revelations, rationalizing Birgitta's wedded and widowed state.[5]

Not only Jesus, but members of Birgitta's *famiglia* were anxious to explain away the taint of sexuality. At the beginning of his *Life* of the saint (the basis for later *Lives*), Birger Gregorius pointed out that there are three ways to holiness—that of the virgin, of the widow, and of the wife. Virginity might be the best, but married persons also could please God through their faith and good works. Birgitta, although wife of Ulf, was the *Sponsa* (or bride) of Christ, and she is usually referred to by that name in the *Revelations*. After all, the Virgin herself had been wife, widow, and virgin, and a humble widow is more pleasing to God than a proud virgin. Birger's *Life* of the saint is noticeably, almost primarily, attentive to Birgitta's sexual attitudes and behavior, which obviously were matters of major concern for the noble Swedish saint as well as the English woman.[6]

In her book, Margery mentioned the births of some of her children, but never the children themselves. The one exception is the son whom she turned away from an evil life, who married overseas, came to her in England with his wife and child at the end of his life, and may have been her first scribe. While he still lived in Lynn and was a sinner, Margery kept urging him to "leave the world and follow Christ, insomuch that he fled her company and would not gladly meet with her" (p. 221) [161]. A lecherous young man (in his mother's opinion), he returned from a trip diseased, "his face waxed full of weals and blubbers as if he were a leper" (p. 222) [161]. He told people that his mother had cursed him and sent him away, and they said "she had done right evil, for through her prayer, God had taken vengeance on her own child". Margery ignored the criticism and felt justified when he begged forgiveness and changed his way of life. Obviously he believed that his mother's curse had caused his illness and that her prayers could cure him, and Margery must have agreed: "When she came to her meditation, not forgetting the fruit of her womb, she asked forgiveness for his sin and release from the sickness. . . . So

5. See, for example, *Revelaciones Extravagantes*, p. 218.
6. See, for example, *Birgerus Gregorii Legenda Sancte Birgitte*, ed. Isak Collijn. Vol. 4 of *Samlingar utgivna au Svenska Fornskrijtsällskapet* (Uppsala, 1956), p. 9.

long she prayed, that he was clean delivered of the sickness and lived many years after . . .". He ascribed not only the cure but his conversion to his mother's prayers, and Margery thanked God for it, although she was skeptical at first. When she realized the change was permanent, however, she was delighted, and when he died within a month of his return to England, she praised God that he had died "in good life and right belief".

Margery's experience with her son is reminiscent of that of Saint Birgitta with her son Karl, the only one of her eight children to provoke tears and worry. In trouble from boyhood, Karl's last sin was the worst: he became the lover of Joanna, the evil queen of Naples. Karl was "punished" by dying of tuberculosis in 1372, just before his mother's pilgrimage to the Holy Land, and Birgitta was tormented by anxiety over the state of his soul. She was reassured by an extraordinary vision in which the Virgin told her that she herself had stood by Karl's deathbed: "as a womman that standith by another womman when sche childeth, to help the chylde that it dye not of flowying of bloode ne be no slayne in that streight place were it cometh oute."[7] (The image of Mary as midwife to the dying soul, revealed to a woman with eight children, is a graphic contribution to "feminine" piety.)

Mary helped Karl because he used to say a prayer to her taught him by Birgitta.[8] The Virgin and the devil fought over his soul, and his many sins were weighed against Mary's intercession and Birgitta's tears and prayers and holy deeds. An angel arguing for Karl's soul said to the devil: "The teres of his madre haue spoiled [thee] . . . so moche hir teeres plesed God."[9] The coincidence of the two sons, dying earlier than their mothers and saved from eternal punishment by their mothers' prayers and tears, is too striking to be overlooked. Both sons, in the eyes of their mothers, were sexual sinners, and their mothers fought their sins—perhaps literally—to the death. It may be that any woman who left her children in order to serve God needed to believe that she could save them through her own sanctity, that her maternal power could be enlarged and transformed.[1] Margery's story, played out on the domestic and local level, is almost a parody of Birgitta's, which took place on a much larger stage, but the shared themes are striking.

Unfortunately for Margery, she did not, like Birgitta, produce a child whose existence could justify the married state. One of Birgitta's daughters, Saint Catherine of Sweden (1331–1381), was another woman saint, and a remarkable one. Like her mother, Catherine was married at about

7. *Revelations*, p. 117.
8. Such an intercession is characteristic of much medieval Marian piety, in which the Virgin serves as an advocate for the members of her own *famiglia*.
9. *Revelations*, p. 121.
1. Despite their very different context, recent studies of maternal power (often the most significant form of power available to women) support this point of view. See esp. Nancy Chodorow, *The Reproduction of Mothering* (Berkeley, 1978), Dorothy Dinnersteen, *The Mermaid and the Mino-taur* (New York, 1976), and Adrienne Rich, *Of Woman Born* (New York, 1976).

twelve years of age; having observed her parents' continence, she persuaded her husband not to consummate the marriage. But she outdistanced her mother, for she was still a virgin at eighteen, when she left her husband for a visit to her mother in Rome. In her own words, "I longed so much for Mother that I could neither eat nor drink nor sleep, and I could no longer find a joy in anything."[2] Birgitta urged Catherine to remain with her in Rome although her husband was ill in Sweden, and God agreed: "Tell your daughter . . . that it is more useful for her to stay in Rome than to go home . . . I will have a care for her husband and bestow upon him the gifts that are best for his soul, for soon I will call him to Me."[3]

The young husband died, and Catherine, with the enviable status of virgin-widow, remained with her mother for the rest of Birgitta's life. Catherine's life was not simple, however, for at eighteen it was attachment to her mother, and not a religious vocation, that brought her to Rome. After her husband's death she forced herself, by horrifying methods, to discover a vocation that would keep her by her mother's side.[4] When Birgitta died, Catherine became abbess of Vadstena, but she spent most of her time and energy in the cause of her mother's canonization and in the fight for the Birgittine order and rule.

* * *

In relation to Margery Kempe, it seems clear that the stories of female saints helped her to live out her vocation by placing before her a group of holy women who not only defied their society but won closeness to Christ by doing so. In a less positive vein, the legends may have exacerbated her fear of sexual violence, a fear that was to some extent a realistic response to the dangers of an unconventional life. It may be, however, that on the unconscious level at least, she feared abuse almost as an adjunct to her vocation and perhaps even as a punishment for its singularity.

Probably because its author lived in the world, and not at home or in a convent, the *Book of Margery Kempe* is populated largely by men. Apart from an occasional figure like the sympathetic jailer's wife of Leicester, Margery encountered only men on her travels. She wrote about her father, her husband, and her son, but said nothing of her mother, of sisters, or of daughters (except for the unsatisfactory daughter-in-law). She visited the nuns at Denny and comforted the woman who went insane after childbirth, but these were exceptions. Margery departed from the conventional female roles of housewife or nun, and as a result, she lived among men or remained solitary. Of course her confessors and advisers

2. Tr. and quoted in Jorgensen, *Bridget*, 2:57.
3. *Ibid.*, 58–59.
4. *Ibid.*, 69–72.

were men, as were all the spiritual authorities to whom she turned, with one notable exception: the anchoress Julian of Norwich. Margery knew Julian by reputation as a spiritual counselor and an expert in the discernment of spirits. When she visited her, they spoke together at length of spiritual matters: "Much was the holy dalliance that the anchoress and this creature had by communing in the love of Our Lord Jesus Christ the many days that they were together" (p. 43) [33].

Julian of Norwich is unique in English religious history. She was a mystic, a theologian, and an educated woman: her description of herself as "unlettered" is an expression of conventional humility.[5] She was deeply learned but not university trained; no hint of scholastic argument enters her book. After about 1403 she lived in a cell in the church of Saints Julian and Edward in Norwich, and she may have been a nun before she became an anchoress. In 1373, at the age of thirty, she fell desperately ill (in response to her own prayer for a serious illness); when she recovered, she received the sixteen "showings" that comprise her revelations. She wrote a short account of her experiences soon after the event; twenty years later, after profound reflection and meditation, she produced an expanded and revised longer version.[6] Her writings are orthodox in content, unorthodox in style—informal, experiential, and written in the first person, characteristics of mystical confession and not of theological argument. Beginning with the revelation of Christ's humanity and Passion, and without departing from her experience, Julian moved toward a spiritual intellectual appreciation of who God is.

Julian's *Book of Showings* consists of description and contemplation of the sixteen revelations, which were vivid, graphic experiences of Christian doctrine, centered on the Passion. The central theme is love, and the central theological problem, or argument, is that of sin and evil. The last "showing" sums up Julian's belief, and her experience: "What, woldest thou wytt thy lordes menyng in this thyng? Wytt is wele, loue was his menyng. Who shewyth it the? Loue. (What shewid he the? Love.) Wherfore shewyth he it the? For loue."[7] To Julian, sin was nothing, for God does everything: "ther is no doer but he" (p. 340), and God does not sin. Sin does cause pain, however, and thus Christ's pain and Passion—revealed to her by direct "showing"—became the resolution of the problem of evil. Unlike sin, "payne is somthyng . . . for it purgyth and makyth vs to know oure selfe and aske mercy" (pp. 406–407). In her own way, Margery Kempe also struggled with the question of sin and evil, and re-

---

5. Edmund Colledge and James Walsh, "Editing Julian of Norwich's *Revelations*: A Progress Report," *Medieval Studies* 38 (1976): 404–27. This article summarizes the full description of Julian's "intellectual formation" given in the introduction to their edition of *A Book of Showings to the Anchoress Julian of Norwich*, 2 vols. (Toronto, 1978), 1:43–59.
6. Colledge and Walsh compare the two versions in their introduction. See also B. A. Windeatt, "Julian of Norwich and Her Audience," *Review of English Studies*, n.s. 27 (1977): 1–17.
7. *Showings*, 2:732–733. The next eight references, indicated by page numbers in the text, are to this volume.

ceived from God a very different resolution. When she refused to believe that some souls were damned, she was punished with demonic visions of sexual abominations until she learned to believe God's word as it was spoken to her soul (see Book I, chapter 59, of Margery's *Book*). The problem of evil became a problem of authority, and Margery's God—a stern Father in this instance—settled her doubts by exerting his power.

Unlike Margery Kempe, whose God was always Father or beautiful young man or boy-child, Julian of Norwich was supreme among those Christian thinkers who have perceived God (and God's relationship to the soul) unrestricted by patriarchal language and masculine imagery. For Julian, God is "the maker, the keper, the louer" (p. 300). In the Trinity she "saw and vnderstode these thre propertes: the properte of the faderhed, and the properte of the mother hed, and the properte of the lordschyppe in one god" (pp. 583-584). Christ is "oure moder in kynd . . . and he is oure moder of mercy . . ." (p. 586). The point is repeated again and again: "As verely as god is oure fader, as verely is god oure moder . . ." (p. 590). This is so for good reason, as Julian explained: "The moders seruyce is nerest, rediest and surest. nerest for it is most of kynd, redyest for it is most of loue, and sekerest for it is most of trewth. This office ne myght nor coulde nevyr none done to þe full but he allone. We wytt that alle oure moders bere vs to payne and to dyeng. A, what is that? But oure very moder Jhesu, he alone beryth vs to joye and to endlesse levyng, blessyd mot he be" (p. 595). Christ died on the Cross in childbirth.

The appreciation of Christ as Mother is not limited to the Cross; it includes the familiar image of Christ as nursing mother: "The moder may geue her chylde sucke hyr mylke, but oure precyous moder Jhesu, he may fede vs wyth hym selfe, and doth full curtesly and full tendyrly with the blessyd sacrament, that is precyous fode of very lyfe . . ." (pp. 596–597). The recognition of God as Mother, experienced directly through mystical revelation and expressed in the ancient imagery of the maternal Saviour, enabled Julian to incorporate the pains of Christ into a profound theology of love and suffering.

Julian of Norwich was an imposing exception to Margery's isolation from other women. Apart from the anchoress, Margery knew about other holy women through story and legend and reputation gathered in church, in pious conversation, and on her travels. The friars of Lynn shared tales of the saints of their orders; in Germany and the Low Countries, where Margery's friends and relatives were merchants and traders, almost every town and cathedral had its special saint, and many of these were women. From the life of Saint Birgitta in particular, Margery was aware that a special sanctity was accessible even to married women, despite the persistent Christian emphasis on virginity. In the lives of such women as Birgitta or Dorothea or Margery Kempe, the ancient saints' battle for virginity was transformed into a struggle for chastity within mar-

riage, and for sufficient freedom from the marriage bond to permit intimacy with Christ. Free of the burdens of marriage and family, women
could move out into the world as prophets and reformers, and a woman
might hope for a special vision or divine revelation. Despite persistent dis-
paragement of the female sex (and of sexuality itself), there were new possibilities of spiritual leadership and adventure for women in the later
Middle Ages. Special promises were made to chosen women, and one of
these was Margery Kempe, to whom God spoke explicitly to comfort and
to reassure: "Daughter, when thou art in Heaven, thou shalt be able to
ask what thou wilt, and I shall grant thee all thy desire. I have told thee
beforetime that thou art a singular lover, and therefore thou shalt have a
singular love in Heaven, a singular reward, and a singular worship" (p.
52) [39]. In a remarkable eschatological vision, Margery and others like
her were linked by a promise to the legendary virgin saints: "And, forasmuch as thou art a maiden in thy soul, I shall take thee by the one hand
in Heaven, and My Mother by the other hand, and so shalt thou dance
in Heaven with other holy maidens and virgins, for I may call thee dearly
bought, and Mine own dearworthy darling" (p. 52) [39].

The holy women of late medieval Europe, who began to appear in substantial numbers after the middle of the thirteenth century, characteristically saw visions, communicated directly with God, and found scribes or
biographers who publicized their experiences. Some of them, in the tradition of Christian female sanctity, were lifelong virgins, but an increasing number were married women and mothers who struggled with the
married state and eventually "transcended" it, becoming in effect "hon-
orary" virgins through their own holiness and the special favor of God.
These women saints, who traveled widely, spoke out publicly, and departed from the traditional roles of Christian women, were a new creation
of the late Middle Ages. Their lives and works form a context in which to
recognize and appreciate Margery Kempe, her book, and her vocation.

LYNN STALEY

Authorship and Authority[†]

* * *

The Book of Margery Kempe is a book of witnesses. It bears witness to
the holiness of the "creatur" whose story it is and the book does so by and

† From *Margery Kempe's Dissenting Fictions* (University Park: Pennsylvania State UP, 1994)
31–38. Copyright 1994 by The Pennsylvania State University. Reproduced by permission of the
publisher. Bracketed page numbers refer to this Norton Critical Edition.

through the scribes who serve as amanuenses for this English "holy woman."[1] The Book begins with a proem that locates Margery in a community in which books serve as tokens of permanency and authority. The proem, which is described as the work of Margery's scribe, who adds it "to expressyn mor openly þan doth þe next folwyng, whech was wretyn er þan þis" (5) [6], serves as a scribal testimonial that underlines Margery's holiness by stressing the scribe's own "conversion." Directly following is a one-paragraph proem that is also focused on the actual composition of the Book. Taken together, the two proems serve to emphasize the authority of the record they introduce. The writer thus describes how the book came to be written:

> Summe of these worthy & worshepful clerkys tokyn it in perel of her sowle and as þei wold answer to God þat þis creatur was inspyred wyth þe Holy Gost and bodyn hyr þat sche schuld don hym wryten & maken a booke of hyr felyngys & hir reuelacyons. Sum proferyd hir to wryten hyr felyngys wyth her owen handys, & sche wold not consentyn in no wey, for sche was comawndyd in hir sowle þat sche schuld not wrytyn so soone (3) [4]

Only after another twenty or so years after her first mystical experience does God command her to write down her feelings so that "hys goodnesse myth be knowyn to alle þe world" (4) [4]. Kempe carefully positions Margery between the learned clerks on the one hand and God on the other. Once Margery knows that God intends to use her words to manifest his goodness, she needs to find a writer who can inscribe her experience for her and thereby give "credens to hir felingys" (4) [4]. Kempe persistently describes Margery as part of a community that values the written word, or the written life. Though he is at first offended by her copious weeping, one priest becomes her supporter because he reads the life of Mary of Oignies (152–53) [112]. The abbot of Leicester wishes to "record" her conversations with him for the benefit of the bishop at Lincoln (117) [86]. Margery herself feels more comfortable about her salvation when she has a vision of her name inscribed in the Book of Life (206–7) [151].

Although she describes a community that derives authority from its books, Kempe's persistent emphasis upon Margery's illiteracy is a key part of her persona. Her description of herself as one of "owyr Lordys owyn secretarijs" (71) [52] points us to her life as the text she "writes," not to an actual book. Notwithstanding the fact that by the first quarter of the fifteenth century it was fairly common for women of her social status to read and not unusual for them to write, Kempe insists that Margery reads and writes only with the aid of a clerk or a scribe. The proem to the Book therefore depicts Margery as a holy woman who is scorned by her worldly

---

1. For discussions of Kempe's scribes, see Atkinson, Mystic and Pilgrim; Ellis, "Margery Kempe's Scribe and the Miraculous Books"; Hirsch, The Revelations of Margery Kempe, all of whom see the scribes as shaping the text in various ways.

contemporaries but cherished by some members of the clergy. Those who recognize her sanctity offer to write down her story "wyth her owen handys" (3) [4], thereby verifying God's presence in Margery by helping her to "make a book" out of her feelings and visions. The vignette provides a highly specific focus upon the life before us by locating Margery within both the conventions of sacred biography and the sanctions of Holy Church. Categorized generically and stamped with orthodoxy, the intricately woven fictions of the *Book* are spun between the poles of a holy *accessus* and an even holier "epilogue," the prayers that complete the volume. Kempe also describes one priest who read to Margery over a period of seven or eight years (143) [106]; a little child who must point out her name in the Book of Life because she cannot recognize her own name (206–7) [151]; a master of divinity who wrote a letter for her (45) [34]; as well as the various scribes she engages in the writing of the *Book* (4–5, 216, 220–21) [4–6, 157, 160–61]. Her presentation of Margery as illiterate may reflect contemporary distrust for those who possessed or could read religious books. Margery's remark that one priest read her "þe Bybyl wyth doctowrys þer-up-on" (143) [106], underlines her devotion to the Scriptures and signals her orthodoxy. In a world where owning or reading a Bible, particularly a copy of the Bible in the vernacular, could be construed as an act of religious and political dissent, Margery's remark that her knowledge of Scripture was mediated through a priest locates her in the bosom of Holy Church. However, Kempe's emphasis upon illiteracy may also indicate her sure understanding of the conventions of spiritual writings by or about women.

In such writings the scribe was an essential component of the authority of the life itself. In this sense, it is less important to ascertain whether Kempe was actually illiterate and therefore dictated her book to a scribe than to seek to understand what function the scribe serves in her book. Since Kempe stresses the amount of time Margery spent with her scribe (216) [157], it is likely she exerted a good deal of control over the text itself: either she wrote it herself and created a fictional scribe, or she had it read back to her and was aware of exactly what was in the text. In other notable accounts of holy women, the scribe tends to lend his authority to the life. Jacques de Vitry in the prologue to his life of Mary of Oignies speaks as a preacher, castigating the spiritual weaknesses of the clergy of his own time and dedicating his work to the bishop of Toulouse in the hopes that the life of this woman may kindle religious fervor in others. Thomas of Cantimpré identifies himself as writing in the tradition of Jacques de Vitry, implicitly justifying his life of Christina Mirabilis by underlining his own veracity as a witness. Philip of Clairvaux describes himself as a witness to the life of Elizabeth of Spalbeck.[2] In a longish proem,

---

2. For Middle English versions, see Horstmann, ed., *Prosalegenden*. Though the translator does not translate Jacques de Vitry's Prologue, he is careful to identify him.

Osbern Bokenham explains that he is turning into English verse the collection of female saints' lives he offers as his "legends" in order to excite
men's affections.[3] The writer thus frequently adopts the role of the
preacher who verifies the significance of the life he recounts by linking
the example of the holy woman to the perceived inadequacies of the present age.[4]

Similarly, the scribes who figure in The Book of Margery Kempe
function as witnesses to her holiness and singularity. However, like
such figures of doubt in medieval mystery plays as the Midwives who
attend Christ's birth and Thomas who doubts the Resurrection,
Kempe's scribes need to be convinced that they have witnessed the
miraculous. She describes Margery's second scribe as a priest who is
initially willing to correct the errors created by her first scribe (4) [5],
but who then refuses, saying he cannot read the manuscript of the first
scribe. Margery says that it is her reputation in the community that
makes him unwilling to appear to sponsor her, observing that cowardice made him fear to be associated with her and her copious weeping. He consequently sends her to a third scribe, who cannot transcribe
the foul manuscript she presents to him. Finally the priest, or the second scribe, "was vexyd in his consciens" (4) [5] and agrees to have
another try at what looked like an unreadable manuscript. Margery
prays for him, and a minor miracle occurs: he is suddenly able to read
the broken English of her first scribe and to do the work he had at first
agreed to do. At the end of the long first book, Kempe notes that here
ends the work of the first scribe, corrected by the priest (220) [160].
The short second book begins with yet another scribal testimonial:

> Afftyr þat owr Souereyn Sauyowr had take þe persone whech wrot
> first þe tretys aforn-seyd to hys many-fold mercy, and þe preiste of
> whom is be-forn-wretyn had copijd þe same tretys aftyr hys sympyl
> cunnyng, he held it expedient to honowr of þe blisful Trinite þat hys
> holy werkys xulde be notifyid & declaryd to þe pepil, whan it plesyd
> hym, to þe worschip of hys holy name. And þan he gan to writyn in
> þe ȝer of owr Lord m.cccc.xxxviij in þe fest of Seynt Vital Martyr
> sweche grace as owr Lord wrowt in hys sympyl creatur ȝerys þat sche
> leuyd aftyr, not alle but summe of hem, aftyr hyr owyn tunge. (221)
> [161]

Having earlier sought to distance himself from her, this priest has become
a true witness to the Lord's grace as it is manifested through the life of
Margery Kempe. He therefore adds a second book, written two years after
the first (see 5 and 221) [6, 161], concluding this second book with a selection of Kempe's prayers (248–54) [180–84].

---

3. Osbern Bokenham, Legendys of Hooly Wummen. See also the much later Lives of Women Saints,
ed. Horstmann, 1–10.
4. On this point, see also Bynum, Holy Feast, 229.

Kempe underlines the important function the scribe fulfills by suggesting that the act of writing is a form of penitential prayer. In answer to Margery's worry that the time spent "in hir chamber wyth hir writer" took time away from prayer in church, God says to her:

> "Drede þe not, dowtyr, for as many bedys as þu woldist seyin I accepte hem as þow þu seydist hem, & þi stody þat þu stodiist for to do writyn þe grace þat I haue schewyd to þe plesith me ryght meche & he þat writith boþe . . . ȝet xulde ȝe not plesyn me mor þan ȝe don wyth ȝowr writyng, for dowtyr, be þis boke many a man xal be turnyd to me & beleuyn þerin."(216)[157]

Both Margery and her scribe are described as sanctified through their labors; in fact, the scribe, like the holy woman whose words he transcribes, is blessed with the gift of tears during the time they worked on the book (219) [159].[5] Finally, Christ, Mary, and many of the saints come into Kempe's soul to thank her for the writing of the book (219) [159]. Kempe's references to scribes and to the process of writing ultimately relate to her emphasis upon the process involved in making a book, a process that, in turn, focuses attention upon the subject of that book, the holy woman.

Just as Kempe uses the voice of God as a screen for the social criticism inherent in many of her descriptions, so the scribe serves to shift attention from her role as a social critic to Margery's status as a holy woman. For example, during her time in the Holy Land, God tells her of her special position: "'Dowtyr, I xal makyn al þe werld to wondryn of þe, & many man & many woman xal spekyn of me for lofe of þe & worshepyn me in þe'" (73) [54]. Kempe follows God's praise for Margery as a singular vessel of his glory with an account of her fellow pilgrims, who do not wish her to accompany them to the River Jordan. By juxtaposing their dislike of her behavior with God's approbation for it, Kempe highlights the disbelief, the spiritual tepidity, of the contemporary English. However, her narrative strategy shields her from charges that she functions as a voice of social and religious criticism. First, God (as he does throughout the *Book*) speaks to Margery directly, using first- and second-person pronouns, thereby giving us the impression that we are eavesdropping on a private conversation. Moreover, Margery's experience is described by an omniscient, third-person narrator, presumably the scribe, whose ability to recount both God's intimate speeches to her, as well as the experience of Margery herself renders him a powerful "witness" to her life. By emphasizing her singularity, the scribe isolates Margery and gives her the freedom, the flexibility, the safety, if you will, to speak against the spiritual

---

5. Atkinson remarks (*Mystic and Pilgrim*, 164) that Brother Arnold, who transcribed the visions of Angela of Foligno, experienced "in the very act of writing a spiritual and new grace." This is not to deny Kempe's priest his tears but to suggest that the detail is one more in a strand linking *The Book of Margery Kempe* to a highly self-conscious culture of the book.

laxities of her own age. Kempe does not directly address the reader; she addresses the reader through the scribe. Only God speaks directly, and he does so only to Margery herself. Where Julian of Norwich becomes her own scribe and speaks with the authority of the seer and thinker, Kempe embodies authority and thus freedom in the scribe who writes Margery's life.

The very presence of a scribe at certain points in the *Book* heightens its bookish quality. With its allusions to other books of spiritual counsel, its attention to its own veracity as a written text, and its careful delineation of the chronological relationship between experience and transcription, it seems to insist upon its own literary authority.[6] In part, this authority rests upon the presence of a scribe whose fear, skepticism, service, and emotive recognition duplicates perhaps any man or woman's reaction to the carefully conceived protagonist of *The Book of Margery Kempe*. I would like to be able to say that the scribe never existed, that Kempe created him, but I can say that, in terms of the shape and function of the *Book*, its author needs a scribe, even a succession of scribes, as witnesses and mediators who authorize the text. Lacking a scribe, we would be left with one woman of forty-something (that age, thought of as post-menopausal and thus less "female,"[7] in which so many medieval women say they began to write), who sits down to record a series of visions and adventures that occurred some years before. How would we class such a work? Would it be it picaresque narrative? Satire? Chaucerian imitation? Heresy? From the very beginning, the scribe mediates, guiding our response to this extraordinary text. If control is one of the issues most pertinent to the subject of scribes, Kempe, like Chaucer, found a way to control scribes by writing them into a work, where they function as keys to authorial strategy and design.

Though scribes obviously existed throughout the Middle Ages, that fact should not prevent us from questioning an author's reasons for employing scribal metaphors within a work. Since the scribe served as a mediator, the relationship adumbrated through a scribe is social or communal. The uses to which authors like Chaucer, Hildegard of Bingen, Christine de Pisan, Julian of Norwich, and Margery Kempe put scribes not only underline the authors' awareness of their relationships to

---

6. Considering the care Julian of Norwich takes to indicate similar matters of chronology as they relate to her own authority, it is tempting to speculate that Margery had not only read and thought about the technique of some version of the *Showings*, but consciously sought to insert herself into a particular authorial company by her own references to time and place.

7. See Bonnie Anderson and Judith Zinsser, *A History of Their Own*, 2 vols. (New York: Harper & Row; 1988); 1:05. See also the very pertinent comments of Peter Brown on the status of widows in the early church and the ways in which a woman who was in some way "de-feminized" attained a flexibility and a freedom she did not have as a sexual being (*The Body and Society*, 144–45). In book 5 of *The Republic*, Plato defines a woman's childbearing years as ending at forty. After menopause, women were supposed to become more male, freer, healthier. The fact that so many women say they begin to write at about this time in their lives suggests that the age itself functioned as a trope of female authorship and thus authority.

their communities, but suggest how a stylus might be trimmed to suit individual needs, needs that were frequently related to gender. An author
might use the scribe as a literary trope to suggest both the public and private aspects of his or her vocation. Sometimes the scribe served as a
screen between the author and the reader and was deliberately used to
mask intent, particularly when the author intended to criticize either civil
or ecclesiastical institutions. The scribe, or the scribe's ghostly presence,
was at other times used to legitimate the author and verify the import of
the work. Since the question of authority would have been particularly
pressing to a woman author, a figure such as a scribe or secretary could
be used as a signifier of vocation. All of these ways of employing the scribe
as a figure of speech relate to the author's perception of the act of producing literature, or of the relationship between author, scribe, and audience. Ultimately, the scribe can be described as a code that at once
conferred authority and denied it, indicated scope and delimited it.

Kempe's use of the trope of the scribe indicates her fundamental
understanding of the terms of the genre in which she worked. What
she offers is best understood, not as an autobiography, but as a biography, a "treatise," written by someone about an exemplary person. As
the following chapter will demonstrate, the precise type of biography
to which Kempe's *Book* can be assimilated is sacred biography, a form
increasingly translated into vernacular languages throughout the late
Middle Ages. The work of Kempe's fellow East Anglians Osbern
Bokenham and John Capgrave provides strong evidence of the growing public for such vernacular lives. By using Margery's life as a means
of scrutinizing not only the foundations of English society but also the
nature of ecclesiastical and political authority, Kempe develops what
was nascent in the traditions of sacred biography she would have inher-
ited from Latin and Continental models. She also reveals her shrewd
grasp of the ways in which the issues and the language of her day could
be used to signify more fundamental truths about societies; like
Chaucer and Langland, she is able to convey a world whose immedi-
acy only appears a reflection of reality. In terms of the *Book's* function,
the scribe is an integral component of the fiction, for by his very existence *in the text* he testifies to the local eminence of the holy, the
exemplary. Written in English about an English "saint," *The Book of
Margery Kempe* dramatizes the weaknesses of the social and ecclesiastical institutions of an age whose need for such sanctity is acute.
Through her scribe, Kempe can speak of the unspeakable, can raise
issues best left alone, can detail the process by which Margery threatens a community that exacts a heavy price for nonconformity, and can
finally question the very process by which we invest authority in communal bodies. Kempe uses her scribe at once to contain the effect and
to underline the urgency of questions she poses through Margery and
her extraordinary life.

KARMA LOCHRIE

From Utterance to Text[†]

* * *

The most significant endorsement of Kempe's visions comes from Julian of Norwich. Kempe shows Julian "very many holy speeches and dalliance that our Lord spoke to her soul" to determine whether there is any deceit in these spiritual locutions. Julian instructs Kempe to measure these experiences according to the worship they accrue to God and the profit to her fellow Christians. She also justifies Kempe's tears as tokens of the Holy Spirit in her soul. Finally, Julian encourages Kempe, "Set all your trust in God and fear not the language of the world" (43)[32]. Kempe's "holy dalyawns" and "comownyng" in the love of God with Julian last several days, providing a kind of oral testimony to the dalliance of God in Kempe's soul. Julian's advice that Kempe not fear the language of the world is a significant one, for it advocates the divine locutions in the soul—dalliance—over and against all those speeches and writings which threaten to silence her.

Kempe's assertion of her own right to speak and teach directly challenges the "language of the world," including the writing of the Church Fathers and the clerical prerogative of speech. This challenge is complicated by the fact that it runs dangerously close to the boundaries of the Lollard heresy in fifteenth-century England. The prescriptions against woman's speech in scriptural and patristic writing are invoked to protect the clerical prerogative to preach.

The most famous scriptural text used to support women's silence is that of St. Paul: "But I suffer not a woman to teach, nor to use authority over the man: but to be in silence. For Adam was first formed; then Eve. And Adam was not seduced, but woman being seduced, was in the transgression" (I Tim. 2:12–14). Various treatises on preaching further reinforce Paul's prohibition of women's assuming the pulpit, signifying as it does, a reversal in the natural hierarchy which leads to the downfall of humanity. In a later elaboration of St. Paul's doctrine by the Dominican Humbert de Romans (d. 1277), Eve herself becomes a sort of false priest who, being corrupted in her own soul, provokes immorality in the souls of others. "'She spoke but once,'" he quotes Bernard, "'and threw the whole world into disorder.'"[1]

---

† From *Margery Kempe and Translations of the Flesh* (Philadelphia: U of Pennsylvania P, 1991) 107–12, 114–19. Copyright © 1991 University of Pennsylvania Press. Reprinted by permission of the publisher. Bracketed page numbers refer to this Norton Critical Edition.
1. Humbert of Romans, *Treatise on Preaching*, ed. Walter M. Conlon, trans. The Dominican Students, Province of St. Joseph (Westminster, MD: Newman Press, 1951), 48. G. R. Owst discusses

Lollard activity in England during the fourteenth and fifteenth centuries circulated the antifeminist fears of woman's speech. One English preacher in Kempe's time, outraged over the growing number of laymen and -women who were usurping the clerical prerogative to read, interpret, and spread the Gospel, exclaimed: "Behold now we see so great a scattering of the Gospel, that simple men & women and those accounted ignorant laymen [laici ydiote] in the reputation of men, write and study the Gospel, as far as they can & know how, teach and scatter the Word of God."[2] Not only were these laywomen and men reading and scattering the gospel, but they were being so presumptuous as to dispute clerks in public.[3]

Records from the diocese of Norwich indicate that women Lollards were in fact "scattering the Gospel" in English translation.[4] While Lollards did not explicitly advocate that women should become preachers, they believed that any lay person could preach and teach the gospel and that all good people, even the laici ydiote, were priests.[5] In the words of one woman Lollard, Hawisia Moone, "every man and every woman beyng in good lyf oute of synne is as good prest and hath [as] muche poar of God in al thynges as ony prest ordred, be he pope or bisshop." The publicity of the Lollard belief in lay preaching can be inferred from Archbishop Courtenay's alarm at the Leicester Lollards, who argued that "any layman can preach and teach the gospel anywhere."[6] While Lollards were being tried and sometimes burnt at the stake at Smithfield, Parliament tried to curb the activities of unlicensed preachers by issuing the statute, De heretico comburendo, which called for their punishment.[7]

Kempe's own preaching and teaching raise the specter of Lollardy, causing townspeople to curse her and clerics to accuse her of Lollard beliefs.[8] After Kempe criticizes some clerics at Lambeth for swearing, she is

---

Humbert's remark in the context of the medieval sermon, Preaching in Medieval England (New York: Russell and Russell, 1965), 5.

2. Quoted in Owst, Preaching in Medieval England, 136. He notes that Robert Rypon, sub-prior of the monastery of Durham and prior of Finchale, also comments on the activities of Lollard lay preachers, 135n. Claire Cross documents the participation of women in the Lollard movement, "'Great Reasoners in Scripture': The Activities of Women Lollards 1380–1530," in Medieval Women, ed. Derek Baker (Oxford: Basil Blackwell, 1978), 359–80.

3. Aston, Lollards and Reformers, 130. Reginald Pecock, bishop of Chicester, complained especially of the arrogance of women Lollards who "make themselves so wise by the Bible, that they "are most haughty of speech regarding clerks" (quoted in Aston, Lollards and Reformers, 51).

4. See Norman C. Tanner, ed., Heresy Trials in the Diocese of Norwich, 1428–31 (London, 1977).

5. See Archbishop Courtney's examination of the Lollards of Leicester, including women, in Cross, "'Great Reasoners in Scripture,'" 362. As Cross points out, Lollard activity in East Anglia where Kempe lived has been especially well documented.

6. For the testimony of Hawisia Moone, see Tanner, Heresy Trials in the Diocese of Norwich, 142. For Archbishop Courtenay's comment, see Margaret Aston, "Lollardy and Sedition, 1381–1431," Past and Present 17 (1960): 12.

7. Aston, "Lollardy and Sedition," 31.

8. For more on Kempe in the context of the Lollard movement, see Clarissa W. Atkinson, Mystic and Pilgrim: The Book and World of Margery Kempe (Ithaca, NY: Cornell University Press, 1983), 103–12; 151–54. David Aers also sees Kempe's resistance to authority as identifying her with the Lollard movement; see Community, Gender, and Individual Identity: English Writing 1360–1430 (London: Routledge, 1988), 84.

confronted with an angry townswoman who says, "I wish you were in Smithfield, and I would carry a fagot to burn you with; it is a pity that you live" (36)[28]. In another encounter with a group of Canterbury monks, she is followed out of the monastery by the same monks who taunt her, "You shall be burned, false Lollard. Here is a cartful of thorns to burn you with" (28)[22]. They are prepared to make good their threat to the encouragement of the Canterbury townspeople until she is rescued by two young men. Her own trembling, quaking, and standing stock still indicate that she, at least, believes their threats and is very much afraid of them.

Kempe's efforts to authorize her own voice are thus very politicized and dangerous. She must assert her own orthodoxy as a Christian at the same time that she argues for her right to speak. Obviously, this is a contradiction which continually threatens to brand her as a Lollard. She has few *auctores* whose writings she can bring to her own defense. If she tries to quote Scriptures, she again incriminates herself, for Lollards were said to have been able to read English translations of the Bible.[9] In fact, when Kempe does quote Luke to justify her speech to the Archbishop of York and his ministers, the clerics respond in unison: "Ah, sir, . . . we know well that she has a devil within her, for she speaks of the Gospel" (126) [93]. Access to vernacular translations of the gospels was tantamount to possession by the devil. Clearly, Kempe's access to the written word, like her bold speech, is both controversial and dangerous.

At issue in Kempe's first arraignment before Henry Bowet, Archbishop of York, is her publicity and her speech. The clerics declare their fears quite openly:

> We knowyn wel þat sche can þe Articles of þe Feith, but we wil not suffyr hir to dwellyn among vs, for þe pepil hath gret feyth in hir dalyawnce, and perauentur sche myth peruertyn summe of hem. (125) [92]

> (We know well that she knows the Articles of Faith, but we will not suffer her to dwell among us, for the people have great faith in her dalliance, and she might by chance pervert some of them.)

Her knowledge and belief in the Articles of Faith seem to be a ruse for her "dalyawnce" by which she perverts her listeners. The choice of words here—"dalyawnce"—is crucial, since dalliance is the source of her mystical and authorial credibility, as we have seen. The charges of the cler-

---

9. Women Lollards often knew Scriptures from having them read to them. In addition, however, they seem to have taught others including their own children passages from the Bible. See Cross, "'Great Reasoners in Scripture,'" 370. Some of these Lollard women boasted of their learning. Margery Baxter claimed to have deceived a Carmelite, while another woman Lollard publicly declared that "she was as well learned as was the parish priest, in all things, except only in saying mass." See Meech and Allen's commentary in *The Book of Margery Kempe*, 315n, and Cross, 371.

ics echo the fears of Humbert de Romans and St. Bernard for the consequences of woman's speech. The archbishop attempts to assuage their fears by demanding that Kempe swear she will neither teach nor challenge the people of his diocese.

Kempe not only refuses to swear: she makes a case for her right to speak which is key to her authorization of herself as a mystic and her book as a whole. She defends her speech by citing a passage from Luke 9:27–28:

> And also þe Gospel makyth mencyon þat, whan þe woman had herd owr Lord prechyd, sche cam be-forn hym wyth a lowde voys & seyd, "Blyssed be þe wombe þat þe bar & þe tetys þat ʒaf þe sowkyn.' þan owr Lord seyd a-ʒen to hir, "Forsoþe so ar þei blissed þat heryn þe word of God and kepyn it.' And þerfor, sir, me thynkyth þat þe Gospel ʒeuyth me leue to spekyn of God. (126) [93]

> (And also the Gospel makes mention that, when the woman had heard our Lord preach, she came before him with a loud voice and said, 'Blessed be the womb which bore you and the teats which gave you suck.' Then our Lord responded to her, 'In truth so are they blessed who hear the word of God and keep it.' And therefore, sir, it seems to me that the Gospel gives me leave to speak of God.)

What is curious is that the Gospel passage does not explicitly endorse woman's speech, but rather her "hearing and keeping" of the word of God. Kempe's gloss of Luke seems rather forced and self-serving. However, there is an interesting precedent for Kempe's interpretation of Luke from a contemporary of hers. The self-confessed Lollard William Brute cites precisely the same passage in his argument for women's right to preach. His extensive gloss of the passage provides us with evidence of the Lollard argument for women preachers, and perhaps, of the subtext of Kempe's gloss. While acknowledging Paul's virtual command that women be silent listeners rather than teachers of the Word, Brute nevertheless makes a clever argument for women preachers:

> Docere et predicare verbum Dei competit sacerdotibus et ad hoc tam a Cristo quam ab apostolis sunt in ecclesia ordinati, et Paulus docet mulieres in silencio discere cum omni subieccione et docere mulieri non permittit neque dominari in virum. Quod tamen non possunt docere neque in virum dominari non dicit Paulus, nec ego audeo affirmare, cum mulieres, sancte virgines, constanter predicarunt verbum Dei et multos ad fidem converterunt sacerdotibus tunc non audentibus loqui verbum, et an predicare verbum Dei sit maius vel minus vel equale cum ministracione corporis Cristi Deus novit qui respondit mulieri dicenti: 'Beatus venter qui te portavit et ubera que suxisti dicendo quin ymmo beati qui audiunt verbum Dei et custodiunt illud,' si beati qui audiunt et custodiunt, magis beati

qui predicant et custodiunt verbum Dei, quoniam beacius est magis dare quam accipere.[1]

(Teaching and preaching the Word of God belongs to the priests and moreover, they are ordained in the Church as much by Christ as by his apostles. Paul teaches that women learn in silence with all subjection and that it is not permitted to woman to teach nor to have mastery over a man. Because, nevertheless, Paul does not say they are not able to teach nor to dominate a man, neither do I venture to affirm it, since women, holy virgins, have constantly preached the word of God and converted many to the faith at times when priests were too faint-hearted to speak the word. God considered the question of whether preaching the word is superior, inferior, or equal to the administration of the body of Christ, when he responded to the woman who said, 'Blessed be the womb that bore you and the breasts which gave you suck,' saying, 'Rather, blessed are they who hear the word of God and keep it.' If they are blessed who hear and keep the word of God, they are even more blessed who preach and keep it, because it is more blessed to give than to receive.)

A two-fold strategy emerges from Brute's defense of women's preaching. Brute negotiates the Pauline prohibition of women's speech by distinguishing between what women are capable of and what they are permitted, between what Paul explicitly forbids and what he fails to affirm. The example of teaching virgins contradicts Paul's prohibition, allowing Brute to insert exceptions to Paul's rule. His second strategy is to conflate the teaching that "it is more blessed to give than to receive" with the Christ's answer to the woman, rendering preaching the word more blessed than hearing and keeping it. In this way, Brute circumvents Paul's prohibition of women preachers.

Brute's defense helps to elucidate Kempe's own argument for her right to speak. Her "reading" of Luke and her assertion of her own teachings could be labeled Lollard. They are, in fact, Lollard arguments. She further threatens to speak of God "until the Pope and Holy Church ordain that no man shall be so bold as to speak of God." However, she does make a distinction between teaching and preaching which Lollards do not make. When a cleric produces the inevitable passage from St. Paul that "no woman should preach," she answers, "I preach not, sir, I come into no pulpit. I use but communication and good words, and that will I do while I live" (126) [93]. Kempe may seem to be quibbling here between preaching—coming into the pulpit—and teaching in order to rescue herself from the damning Pauline edict. Her distinction is not entirely orig-

---

1. William W. Capes, *The Register of John Trefnant, Bishop of Hereford* (Hereford, 1914), 345. The translation is my own. Meech and Allen cite Brute's feminism in connection with Lollard advocacy of women preachers, but they do not mention the parallel between Kempe's argument and Brute's, 315n. Margaret Aston summarizes Brute's defense of women's preaching, *Lollards and Reformers*, 52.

inal, though. In the beginning of the popular fifteenth-century treatise, *Speculum Christiani*, the author marks similar boundaries between preaching and teaching:

> A Grete differens es be-twene prechynge and techynge. Prechynge es in a place where es clepynge to-gedyr or foluynge of pepyl in holy dayes in churches or othe[r] certeyn places and tymes ordened ther-to. And it longeth to hem that been ordeynede ther-to, the whych haue iurediccion and auctorite, and to noon othyr. Techynge is that eche body may enforme and teche hys brothyr in euery place and in conable tyme, os he seeth that it be spedful. For this es a gostly almesdede, to whych euery man es bounde that hath cunnynge.[2]

> (There is a great difference between preaching and teaching. Preaching occurs in a place where there is a summoning together or following of people on holy days in churches or other special places and times ordained thereto. And it belongs to them who are thereto ordained, who have jurisdiction and authority, and to no one else. Teaching means that each body may inform and teach his brother in every place and at a suitable time, as he sees it necessary. For this is a spiritual almsdeed, to which every man who possesses cunning is bound.)

Whether or not the author meant to include women among those bound to the spiritual almsdeed of teaching, his argument is very similar to Kempe's. The basic difference between teaching and preaching is the institutionalization of the words by means of specified places, times, and circumstances. The authority and jurisdiction of preaching belongs, the *Speculum Christiani* author is quick to remark, only to ordained priests. Teaching confers no such authority or jurisdiction on its speaker, yet it occupies the dangerously vast position of any place which is outside the pulpit. Kempe's appeal to this argument allows her to claim that crucial positionality of the mystic voice as separate from the magisterium one, and as legitimate in the eyes of God. It is also, then, a marginal, straying position which threatens to blur the boundaries between authorized and heretical speech.

Obviously, such a distinction does not diminish the threat which her speech poses for the clerics who oppose her and the archbishop, who merely wishes his diocese to be left in peace. In fact, it renders her speech immune from their authority and jurisdiction. We can observe clerical frustration when one monk curses her, saying that he wished she were closed up in a house of stone so that no man could speak with her (27) [22], or when some men of Beverley gently suggest that she return to spinning and carding (129) [96]. Attempts to silence Kempe, however, are not always so innocuous. The Steward of Leicester tries to intimidate Kempe

---

2. G. Holmstedt, ed., *Speculum Christiani*, EETS, o.s. 182 (London: Oxford University Press, 1933; rpt. 1971), 2.

by speaking to her in Latin, and when that fails, by threatening to rape her (112–13) [83].

Kempe's argument for woman's speech makes use of a popular debate of her time. But she is not the last to use the Lucan passage to authorize her own speech. In her *Book of the City of Ladies*, Christine de Pizan in the fifteenth century searches likewise for an argument for woman's speech which would refute the cultural idioms identifying it as "blame-worthy and of such small authority." The allegorical figure of Reason, who appears to the despairing Christine, points to Christ's favoring of woman's speech by having his resurrection announced by a woman, Mary Magdalene, as well as to other examples from the Gospels. She concludes her testimony to woman's blessed speech with the same passage from Luke cited by Kempe. Interestingly, Christine does not include Christ's response, which is so crucial to Brute's exegesis of the passage. Instead she considers the woman's speech itself as a model of wisdom, boldness, and "great force of will." From this and her other examples she infers, "Thus you can understand, fair sweet friend, God has demonstrated that He has truly placed language in women's mouths so that He might be thereby served."[3]

* * *

Kempe dislocates herself as author by breaking with written authority. In the place of textual authority she substitutes the *volo* of mystical desire which gives habitation to her speech.

This does not mean, however, that Kempe makes no reference to textual authorities; in fact, her *Book* does draw upon spiritual texts, and, oddly enough, she clearly views it in the context of a Latin tradition. On two separate occasions in her *Book*, a collection of texts is cited in connection with Kempe's own spiritual practices, including the *Scala Perfectionis* by Walter Hilton, the *Liber Revelationum Celestium S. Birgitta* of St. Bridget, Rolle's *Incendium Amoris* and the Pseudo-Bonaventure text, *Stimulus Amoris*.[4] As we have seen, some scholars would simply attribute these Latin sources to Kempe's scribe.[5] Meech and Allen note that Kempe could have known these Latin works only through "extempora-

3. Christine de Pizan, *The Book of the City of Ladies*, trans. Earl Jeffrey Richards (New York: Persea Books, 1982), 30. I have discussed this passage in connection with Kempe's search for authority elsewhere, "The *Book of Margery Kempe*: A Marginal Woman's Quest for Literary Authority," *Journal of Medieval and Renaissance Studies* 16 (1986): 33–56.
4. Hilton's text is not mentioned by title in either place, but the *Incendium Amoris* is twice referred to by its Latin title, as is the *Stimulo Amoris*, 39 and 154. As I will show, Kempe's use of these references differs in these two passages in important ways.
5. Lawton is the only one to point to the "signs of Latinity" in Kempe's text, particularly to her use of the *Meditationes Vitae Christi*. Lawton argues that this Latinity needs to be explored in more detail and that it signifies "a certain far from naive intertextuality in the work of Margery Kempe," "The Voice of Margery Kempe's *Book*," paper presented at the Modern Language Association Convention, New Orleans, 1988.

neous translations" by the priest who reads to her over a period of seven or eight years or through actual English translations.[6]

These references are further complicated by Kempe's own testimonies. She asks the Steward of Leicester to direct his questions to her in English instead of Latin because she cannot understand it (113) [83]. Yet when another clerk asks her what the biblical command, "Crescite & multiplicamini," means in order to see whether she advocates the heretical interpretation of this passage to justify free love, she responds without difficulty (121) [89]. In Book II, when she is chided for her weeping, she quotes the Latin Psalm 126:5 and 6: "'Qui seminant in lacrimis' & cetera 'euntes ibant & flebant' & cetera, and swech oþer" (235) [172]. She clearly understands some Latin phrases and scriptural texts even if she cannot speak or hear in Latin. Nevertheless, it is remarkable in her book that Latin seems to comprehend her whether she comprehends it or not. A German priest who becomes Kempe's confessor in Rome understands no English, yet he is able to translate Kempe's stories into Latin to the astonishment of a group of her fellow pilgrims (97) [71].

Though we cannot know how much Latin Kempe knew, neither can we ignore the Latinity of her book. We need to be aware of the fact that the priest who read to her probably read from Latin texts of Hilton, Rolle, and Bridget even if he then translated or paraphrased his readings. Kempe's own spirituality seems to be most markedly influenced by the writings of Richard Rolle, particularly the *Incendium Amoris*. This is one of the works which Kempe had read to her before the Latin text was translated into Middle English by Richard Misyn in 1434–35.[7] In fact, traces of Rolle's Latin work survive in Kempe's book, not only in her images and mystical concepts but in her mystical idioms.

Kempe's text frequently makes reference to the "fire of love," a very common mystical idea attributed to Rolle in the *Incendium Amoris*.[8] Early in her book, she describes how her heart was consumed by the "ardowr of lofe." Since most other references are made to the fire, rather than the ardor, of love, Hope Emily Allen speculates that maybe Kempe is making a distinction between two types of fires (271n). Yet a reading of the Latin text of Rolle's treatise reveals that the Latin *ardor* was often used as a synonym for *ignis (fire) and amor (love)*. Rolle explains in his prologue that he uses *ignis* metaphorically to describe *ardor*, the flame or heat of love.[9] It is interesting to note that Misyn translates the *ardor* of the

6. Meech and Allen, 276n. H. E. Allen also speculates that local copies of English translations might have existed at one time and have since vanished.
7. She mentions having this book read to her after she returns from her visit to the Holy Land, which was at least fifteen years before Misyn's translation (153).
8. While this work is the main source for the "fire of love," other Latin and English writings by Rolle elaborate on this mystical experience, including the *Melos Amoris, Emendatio Vitae, The Form of Living, The Commandment*, and the lyrics.
9. *The Incendium Amoris of Richard Rolle of Hampole*, ed. Margaret Deanesly, Publications of the University of Manchester, Historical Series, 26 (London, 1915): "Necessitas quoque corporalis

Latin text as "hete," "lufe," and "flaume," but not the English derivate, "ardor." Clearly, more than one translation of the Latin text is possible in Middle English. Kempe's use of the word "ardowr" follows the Latin more closely than Misyn's does, even though the word in Middle English does not have the same meaning as the Latin word. This could be the result of a literal translation of the Latin, either the priest's or her own. Whichever is the case, this is just one example of the Latin residues in Kempe's text.

Other borrowings from Rolle likewise recall the Latin text of the *Incendium Amoris*. Kempe's description of the first visitation of the fire of love, for example, is very close to Rolle's description of the same in his prologue. Kempe experiences the fire she feels in her breast and heart as truly "as a man would feel the material fire if he put his hand or his finger in it" (88) [65]. This material analogy is provided by Rolle as well in his prologue and in his English work, *The Form of Living*,[1] In this case, Kempe's use of Rolle could have come from either his Latin or his English writings.

She also renders the Rollean experience of the fire of love in her use of the verb "languryn." Rolle's fullest explication of the mystical lover's languor appears again in the *Incendium Amoris*. His explication of languishing comes from the declaration from the Song of Songs 5:8: "I adjure you, O daughters of Jerusalem, if you find my beloved, that you tell him that I languish for love." Rolle attributes this languishing to the lover's abundant love, which lacks the object of his love. More importantly, this languishing accompanies the fire of love, according to Rolle:

> Amoris ergo diuini incendii est mentem quam capit uulnerare: ut dicat, 'Uulnerata sum ego caritate,' et eciam languidam facere pro amore, (unde dicitur *Amore langueo*,) et inebriare: ut sic tendat ad dilectum, quod sui ipsius et omnium rerum obliuiscatur preter Christum.[2]

> (Therefore it is the mind which is wounded by the fire of divine love that is meant by, "I am wounded with love." Also when one is made languid and intoxicated for love, it is said, "I languish for love." For this is how one strives towards the beloved to the extent that he forgets himself and all things apart from Christ.)

Elsewhere in his Latin works, Rolle likewise attributes this "languor" to the wounding of the heart and the unsatisfied longing of the lover for his

atque affecciones humanitus impresse, erumpuosique exilii anguscie ardorem ipsum interpolant, et flamman quam sub metaphora ignem appellaui, eo quod urit et lucet, mitigant et molestant" (146). Rolle also calls this warmth or love a "spiritual ardor" (147).

1. *English Writings of Richard Rolle, Hermit of Hampole*, ed. Hope Emily Allen (Oxford: Clarendon Press, 1931), 105.
2. *Incendium Amoris*, 195. The subject of languishing also comes up in the English work, *The Form of Living*, but it is more fully elaborated in the Latin works, see *English Writings*, ed. H. E. Allen, 103–4.

beloved.[3] Kempe's understanding of mystical languor closely approaches Rolle's, for she reserves the English verb *languren* only for her experience of the terrible lack of the object of her love. When she desires to be rid of the world, Christ instructs her that she must remain and "languren in lofe" (20) [16]. Her "languor" is often triggered by the "gret sowndys & gret melodijs" reminding her of Heaven and her own impatience for it (185) [135]. She needs only to hear the words uttered in a sermon, "Owr Lord Ihesu langurith for lofe" to be reduced to boisterous weeping (185) [135]. Her choice of words again invokes the Latin works of Rolle to her text. It is interesting to note that Kempe uses the verb "languryn" where the Middle English translation of the *Incendium Amoris* consistently translates *langueo* into "longyn."[4] Her choice of the English cognate for the Latin words *languor and ardor* echoes Rolle more directly than does the Middle English translation by Misyn.

Kempe's clearest echoes of Rolle occur in her metaphorical renderings of mystical union in terms of song or melody and smell. Rolle's three-fold distinction among the stages of mystical ascent—*calor, dulcor, and canor*, fire, sweetness, and song—is made in his *Incendium Amoris*, although it appears in his Middle English works as well.[5] Kempe experiences the heavenly melody described by Rolle in his Latin work when she awakens in the middle of the night to "a sound of melody so sweet and delectable, she thought, as though she were in Paradise" (11) [10]. She later speaks of the "sowndys & melodijs" which she heard over a period of twenty-five years and which were so loud as to interfere with her conversations with people (87–88) [64–65]. These mystical references compare with Rolle's account of his own experience while he is reading the Psalms of a "suavitatem inuisibilis melodie" (sweet invisible melody) which overwhelms him. Not only does the divine voice become transformed into this invisible music, but the human response is also converted into song.[6]

More significant is Kempe's reference to the heavenly smells, because she could have been familiar with this mystical sensation in Rolle only through his Latin works.[7] The mystical comfort Kempe receives comes

---

3. See Rolle, *Emendatio Vitae* in *The Fire of Love and the Mending of Life*, trans. M. L. Del Mastro (Garden City, NY: Image Books, 1981); and *Melos Amoris*, ch. 55, in *The Melos Amoris of Richard Rolle of Hampole*, ed. E. J. F. Arnould (Oxford: Basil Blackwell, 1957).

4. For a comparison with the Latin passage quoted, see ch. 18, 40, where even *Amore langueo* is translated "for lufe I longe." For another example, compare Deanesly's edition of *Incendium Amoris*, 216–19, with Richard Misyn's Middle English translation, *The Fire of Love and the Mending of Life, or the Rule of Living*, ed. Ralph Harvey, EETS, o.s. 106 (London, 1896; rpt. 1973), 56–58.

5. See Rolle, *Incendium Amoris*, 182–91; also *The Form of Living* in *Richard Rolle*, trans. R. S. Allen, 170–180.

6. See Wolfgang Riehle's discussion of Rolle's musical imagery, *The Middle English Mystics*, trans. Bernard Standring (London: Routledge and Kegan Paul, 1981), 119–22. The *Melos Amoris* as well as the *Incendium Amoris* uses the related notions of song and melody to convey mystical dalliance; see Arnould, *Melos Amoris*, 20, 138–40.

7. In fact, Riehle claims that this particular mystical sensation is limited in English mysticism to the Latin works of Rolle, except for the negative experience of the devil's stench in Julian of Norwich's *Showings: Middle English Mystics*, 115–16.

in the form of "sweet smells" which exceed all earthly odors and the power of speech to describe (87) [64]. Christ also offers Kempe the comfort of knowing that at her death he will remove body from soul "with great mirth and melody, with sweet smells and good odors" (51) [38]. The mysterious odors of divine visitation infuse Rolle's *Melos Amoris* as they do few of his other Latin or English works.[8] While these heavenly scents may be found in continental mysticism, in England they are almost exclusively characteristic of Rolle and Kempe.

This brief overview suggests that Kempe draws upon the Latin writings of Richard Rolle to characterize her mystical experiences. Her references to divine fragrances, heavenly melodies, and the "ardor" and "languor" of love are only a few examples of the Latinity of her *Book*. Other examples from Hilton, Pseudo-Bonaventure, Bridget's *Liber Revelationum Celestium*, and the *Stimulus Amoris* need to be explored more seriously in Kempe's text than they have been previously. Although the *Book's* Latinity rarely surfaces, we can observe the process in the scribe's own authorization of Kempe's tears. After suffering from doubt about Kempe's tears because of a friar's preaching against her, the scribe reads several works which restore his faith in her, including the biography of Marie d'Oignies and the *Stimulus Amoris*. The scribe refers to the Pseudo-Bonaventure text, *Stimulus Amoris*, by its English title, "þe Prykke of Lofe." Walter Hilton translated this Latin work into English using the same title, but the scribe's quotation in Middle English actually corresponds more closely to the Latin than it does to the English text. Compare the Middle English version with the Latin:

> A, Lord, what xal I mor noysen er cryen? þu lettyst & þu comyst not, & I, wery & ouyrcome thorw desyr, begynne for to maddyn, for lofe gouernyth me & not reson. I renne wyth hasty cowrs wher-þat-euyr þu wylte. I bowe, Lord, þei þat se me irkyn and rewyn, not knowyng me drunkyn wyth þi lofe. Lord, þei seyn 'Lo, ȝen wood man cryeth in þe stretys,' but how meche is þe desyr of myn hert þei parceyue not (154) [113].

> (Sed quid vociferabor amplius? Tardas, et non venis, et jam lassatus desiderio incipio insanire. Amor regit, et non ratio, et curro cum impetu, quocumque me volueris inclinare. Nam qui me vident, derident, et quod tuo amore sim ebrius, non cognoscunt. Dicunt enim: Quid iste insanus vociferatur in plateis? Et quantum sit desiderium non advertunt.)[9]

---

8. *Melos Amoris*, ed. Arnould, 49, 83, 99, 119. Riehle also finds reference to smells in conjunction with the fire of love in *Emendatio Vitae: Middle English Mystics*, 116. The Misyn translation of this work describes the mystic's love as "swete smelland" and a "plesand odur," *The Mending of Life*, 125, 126.

9. The Middle English reads: "Ah, Lord, what shall I more make noise or cry out? You delay and you come not, and I, weary and overcome through desire, begin to go mad, for love governs me and not reason. I run with hasty course wherever you wish. I bow, Lord, and they who see me are irked and pity me, not knowing that I am drunk with your love. Lord, they say, 'Lo, yonder

The scribe seems to be translating from the Latin rather than quoting from Hilton's Middle English translation, for there are some distinct differences in Hilton. Instead of the clause, "I run with a hasty course wherever you wish," Hilton's text has "I run with great noise witherso my love inclines." Further, Hilton inserts a phrase found in none of the Latin texts, substituting for "desire" "desire of Jesus burneth in my heart."[1] Although the Latin text cannot be established conclusively as a source for the scribe's quotation, it can be seriously considered. It is possible that he translates from a text at hand as he writes this portion of the narrative. Since Kempe mentions the Latin title elsewhere, there is a good chance she was familiar with both.[2]

We have evidence that the scribe's memory of another Latin text fails him even though there is a clear resemblance between the Middle English and its source. The story of Marie d'Oignies, like the Pseudo-Bonaventure text, restores the scribe's faith in Kempe's tears. He quotes the *incipit* of chapter 18 and paraphrases the contents of chapter 19 of Jacques de Vitry's *Vita Maria Oigniacensis*. A comparison of the Latin source and the scribe's recollection again reveals a correlation:

> Of þe plentyuows grace of hir teerys he tretyth specyaly . . . in þe xix capitulo wher he tellyth how sche, at þe request of a preyste þat he xulde not be turbelyd ne distrawt in hys Messe wyth hir wepyng & hir sobbyng, went owt at þe chirche-dor, wyth a lowde voyse crying þat sche myth not restreyn hir þerfro. & owr Lord also visityd þe preyste beyng at Messe wyth swech grace & wyth sweche deuocyon whan he xulde redyn þe Holy Gospel þat he wept wondirly so þat he wett hys vestiment & ornamentys of þe awter & myth not mesuryn hys wepyng ne hys sobbyng, it was so habundawnt, ne he myth not restreyn it ne wel stande þerwyth at þe awter (153) [112–13].
>
> (Quadam autem die ante Parasceven, cum jam imminente Christi Passione majori lacrymarum imbre, cum suspiriis et singultibus, se cum Domino mactare inchoasset; quidam de Sacerdotibus ecclesiae eam ut oraret cum silentio, et lacrymas cohiberet, quasi blande increpando hortabatur. Illa . . . impossibilitatis [*sic*] suae conscia,

---

crazy man cries in the streets,' but how great my heart's desire is, they perceive not." The Latin text appears in Meech and Allen, 323n. Although Hilton's text has not been edited, it has been translated by Clare Kirchberger, *The Goad of Love* (London, 1952): "But whereto shall I cry more thus? Thou tarriest and comest not and I as man weary in yearning begin for to fonne. For love stirreth me and no reason and I run with great noise whitherso my love holdeth. And they see me, scorn me, for they know not that I am made as I were drunken, for longing in love. They say thus: 'Why crieth this wood man thus in the streets? but they take no heed how that "desire of Jesus burneth in my heart" (59).

1. The additions to the Middle English versions seem to be present in all of the ten surviving manuscripts, according to Kirchberger, *The Goad of Love*, 20. This makes the added phrase in this modern English translation particularly important for distinguishing between the scribe's Latin and English sources.

2. As Kirchberger points out, the Latin and Middle English texts are quite different, for Hilton tempered much of the excessive affectivity of the Latin texts, *The Goad of Love*, 28–44. Clearly, Kempe would have found more affinities with her own spirituality in the Latin texts than she would have in Hilton's.

egressa clam ab ecclesia in loco secreto et ab omnibus remoto se abscondit, impetravitque a Domino cum lacrymis, ut praedicto Sacerdoti ostenderet, quia non est in homine lacrymarum impetum retinere, quando flante spiritu vehementi fluunt aquae.)[3]

The basic elements of de Vitry's story survive in Kempe's version, including the priest's prohibition against Marie's weeping, her inability to restrain her tears which forces her to leave the church, and, finally, the priest's own experience of uncontrollable tears. Yet the Middle English here does not follow the Latin syntax and wording the way the previous passage did. Is this an example of the scribe's faulty memory, or is he reading from a different text of Marie's life?

Kempe offers a parenthetical explanation which, because it is so uncharacteristic, should alert us to an important distinction between texts alluded to by memory, which need justification, and texts more directly available, which need no justification:

> Than þe preste whech wrot þis tretys . . . had seyn & red þe mater befornwretyn [the story of Marie d'Oignies] meche mor seryowslech & expressiowslech þan it is wretyn in þis tretys (for her is but a lityl of þe effect þerof, for he had not ryth cler mende of þe sayd mater whan he wrot þis tretys, & þerfor he wrote þe lesse þerof). (153) [113]

> (Then the priest who wrote this treatise . . . had seen and read the matter before written [the story of Marie d'Oignies] much more seriously and in more detail than is written in this treatise [for here is but a little of the story's meaning, because he did not have a very clear memory of the said matter when he wrote this treatise, and therefore he wrote less about it.])

Kempe points out two important things in this passage, both of which are instructive as exceptions to the rule of her dictation. First, the story of Marie d'Oignies is the scribe's and not her own; and second, the written account is but a trace of the Latin story because the scribe's recollection was "not ryth cler." The clear attribution of the Latin texts to the scribe's reading (and not Kempe's), along with her apology for his faulty memory, suggests by way of exception her own relationship as author to her text and to her Latin sources. The Latin traces of Rolle's works are not the result of scribal mediation, nor do they reflect the efforts of Kempe to authorize her own discourse. Rather, they represent Kempe's own

3. The Middle English passage reads: "Of the plenteous grace of her tears he treats especially . . . in the 19th chapter where he tells how she, at the request of a priest so that he would not be troubled nor distraught in his Mass with her weeping and her sobbing, went out at the church door, with loud voice crying because she could not restrain herself. And our Lord also visited the priest at Mass with such grace and with such devotion when he would read the Holy Gospel that he wept wondrously so that he wet his vestment and the ornaments of the altar and he could not measure his weeping nor his sobbing, it was so abundant, nor might he restrain it nor well stand therewith at the altar." The Latin is quoted in H. E. Allen's notes to *The Book of Margery Kempe*, 323n. The corresponding passage in the Middle English version of Marie's life may be found in C. Horstmann, *Prosalegenden: Die Legenden des MS Douce 114. Anglia* 8 (1885): 135–36.

inscription of the Latin culture which excludes her into her text by way
of translation. At the same time that her own text echoes Rolle, it rejects
Latinity and authorization of written discourse altogether.

DAVID AERS

The Making of Margery Kempe: Individual and Community[†]

3e arn no good wyfe

(John Kempe to Margery Kempe)

'Why gost þu in white? Art þu a mayden?'
Sche, knelyng on hir knes be-for hym, seyd, 'Nay, ser, I am no mayden;
I am a wife.' He comawydyd hys mene to fettyn a peyr of feterys & seyd
she xuld ben feteryd, for sche was a fals heretyke.

(Archbishop of York and Margery Kempe)

forsake þis lyfe þat þu hast, & go spynne & carde as oþer women don.

('men of þe cuntre', in Yorkshire, to Margery Kempe)

Margery Kempe belonged to a cultural domain which Langland viewed
with dismay. But the mercantile world that seemed such an ominous de-
viation from traditions he cherished, was Margery's 'natural' and un-
questioned element. Born about 1373, she was the daughter of a very
powerful burgess in Lynn, one of England's largest towns and part of a
European economic system. Her husband, though lacking the promi-
nence and wealth of her father, came from the same class, and with him
she had fourteen children. She herself was, for a time, an independent
businesswoman, but gradually became as mobile as the fictional Wife of
Bath or the figure of the poet in *Piers Plowman*, a pilgrim to Jerusalem
and Europe, a visionary and a mystic. She dictated what she considered
the most significant experiences of her life in a work from which she
hoped readers would derive 'gret solas and comfort', witnessing the divine
mercy and revelation she felt her life exemplified. Her book, as Sarah
Beckwith notes, 'contains an account of its own difficult genesis and
Margery's difficulties in persuading her male scribe to take down her revelations: "for þer was so mech obloquie & slawndyr"'.[1] It is one of the

---

† From *Community, Gender, and Individual Identity* (London: Routledge, 1988) 73–74, 75–80.
  Reprinted by permission of the publisher. Bracketed page numbers refer to this Norton Critical
  Edition.
1. All quotations from Margery Kempe are to S. B. Meech and H. E. Allen (eds) (1961) *The Book of
   Margery Kempe*, Oxford: Early English Text Society, o.s., 212. References to this edition now in the
   text. Sarah Beckwith, 'A very material mysticism: the medieval mysticism of Margery Kempe', in
   David Aers (1986) *Medieval Literature: Criticism, Ideology and History*, Brighton: Harvester, here
   p. 37. For Margery's life, see Clarissa Atkinson (1983) *Mystic*, Cornell: Cornell University Press.

most fascinating English texts of the later Middle Ages, a precious work for anyone interested in the history of gender, subjectivities, and English culture. More than any other writing from this era, Margery Kempe's draws attention to many of the complex processes through which female identity might be made in a particular community and class. The book resists conventional sublimations of such processes and the painful conflicts they entailed. This resistance makes it often an extremely moving text, after all these years, across the most thorough transformations of economic systems and mentalities. Thorough, undoubtedly, but perhaps less than total: could it be that at least some of her struggles resonate in our own domestic culture and have not been transcended?

Sadly, but predictably, the book's very resistance to sublimation has been the main reason it has aroused such condescension and hostility among medievalists, ones quite able to keep a calm, scholarly respect when writing about texts exhibiting pathological anti-feminism or dehumanizing class hatred. The hostility has been amply documented in Clarissa Atkinson's indispensable study of Margery Kempe and well analysed in an important essay by Sarah Beckwith. Commentary, the two critics show, has been dominated by terms such as these: 'terrible hysteria', 'neuroticism', 'a hysteric, if not an epileptic', a sufferer from 'morbid self-engrossment', lacking in 'spiritual wisdom' or 'true [!] mystical experience', 'quite mad—an incurable hysteric with a large paranoid trend'.[2] Still emerging in the 1980s one continues to find the extraordinarily uncritical deployment of such obscure but loaded terms by critics: 'a hysterical personality organization', 'a woman whose preoccupation with herself and pervasive hysterical fear come close to insanity'.[3] From their very different theoretical perspectives both Atkinson and Beckwith disclose the resentment of such commentators against Margery's engagement with the social world, her refusal to obey the wishes of the monk at Canterbury: 'I wold þow wer closyd in an hows of ston þat þer schuld no man speke wyth þe' (27) [22]. They analyse the way modern scholars, like the medieval monk, have desired to lock her up, to deprive her of her social mobility, her relative independence of masculine control (as we shall see, relative must be stressed). Those disapproving scholars explicitly prefer the path of negative mysticism, the mysticism of the pseudo-Dionysius or *The Cloud of Unknowing*, to the affective or positive mystical tradition to which Margery belongs, and Beckwith's comment on this preference is very illuminating: 'Negative mysticism, by insisting on the

2. Atkinson, *Mystic*, chapter 7, quotations from pp. 197, 200, 210; Beckwith, 'Material mysticism', pp. 37–40.
3. S. Medcalf (1981) *The Later Middle Ages*, London: Methuen, p. 115; and D. E. Hinderer (1982) 'On rehabilitating Margery Kempe', *Studia Mystica* 5: 27–43, quoted in Kieckhefer (cited in note 4 below), p. 196. On 'hysteria' see Luce Irigaray's reflections in 'Plato's hysteria' in (1985) *Speculum of the Other Woman*, trans. G. C. Gill, Cornell: Cornell University Press; Ilza Veith (1965) *Hysteria: The History of a Disease*, Chicago: Chicago University Press; and Alan Krohn (1978) *Hysteria*, New York: International Universities Press.

unrepresentability of the Other (God) refuses the return to the social sphere.'[4] This can hardly be said of Margery. Even though her 'return' is very different from Langland's, her book, like the self or selves projected in it, actually works over and is produced by cultural forces and problems which are of great significance, in her own time and, so it seems to me, beyond.

I

It was just this awareness that led Sheila Delany to begin her stimulating essay on Margery Kempe and Chaucer's Wife of Bath 'by placing Margery Kempe in her social milieu.'[5] Eight years later, during which time Delany's essay seems largely to have been ignored, Clarissa Atkinson included an outline of the social, economic, and political features of Lynn, paying due attention to the place of women in the merchant class. Given the accessibility of these excellent descriptions of Margery's Lynn, now to be used with the invaluable documentary survey edited by Dorothy Owen, there is no need to go over this ground here.[6] What seems worth recalling, however, is the significance and representativeness of such a community in late medieval culture and society. Late medieval England contained, and had done for many years before Margery Kempe, many communities governed by men whose wealth came from trade, industry, and renting out of property in town and country. In such communities, which varied greatly in size, markets were central—urban markets, rural markets, and, in Lynn's case, international markets. Their élite was driven by the desire for economic success and security, for political power and social recognition. Perceptions, desires, and discourses were shaped by a web of economic and social relationships organized around market transactions and values.[7]

Few observations about Margery Kempe's book are more just than Delany's; 'one is kept constantly aware of the "cash nexus"; it pervades her consciousness as it pervaded her world, part of every human endeavour

---

4. Atkinson, *Mystic*, p. 201; here I quote Beckwith, 'Material mysticism', pp. 39–40; her comments on the monk's wishes, pp. 38–9, and the quotation from Knowles on p. 39 should be savoured. On Margery Kempe's place in tradition, Atkinson's invaluable work is well supplemented by R. Kieckhefer (1984) *Unquiet Souls: Fourteenth-century Saints and their Religious Milieu*, Chicago: Chicago University Press.

5. Sheila Delany (1975) 'Sexual economics, Chaucer's Wife of Bath and *The Book of Margery Kempe*', *Minnesota Review* 5, reprinted in her collection (1983) *Writing Woman*, New York: Schocken, to which references here are made, pp. 80–1.

6. Atkinson, *Mystic*, pp. 67–80, 86–101: also relevant, unavailable to Atkinson, D. Owen (ed.) (1984) *The Making of King's Lynn*, Oxford: British Academy, Oxford University Press.

7. On pre-capitalist market economies and society see my Introduction, with relevant references. For studies cited there of special relevance to the culture of Margery Kempe's class see Sylvia Thrupp (1948) *The Merchant Class of Medieval London*, Chicago: Chicago University Press, 1962; Jennifer Kevmode, "The Merchants of Three North England Towns," in *Profession, Vocation & Culture in Late Medieval England*, ed. Cecil H. Cloush, Liverpool: Liverpool University Press, 1982; and Martha Howell, *Women, Production & Patriarchy in Late Medieval Cities*, Chicago: Chicago University Press, 1986.

and confrontation. No one is immune from money consciousness.'[8] The accuracy of this remark suggests how her work resisted the sublimation of its enabling community. In the account of 'conversion' something emerges of her experience as a female within an urban class which fostered a strong sense of class identity and self-value.[9] This is the ground of her 'grett pompe & pride', her 'pompows aray', the head dress and cloaks she described in such vivid detail (9) [8]. As much as for the aristocracy or rural gentry the maintenance of oligarchic identity in towns depended on maintaining social and class differentiations expressed through display.[1] This had to be very visible and aggressively competitive, 'þat it schuld be þe mor staryng to mennys sygth and hir-self þe mor ben worshepd'. As befits those who attempted to control the townspeople, 'Alle hir desyr was for to be worshepd of þe pepul'. She was also acutely conscious of gradations within the ruling class, sharply reminding her husband 'þat sche was comyn of worthy kenred—hym semyd neuyr for to a weddyd hir, for hir fadyr was sum-tyme meyr' (9) [8].

She indicates the personal and psychological drives within her class and community when she recalls how she seemed compulsively driven to accumulate: refusing to 'be content with þe goodys þat God had sent hire' she 'evyr desyrd mor & more' (9) [9]. The trouble with such conventional moralizing is that it quite fails to engage with the complexities of the situation. For the goods that God had sent her were only sent through the competitive practices and mercantile mentality of her successful father, without which neither goods nor status could be retained. So while she came to judge her motives hostilely, 'for pure covetyse & for to maynten hir pride', she proved herself a true daughter of her class in her drive to become 'on of þe grettest brewers in þe town' (9) [9], more than Langland's Rose the regrator.[2] When this successful business collapsed after three or four years she defied her husband's 'cownsel' and set up a milling enterprise (9–10) [9].

It is important that we understand how normal were the values she exhibited in these episodes, and how marginal the moralizing clerical grid she later applied. Nor are they utterly alien to our own infinitely more in-

8. Delany, 'Sexual economics', p. 86.
9. Similarly, Atkinson, *Mystic*, pp. 78–9, 101.
1. On display in the merchant class, see Sylvia Thrupp (1948) *The Merchant Class of Medieval London*, Chicago: Chicago University Press, 1962, pp. 130–54, 234–56, 317–18; Elspeth M. Veale includes a relevant discussion of sumptuary legislation in chapter 1 of (1966) *The English Fur Trade in the Later Middle Ages*, Oxford: Oxford University Press; relevant to these aspects of her milieu is M. James (1983) 'Ritual, drama and social body in the late medieval English town', *Past and Present* 98: 3–29, and R. B. Dobson, 'The risings in York, Beverly and Scarborough, 1380–1381', in R. H. Hilton and T. H. Aston (eds) (1984) *The English Rising of 1381*, Cambridge: Cambridge University Press.
2. On women in the urban economy, see Martha C. Howell (1986) *Women, Production and Patriarchy in Late Medieval Cities*, Chicago: Chicago University Press; David Nicholas (1985) *The Domestic Life of a Medieval City: Women, Children and the Family in Fourteenth-Century Ghent*, Lincoln, NE: Nebraska University Press; on brewing and Rose the regrator, see R. H. Hilton (1985) *Class Conflict and the Crisis of Feudalism*, London: Hambledon, pp. 203–4. What was the relation between Margery's brewing and John's (*Book of Margery Kempe*, p. 364)?

tensive and extensive market society where the pursuit of economic self-interest and the accumulation of commodities are perceived as the greatest human good, one which should determine collective decision and personal values. However, in that pre-capitalist and predominantly agrarian society such market values were far from achieving the virtual hegemony they have acquired in contemporary capitalist societies. Granted, historians such as Toussaert, Thomas, and Delumeau have demonstrated an immense disparity between the religion of a tiny clerical élite and the religion of the vast majority of people, suggesting how there never was a 'golden age' of medieval Christianity preceding some post-medieval 'fall'.[3] Nevertheless, whatever the current cultural tendencies, aspects of the Gospels could still be heard—at least enough to induce some anxiety amongst urban middle classes and élites about the final justice of their form of life. It is in this framework that Margery interpreted the collapse of her second business enterprise as a divine warning that she should forsake 'hir pride, hir coueytyse, & desyr þat sche had of þe worshepys of þe world' (11) [10]. As usual such condemnation attacks the individual sinner without bringing into question the system of relationships which organizes social life in a way that demands the behaviour judged as sinful if the existing order is to be maintained. Here, understandably, Margery does not put the habitual practices and values of her own class into question. Even if God judges her own enthusiastic participation in her class's practices as sinful, they themselves remain fundamental and untroubling presuppositions of her world, a naturalized part of her daily experience.

It is hardly surprising, then, that they played a decisive role in shaping her identity through all transformations. One of the potential effects of the thirteenth-century expansion of markets for those not too destitute to enter the circuits of exchange, was to encourage the exercise of individual choice, one that potentially instigates a development of individual consciousness, responsibility, and *relative* autonomy (all 'autonomy' always being thoroughly relative).[4] One of the consequences of the mid-fourteenth-century demographic collapse, as we observed in the previous chapter, was to make this potential more widely available, much to the chagrin of employers and their allies. Appreciation of potential advantages of free access to markets, including the freedom to sell labour-power, was among the motivations of those rising in 1381, a rising that was concentrated in 'the most industrialised and commercialised part of

---

3. See Jean Delumeau (1971) *Le Catholicisme entre Luther et Voltaire*, Paris: Presses Universitaires, part 3, chapter 3, 'La legende du Moyen Age Chrètien', especially pp. 234–7; Jacques Toussaert (1963) *Le Sentiment religieux en Flandre à la fin du Moyen Age*, Paris: Plon; Keith Thomas (1973) *Religion and the Decline of Magic*, Harmondsworth: Penguin, chapters 2, 3, 6, 9; Ronald Finucane (1977) *Miracles and Pilgrims*, London: Dent. Grave reservations, which I fully share, are offered concerning J. Bossy (1985) *Christianity in the West*, Oxford: Oxford University Press, by R. W. Scribner (1986) in *English HR*, 100: 683–6.
4. The tricks and relativity in any notion of autonomy, whether of individuals, 'elements', 'levels', or whatever is made clear in most theoretical traditions, including marxist, Hegelian, psychoanalytic, structuralist and poststructuralist.

the country' where the peasant market and its potentials were most developed.⁵ Despite being a woman, Margery's own access to the market as owner of money enabled her to act as a relatively free agent, and to act in the public sphere of production and exchange. She invested capital, organized public work, employed men, defied her official domestic master, made thoroughly individualistic and independent choices (within the current horizons), and exercised power which was inextricably bound up with her specific class and its position in a pre-capitalist market economy. This power even, as we shall see, enabled her to *buy* the sexual and physical autonomy from her husband that she longed for, a longing itself, perhaps, fostered by the class outlook and practice just outlined.

Nowhere is Delany's observation that the 'cash nexus . . . pervades her consciousness' more explicitly illustrated than in the categories and metaphors through which Margery Kempe thinks about and experiences some of the basic interactions between God and humanity. While St Paul certainly uses symbolism drawn from the transactions of slave markets, there is nothing approaching the scope and detailed literalism with which Margery applies market models. As Clarissa Atkinson remarks: 'Unlike the feudal lord of Anselmian theology, Margery's God, who controlled the economy of salvation, functioned as a great banker or a merchant prince.⁶ Some of the passages now to be considered may seem idiosyncratic, but Margery's outlook is perfectly representative of versions of consolation and salvation sponsored in conventional religious practices and discourses in her culture. Her writing suggests the feelings involved in the formulaic evidence concerning what Rosenthal called the 'purchase of paradise' and Chiffoleau 'la comptabilité de l'au-delà,' evidence found copiously in wills, indulgences, sermons, and conventional verses, like those on Gregory's trental.⁷

When Margery Kempe records how she wished to go back to Jerusalem 'to purchasyn hir mor pardon' (75) [55], we witness an example of the links between someone's religious consciousness and their culture's profane economic practice, so habitual as to be naturalized. As her class fostered restless drives to acquire money enabling power over consumption (rather than capitalist accumulation) so the religion it sup-

---

5. R. Hilton (1973) *Bond Men Made Free*, London: Temple Smith, p. 174, see pp. 171–95, 154–6: most studies of peasant communities reveal the market's role in increasing polarization in post-plague England, whether the studies are done from within the Toronto school paradigm (e.g., E. B. Dewindt (1972) *Land and People in Holywell-cum-Needingworth*, Toronto: Pontifical Institute), or a neo-marxist one (e.g., Z. Razi (1980) *Life, Marriage and Death in a Medieval Parish*, Cambridge: Cambridge University Press), or neither (Marjorie K. McIntosh (1986) *Autonomy and Community*, Cambridge: Cambridge University Press, chapter 3 and pp. 226–8).
6. Atkinson, *Mystic*, p. 60; similarly Delany, 'Sexual economics', pp. 86–7.
7. On the upper-class economy of purgatory, see J. T. Rosenthal (1972) *The Purchase of Paradise*, London: Routledge & Kegan Paul; the most culturally resonant study known to me on this subject is Jacques Chiffoleau's haunting study (1980) *La comptabilité de l'au-delà: les hommes, la mort et la religion dans la région d'Avignon à la fin du Moyen Age*, Rome: L'Ecole Française de Rome. Note also: M. Mollat, *The Poor in the Middle Ages*, Connecticut: Yale University Press, pp. 259, 263–5; M. Rubin (1987) *Charity and Community*, Cambridge: Cambridge University Press, pp. 259, 279, 280, 281. Despite warnings such as those in *Dives and Pauper* (I 186), the Church's accommodation to these extensions of the market economy seems to have been as total as Langland feared.

ported and paid for fostered the congenially congruent idea that 'mor' was better, could be purchased and would afford efficacious credit on distant shores where the final accounts would be settled. True enough, the restless drive for economic gain was in a system where failure or refusal to compete entailed decline, decay, and the disaster of downward declassment for self and family: not to pursue 'mor' would inevitably breed anxiety and insecurity, yet the very pursuit of 'mor' was itself a cause and source of anxiety and insecurity, as moralists safely removed from direct participation had always noted. This dialectic has a potentially disturbing religious form. The very drive for 'mor' that Margery's wish on the road from Jerusalem illustrates (more pardon, more absolution, more indulgences), is potentially both effect and cause of a compulsive discontent, a haunting anxiety which seeks alleviation from the very processes that stimulate it. It is the economic, institutional, and psychological matrix that Chaucer mediates as his pardoner mockingly invites the Canterbury pilgrims to give thanks for having an ecclesiastical official with them, one who possesses the means to ease their passage through purgatory:

> taketh pardoun as ye wende,
> Al newe and fressh at every miles ende,
> So that ye offren, alwey newe and newe,
> Nobles or pens, whiche that be goode and trewe.
> It is an honour to everich that is heer
> That ye mowe have a suffisant pardoneer
> T'assoille yow, in contree as ye ryde,
> For aventures whiche that may bityde.
> Paraventure ther may fallen oon or two
> Doun of his hors, and breke his nekke atwo.
> Looke which a seuretee is it to yow alle
> That I am in youre felaweshipe yfalle,
> That may assoille you . . .

The very means for attaining 'seuretee' is the means for inducing anxiety and guilt which in turn drives the penitent to seek or purchase more securities in the matrix which induces more guilt and anxiety.[8]

For Margery Kempe, however, a return to Jerusalem 'to purchasyn hir mor pardon' is made unnecessary by Christ's direct intervention to tell her that by saying or thinking reverend sentiments about those holy places, she will receive the same pardon as if she went physically (75) [55]. While this could sponsor a significant deinstitutionalization of par-

8. F. N. Robinson (ed.) (1979) *The Works of Geoffrey Chaucer*, Oxford: Oxford University Press, all quotes to this edition, here *Pardoner's Prologue and Tale*, ll. 927–40. On the details of this dialetic, see T. N. Tentler (1977) *Sin and Confession on the Eve of the Reformation*, Princeton: Princeton University Press. There are examples of compulsive and anxious daily and more than daily confession among Margery Kempe's fourteenth-century antecedents studied by Kieckhefer, *Unquiet Souls*, pp. 127–35. Also see the comments on such practice by Jennifer Kermode, 'The merchants of three northern English towns', in C. H. Clough (ed.) (1982) *Profession, Vocation and Culture in Late Medieval England*, Liverpool: Liverpool University Press, pp. 23–4.

don, not for the first or last time in the book, it still shows the effects of Margery's market model since the 'mor' pardon granted her can now be put to further philanthropic uses, charitably bestowed on others—the only justification Langland could find for mercantile wealth.[9]

Saved the journey back to Jerusalem, Margery travelled on, coming to Assisi in late summer 1414 where the model we are considering is clearly exemplified: 'Sche was þer also on Lammes Day, when þer is gret pardon of plenyr remyssyon, for to purchasyn grace, mercy, & forȝeueness for hirself, for alle hir frendys, for alle hir enmys, & for alle þe sowlys in Purgatory' (79) [58]. Here we meet the ecclesiastic underpinning of Margery's vocabulary, as of Chaucer's pardoner. The special indulgence she refers to was tied in with pilgrimage to the chapel of the Portiuncula.[1] Outlining the history of indulgences, R. W. Southern traces their development from Urban II's use of them to encourage men to join the Crusade to the later medieval extension of grants of plenary indulgence to individuals purchasing them from confessors. He shows that by 1344 'this free use of the papal power had grown to massive proportions' and from the later fourteenth century plenary privileges extended to local churches, as the one Margery visited in Assisi, 'had become very common', as had individually obtainable plenary indulgences.[2] Whereas this situation was scandalous or hilarious to some, it caused no qualms for Margery, and the public setting she evokes in Assisi reminds us of the utter normality of her mentality and the scene: '& þer was a lady was comyn fro Rome to purchasyn hir pardon. Hir name was Margaret Florentyne. & sche had wyth hir many Knygtys of Roodys, many gentyl-women, & mekyl good caryage' (79) [58]. Her own son, after his conversion, 'went many pilgrimagys to Rome & to many oþer holy placys to purchasyn hym pardon' (224) [163], and it is appropriate that one of the final events in the book is Margery's visit to Syon Abbey in 1434 'to purchasyn hir pardon'.[3] Continually accumulating, continually spending, continually needing to purchase 'mor', the model of the market and the relationships it sponsors determines this version of guilt, forgiveness, and salvation.

* * *

9. G. Kane and E. T. Donaldson (eds) (1975) *Piers Plowman: B version*, London: Athlone, VII 24–33; on this aspect see Thrupp, *Merchant Class*, pp. 174–80, 188–90, 311–12, and the Norwich wills around which N. P. Tanner builds his study (1984) *The Church in Late Medieval Norwich*, Toronto: Pontifical Institute, chapter 3 and appendix 14.

1. *The Book of Margery Kempe*, p. 298.

2. R. W. Southern (1970) *Western Society and the Church in the Middle Ages*, Harmondsworth: Penguin, pp. 136–43, quoting from pp. 137–8, 139.

3. She gets there on Lammas Day, 'þe principal day of pardon' (p. 246): there is a classic list of pardons printed in George J. Aungier (1840) *The History and Antiquities of Syon Monastery*, London: J. B. Nichols, pp. 424–5; for example: 'in the fest of Sent Peter, whiche is called Lammas or Advincula, shall have . . . playne remission in all casis reserued and unreserued, thre owte take, that is, the voo of chastite, beheste to Sent James, and violently smytyng and killing a preste, this except shall haue playne remission, and the thirde parte of pennans enyoyned and relesid, with a thousant yere of pardoune, CCCCCCC daies and fifte.'

KATHLEEN ASHLEY

Historicizing Margery: *The Book of Margery Kempe* as Social Text[†]

The Book and the Canon

The Book of Margery Kempe, usually regarded as "the first autobiography in English,"[1] is one of those richly enigmatic texts about which much has been written but whose circumstances of initial production and reception we know mainly from internal textual evidence.[2] It has been difficult to locate the *Book* with any specificity in a late medieval setting, and we might even say that this text, like its subject Margery, has been in search of an appropriate and appreciative interpretive community.[3] * * *

The most significant intertext for Margery's *Book* has been provided by hagiography, the narrative of a saint's life. Sidonie Smith argues that the "*Book's* very legibility (for herself, her amanuensis, and her projected reader) derived from its resonance with biographical and hagiographical representations of female mystics."[4] Margery's autobiography is, we might say, "failed hagiography"—a substitute for the sacred biography no one else would authorize. The narrative makes a case for Margery as a holy woman who could be officially recognized as a saint. It must be seen, therefore, not simply as the protest of an embattled woman against a system that excludes her, but more specifically as a text whose rhetorical strategies are impelled by the political goal of obtaining canonization from the Church. Conveniently located at the intersection of hagiography, autobiography studies, and social history, this unusual account of one woman's spiritual pilgrimage through fifteenth-century Europe has proved an irresistible subject for contemporary academic discourse since its rediscovery earlier in this century.

---

† From *Journal of Medieval and Early Modern Studies* 28 (1998): 371–88. Copyright © 1998, Duke University Press. All rights reserved. Reprinted with permission. Bracketed page numbers refer to this Norton Critical Edition.
1. The term is Mary G. Mason's in "The Other Voice: Autobiographies of Women Writers," *Autobiography: Essays Theoretical and Critical*, ed. James Olney (Princeton: Princeton University Press, 1980), 207–34; repr. in *Life/Lines: Theorizing Women's Autobiography*, ed. Bella Brodzki and Celeste Schenck (Ithaca: Cornell University Press, 1988), 19–44.
2. Two severely abridged versions of the *Book* were made, one printed by Wynkyn de Worde in 1501 and then reprinted by Henry Pepwell in 1521, both within a framework of devotional reading; see the analysis of Sue Ellen Holbrook, "Margery Kempe and Wynkyn de Worde," in *The Medieval Mystical Tradition in England*, ed. Marion Glasscoe (London: D. S. Brewer, 1987), 27–46. The unique complete manuscript of Margery's *Book* includes a Carthusian reader's marginal comments in a late-fifteenth or early-sixteenth-century hand and three other sets of notes that, according to Karma Lochrie, provide us with "early readings" of Kempe's text. For insightful discussion of this stage of reception, see Karma Lochrie, *Margery Kempe and Translations of the Flesh* (Philadelphia: University of Pennsylvania Press, 1991), 120–23, 203–28.
3. The phrase was popularized by Stanley Fish, *Is There a Text in This Class? The Authority of Interpretive Communities* (Cambridge: Harvard University Press, 1980).
4. Sidonie Smith, *A Poetics of Women's Autobiography: Marginality and the Fictions of Self-Representation* (Bloomington: Indiana University Press, 1987), 66.

* * *

Building on recent interpretations, which have emphasized Margery's gender and spirituality, I would like to position the *Book* centrally as a key text for our understanding of other cultural changes also taking place in the fourteenth through the seventeenth centuries. We could well apply to Margery Kempe's text the description Mark Amsler gives of Chaucer's Wife of Bath: "the narrative performance of the Wife of Bath, the only secular female on the pilgrimage, marks the textual space of the urban and commercial bourgeoisie whose power and autonomy are defined largely by lay literacy, economic mobility, revised inheritance laws, consensual marriage, and religio-political reform in the fourteenth century."[5] Analyzed within this broad historical framework, *The Book of Margery Kempe* is, to use Fredric Jameson's definition, "a form of social praxis . . . a symbolic resolution to a concrete historical situation."[6] It is a liminal text we can read for its unintentional representation of the profound shift that validated the new set of practices—lay literacy, economic mobility, revised inheritance laws, consensual marriage, and religio-political reform—by producing what I will call a "bourgeois ideology."[7]

Bourgeois Dilemmas

Margery's representation of female mystical experience has a crucial relationship to the urban bourgeoisie of which she was a member, for—despite first impressions to the contrary—Margery's social class is not incidental to her story. She was the daughter of John Brunham, a leading citizen and several times mayor of Lynn, she was the wife of another bourgeois, and she was an active member of commercial society in her youth.[8]

5. Mark Amsler, "The Wife of Bath and Women's Power," *Assays* 4 (1987): 72.
6. Fredric Jameson, *The Political Unconscious: Narrative as a Socially Symbolic Act* (Ithaca: Cornell University Press, 1981), 117. For a discussion of the Marxist term *praxis*, see *A Dictionary of Marxist Thought*, ed. Tom Bottomore et al. (Cambridge: Harvard University Press, 1983), 384–89.
7. According to Rosalind Coward and John Ellis, ideology fixes "the individual in place as subject for a certain meaning. This is simultaneously to provide individuals with a subject-ivity, and to subject them to the social structure with its existing contradictory relations and powers." See *Language and Materialism: Developments in Semiology and the Theory of the Subject* (London: Routledge and Kegan Paul, 1977), 76. As I am using the term *bourgeois ideology* here, it refers to the incipient articulations during the fifteenth and sixteenth centuries of a construct that will be fully functional only in the seventeenth century, when it would be called the *Protestant ethic*. As Thomas M. Safley puts it, "Max Weber hypothesized that the 'ascetic' individual—the person who could view material success as a sign of divine election—was the unique Protestant contribution to capitalist, economic development." See "Civic Morality and the Domestic Economy," in *The German People and the Reformation*, ed. R. Po-Chia Hsia (Ithaca: Cornell University Press, 1988), 174. My rereading of *The Book of Margery Kempe* as an early example of this emergent "bourgeois ideology" was enabled by my current research on the history of conduct books addressed to women from the fourteenth to the late sixteenth century—a project that reveals the ideological centrality of gender to the self-definition of urban bourgeois elites.
8. Local documents naming Margery's father or her husband are included in Appendix 3 of the EETS edition of the *Book*, 358–75. Only one extant document mentions a Margery Kempe who joined the most prestigious guild in King's Lynn in 1438; otherwise, Margery herself does not appear in civic or ecclesiastical records. Despite the many topical references in her narrative,

Sheila Delany first pointed out that the "cash nexus" permeated Margery's consciousness and language, whether she was buying spiritual benefits or paying off her husband's debts in exchange for her sexual freedom; and Sarah Beckwith notes that in Margery Kempe the worlds of the sacred and the secular "are incomprehensible other than through their mutual relation. Her *habitus* is one that readily converts symbolic capital into economic capital and economic capital back into cultural capital."[9] David Aers has also emphasized Margery's economic autonomy as a member of this new commercial class:

> Despite being a woman, Margery's own access to the market as owner of money enabled her to act as a relatively free agent, and to act in the public sphere of production and exchange. She invested capital, organized public work, employed men, defied her official domestic master, made thoroughly individualistic and independent choices . . . and exercised power which was inextricably bound up with her specific class and its position in a precapitalist market economy.[1]

Though she critiques her own greed and that of others, and though she appears to reject commerce for contemplation,[2] Margery's saga can be read as offering metaphorical resolution to ideological dilemmas faced by the urban middle classes in the late Middle Ages. The bourgeoisie had won both economic and political power in urban settings by the fifteenth century, but that power had not yet produced a positive class identity to rival its well established competitors—ecclesiastical and aristocratic ideologies—both of which still had cultural caché in the fifteenth century.[3] An essentially monastic value system that underpinned religious ideologies denigrated involvement in the world and privileged withdrawal from the active life to contemplation.[4] In the

---

Margery's controversial activities are "not referred to in any contemporary source," as Staley has observed (*Margery Kempe's Dissenting Fictions*, 173).

9. Delany, *Writing Woman*, 86; Beckwith, *Christ's Body*, 110.

1. David Aers, *Community, Gender, and Individual Identity: English Writing, 1360–1430* (London: Routledge, 1988), 77–78.

2. Staley, *Margery Kempe's Dissenting Fictions* makes a strong case that the author of the *Book* (whom she calls Kempe) characterizes her community as "stifling, conformist, mercantile, violent, and superficial" (40), and deploys her persona (Margery) as the distracting foreground of her narrative. In other words, "Kempe avails herself of the freedom of the social critic by drawing upon the conventional elements of female sacred biography" (40). Staley argues that Margery is not marginal, as critics have suggested, but is represented as "a figure whose liminal status is ultimately resolved, not by reintegration into the community, but by her rejection of its demands and practices" (40 n. 2).

3. See comments by Larissa Taylor, *Soldiers of Christ: Preaching in Late Medieval and Reformation France* (New York: Oxford University Press, 1992), 148–49, that preachers' attitudes toward the new professional groups (public officials, lawyers, merchants, etc.) in this period are uniformly negative.

4. Obviously, in making this statement, I am ignoring the existence of the fraternal orders, who led mixed lives of religious commitment and social activity in urban settings; but I would suggest that the paradigm of religious withdrawal from the world was still ideologically hegemonic and may account for the popularity of satires against these liminal religious. On the late medieval *mentalité* that excluded the merchant and professional classes from approbation, see essays in Jacques Le Goff, *Time, Work, and Culture in the Middle Ages*, trans. Arthur Goldhammer

secular realm aristocratic values were still hegemonic as objects of cultural desire, although the actual economic and political powers of the aristocracy had dwindled considerably.

As social text, Margery's *Book* has little to say about aristocratic values, but it is intensely revealing of the boundary between religious norms and bourgeois values. Sarah Beckwith's formulation is that the *Book* "can be considered a complex examination" of the "interconnection [between clerical and bourgeois values] across the body of a bourgeois religious woman, and the struggle for cultural hegemony by means of it."[5] I would emphasize the still-conflicting associations of the concepts of "bourgeois" and "religious" in the fifteenth century and read the text as praxis; Margery's autobiography symbolically enacts a solution to the cultural dilemma of how to achieve spiritual validation while remaining an active member of mercantile society. This is not just a female problem, but *the* late medieval ideological dilemma for the bourgeoisie.

The Discourse of "Woman" and the Liminal Text

The centrality of gender to social change in the fifteenth century has been suggested by Alice Jardine, who says that the transition between the late Middle Ages and the Renaissance was "a period when 'woman' was at the height of discursive circulation."[6] As most critics have noted, Margery's *Book* represents her gender as controversial since Margery refuses to model her conduct either on anchorite behavior (enclosed in a sacred space) or on that of the urban goodwife (enclosed in the domestic space). Instead, Margery roams across eastern England and the Continent in her restless search for fulfillment and justification beyond ac-

---

(Chicago: University of Chicago Press, 1980). Le Goff comments on the merchants who were "irked that they did not occupy a place in the social hierarchy commensurate with their economic strength" and defines the pre-fifteenth-century tendency for revolts against the Church to take the "form of mystical religiosity, one of whose principal characteristics was to exclude material, and consequently professional, life from integration into the religious universe" (109).

5. Beckwith, *Christ's Body*, 102.

6. Alice Jardine, *Gynesis* (Ithaca: Cornell University Press, 1985), 93. Cora Kaplan, writing as a cultural materialist critic about nineteenth- and twentieth-century literature in *Sea Changes: Culture and Feminism* (London: Verso, 1986), has critiqued contemporary feminist criticism for overvaluing gender and ignoring class and race: "for without the class and race perspectives that socialist feminist critics bring to the analysis of both literary texts and of their conditions of production, liberal feminist criticism, with its emphasis on the unified female subject, will unintentionally reproduce the values of mass market romance. In that fictional landscape the other structuring relations of society fade and disappear, leaving us with the naked drama of sexual difference as the only scenario that matters" (148). A similar critique has been made by Margaret Ezell, "Re-visioning the Restoration: Or, How to Stop Obscuring Early Women Writers," in *New Historical Literary Study: Essays on Reproducing Texts, Representing History*, ed. Jeffrey Cox and Larry Reynolds (Princeton: Princeton University Press, 1993), 136–50. Ezell notes "the emotional impact of material which is perceived as transhistorical and autobiographical" (143). The tendency to de-historicize writing by women and discover female commonalities in a "feminist retelling of the past" has also characterized the criticism of Margery Kempe. In this essay I will be following Christiane Klapisch-Zuber, who has investigated the "interaction of sex-based differences and politics" as she studies "how a set of gender-based symbols came to be written into a good part of history." See *Women, Family, and Ritual in Renaissance Florence*, trans. Lydia Cochrane (Chicago: University of Chicago Press, 1985), iv.

cepted female roles.[7] Following the dictum of cultural anthropology that what is socially marginal is often symbolically central, many critics have assumed that the symbolic potency of gender issues in the *Book of Margery Kempe* correlates with Margery's literal marginality, a position from which Margery offers critiques of both the religious establishment and secular values.[8]

Even granted that her marginality is self-elected, I'd argue that the binary language of *margin and center* is not adequate to capture the complexity of late medieval constraints and possibilities within which Margery Kempe acted. Scholars like Clarissa Atkinson, David Aers, and Anthony Goodman have called attention to the far from monolithic religious and social context of Margery's various activities.[9] The religious authorities did not speak with one voice but articulated diverse and competing positions, especially on female spirituality. If Margery encounters resistence from one churchman, she is able to find another who supports her. The picture of her fellow pilgrims that emerges from her narrative is similarly fragmented. Some of the groups or individuals she travels with recognize her spiritual gifts while others reject her. Even her husband is at times supportive and at others resistent to her devotional goals. A reader of this text would be hard pressed to find coherent communities of any kind in fifteenth-century Europe.

While her rhetoric emphasizes her hard won "singularity,"[1] Margery moves through the multiple fissures of her society in a mode more characteristic of liminality than marginality (where marginality connotes only negative exclusion from normative categories).[2] In Victor Turner's defin-

7. Sidonie Smith notes that "the rather stable story of spiritual conversion is syncopated by the constant mobility, the unending quest to gain exoneration, blessing, and support and to avert condemnation and burning" (*A Poetics of Women's Autobiography*, 79).
8. See especially Staley, *Margery Kempe's Dissenting Fictions*, 177–78: "Just as the *Book's* testimonies to Margery's sanctity at once provide an image of holiness and comment upon the society that will not recognize what is in its midst, so Kempe's emphasis on the gender of her protagonist—and thus upon gender conflict—gives her the scope to glance at the foundations of both spiritual and civil authority. . . . Moreover, both parts of the *Book* conclude with depictions of Margery as having attained a necessary and objective distance from her world."
9. Anthony Goodman, who is unsympathetic to Margery's eccentricity, notes the spiritual and political patronage provided her mysticism by clerics in Lynn and Norwich: "*The Book of Margery Kempe* reveals a glimpse of what may have been a significant division of opinion between conservative-minded burgesses and the people of Lynn, encouraged by like-minded clerics, and a group of clerical radicals drawn together from various religious disciplines." See "The Piety of John Brunham's Daughter, of Lynn," in *Medieval Women*, ed. Derek Baker (Oxford: Basil Blackwell, 1978), 357; also Atkinson, *Mystic and Pilgrim*, 103–28. Aers, *Community, Gender, and Individual Identity*, says it is "noticeable that we get an image of a clerical community whose responses to her were so far from homogeneous that they could range from the most intimate and reverential support to the most aggressive dismissal" (109).
1. The term is Lynn Staley's, *Margery Kempe's Dissenting Fictions*, 33.
2. Barbara Babcock writes, "All too often 'marginality,' like 'deviant,' has connoted being outside in a solely negative sense, being dangerous to or somehow below 'normal' boundaries." "'A Tolerated Margin of Mess': The Trickster and His Tales Reconsidered," *Journal of the Folklore Institute* 11 (1975): 149. Nevertheless, Babcock prefers to use the term *marginal* with a meaning closer to Victor Turner's *liminality*. Karma Lochrie uses the term *marginality* to describe Margery in "*The Book of Margery Kempe*: A Marginal Woman's Quest for Literary Authority," *Journal of Medieval and Renaissance Studies* 16 (1986): 33–56.

ition, *liminality* is the mediating state between customary categories in a transformative process. It is characterized by ambiguity or paradox, and—as a "realm of possibility"—allows for new cultural combinations and new paradigms.[3] Not only is Margery a liminal character, the text itself is liminal as a narrative that represents a cultural transformation and models the construction of validating ideologies.

The Text as Authorizing Document

Margery's autobiographical narrative, like the phenomenon of female mysticism, prefigures the kind of text that will allow individuals and groups to authorize themselves—a crucial step beyond the mediated structures of late medieval authority. To see this, we need to read mysticism as a socially symbolic language and focus on the necessity of producing a *written* text. Margery may invoke ineffability topoi in claiming inability to describe her mystical experiences,[4] but the materiality of the written document is crucial to the personal validation of her life; she must produce a hagiographic text to record her mystical visions and substantiate her claims to sanctity.[5]

Margery's personal need represents the late medieval cultural mandate of literacy upon which the bourgeoisie based its evolving status. The clerical monopoly on writing was no longer a literal fact, but it remained an ideological trope in the fifteenth century. The writing of the laity—especially of women—remained culturally invisible, although of course the livelihoods of urban artisan and bourgeois often depended upon literacy and numeracy. The rise to power of these new classes was predicated upon independent control over written texts and documents.

My rereading of mysticism as cultural text suggests that the mystic who could either write her own life experiences or, more often, gain the support of others to write a hagiographic text was appropriating clerical powers of literacy. The Church attempted to control religious experiences like visions through the confessional, individual supervision, and other monitoring techniques, but the ability of literate nonclerics to circulate a

---

3. See my introduction to *Victor Turner and the Construction of Cultural Criticism: Between Literature and Anthropology* (Bloomington: Indiana University Press, 1990), xviii. Without using anthropological terminology, and within a feminist framework, Nona Fienberg in "Thematics of Value in *The Book of Margery Kempe*," *Modern Philology* 87 (1989): 132–41, perceives that Margery, "through a subtle and dynamic series of calculated transactions," transforms herself (132). Those changes in her "personal economy" are correlated to the liminality of late medieval society.

4. Margery says in her opening remarks, "Ne hyr-self cowd nevyr telle þe grace þat sche felt, it was so hevenly, so hy a-bouen hyr reson & hyr bodyly wyttys, and hyr body so febyl in tym of þe presens of grace þat sche myth nevyr expressyn it wyth her word lych as sche felt it in hyr sowle" (3) [4].

5. On the context in which she does this, see Aviad Kleinberg, "Proving Sanctity: Selection and Authentification of Saints in the Later Middle Ages," *Viator* 20 (1989): 183–205. For a male mystic using similar strategies, see Nicholas Watson, "Translation and Self-Canonization in Richard Rolle's *Melos Amoris*," in *The Medieval Translator: The Theory and Practice of Translation in the Middle Ages*, ed. Roger Ellis (Cambridge: D. S. Brewer, 1989), 167–80.

written text challenged ecclesiastical authority.[6] Though eminent the-ologians like Jean Gerson warned against the multitude of silly women who ran to their confessors to chatter about their latest vision or revela-tion, even Gerson had to acknowledge that mysticism had developed a force independent of clerical sanction and that the Church would attack it to its own detriment.[7] Textual documentation of miracles or visions was essential to the ecclesiastical canonization procedure, but it also provided social validation whether or not the holy person received official recog-nition. The ability to produce the written discourses of mysticism in the late Middle Ages brought independent social power.

The prefatory narratives in *The Book of Margery Kempe* represent the autobiography as a text produced outside regular ecclesiastical or clerical structures. The *Book's* introduction, composed by Margery and her pries-tamanuensis, shows how the writing of Margery's life and revelations was itself founded on divine sanction, beyond the advice and power of mere humans.

* * *

Neither the urgings of religious authorities (which she resists for twenty years) nor the hostility, ineptitude, and physical incapacity of her amanuenses (which delay her for several more years) are shown to inhibit production of Margery's *Book*. Rather, by the power of divine instruction given directly to Margery the narrator and through her

6. The most striking example of this is heretical movements like Lollardy, with their deliberate de-ployment of vernacular literacy to enable the laity to resist ecclesiastical control. See Margaret Aston, *Lollards and Reformers: Images and Literacy in Late Medieval Religion* (London: Ham-bledon, 1984), especially chapters on "Devotional Literacy" and "Lollardy and Literacy," 101–33, 193–217; also Anne Hudson, "Lollardy: The English Heresy?" and "Some Aspects of Lollard Book Production," in her *Lollards and Their Books* (London: Hambledon, 1985), 141–63, 181–91. Given her transgressive liminality in religious matters, Margery is often accused of being a Lollard. See Lochrie, *Margery Kempe and Translations of the Flesh*, 106–13. How-ever, what is at issue is preaching and teaching, not Margery's writing. Lochrie argues that Margery privileges "her own voice—and the oral/aural text of her dialogues with Christ—over the textual witness of her *auctoritees*" (204), but I would suggest that the impetus to produce her own written narrative recording those authorizing dialogues is not less important to Margery's self-authorization.
7. Jean Gerson wrote the *De probatione spirituum* at the Council of Constance in 1415, where papal schism and mysticism were discussed. In section 49, Gerson says, "If the visionary is a woman, it is especially necessary to learn how she acts toward her confessors or instructors. Is she prone to continual conversations, either under the pretext of frequent confession or in relating lengthy accounts of her visions . . . ?" trans. in Paschal Boland, *The Concept of Discretio Spir-ituum in John Gerson's "De Probatione Spirituum" and "De Distinctione Verarum Visionum a Falsis"* (Washington, D.C.: Catholic University of America Press, 1959), 36. In sections 11–12, Gerson writes, "Of special interest is the case of Bridget (of Sweden), who claims to have en-joyed visions not only of angels, but also of Jesus Christ, Mary, Agnes, and other saints, who talk to her with the familiarity of friends, or as a bridegroom to his bride. . . . Truly there is danger here, either in approving or in disapproving such writings. For what would be more disgraceful or incongruous for this Sacred Council than to declare that false, imaginary, or foolish visions are true and genuine revelations? On the other hand, to denounce those revelations which are declared authentic in many places and by different peoples, after various and numerous exami-nations, would pose a threat, perhaps great, of spiritual harm to the Christian faith and the de-votion of the faithful" (28).

scribes—who function as internal witnesses to Margery's holiness[8]—the text of her holy life is finally written. The text contains its own authorization as it seeks to validate Margery's experiences, and thus may be seen as prototype of the kinds of writing that would eventually undermine clerical textual authority. Furthermore, the life it describes is ostensibly directed toward the sacred to the exclusion of mundane social obligations, but it ultimately represents the active life as one of the bases for Margery's claim to sanctity.

Mysticism as Cultural Text

Accounts of mystical experiences (which might seem individual and private) nevertheless provided a privileged site for testing *social* identities in the later Middle Ages. Laurie Finke has recently summarized research suggesting that the discourse of late medieval mysticism empowered women to speak with an authority that challenged that of the institutional church. She sees mysticism as a "site of struggle between the authoritative, monologic language of a powerful social institution and the heteroglossia of the men and women who came under its sway and sometimes resisted it."[9] Finke's argument remains bound to a model of the church as controller of dominant discourse, against which women mystics' words and bodies became "the sites of a struggle to redefine the meaning of *female* silence and powerlessness [my emphasis]."[1] I'd propose instead a model in which late medieval female mysticism becomes a site of *cultural* struggle to redefine social ideologies, with mysticism and gender as languages in which the conflicts are articulated.

For both genders religious experience was a site of contention, where the late medieval crisis of interpretation and authority could be enacted in the symbolic language of mystical experience. Margery's devotional behaviors provide texts for contested interpretation—in her century as well as ours. Earlier scholars were puzzled by the phenomenon of Margery's "cryings," her socially disruptive expression of affective devotion to Christ; her loud wailing was also an idiosyncratic sign of holiness for Margery's peers. Even her amanuensis had difficulty interpreting her behavior until he discovered, to his relief, the precedent of Marie d'Oignies in Jacques de Vitry's hagiographic text.[2] The trope of copious tears recurs in a majority of the chapters of Book One, and in each case

---

8. See Staley, *Margery Kempe's Dissenting Fictions*, 33–38. She summarizes her arguments by saying that "the scribe is an integral component of the fiction, for by his very existence *in the text* he testifies to the local eminence of the holy, the exemplary" (38).
9. Laurie Finke, *Feminist Theory, Women's Writing* (Ithaca: Cornell University Press, 1992), 78.
1. Ibid., 98.
2. See the *Book*, 152–53; also on responses to Margery's tears by inscribed readers and later manuscript annotators, see Lochrie, *Margery Kempe and Translations of the Flesh*, 118–27. Lochrie points out that Margery's "boistrous weeping" dates from her visit to Mount Calvary and "suggests a continual engagement in meditation on Christ's crucified body" (172, 177).

it triggers an examination not only of *how* to interpret the phenomenon but of *who* is authorized to do so.

What the *Book* shows is a society with no common ground for understanding Margery's "roarings." In the absence of coherent interpretive communities, authoritative interpretation can only be found by displacing it from the conflicting views of her contemporaries to Margery's visionary conversations with Christ. There Christ reassures Margery with monotonous regularity that her tears are "fre ʒyftys of God" apart from her merit, for "terys of compunccyon, devocyon, & compassyon arn þe heyest & sekerest ʒftys þat I ʒeve in erde" (30, 31) [24].

The tears resolve the paradoxes of Margery's social identities into a multivalent yet unified relationship with Christ:

> Whan þow stodyst to plese me, þan art þu a very dowtyr; whan þu wepyst & mornyst for my peyn & for my Passyon, þan art þow a very modyr to have compassyon of hyr chyld; whan þow wepyst for oþer mennys synnes and for adversytes, þan art þow a very syster; and, whan thow sorwyst for þow art so long fro þe blysse of Hevyn, þan art þu a very spowse & a wyfe. (31) [24]

The explicitness of Christ's comforting resolutions only highlights the social disagreements over Margery's behaviors and identities, and reveals how little consensus there was about the role of lay female mystics in the fifteenth century.

Within the late medieval hagiographic code that Margery's text employs, visions were the mark of the holy person.[3] Given that fact, Margery's visions (and within them her conversations with Christ) have elicited surprisingly little critical analysis except to note that Christ as male authority figure is unfailingly supportive and helpful to Margery. What I would emphasize is Margery's fluent access to divine assistance, which provides her with a strong sense that she can become her own spiritual interpreter and agent despite external harrassment and skepticism.

The threshold between Margery's physical and her spiritual lives is thin, and she can "cross over" virtually at will. In one memorable incident, she and her husband are coming from York on a Friday, Midsummer's Eve, "in very hot weather." She is carrying a bottle of beer and her husband has a cake tucked inside his clothes. He urges her to resume marital relations, but she tells him she wants to take a vow of chastity before a bishop. He presses his case urgently; he wants to sleep with her, wants her to pay his debts before she goes off on pilgrimage, and wants her not to fast on Friday but to eat and drink with him. When she refuses

---

3. In earlier hagiography, miracles were a more significant sign of holiness, as Andrè Vauchez has shown in *La Saintetè en Occident aux derniers siécles du moyen agê d'aprés les procés de canonisation et les documents hagiographiques* (Rome: Ecole Francaise de Rome, 1981). By the fourteenth and fifteenth centuries, *miracula* had largely been replaced by visions as the requisite sign of sanctity, as Margery's *Book* demonstrates. Margery does work a few miracles, including the snowstrom that quenches a fire at St. Margaret's Church in response to her prayer (162–64).

to break her fast, he threatens to force her to have sex. At this point in the tense marital argument, Margery—who obviously fears rape—kneels down to pray and ask Christ for a resolution to her dilemma. As if immediately at her side, he tells her that the fast can be a negotiating tool; she can now break her fast in return for her sexual freedom. Although these features of Margery's visionary conversations appear distinctive—the lack of conventional meditative apparatus and an intimate spiritual advisor available whenever Margery needs it—they were also features of the visions of Bridget of Sweden, whose canonization was being debated during the early fifteenth century.[4] What they convey is the privileged and independent position of the female mystic, whose spiritual needs are being met without ecclesiastical mediation.

Typically, too, the conversations with Christ reinterpret social and religious conventions, putting in place new definitions that are consistent with the needs of lay piety. When Margery laments to Christ, "A, Lord, maydenys dawnsyn now meryly in Heven. Xal not I don so?" (50) [38], she registers her distress that her marital and maternal roles have removed from her the possibility of being holy according to the norms of late medieval Christianity. Christ replies, however, that "tor-as-mech as þu art a mayden in þi sowle, I xal take þe be þe on hand in Hevyn & my Modyr be þe oþer hand, & so xalt þu dawnsyn in Hevyn wyth oþer holy maydens & virgynes" (52) [39]. The external definition of virginity given by conventional religion has been replaced by a chastity of soul which can co-exist with the demands of married life in the world.[5]

Margery's problems often center on conflicts between her social roles of wife and mother and her religious mission. The narrative describes a time, "whyl thys creatur was beryng chylder & sche was newly delyveryd of a chyld, owyr Lord Cryst Jhesu seyd to hir sche xuld no mor chyldren beryn, & þerfor he bad hyr gon to Norwych" (38) [29]. She resists at first, claiming to be weak from childbirth, but he promises to give her strength for the trip. Similarly, on another occasion (48) [36], Christ promises to find Margery a babysitter when he asks her to take on a spiritual task at a time when she has just had a baby that needs care. Margery's conversations with Christ focus on the problematics of the active life in the *female* terms of childbearing, childrearing, and marital obligation.

---

4. Margery's pilgrimage to Rome in 1414 coincided with ceremonies reaffirming Bridget's canonization and prompted visions obviously modeled on Bridget's. The tone of Margery's visionary scenes is, like Bridget's, "homey" and intimate; see quotation from Gerson on Bridget's revelations in note 7 above.
5. On this topic, see Clarissa W. Atkinson, "'Precious Balsam in a Fragile Glass': The Ideology of Virginity in the Later Middle Ages," *Journal of Family History* 8 (1983): 131–43. Without making the same argument I do that Margery's autobiography demonstrates a new "bourgeois" ideology, Janel Mueller has seen how the text sponsors a spirituality in which "there is no inherent incompatibility between becoming a bride of God and being acknowledged as the wife of John Kempe, burgess of Lynn, and the mother of his fourteen children." See "Autobiography of a New 'Creatur': Female Spirituality, Selfhood, and Authorship in *The Book of Margery Kempe*," repr. in *Women in the Middle Ages and the Renaissance: Literary and Historical Perspectives*, ed. Mary Beth Rose (Syracuse: Syracuse University Press, 1986), 155–71.

In a text ostensibly about a female's desire to abandon her family responsibilities to serve God, we have a vivid representation of the opposite position: the validation of holiness as an outcome of the active life. David Aers argues strenuously that "Margery's religious identity involved a rupture with the earthly family, an energetic struggle against the nuclear family, its bonds, its defenses in the lay community and its legitimating ideologies."[6] He notes that her imaginary life "enabled both an affirmation of her community's conventional stereotypes and their negation."[7] This reading of Margery's paradoxical resolution reduces her dilemma to a female dilemma. Mary Mason, too, has identified the "dual sense of vocation: the wife-mother, pilgrim-mystic roles which were continuous throughout Margery Kempe's life." Mason sees the duality as a "common pattern of women's perception of themselves."[8]

I would reinterpret Mason's feminist insight in more broadly cultural terms; the *Book* may talk about the problematics of a "dual sense of vocation" in the female terms of childbearing, childcare, and marital sexual obligation, but for late medieval bourgeois culture those were the very terms in which it was defining a new family- and work-centered ideology that would allow them to be pious without leaving their secular activities. In one of the more extended visionary sequences of the *Book*, Margery becomes the attendant to St. Anne on the birth of Mary, and to Mary on the birth of Christ. She is included in the sacred events, and she is appreciated for her role as assistant to childbirth. On the birth of John the Baptist, which she witnesses, she asks Elizabeth to recommend her to Mary as a servant. Elizabeth tells her, "Dowtyr, me semyth . . . þu dost ryght wel þi dever" (19) [15], a comment that validates the role of charitable service in the active life.

Despite Margery's repeated gestures of separation from her social roles as urban bourgeoise and wife in order to pursue her vocation as a holy woman, she is finally to play out her spiritual commitments through nursing her ill and senile husband. This episode is usually interpreted as a step backward into the role of human wife for Margery, who wants to serve Christ alone.[9] Margery certainly articulates those fears when she holds a conversation with Christ on the subject and he tells her, "I bydde þe take hym hom & kepe hym for my lofe" (180) [132]. She responds that she cannot do that for she would have to neglect her spiritual husband: "I xal þan not tendyn to þe as I do now." Christ then offers a resolution to her

6. Aers, *Community, Gender, and Individual Identity*, 99.
7. Ibid., 108.
8. Mason, "The Other Voice," 22.
9. See, for example, Smith, *A Poetics of Women's Autobiography*, who says that Margery serves her husband as "a martyr of Christ rather than a wife" (72). Lynn Staley in *Margery Kempe's Dissenting Fictions* interprets Margery's return to the household as caretaker of her ailing husband as hinting at "a conception of Christian community" that accepts social bonds (63), though one limited by the constraints of the surrounding social environment (64). Staley does not explicitly connect this concept of community with bourgeois ideologies.

dilemma: "þu xalt have as meche mede for to kepyn hym & helpyn hym in hys nede at home as ȝyf þu wer in chirche to makyn þi preyerys. . . . I preye þe now kepe hym for þe lofe of me." In serving him, her *Book* shows, she serves "as sche wolde a don Crist hym-self" (181) [132].

By the end of her first book, Margery as exemplary figure through her active service has become a mediator for others. Christ assures her that "for þe gret homlynes þat I schewe to þe þat tyme þu art mekyl þe boldar to askyn me grace for þi-selfe, for þin husbond, & for þi childryn, & þu makyst every Cristen man & woman þi childe in þi sowle for þe tyme & woldist han as meche grace for hem as for þin owyn childeryn" (212) [154]. In this long culminating speech, which articulates a new ideology of spiritual value through the active life, he also tells her that he thanks her for all the ill people she has cared for in his name, "& for al þe goodnes & servyse þat þu hast don to hem in any degre, for þu schalt havyn þe same mede wyth me in Hevyn, as þow þu haddist kept myn owyn self whil I was her in erde" (213–14) [155]. It is not necessary, in other words, to reject the world totally in order to achieve holiness. As the ultimate authorizing voice in this text, Christ confirms that service in this world "counts" spiritually.

To put Margery's *Book* in broad historical perspective, we might contrast its ideological situation to that of Augustine's *Confessions*, written one thousand years earlier. Augustine represents the ideal of personal chastity as his solution to the battle against lust—this at the very moment when Ambrose and other leaders of the early Christian church were making celibacy the mark of the spiritual elite. Augustine's narrative, like Margery's, can be historicized. Both portray the struggles of an individual that are at the same time illustrations of ideological programs being enacted in their societies. In Augustine's case, the new Christian elites were attempting to undermine dominant Roman family and civic ideologies. One thousand years later, Margery's autobiography is part of a bourgeois rewriting of the cultural script, which by the seventeenth century had reinstated family ideologies very similar to Roman ones that analogously linked family and state in patriarchal governance.[1]

Margery's *Book* culminates not with a rejection of history but with an immersion in it. Her social text thus speaks for her contemporaries, lay

1. John Freccero argues that Augustine's *Confessions* is the founding text of (traditional male) autobiography, where the conversion from and total rejection of the sinful self leads to the atemporal or allegorical self that authors the book; "Autobiography and Narrative," in *Reconstructing Individualism: Autonomy, Individuality, and the Self in Western Thought*, ed. Thomas C. Heller, Morton Sosna, and David E. Welbery (Stanford: Stanford University Press, 1986), 16–29. Margery's *Book* seems to provide an alternative (female) model for autobiography as a text that remains firmly within history. But I would suggest that the differences between Augustine's and Margery's autobiographies have little to do with gender as an implicit poetic structure and everything to do with their ideological positions within a culture which was—in Augustine's case—breaking with secular and familial norms of Roman culture and—in Margery's case—reinstating them. On early modern "domestic politics," see Susan Dwyer Amussen, *An Ordered Society: Gender and Class in Early Modern England* (New York: Columbia University Press, 1988), esp. 34–66.

men and women who were seeking to validate their secular lives according to dominant religious norms. In historicizing Margery, that is, in reading her *Book* and life as social texts, we can see that her gender and her
mysticism are "about" not just the status of Margery the individual female
mystic, but are products of the symbolic imagination of Western culture
at a crucial moment of transition. During that several hundred year period—from roughly 1300 to 1650—a new group we now call the "middle class" consolidated their socioeconomic power by developing a
self-conscious identity. As a window onto this process, Margery Kempe's
Book is invaluable. An unsuccessful piece of autohagiography that was
never sanitized or polished by cult followers, it remained as it was originally produced; for this reason, it is one of our most revealing texts for the
crisis that broadly affected medieval society in the fourteenth and fifteenth centuries. This was a crisis in interpretation and authorization, as
clerical ideologies and institutions that had inspired a set of practices by
an ascetic elite were appropriated—and in the process transformed—by
a lay and predominantly bourgeois class that sought an explicit validating
ideology for their own economic and political power.

GAIL McMURRAY GIBSON

St. Margery: *The Book of Margery Kempe*†

Margery Kempe was the troublesome and pious wife of John Kempe, a
burgess of the bustling Norfolk port of Lynn, and the daughter (born
about 1373) of John Brunham, who had five times been mayor of the city.
Margery Kempe was the mother of fourteen children. She had tried her
hand at running a brewing business, then at milling corn. She was also a
self-proclaimed visionary and mystic. It was Margery Kempe's cross to
bear that, in her own time as well as in most modern scholarship, she
would be maligned, misunderstood, and alternately charged with hysteria and with hypocrisy.[1] It would be far more accurate, however, to say
that Margery Kempe of Lynn possessed an unswerving sense of devo-

---

† From *The Theater of Devotion* (Chicago: U of Chicago P, 1989) 47–53. Reprinted by permission of the publisher. Bracketed page numbers refer to this Norton Critical Edition.
1. Despite several recent and very sympathetic studies by such scholars as Clarissa Atkinson, Susan
Dickman, Deborah Ellis, and Karma Lochrie, of Margery Kempe's piety and its relationship to
late medieval social history and the continental "feminist movement" (e.g., Susan Dickman,
"Margery Kempe and the English Devotional Tradition," in *The Medieval Mystical Tradition in
England: Papers Read at the Exeter Symposium, July 1980*, ed. Marion Glasscoe [Exeter: University of Exeter Press, 1980], 151) and despite the quite remarkable fact that selections from *The
Book of Margery Kempe* were included in the new fifth edition of that arbiter of the literary
canon, *The Norton Anthology of English Literature*, most scholars, especially male scholars, re-
main curtly dismissive. Cf. Derek Brewer, *English Gothic Literature* (New York: Schocken
Books, 1983), p. 253. "Religion was to Margery what sex was to Chaucer's Wife of Bath."

tional theater and that she embraced her martyrdoms deliberately and self-consciously.

The Book of Margery Kempe, in which Margery dictated to a sympathetic fifteenth-century scribe the litany of her tribulations in Norfolk and far beyond, is the first autobiography in the English language. Lost for centuries and only rediscovered in 1934, Margery Kempe's *Book* is also a calculated hagiographical text, a kind of autobiographical saint's life. Its rambling and conversational style should not distract us from the fact that its true literary as well as spiritual models were the *legenda*—lives—of late medieval saints, especially the fourteenth-century Swedish wife, mother, and mystic, St. Bridget, to whom Margery quite explicitly compares herself—and with whom she often competes. ("As I spak to Seynt Bryde [Bridget] ryte so I speke to þe, dowtyr," Jesus more than once assures Margery in her visions.[2]) There is no doubt that Margery Kempe was an audacious and feisty lady who made her fair share of enemies; but there is also documentary proof that a Margery Kempe of Lynn was admitted to membership in the powerful and prestigious Trinity guild of Lynn in 1438, at the very time that she was dictating her story of persecutions and rejections.[3] If martyrdom by sword was not available to qualify her for sainthood, martyrdom by slander was, and Margery's *Book* seems quite conscious of the validating implications of such suffering. When, for example, she finds herself imprisoned in a kind of casual house arrest by her uneasy accusors in Beverly, Margery Kempe reports that God reassures her that such inconvenience is more precious to him than actual martyrdom by sword: "Dowtyr, it is mor plesyng vn-to me þat þu suffyr despitys & scornys, schamys & repreuys, wrongys & disesys þan ʒif þin hed wer smet of thre tymes on þe day euery day in sevyn ʒer."[4] Such despisings are not only reported as proof of her future sanctity and triumph (indeed, Margery tells us that God has revealed that someday in her parish church in Lynn, Norfolk, she will be reverenced as a saint, that "I [God] xal ben worschepyd in þe"[5]), but also as the source of much of her privileged spiritual knowledge. In one of her intimate conversations with Christ, she is assured that because of her hardships "þu xalt knowe þe bettyr what sorwe & schame I suffyrd for thy lofe and þu schalt have þe more compassyon whan þu thynkyst on my Passyon."[6] An attentive look at the language in Margery's accounts of her sufferings and trials shows her pervasive verbal as well as typological indebtedness to gospel Passion narratives.[7] Margery's spiritual compassion is manifested by phys-

2. *Book of Margery Kemp,* p. 47 [36].
3. See appendix 3 in *Book of Margery Kempe,* pp. 358–59.
4. *Book of Margery Kempe,* p. 131 [97].
5. *Book of Margery Kempe,* p. 156 [115].
6. *Book of Margery Kempe,* p. 156 [115].
7. On the "recurrence of divine pattern" in hagiographic texts see David L. Jeffrey, "English Saints' Plays," in *Medieval Drama,* ed. Neville Denny, Stratford-upon-Avon Studies, no. 16 (London: Edward Arnold, 1973), esp. pp. 72–73, and James W. Earl, "Typology and Iconographic Style in Early Medieval Hagiography," *Studies in the Literary Imagination* 8 (1975): 15–46.

ical experience which mirrors Christ's own sufferings; if she cannot be, like St. Francis, actually imprinted with Christ's wounds, she struggles for her own version of the *imitatio Christi*. Like Christ's on the Cross, her body is wrenched violently to one side in the extremity of her weeping meditations on the Passion. Like Christ, she is spit upon and scorned by her contemporaries. In the triumph of her conviction, like Christ himself, she magnanimously begs forgiveness for those who know not what they do:

> Sum seyde þat sche had þe fallyng euyl, for sche wyth þe crying wrestyd hir body turnyng fro þe o syde in-to þe oþer & wex al blew and al blo as it had ben colowr of leed. & þan folke spitted at hir for horrowr of þe sekenes, & sum scornyd hir and seyd þat sche . . . dede meche harm a-mong þe pepyl. . . . & þan wept sche ful sor for hir synne, preying God of mercy & forȝeuenes for hem, seying to owr Lord, "Lord, as þu seydyst hangyng on þe Cros for þi crucyfyerys, 'Fadyr, forȝeue hem; þei wite not what þei don,' so I beseche þe, forȝeue þe pepyl al scorne & slawndrys & al þat þei han trespasyd, ȝyf it be thy wille, for I haue deseruyd meche mor & meche more am I worthy."[8]

Margery's protestations of the public hostility she faced must thus be read in the context of her deliberate attempt to participate in the martyrdom pattern of Christ and his saints; indeed, her qualifications for sainthood depend upon that participation. It is largely, I think, because modern readers have been so quick to accept Margery Kempe's own words uncritically that they have also thoughtlessly characterized her piety as aberrant and eccentric, and have thus underestimated the usefulness of her *Book*, not as historical fact, but as an indispensable guide to fifteenth-century English lay spirituality.

In fact, what Margery Kempe's *Book* discloses is not "pathologically neurotic" or eccentric visions of her own invention,[9] but rather a life of extremely literal and concrete achievement of those very spiritual exercises which the thirteenth-century writer of the *Meditationes vitae Christi* had once urged upon the Franciscan nun for whom that devotional text was first written. Nicholas Love's enormously popular English adaptation of the *Meditationes*, *The Mirrour of the Blessed Lyf of Jesus Christ* (1410), had helped perform the transformation of this contemplative text into a model for the lay devotions of men and women who lived very much in the world. Margery's sacred conversations, her noisy and physical participation in sacred events, her restless hankerings and pilgrimages to

---

8. *Book of Margery Kempe*, pp. 105–7 [77–78].
9. Cf. Wolfgang Riehle, *The Middle English Mystics* (London: Routledge and Kegan Paul, 1981), II: "The excessive emotional piety of this wife of a citizen of Lynn shows pathologically neurotic traits. Nevertheless some of the mystical passages in her autobiography are of some value. The very fact that Julian [of Norwich, another East Anglian mystic], who had a conversation with her, considered her piety to be genuine, forces us to include Margery in our study."

shrines and relics and to the Holy Land itself, are all manifestations of her determined attempts to live out a series of homely and affective meditations which were originally addressed to a Poor Clare in Italy more than a century before her birth. That Margery's living out of these spiritual exercises has seemed to modern readers like personal and idiosyncratic mysticism is largely testimony to the zeal with which she seized for her own life and time these Incarnation meditations.

It is often when Margery Kempe sounds most like her inimitable self that she is, in fact, most the Pseudo-Bonaventure. When, for example, Margery is present in meditational vision when the resurrected Christ appears to his mother, Margery's report of the spiritual dialogue between Mother and son—Mary's solicitous questions about Christ's wounds, her grudging approval to Christ's request for permission to leave so that he can appear (in canonical fashion) to Mary Magdalene—all has the ring of Margery Kempe's own and unique imagination. But in fact, the whole scene and suggestions for mentally producing it existed in the *Medita tiones vitae Christi*, in the authority of a revered text and not in Margery's own psychology. It was the author of the *Meditationes* who was first to invent this Resurrection meditation in which Christ appears to his mother. Obviously dissatisfied with the silence of the Gospels about the matter, the Pseudo-Bonaventure presented a sweetly moving scene in which the risen Christ and his mother "stayed and conversed together, mutually rejoicing" until Christ begs leave to appear to Mary Magdalene and so return to historical veracity.[1]

The Pseudo-Bonaventure's determination to leave the Virgin Mary out of no crucial moment of Incarnation history is everywhere apparent in the *Meditationes*. In fact, it might be argued that the primary devotional model offered by the *Meditationes vitae Christi* is *imitatio Mariae* instead of *imitatio Christi*; that is, although the text renders the humanity and suffering of the life of Christ in lingering and loving detail, the paradigm urged upon the reader is the life of she who had defined her paradoxical exaltation by humility, by proclaiming at the moment of Annunciation, "Behold the handmaid of the Lord" (Luke 1:38).

It is as handmaid of God's handmaiden that the Franciscan nun to whom the *Meditationes* was first addressed is to meditate upon the Incarnation. Likewise, in Margery Kempe's *Book*, just as to proclaim Margery's martyrdoms is to proclaim her Christ-likeness, so to serve humbly as handmaiden is to be like Mary, the very Queen of Heaven. The domestic and housewifely services which Margery Kempe repeatedly performs for the Virgin Mary and the Christ Child in her visionary life are not naive or childish attempts at mysticism, as they have so often been interpreted, but rather deliberate and self-conscious emulation of the Marian model. The Poor Clare addressed by the

---

1. *Meditations on the Life of Christ*, p. 360.

Meditationes was urged to be handmaiden in her soul; so concretely does that advice live in Margery's visionary imagination that she serves in her soul with no less pragmatism, clarity, and domesticity than she will serve her bedridden husband in his old age. Indeed the point is precisely that there is no great difference for Margery in the two prayerful acts of service. To attend to her incontinent husband's diapers is just as much a spiritual exercise for Margery Kempe as to swaddle the infant Christ is an incarnational reality.

In the early pages of her *Book*, Margery tells how God directed her to think upon the birth and childhood of the Virgin Mary, and how in doing this she prayed to Mary's mother, St. Anne, that she might be "hir mayden & hir seruawnt" and so help care for the infant Mary."[2] Margery also reports overhearing Mary's girlhood wish that she could be worthy enough to "be þe handmayden of hir þat xuld conseive þe Sone of God."[3] Mary's longing is here reported not so much for its dramatic irony (as is the case in the *Meditationes* and in the N-Town play "The Presentation of the Virgin"[4]) as for the apt commentary it offers on Margery's own sanctity. Margery has been chosen worthy handmaiden by St. Anne herself; it is *she* who has fulfilled the longing of Mary to be handmaiden of God's handmaiden. Indeed, since exaltation comes from service, Margery has, in a sense, out-humbled and out-performed the Virgin Mary herself by being not just handmaiden but handmaid to the handmaiden, as in being chosen by Mary to carry the baggage when Mary and Joseph go on their family visit to St. Elizabeth.[5]

Such visionary participation in Incarnation history becomes ever more energetic and more concrete as Margery follows as literally as possible the devotional exercises outlined in the *Meditationes*. From the passive service of bearing the holy baggage, Margery assumes roles of active handmaidenship, as, for example, in the vision in which she acts as comforter to the Virgin Mary, distraught with grief after the burial of her son.[6] Margery does this, in her typical womanly way, by bringing Mary nourishing food. A delightful detail in her *Book*, it is not Margery's invention at all but a suggestion of the author of the *Meditationes*, who had urged the Franciscan nun meditating on Mary's sorrow to "serve, console and comfort so that she may eat a little."[7] It is, however, a telling difference

---

2. *Book of Margery Kempe*, p. 18 [15].
3. *Book of Margery Kempe*, p. 18 [15].
4. See the discussion of the N-town play of Mary's Presentation in the Temple in chapter 5.
5. *Book of Margery Kempe*, p. 18 [15].
6. *Book of Margery Kempe*, pp. 194–95 [142–43].
7. *Meditations on the Life of Christ*, p. 347. Deborah S. Ellis in her otherwise perceptive article, "Margery Kempe and the Virgin's Hot Caudle," *Essays in Arts and Sciences* 14 (1985):I–II, does not appear to realize the textual authority for Margery's vision of the Virgin's sickbed. Cf. Ellis, p. 7, "When presented with a formal occasion for piety—a Good Friday sermon or a Corpus Christi procession, for instance—Margery reduces the public vision into a private domestic scene: 'Than þe creatur thowt . . . sche mad for owr Lady a good cawdel & browt it hir to comfortyn hir . . .'"

between Margery's thirteenth-century devotional model and her practical and concrete fifteenth-century East Anglian spirituality that Margery's account of her vision actually names the food that she prepares and brings to the Virgin Mary's sickbed—a "cawdel," or mixture of warm spiced wine, egg, and gruel. Indeed it would not be surprising if the fragmentary fifteenth-century recipe (ground sugar and cinnamon are among its ingredients) that appears on the verso of the last folio of the Kempe manuscript was intended to be the recipe for Margery's wine caudle, a kind of spiritual chicken soup.[8] So completely has all human life been touched by Margery Kempe's conversations with the Holy Family that instructions for making sickbed food for Christ's grieving mother seem entirely reasonable and appropriate—and the restoring caudle seems a likely and convincing symbol, resonant with particularity, of the restoring food and drink of the Eucharist, of the body of Christ that will itself become spiritual food.[9]

Margery's service to the Holy Family more often involves being nursemaid than cook. But again, it is the Virgin Mary herself who offers the model. Margery tells how as she stood at her prayers in the Lady Chapel of the "Frer Prechourys" she saw a vision of Mary "holdyng a fayr white kerche" in her hand and inviting Margery to watch as she swaddled the infant Christ. The sight of the Virgin at her motherly task brings Margery such joy and spiritual comfort, she tells us, that "sche cowde neuyr tellyn it as sche felt it."[1] In another meditation, Margery herself begs Mary for the "fayr whyte clothys & kerchys" so that she, herself might swaddle the newborn Christ in her devotions, a task she performs not only with love, but with "byttyr teerys of compassyon, hauyng mend of þe scharp deth þat he schuld suffyr for þe lofe of synful men."[2] The late medieval preoccupation with juxtaposing the joyful Nativity event with forebodings of the sorrows of the Passion is here focused in Margery's imagination on the physical act of wrapping the Child's body. The fair white cloth she sees in her vision is at once swaddling cloth and shroud.

What is particularly interesting about Margery's vision of the swaddling clothes is that it is based not only upon the text of the Gospel of Luke but upon an actual relic which Margery had seen on her pilgrimage to Assisi: "Vp-pon a tyme as þis creatur was in cherche at Assyse, þer was shewyd owyr Ladys kerche whech sche weryd her in erth wyth gret lygth and gret

---

8. See *Book of Margery Kempe*, p. xliv.
9. As Caroline Walker Bynum observes in her fascinating study, *Holy Feast and Holy Fast: The Religious Significance of Food to Medieval Women* (Berkeley: University of California Press, 1987), 294–95, the late medieval world was one "whose central ritual was the coming of God into food as macerated flesh, and it was compatible with, not contradictory to, new philosophical notions that located the nature of things not in their abstract definitions but in their individuating matter or particularity." In this sense the restoring caudle given to the grieving Virgin Mary is both a homily about Margery's affective participation and handmaidenship—and a foreshadowing symbol of the restoring food and drink of the Eucharist.
1. *Book of Margery Kempe*, p. 209 [152].
2. *Book of Margery Kempe*, p. 19 [15].

reuerens. Pans þis creatur had gret deuocyon. Sche wept, sche sobbyd, sche cryed wyth gret plente of teerys & many holy thowtys."[3] This "kerche" or head veil of the Virgin Mary was one of the most venerated relics of the Lower Church of St. Francis at Assisi. It had been presented to the church in 1319 by Tomasso degli Orsini, who claimed to have obtained the veil from the Pasha of Damascus, an Islamic prisoner of war. It was further claimed that this was the very cloth Mary had swaddled the Christ Child with at the Nativity; the holy relic, it was said, had been stolen by the Pasha from a church in Jerusalem.[4] The real source of the Virgin's relic was almost certainly not a prisoner of war, but a revered text—again, the *Meditationes vitae Christi*. For it was the *Meditationes*, written some fifty years before the mysterious reappearance of the Christ Child's swaddling cloth, which explained and gave canonical validity to the relic. The Pseudo-Bonaventure had urged his reader to pay particularly close attention to his meditation on the Nativity "especially as I intend to recount what the Lady revealed and disclosed, as told to me by a trustworthy holy brother of our order, to whom I think it had been revealed."[5] This special revelation included the information that the Christ Child was born on a Sunday at midnight, that he emerged from Mary's womb soundlessly and painlessly, that the Virgin Mary embraced the Child, washed him with the sacred milk from her breasts, and then "wrapped Him in the veil from her head and laid Him in the manger."[6]

The Pseudo-Bonaventure's purpose in revealing the swaddling clothes to be the veil from the Virgin's own head was to emphasize, as he does throughout the Incarnation meditations, the poverty and humility of the Holy Family, a favorite Franciscan theme that distinguishes this swaddling scene from, for example, that in the Nativity revelation of St. Bridget, who reported that the Virgin had brought with her to Bethlehem "two small linen cloths and two woolen ones of exquisite purity and fineness" to serve as Christ's swaddling clothes.[7] But the Virgin's veil in the *Meditationes vitae Christi* is not only a sign of humility but a visual emblem linking the joyful maternity of the Virgin with her anguish at Calvary. With a terrible symmetry, the Virgin's head veil again appears in the Pseudo-Bonaventure's *Meditationes*, this time in the midst of the Crucifixion narrative:

> Again He is stripped, and is now nude before all the multitude for the third time, His wounds reopened by the adhesion of His garments to His flesh. Now for the first time the Mother beholds her Son thus taken and prepared for the anguish of death. She is saddened and shamed beyond measure when she sees Him entirely

3. *Book of Margery Kempe*, p. 79 [58].
4. Francis Newton, *St. Francis and His Basilica Assisi* (Assisi, 1926), 136, and *Book of Margery Kempe*, p. 298n.
5. *Meditations on the Life of Christ*, p. 32.
6. *Meditations on the Life of Christ*, p. 33.
7. Translated by Henrik Cornell in *The Iconography of the Nativity of Christ*, Uppsala Universitets Arsskrift (Uppsala: A. B. Lundequistska Bokhandeln, 1924), 12.

nude: they did not leave Him even His loincloth. Therefore she hurries and approaches the Son, embraces Him, and girds Him with the veil from her head.[8]

Although it is difficult to know precisely where and when the medieval tradition originated that Mary's veil covered Christ's loins after he had been stripped for the Crucifixion, it seems to have been the *Meditationes vitae Christi* which invented, or at least popularized, that veil as an image linking Christ's Nativity to his Passion.[9] It would perhaps be more accurate to say that the Pseudo-Bonaventure's text popularized the head veil as an important symbolic detail of Incarnation history, for rhetorical juxtaposition of the Virgin's joy at swaddling the infant Christ and her anguish as she shrouded the crucified Christ had been commonplace in sermon meditation in the Eastern Church far before the thirteenth century.[1] Indeed, both at the Nativity and at the Crucifixion, Mary's use of her own veil to clothe Christ is literal manifestation of the ancient and widespread metaphoric explanation of Christ's incarnate body as a "garment" bestowed upon him by his human mother. The poor frail cloth of humanity is what actually swathes the Christ Child in the *Meditationes vitae Christi* and in devotional texts like the fourteenth-century English lyric in which Mary sings

> Iheus, suete, be nout wroth,
> I haue neiþer clut ne cloth
> þe inne for to folde;
> I ne haue but a clut of a lappe,
> þerfore ley þi feet to my pappe,
> And kep þi from þe colde.[2]

8. *Meditations on the Life of Christ*, p. 333.
9. Mary's girding Christ at Calvary with the veil from her head is also reported in another popular thirteenth-century meditation on the Passion, the so-called *Dialogus Beatae Mariae et Anselmi de Passione Domini*, a text attributed to St. Anselm (c. 1033–1109) in the Middle Ages, but which is probably contemporary with the Pseudo-Bonaventure's *Meditationes*. In this supposed dialogue between the Virgin Mary and St. Anselm, Mary reveals how "when they had arrived at that most ignominious of places, Calvary, where dead dogs and carrion were thrown, they stripped my only son of all his clothes; and I, made faint by it, nevertheless took my headcloth and bound it around his loins." See Pseudo-Anselm, *Dialogus Beatae Mariae et Anselmi de Passione Domini* 10 (*PL* 159:282): "Cum venissent ad locum, Calvariae ignominiossimum, ubi canes et alia morticina projiciebantur, nudaverunt Jesum unicum filium meum totaliter vestibus suis, et ego exanimis facta fui, tamen velamen capitis mei accipiens circumligavi lumbis suis."
1. Simon Metaphrastes, a Byzantine theologian of the tenth century, for example, wrote of the Virgin's lament at the Cross in the form of an imagined monologue in which Mary contrasts the joys of Bethlehem with the sorrows of Calvary. One of the images in this monologue is the cloth of swaddling garment and of shroud, though it is not here specifically identified with any garment of the Virgin's. In the Simon Metphrastes text, the cloth which wraps Christ was simply one of a number of affective details whose purposes were to arouse the reader to compassion and sympathetic participation in the joys and sorrows of the Virgin: "Formerly I zealously wrapped the infant's swaddling bands around you, and now I prepare your shroud. . . . As a child you often slept against my breast, and now you sleep there in death." See Simon Metaphrastes, *Oratio in Lugubrem Lamentationem Sanctissimae Deiparae Pretiosum Corpus Domini Nostri Jesus Christi Amplexantis*, in J. P. Migne, ed., *Patrologiae cursus completus: series graeca* (Paris: J. P. Migne, 1857–66), hereafter referred to as *PG*), 114:215.
2. Carleton Brown, ed., *Religious Lyrics of the XIVth Century* (Oxford: Oxford University Press, 1924), 91 (ll. 13–18). The lullaby is from Advocates Library MS 18.7.21, a commonplace book of 1372 which belonged to the English Franciscan preacher John Grimestone.

Whatever the historical and symbolic explanations of the veil tradition, for the purposes of understanding Margery Kempe's meditations on the swaddling clothes it is sufficient to note that the cloth's significance lies in its substitution for an abstract theological concept—Mary as the mother who clothes the Logos in fleshly mortality—of an extremely concrete image for the Incarnation mystery. It is probable that Margery Kempe's veneration of the famous veil relic on her pilgrimage to Assisi reinforced a devotional image already familiar to her and to her English contemporaries, not only through Nicholas Love's translation of the *Meditationes vitae Christi*, but also through popular sermons like those in John Mirk's well-known anthology of vernacular sermons for parish priests.[3]

* * *

SARAH BECKWITH

Margery Kempe's *Imitatio*[†]

The licensing force of Kempe's religiosity is of course the figure of the incarnated God, Christ. The mimesis of Christ is at the very centre of Kempe's book. In a society which prohibited women from writing and preaching, from adjudicating the authoritative scriptural word, it was only the direct word of God and Christ, prophetically authorized, that could make a woman's words worth the listening or transcribing.[1] So in *The Book of Margery Kempe* Kempe can speak to those around her and get her book written only through an arduous apprenticeship in the discernment of spirits.[2] What licenses her piety is the accompanying apprenticeship in suffering enjoined by her imitation of Christ.

---

3. In Mirk's *Festial* (c. 1400), the "Homily on Lent" describes how "Cristis cloþys wern drawn of hym and don all naked, saue hur lady, his modyr, wonde hyr kerchef about hym to hyll his membrys." *Mirk's Festial: A Collection of Homilies*, Part I, ed. Theodore Erbe, EETS, o.s., 96 (London: Oxford University Press, 1905), 247.

† From *Christ's Body* (London: Routledge, 1993) 80–83. Reprinted by permission of the publisher. Bracketed page numbers refer to this Norton Critical Edition.

1. In this connection see Karma Lochrie's article, 'The Book of Margery Kempe: The Marginal Woman's Quest for Literary Authority', *Journal of Medieval and Renaissance Studies*, 1986, vol. 16, pt 1, pp. 33–55.

2. The 'discernment of spirits' was the procedure whereby authentic revelations were distinguished from false ones. For a discussion roughly contemporary with Margery Kempe, see *The Chastising of God's Children and the Treatise of Perfection of the Sons of God* ed. Joyce Bazire and E. Colledge, Oxford, Blackwell, 1957, pp. 173–82, which deals with the tokens by which good spirits may be distinguished from bad ones. One such sign is 'whether he submitteth hym or his visions loweli to the doom of his goostli fadir, or of other discreet and sad goostli lyuers, for drede of illusion, or ellis kepith hem priuey and shewith hem not, but stondith to his owne examyneng, and to his owne doom'. Christ gives Margery five 'tokyns' that are the signs of her special grace (see Kempe, p. 183) [133–34]. The issue of the discernment of spirits was at stake in the discussions over the canonization of Birgitta, a notable influence on Margery Kempe. The anxiety

From the very beginning the figure of Christ in her book exists in complex relation to the clerical establishment. Her book, after all, begins with a refusal of the mediating counsel of the clergy. She refuses to confess a particularly heinous sin to a confessor after the birth of her first child. Christ's first 'visitation' to Kempe coincides in her narrative with that refusal. Christ enters 'in lyknesse of a man, most semly, most bewtyuows, & most amyable þat euyr mygth be seen wyth mannys eye'.[3] Christ the man is juxtaposed with the institutional church as an alternative source of mercy, forgiveness and redemption. And he appears at his most familiar and speaks in a language to which she can respond. Although she understands the basics of Trinitarian doctrine, her interest is entirely in the Second Person. She talks about accompanying Mary and Joseph to visit Elizabeth to help her bear St John, and assists Mary at the nativity in the very same tone used to discuss her life in Lynn. It is a seamless rendition of the meditations enjoined by Nicholas Love in his *Mirrour of the Blessyd Lyf of Jesu Christ*, and bespeaks an extraordinary continuity of her life and Christ's.[4] That continuity is a continuity of shared fleshliness, for as Christ says to her: 'for þu hast so gret compassyon of my flesche I must nede haue compassyon of þi flesch.'[5] It is no surprise, then, that she should wish to concentrate on those parts of his life which emphasize that embodiedness most completely. Her text returns repeatedly to the moments of Christ's birth and death, and sometimes, as in her contemplation of the *pietá*, that image which depicts Christ dying in the arms of his mother, where birth and death coalesce. Having then been present at, indeed having aided in, the very parturition of Christ as baby, she becomes most interested in him at the moment of his death, his crucifixion. This is where her identification is at its most literal and empowered. So, when she goes to Calvary, the meditations of her mind assume an utterly literal actuality: 'Sche had so very contemplacyon in þe sygth of hir sowle as yf Crist had hangyn befor hir bodily eye in hys manhode.'[6] Similarly, as there is no difference for her between the

---

about women's revelations is discussed in relation to the 'discernment of spirits' by Jean Gerson. Gerson's 'De probatione spiritum' was written during the Council of Constance against the claims put forward on behalf of St Birgitta (see Eric Colledge, '*Epistola solitarii ad reges*: Alphonse of Pecha as Organizer of Brigittine and Urbanist Propaganda,' *Medieval Studies*, 1956, vol. 18, p. 43. Adam Easton, monk of Norwich, and later cardinal, writes a defence of St Birgitta, *Defensorium S. Birgittae* addressed to Boniface IX. The text can be found in three manuscripts: Bodleian MS Hamilton 7, Oxford University, folios 229–48; Lincoln Cathedral MS, 114, folios 23ᵛ to 53ᵛ and Universitätbibliothek Uppsala MS, c518 folios 248–73. For a discussion of Easton's defence see James A. Schmidtke, '"Saving" by Faint Praise: St Birgitta of Sweden, Adam Easton and Medieval Antifeminism', *American Benedictine Review*, 1982, vol. 33, pt 2, pp. 149–61. Margery's Carmelite confessor, Alan of Lynn, made indexes to Birgitta's *Revelations*. See Kempe, pp. 259 and 268, Goodman, p. 353 for a discussion of 'orthodox' local clerical interest in revelatory phenomena in the 1410s.
3. Kempe, p. 8 [8].
4. Ibid., pp. 18–20 [15–17].
5. Ibid., p. 183 [134].
6. Ibid., p. 70 [51].

sights of her soul and her bodily eye, so graphic are her imaginings, so there is no difference between a crucifix and the object of its memorial signification:

> & sumtyme, whan sche saw þe Crucyfyx, er yf sche sey a man had a wownde er a best wheþyr it wer, er yf a man bett a childe be-for hir er smet an hors er an-oþer best wyth a whippe, ȝyf sche myth sen it er heryn it, hir thowt sche saw owyr Lord be betyn er wowndyd.[7]

A priest, amazed at the cries she utters at the sight of a *pietà* tells her that 'Ihesu is ded long sithyn.' She replies, 'Sir, hys deth is as fresch to me as he had deyd þis same day.'[8]

Ultimately the concreteness of these imaginings is rooted in the visceral compassion with the passion of Christ as she *becomes* him on Calvary:

> &, whan þei can up on-to þe Mownt of Caluarye, sche fel down that sche mygth not stondyn ne knelyn but walwyd & wrestyd wyth hir body, spredyng hir armys a-brode, & cryed wyth a lowde voys as þow hir hert xulde a brostyn a-sundyr, for in þe cite of hir sowle sche saw veryly and freschly how owyr Lord was crucifyed.[9]

And it is these cries, uttered for the first time at this moment of maximal identification, in the very pose of crucifixion on Calvary, the historic point of Christ's death renewed in the culmination of her pilgrimage, that reproduce and repeat that mimesis at every utterance. They become, for Kempe at least, the proof of her sanctity.[1]

But if this is the moment of most literal identification, Kempe's *imitatio Christi* also consists in her willing assumption of suffering, and the way she functions as an object of scorn to those around her. Several times during the early parts of the book, she imagines ways to die[2] for the love of God, but as her narrative continues, it is no longer so necessary to invent or imagine her own persecution, for she has successfully constructed herself as the object of scorn she craves to be. Thus, in an irritating, albeit Christlike fashion, she thanks people for the abuse they heap on her head, and the book comes to read more and more like a trial, a test of her sanctity where sanctity is proved by the act of testing itself. She is of course tried as a Lollard, and catechized several times, in Bristol, Leicester, York, and Hull,[3] and each of these tests forms the occasion for an enforcement of her identification with Christ as the object of persecution. These trials are an important part

---

7. Ibid., p. 69 [51].
8. Ibid., p. 148 [109].
9. Ibid., p. 68 [50].
1. See pp. 89ff. [63ff].
2. E.g. Kempe, p. 142 [105].
3. For incidents at Bristol pp. 107–9 [179–81]; for Leicester, p. 111 [81–82]; for York, pp. 120–2 [89–90], 124–5 [90–95]; and Hull, p. 129 [100].

of the fabric of her book and her life, but more than the actual events themselves, they are organizing tropes for a hagiography, whereby each act and event is an opportunity for an enactment of virtue or resistance to temptation:

> Than thys creatur þowt it was ful mery to be reprevyd for Goddys lofe; it was to hir gret solas & cowmfort whan sche was chedyn & fletyn for þe lofe of Ihesu for repreuyng of synne, for spekyng of vertu, for comownyng in Scriptur whech sche lernyd in sermownys & be comownyng wyth clerkys. Sche ymagyned in hir-self what deth sche mygth deyn for Crystys sake. Hyr þowt sche wold a be slayn for Goddys lofe, but dred for þe poynt of deth, & þerfor sche ymagyned hyrself þe most soft deth, as hyr thowt, for dred of inpacyens, þat was to be bowndyn hyr hed & hir fet to a stokke & hir hed to be smet of wyth a scharp ex for Goddys lofe.[4]

In this passage, for example, her torments from her reprovers and scolders immediately lead to an imagining of her own martyrdom. On one level, of course, this is an identification with Christ, but it is also characteristically a taking of his place, in a redemptive substitution, a replacement of his suffering.[5]

Kempe's prolonged identification with Christ also organizes the very timing of the events of her book, most of which, as Atkinson has pointed out, take place on a Friday, the day in which Christ's passion is commemorated in ecclesiastial ceremonial.[6] The rhythms and tempo of her life are governed by the time of the passion in just the kind of mixing of past and present time recommended by Nicholas Love.[7]

Margery Kempe's very identity is osmotically absorbed in Christ's. As she tells us at the very beginning of her treatise, her book will deal 'in parcel of hys wonderful werkys' and 'in party the leuyng' of his creature Margery Kempe.[8] And it will treat the one through the other, for, as Christ says to her: 'I am in þe and þow in me. And þei þat heryn þe þei heryn þe voys of God.[9] The identification with Christ then engenders a porosity of identity, an exchange between Christ and Margery, and it also enjoins a remarkable lability of social roles created by this very porosity. Kempe renegotiates her own cultural position by means of such identification and role playing.

---

4. Ibid., pp. 29–30 [23].
5. See pp. 96, 108 [70, 79].
6. See Clarissa Atkinson, *Mystic and Pilgrim: The Book and The World of Margery Kempe*, Ithaca, Cornell University Press, p. 114 and see also Sue Ellen Holbrook, 'Order and Coherence in *The Book of Margery Kempe*' in *The Worlds of Medieval Women: Creativity, Influence, Imagination*, ed. Constance H. Berman, Charles W. Connell and Judith Rice Rothschild, Morgantown, West Virginia University Press, 1985, pp. 97–112.
7. See chapter 3.
8. Kempe, pp. 1–2 [3].
9. Ibid., p. 23 [18].

CAROLINE WALKER BYNUM

Late Medieval Eucharistic Doctrine[†]

Sancti uenite, Christi corpus sumite,
sanctum bibentes, quo redempti sanguinem.

saluati Christi corpore et sanguine,
a quo refecti laudes dicamus Deo.

hoc sacramento corporis et sanguinis
omnes exuti ab inferni faucibus.

. . . .

pro universis inmolatus Dominus
ipse sacerdos exstitit et hostia

. . . .

caelestem panem dat esurientibus,
de fonte uiuo praebet sitientibus.

. . . .

(Come, holy people, eat the body of Christ, drinking the holy blood by
which you are redeemed. We have been saved by Christ's body and
blood; having feasted on it, let us give thanks to God. All have been rescued from the jaws of hell by this sacrament of body and blood. . . .
The Lord, offered as sacrifice for us all, was both priest and victim. . . .
He gives the celestial bread to the hungry and offers drink from the living fountain to the thirsty.)[1]

Exactly how Christ was present in the bread and wine was not a question that animated early theologians. Between the ninth and twelfth centuries, however, it became such a question. Preachers and schoolmen
argued over what sorts of metaphors were acceptable for expressing the
nature of God's presence.[2] The majority clearly favored language that was
frankly literal and physical. When the Fourth Lateran Council (1215)
stated—in phrases neither as scholastic nor as Aristotelian as they might
have been—that Christ is present in substance on the altar at the consecration, it was merely making explicit what theologians and layfolk had
assumed for centuries:

There is one universal church of the faithful, outside which no one
at all is saved. In this church, Jesus Christ himself is both priest and
sacrifice, and his body and blood are really contained in the sacrament of the altar under the species of bread and wine, the bread

† From *Holy Feast and Holy Fast* (Berkeley: U of California P, 1987) 50–60. Reprinted by permission of the publisher.

1. A. S. Walpole, *Early Latin Hymns* (London: Cambridge UP, 1922), pp. 345–46. The "Sancti,
uenite" is the oldest eucharistic hymn in existence.

2. Edouard Dumoutet; *Corpus Domini: Aux Sources de la piétè eucharistique médiévale* (Paris:
Beauchesne, 1942); F. Baix and C. Lambot, *La Dévotion à l'eucharistie et le VIIᵉ centenaire de la
Fête-Dieu* (Gembloux: Duculot, 1964); Peter Browe, *Die Verehrung der Eucharistie im Mittelal-
ter* (Munich: Hueber, 1933); Jules Corblet, *Histoire dogmatique, liturgique et archéologique du
sacrement de l'eucharistie*, 2 vols. (Paris: Société Générale de Librairie Catholique, 1885–1886).

being transubstantiated into the body and the wine into the blood by the power of God, so that to carry out the mystery of unity we ourselves receive from him the body he himself receives from us [*accipiamus ipsi de suo, quod accepit ipse de nostro*].[3]

The proliferating eucharistic miracles of the twelfth and thirteenth centuries—in which the host, lying on the paten, shut away in the tabernacle, or raised on high in the priest's hands, turned visibly into Christ—were not (as some have argued) the result of the doctrine of transubstantiation. Rather, they were an expression of the sort of piety that made such doctrinal definition seem obviously true.[4] As Peter of Poitiers (d. 1205) put it: Christ is present beneath the veil of the species "like a hand in a glove." Peter the Chanter even went so far as to ask: "If we concede, without reservation, that the body of Christ is eaten, as Augustine says, why not say absolutely that one sees God?" (But Peter did not quite dare to answer that, yes, the faithful do literally see God through the elements as through a transparent veil.)[5]

The conviction that God was present in the eucharist more literally than in any other sacrament, that behind the veil of the "accidents" of "wine-redness" or "crumbliness" lay the substance of the body of God, raised certain problems for theologians. How could the *totus Christus* be present in physical elements so distressingly fluid or breakable? Would not the pious draw the risible conclusion—as they unquestionably did on occasion—that little bits of Jesus fell off if crumbs were spilled or that one hurt God by chewing the host? Desiring to avoid the implication, found in some eleventh- and twelfth-century supporters of the real presence, that the faithful do eat little pieces of God's flesh, theologians such as Aquinas affirmed that Christ's entire body was present in every particle. Thus his body was not physically broken in the fraction of the host. They also elaborated the doctrine of "concomitance"—the idea that both the body and the blood of Christ are present in each element. Faced with growing devotion to the bread and wine themselves, exactly because the crumbs and drops masked (thinly) the substance of Christ, theologians struggled to retain a firm emphasis on Christ's body as one, because one church and one humanity are saved in it.[6] In the Corpus Christi hymns associated with Aquinas, we hear echoing again and again not only the doctrine of transubstantiation but also the insistence on one Christ in two species. Only thus is total human nature (sensual as well as spiritual) saved:

3. Decrees of the Fourth Lateran Council, in Henry Denzinger, *Enchiridion symbolorum: Definitionum et declarationum de rebus fidei et morum*, 34th ed., ed. A. Schönmetzer (Freiburg: Herder, 1967), document 802, p. 260. Note the close connection between the notion of the unity and exclusivity of the church and the doctrine that the eucharist *is* God's body and blood.
4. See Browe, *Die Eucharistischen Wunder; des Mittelalters* (Breslau: Müller and Seihhert 1938) Dumoutet, CD. See also Edouard Dumoutet, *Le Désir de voir l'hostie et les origines de la dévotion au Saint-Sacrement*, Université de Strasbourg (Paris: Beauchesne, 1926).
5. Dumoutet, CD, pp. 109–10.
6. See Thomas Aquinas, *Summa theologiae*, Blackfriars ed., 61 vols. (New York: McGraw-Hill, 1964–81), III, qq. 75–76, vol. 58, pp. 52–122. See also Dumoutet, CD.

> Verbum caro panem verum verbo carnem efficit
> Fitque sanguis Christi merum; et, si sensus deficit,
> Ad firmandum cor sincerum sola fides sufficit.

(The Word made flesh by a word changes true bread into flesh, and wine becomes the blood of Christ; and if sense is deficient [in perceiving the change] faith alone suffices to make the sincere heart firm [in believing it].)[7]

> Post agnum typicum, expletis epulis,
> Corpus dominicum datum discipulis,
> Sic totum omnibus, quod totum singulis,
> Ejus fatemur manibus.

(After [they had eaten] the lamb, which is a type [i.e., a foreshadowing], and when the meal was over, the body of the Lord was given to the disciples in such a way that the whole was given to all and the whole given to each, and this was done by his own hands.)[8]

> Quibus sub bina specie
> Carnem dedit et sanguinem
> Ut duplicis substantiae
> Totum cibaret hominem.

([To his disciples] he gave, under two species, his flesh and blood, so that it might feed the whole man, who is of twofold substance.)[9]

Sometimes the hymns become veritable theological tractates:

> Sub diversis speciebus,
> Signis tantum et non rebus,
>   Latent re eximiae.
> Caro cibus, sanguis potus,
> Manet tamen Christus totus
>   Sub utraque specie.
>
> . . . .
>
> Fracto demum sacramento
> Ne vacilles, sed memento
> Tantum esse sub fragmento
>   Quantum toto tegitur.

---

7. "Pange, lingua" in Stephen Gaselee, ed., *The Oxford Book of Medieval Latin Verse* (repr. Oxford: Clarendon Press, 1937), p. 144; and Aquinas Byrnes, ed., *The Hymns of the Dominican Missal and Breviary* (St Louis: Herder, 1943), p. 168; trans. adapted from Joseph Connelly, *Hymns of the Roman Liturgy* (Westminster, MD: Newman Press, 1957), p. 120. In writing the office for Corpus Christi, Thomas borrowed from an earlier office. The extent of his "authorship" of these hymns is in doubt; see Baix and Lambot, *La Dévotion*, pp. 89–91. See also F.T.E. Raby, *A History of Christian Latin Poetry from the Beginnings to the Close of the Middle Ages*, 2d ed. (Oxford: Clarendon Press, 1953), pp. 402–14.
8. "Sacris solemniis," in Byrnes, *Hymns*, p. 172; trans. adapted from Connelly, *Hymns*, pp. 121–23.
9. "Verbum supernum prodiens," in Gaselee, *Medieval Latin Verse*, p. 145; trans. adapted from Connelly, *Hymns*, p. 123.

(Under the different species, which are only signs, not things [i.e., realities], lie hidden wonderful things. The flesh is food, the blood is drink, and yet the whole Christ remains under each species. . . . Finally, when the sacrament is broken, do not doubt, but remember: there is as much hidden in a fragment as in the whole.)[1]

The theological questions of transubstantiation and concomitance were not merely schoolroom problems. They arose from and had grave implications for Christian practice, as is demonstrated by a controversy that erupted in Paris in the later twelfth century—years before transubstantiation was defined. The question was whether Christ was present from the moment of the first words of institution: "Hoc est enim corpus meum." Since a body cannot exist without blood and since the blood was clearly not yet present, the wine not having been consecrated, Peter the Chanter concluded that the body could not be present until the words over the wine were said. Both elements were necessary for Christ to be present. Indeed, Peter held, both elements were necessary for the consecration of either to occur. If, during the mass, the priest discovered that he had forgotten to put wine in the chalice, he had to repeat the entire consecration.

Peter's argument met with outraged rebuttal in sermons, in theological analyses, and even in the glosses provided to accounts of miracles. It annoyed both learned and popular opinion, partly because it ran afoul of common liturgical practice (which was simply to fill up the empty chalice and go on) but mostly because, as Guy of Orchelles said, it made existing piety into idolatry. Priest and people alike had begun to practice adoration of the host from the moment of its consecration. If it was not yet Christ, then the faithful were worshiping flour. While no one involved denied that the elements were in some sense Christ's body and blood, the exact moment of the change mattered enormously because people were behaving as if Christ appeared, substantially and totally, in the wafer when the words "Hoc est corpus meum" were said.[2]

This rather minor theological debate reflects a great medieval change. By the thirteenth century the eucharist, once a communal meal that bound Christians together and fed them with the comfort of heaven, had become an object of adoration. The physical appearance of food on the altar was in fact a veil through which holy flesh was spiritually or mystically seen. Since Christ arrived at the moment of consecration, not of communion, he arrived in the hands of the priest before he appeared on the tongue of the individual believer. Whether or not one held or tasted the wafer, one could meet Christ at the moment of his descent into the elements—a descent that paralleled and recapitulated the Incarnation.

1. "Lauda, Sion, Salvatorem," in Gaselee, *Medieval Latin Verse*, pp. 146–47; and Byrnes, *Hymns*, pp. 180–88; trans. adapted from Connelly, *Hymns*, p. 126.
2. Dumoutet, CD, pp. 1–50.

Despite the new focus on "seeing" rather than "receiving," on consecration rather than communion, medieval men and women did not lose
their sense of the religious significance of food and hunger, both as facts
and as metaphors. If anything, food became a yet more powerful and awe-
ful symbol, for the bread and wine that lay on the altar were now even
more graphically seen to be God. But the meaning of *food and hunger*
changed. To patristic poets and theologians, the food on the altar had suggested that Christ himself came as bread to hungry humankind or that
he "digested" Christians, binding them to him as his body—i.e., the
church. Hunger meant human vulnerability, which God comforted with
food, or it meant human self-control, adopted in an effort to keep God's
commandments. In the sermon and song, theology and story, of the high
Middle Ages, however, the food on the altar was the God who became
man; it was bleeding and broken flesh. Hunger was unquenchable desire;
it was suffering. To eat God, therefore, was finally to become suffering
flesh with his suffering flesh; it was to imitate the cross.

Many changes in piety—some coming as early as the ninth century—
foreshadowed, accompanied, and reflected the shift from communion to
consecration as the focal point of devotion. Early medieval Christians
had sometimes reserved the sacrament on the altar in a pyx (for carrying
to the sick) and had combined it with or substituted it for relics in the
consecration of churches. Perhaps as early as the eleventh century, at Bec
and at Canterbury, they venerated it with genuflection, incense, and procession. But the cult of the sacrament, of devotion to the consecrated host
itself, did not really begin until the twelfth century. It then developed
rapidly. The pyxes and reliquaries in which the host was reserved became
more and more elaborate, both to protect the host from profanation and
to allow the faithful to adore it outside the mass. Lamps and candles were
burned before it. Small, usually circular openings (*oculi*), were placed in
the exterior walls of the apse, so that the pious could look directly into the
eucharistic chest and venerate the host from outside the church. From
Germany come stories of knights and peasants galloping up on horseback
so that the horses might adore God also, in a kind of equine communion
known as the *Umritt.*[3] Perhaps as early as the ninth century, recluses had
their cells in churches positioned so they could adore the host each day.[4]
Visits to the host began in the twelfth century; some writers suggested that
such visits might substitute for going on crusade.

The first evidence for the elevation of the host after consecration
comes from Paris about 1200.[5] The practice spread rapidly, and with it
the conviction that seeing the host had spiritual value—that it was a "sec-

---

3. Lionel Rothkrug, "Popular Religion and Holy Shrines: Their Influence on the Origins of the
   German Reformation and Their Role in German Cultural Development," in James Obelkevich,
   ed., *Religion and the People, 800–1700* (Chapel Hill: University of North Carolina Press, 1979),
   pp. 30–32.
4. Louis Gougaud, "Etude sur la réclusion religieuse," *Revue Mabillon* 13 (1923): 86–87.
5. See Baix and Lambot, *La Dévotion*, p. 67.

ond sacrament," alongside receiving. Prayers were composed for the moment of seeing, which was honored by the ringing of bells, genuflection, and incense. By the thirteenth century we find stories of people attending mass only for the moment of elevation, racing from church to church to see as many consecrations as possible, and shouting at the priest to hold the host up higher.[6] An account even survives of guild members bringing charges against a priest for assigning them places in church from which they could not see the elevated host.[7] When John Marienwerder, Dorothy of Montau's confessor, wrote his account of her visions and teachings, he especially emphasized the saint's devotion to "seeing" Christ:

> The spouse [of Christ], compelled by the odor of this vivifying sacrament, had from her childhood to the end of her life the desire to see the blessed host. And if she managed to view it a hundred times in one day, as sometimes happened, she still retained the desire to view it more often.[8]

The cult of the eucharistic host was fully established by the late thirteenth century, with the institution in 1264 of the feast of Corpus Christi (revealed to Juliana of Cornillon and long worked for by Juliana and her friends Eva of St. Martin and Isabelle of Huy).[9] Despite the intense eucharistic enthusiasm of the area around Liège, Juliana's home, the feast made little headway at first, in part because some argued that a special festival for Christ's body might imply less reverence for it at every mass. But after the feast was re-promulgated in 1311/12, and again in 1317, it spread rapidly. In the fourteenth century, "showing" was separated entirely from the mass, with the introduction of the monstrance, a special vessel for displaying the consecrated wafer. The host was now carried uncovered in procession on Corpus Christi and left exposed on the altar for adoration, sometimes for the entire octave. By the fifteenth century certain feasts ended with the exposition and benediction of the blessed sacrament. Even before the promulgation of Corpus Christi, orders and confraternities appeared whose purpose was to promote the cult of the host and to make reparation for the sacrilege of heretics. One such con-

6. Browe, *Die Verehrung*; Josef Jungmann, *The Mass of the Roman Rite; Its Origins and Development (Missarum Sollemnia)*, trans. F. A. Brunner, 2 vols. (New York: Benziger, 1951, 1955), vol. 1, pp. 119–21, and vol. 2, pp. 206ff.

7. The incident is cited by Rothkrug, "Popular Religion," p. 36, and by Anton Mayer, *Die Liturgie in der europäischen Geistesgeschichte: Gesammelte Aufsätze*, ed. E. von Severus (Darmstadt: Wissenschaftliche Buchgesellschaft, 1971), p. 45.

8. See John Marienwerder, *Septililium B. Dorotheae*, treatise 3: *De eucharistia*, chap. 2, ed. Franciscus Hipler, in AB 3 (1884): 409. In his work on the life of Christ, Ludolf of Saxony assimilated "eating" to "seeing": "Venias et nihilominus quotidie ut videas Jesus in praesepio spirituali, scilicet in altari, ut carnis suae frumento mercaris cum animalibus sanctis refici" (quoted in Mary Immaculate Bodenstedt, *The "Vita Christi" of Ludolphus the Carthusian*, Catholic University of America Studies in Medieval and Renaissance Latin Language and Literature 16 [Washington, D.C.: Catholic University of America Press, 1944], p. 133 n. 94).

9. See esp. Baix and Lambot, *La Dévotion*, pp. 75ff.; and Bertaud, "Dévotion eucharistique," cols. 1621–37.

fraternity, itself perhaps not the first, was the gray penitents of Avignon, founded in 1226.[1]

Elevation of the chalice emerged more slowly. The feasts of the Sacred Heart and of the Precious Blood were established only in modern times. But the roots of these festivals go back to the intense devotion to the heart of Jesus found among the Saxon nuns and Flemish holy women of the thirteenth century.[2] * * *

In the mass itself, reception and consecration were increasingly separated, and the elements treated with increasing awe. More and more the rhythm of the service itself, the liturgical practices surrounding it, and even the architecture of churches suggested that God came "through" and even primarily "to" priests. In the early church the altar had been a simple table, and the priest had celebrated facing the people. By the twelfth century the altar stood against the wall of the apse and was often surmounted by a retable. A cross (usually not yet a crucifix) and candles adorned it. The priest celebrated with his back to the people, reciting the canon of the mass in an inaudible whisper, while the people engaged in all sorts of personal devotions (or daydreaming) loosely connected with the ceremony. Communion was given before, after, or completely apart from mass. Monks and nuns might go to the high altar; layfolk usually received at the side altar, where the sacrament was sometimes placed beforehand. Women had been prohibited since the days of the early church from receiving in their bare hands. From the ninth century, women and laymen usually received directly on the tongue. By the eleventh century only priests could take God in their hands.[3]

Moreover, changes in the physical elements themselves made them seem more awesome, magical, and remote. Since the ninth century the wafer had been made from unleavened bread, perhaps because it adhered more easily to the tongue than did leavened bread. In the early twelfth century the host began to be stamped with pictures of Christ rather than with the simple monograms common earlier.[4] In the twelfth and thirteenth centuries the chalice sometimes contained merely a drop of the precious blood mixed with unconsecrated wine (the so-called lay chalice). The cup was sometimes withheld entirely. In the thirteenth century the people were sometimes offered simply a cup of unconsecrated wine for cleansing the mouth after communion. The interchange of the various chalices often went unnoticed, and theologians argued

1. Bertaud, "Dévotion eucharistique," col. 1632.
2. Baix and Lambot, La Dévotion, pp. 113–23.
3. Theodor Klauser, A Short History of the Western Liturgy: An Account and Some Reflections, trans. John Halliburton (2d ed., Oxford: Oxford University Press, 1979), pp. 98–103, 120; Jungmann, Mass of the Roman Rite, vol. 2, pp. 374–80; C.N.L. Brooke, "Religious Sentiment and Church Design in the Later Middle Ages," Bulletin of the John Rylands Library, 50.1 (Autumn 1967): 13–33.
4. Klauser, Western Liturgy, p. 110; Jungmann, Mass of the Roman Rite, vol. 2, pp. 381–82; Baix and Lambot, La Dévotion, pp. 40–41; Corblet, Histoire dogmatique, vol. 1, pp. 188–91; Browe, Die Wunder, pp. 97–98.

over whether the faithful should be taught that they received the body and blood in the wafer and mere wine in the chalice, or whether the cup of the laity indeed held the blood of the Lord.[5] Thomas Aquinas justified the withholding of the cup by pointing out that the priest received both species.[6]

The theory that the priest received for the people was elaborated gradually. Otto of Bamberg (d. 1139) said that the converted Pomeranians should communicate through their priests if they could not receive themselves. Berthold of Regensburg (d. 1272) explained that the communicating priest "nourishes us all," for he is the mouth and we are the body. William Durandus the Elder (d. 1296) suggested that the faithful receive three times a year "because of sinfulness" but "priests [receive] daily for us all." Ludolf of Saxony (d. 1377) argued that the eucharist is called our daily bread because ministers receive it daily for the whole community.[7]

Not only was the priest the channel through which God descended, he was also seen as assimilated to Christ (or the Virgin Mary) in the act of consecration, as deified at the moment in which God arrived between his hands. "Oh revered dignity of priests, in whose hands the Son of God is incarnated as in the Virgin's womb," reads an often-cited twelfth-century text.[8] And the following lines have been attributed to the wandering preacher Norbert of Xanten, who founded an order of clerics:

> Priest, you are not you, because you are God.
> You are not yours, because you are Christ's servant and minister.
> You are not of yourself because you are nothing.
> What therefore are you, oh priest? Nothing and all things.[9]

In the early thirteenth century, Francis of Assisi expressed the same awe of priests:

> If it is right to honour the Blessed Virgin Mary because she bore him in her most holy womb; if St. John the Baptist trembled and was afraid even to touch Christ's sacred head; if the tomb where he lay for only a short time is so venerated; how holy, and virtuous, and worthy should not a priest be; he touches Christ with his own hands. . . . A priest receives him into his heart and mouth and offers him to others to be received.[1]

---

5. Jungmann, *Mass of the Roman Rite*, vol. 2, pp. 381–85, 412–14.
6. Aquinas, ST, III, q. 80, art. 12, reply obj. 3, vol. 59, pp. 84–85. See also III, q. 76, art. 2, vol. 58, pp. 96–100.
7. Jungmann, *Mass of the Roman Rite*, vol. 2, p. 364.
8. Quoted in Yves Congar, "Modèle monastique et modèle sacerdotal en Occident de Grégoire VII (1073–1085) à Innocent III (1198)," *Études de civilisation médiévale (IX⁰–XII⁰ siècles): Mélanges offerts à Edmond-René Labande* (Poitiers: C.E.S.C.M., 1973), p. 159.
9. Quoted in ibid.
1. Francis of Assisi, "Letter to a General Chapter," in Francis, *Opuscula sancti patris Francisci Assisiensis*, ed. the Fathers of St. Bonaventure's College, Bibliotheca Franciscana Ascetica Medii Aevi 1, 2d ed. (Quaracchi: Collegium S. Bonaventurae, 1949), pp. 102–3; trans. B. Fahy in *Omnibus*, p. 105.

As the role of the priest was exalted, the gap between priest and people widened. By the late Middle Ages in northern Europe, elaborate screens were constructed to hide the priest and the altar.[2] Thus, at the pivotal moment of his coming, Christ was separated and hidden from the congregation in a sanctuary that enclosed together priest and God.

In such an atmosphere, deep ambivalence developed about the reception of communion.[3] On the one hand, theologians and canon lawyers encouraged frequent reception. The requirement of at least yearly confession and communion established at the Fourth Lateran Council (1215) was intended to set forth a minimum of observance. And a number of the new monastic orders required frequent communion. But, on the other hand, theologians feared that frequent reception might lead to loss of reverence, to carelessness, even to profanation of the elements. Familiarity might breed contempt. Albert the Great, for example, who supported the practice of daily communion, argued against it for women, fearing that frequent reception would trivialize response.[4] Theologians often asserted that abstaining out of awe was equal to receiving with confidence and joy. Quoting Augustine, they urged an interior seeing and feeding, which became the notion of "spiritual communion."[5]

Faced with such ambiguous advice, many pious people in the later Middle Ages developed, along with a frenzied hunger for the host, an intense fear of receiving it. Margaret of Cortona, for example, pled frantically with her confessor for frequent communion but, when given the privilege by Christ, abstained out of terror at her unworthiness.[6] Gertrude the Great expressed a sense of Christ and sacrament as truly awe-ful when she wrote:

> You, who are the splendor and the crown of celestial glory, you appeared to descend from the imperial throne of your majesty with a movement full of sweetness, and flooded the width of the sky with a sweet liquor so that the saints hastened to drink. . . .
> And you added this understanding [to the vision just recounted]: that one ought to approach the sacrament of your body and blood in such love for your communion (even beyond the love for your glory, if that is possible) that one would be willing to eat the sacrament to one's own condemnation.[7]

2. Brooke, "Religious Sentiment."
3. Joseph Duhr, "Communion fréquente," DS, vol. 2 (1953), cols. 1234–92, esp. cols. 1236–71.
4. Albert the Great, *Commentarii in IV Sententiarum*, dist. 13, art. 27, in Albert, *Opera omnia*, ed. August Borgnet, vol. 29 (Paris: Ludovicus Vivès, 1894), pp. 378–80; and *Liber de sacramento Eucharistiae*, Dist. 4, tract. 4, chap. 3, in *Opera omnia*, vol. 38 (1899); p. 432.
5. The crucial text from Augustine, quoted over and over in the discussions of frequent communion, is "Crede et manducasti," Tractate 25 on the Gospel of John, chap. 12, PL 35, col. 1602.
6. Life of Margaret of Cortona, AASS February, vol. 3, pp. 341, 344. Desire for the eucharist and obsessive fear of receiving it unworthily are themes throughout Margaret's *vita* (see pp. 304–63 passim).
7. Gertrude the Great, *Oeuvres spirituelles*, ed. Pierre Doyère, vol. 2: *Le Héraut*, SC 139, Sér. mon. 25 (1968), pp. 303–7.

Gertrude took comfort for her own feelings of unworthiness from words that God supposedly sent to her when she tried to explain why a friend abstained: "I heard your [i.e., God's] blessed response: 'It is impossible that anyone receiving with such an intention [i.e., the intention to abstain from fear] could be irreverent.'"[8]

For all the terror the eucharist inspired, however, reception of God as food between one's lips remained a uniquely important mode of spiritual encounter. Late medieval saints, especially women, frequently received from confessors, or even the pope himself, the privilege of daily communion as an almost official recognition of their reputations for sanctity. Religious superiors, bishops, and canon lawyers legislated against reception during ecstasy, in an effort to control the waves of frenzy for the eucharist that shook religious houses. The deathbeds of pious people sometimes became the setting for bitter struggle between priest and recipient over how often the holy food could be taken.[9] Indeed, as the moment of consecration became increasingly fraught with meaning, as the power of priests grew ever more awesome, as the notion of eating God seemed more and more audacious and the drink of Christ's blood was permanently withdrawn, some of the devout found that their hunger, seasoned and impelled by fear, merely intensified.[1] The more church architecture, liturgical practice, and priestly power contrived to make the elements seem distant, the more some people luxuriated in them in private, ecstatic experiences. James of Vitry's description of the eucharistic piety of Mary of Oignies could be matched by dozens of similar descriptions from the next two hundred years:

> Thus [Mary] languished in exile. The sole and highest remedy was the manna of celestial bread, until she could come to the promised land [heaven]. In it, the anxiety and desire of her heart were tempered; in it, all her sorrows were appeased. . . . In the highest and most excellent sacrament, she patiently bore all the hardships of her enforced wandering. . . . The holy bread strengthened her heart; the holy wine inebriated her, rejoicing her mind; the holy body fattened her; the vitalizing blood purified her by washing. And she could not bear to abstain from such solace for long. For it was the same to her to live as to eat the body of Christ, and this it was to die, to be separated from the sacrament by having for a long time to abstain. . . . Indeed, she felt all delectation and all savor of sweetness in receiving it, not just within her soul but even in her mouth. . . . Sometimes she happily accepted her Lord under the appearance of

8. Ibid.
9. See the case of Dorothy of Montau, discussed by Kieckhefer, UnS, pp. 22–23.
1. John Marienwerder comments that Dorothy of Montau's hunger for the eucharist was so vast that, if she had been permitted, she would have snatched the host from the hands of the priest with her teeth (*Septililium B. Dorotheae*, treatise 3, chap. 2, in AB 3, p. 409).

a child, sometimes as a taste of honey, sometimes as a sweet smell, and sometimes in the pure and gorgeously embellished marriage bed of the heart. And when she was not able to bear any longer her thirst for the vivifying blood, sometimes after the mass was over she would remain for a long time contemplating the empty chalice on the altar.[2]

Despite the aura of majesty that surrounded the eucharist in the later Middle Ages, it seemed to the faithful to offer itself to their senses with astonishing familiarity.[3] It rang with the music of bells, glowed with light, dissolved on the tongue into honeycomb or bloody flesh, and announced its presence, when profaned or secreted away, by leaving a trail of blood. Christ appeared again and again on the paten and in the chalice as a baby, a glorious youth, or a bleeding and dying man.[4]

The changes in liturgy, theology, and even architecture discussed above help explain why so many visions of Christ came at mass. In an atmosphere where confessors and religious superiors controlled access to the eucharist and stressed scrupulous and awe-filled preparation, recipients naturally approached the elements in a spiritually and psychologically heightened state. When, after mumbling inaudibly, the priest suddenly and to the accompaniment of incense and bells raised on high a thin, shimmering wafer of unleavened bread embossed with the image of Christ, it is small wonder that the pious sometimes "saw" Jesus. When, after hours of self-examination and doubt, anxious nuns or laypeople took God on their tongues, it is small wonder that the bit of bread sometimes swelled "with marvelous sweetness" to choke them. Gazing aloft at a hanging pyx shaped in the form of a dove, some mystics thought they saw the Holy Spirit winging toward them, the wafer in his beak. Contemplating the new devotional object, the crucifix, in dim and damp churches, pious people sometimes thought it dripped blood because of their own private sins. Denied the cup or even the host by ecclesiastical regulation, many of the devout thought, when they at least obtained release from their inner distress and longing, that the comfort of Christ was in their mouths or hearts immediately—without the priest's enabling hands or words.

* * *

2. James of Vitry, Life of Mary of Oignies, AASS June, vol. 5, p. 568.
3. Browe, Die Wunder; Bynum, "Women Mystics."
4. The new emphasis on "seeing" God is reflected in the increasing number of miracles connected with elevation rather than reception. In orders (e.g., Franciscan nuns or tertiaries) where communion was infrequent, ecstasies tended to come at the elevation. Eucharistic miracles could even involve knowing whether "Christ" (i.e., the consecrated host) was present on the altar, or being transported, when there was no service, into the tabernacle to taste Christ.

NICHOLAS WATSON

Arundel's Constitutions[†]

* * *

The Constitutions themselves consist of a series of articles that lay down new regulations for various aspects of the preaching and teaching life of the Church in general and the University of Oxford in particular. The articles of the legislation dealing with Oxford concern us here for the most part only as evidence of how detailed and broadly based Arundel felt his attack had to be. These impose limits on the discussion of theological questions in the schools, provide for a monthly inquiry (no less) into the views of every student at the university, and forbid the study not simply of Wycliffe's books but of all recent texts that have not been approved unanimously by a panel of twelve theologians appointed by the archbishop (articles 6, 9–11).[1] Less detailed but as stringent are a set of articles (1–5, 8) dealing with preaching and with teaching in grammar schools and other contexts. These affirm the illegality of preaching without a license (to be granted only after examination of the preacher's orthodoxy); forbid preachers to discuss the sins of the clergy or the sacraments in their sermons, confining them to the topics listed in Pecham's Syllabus; extend this ban to cover schoolmasters and other teachers; and, finally, forbid all argument over matters of faith outside universities.[2] The specific invoca-

---

† From "Censorship and Cultural Change," *Speculum* 70 (1995): 827–29. Reprinted by permission of the Medieval Academy of America.

1. Article 6 is especially relevant: "Item, For that a new way doth more frequently lead astray, than an old way, we will and command, that no book or treatise made by John Wickliff, or others whomsoever, about that time, or since, or hereafter to be made, be from henceforth read in schools, halls, hospitals, or other places whatsoever, within our province of Canterbury aforesaid, except the same be first examined by the university of Oxford or Cambridge; or, at least, by twelve persons, whom the said universities, or one of them, shall appoint to be chosen at our discretion, or the laudable discretion of our successors; and the same being examined as aforesaid, to be expressly approved and allowed by us or our successors, and in the name and authority of the university, to be delivered unto the stationers to be copied out, and the same to be sold at a reasonable price, the original thereof always after to remain in some chest of the university. But if any man shall read any such kind of book in schools or otherwise, as aforesaid, he shall be punished as a sower of schism, and a favourer of heresy, as the quality of the fault shall require" (John Foxe, *Acts and Monuments*, 3:245). Note the careful provisions made here for the possibility of an approved text's being subsequently corrupted by interpolation and for the more or less systematic distribution of approved texts.

2. Article 1: "We will and command, ordain and decree: That no manner of person, secular or regular, being authorized to preach by the laws now prescribed, or licensed by special privilege, shall take upon him the office of preaching the word of God . . . whether within the church or without, in English, except he first present himself, and be examined by the ordinary of the place, where he preacheth. . . . Moreover the parish priests or vicars temporal, not having perpetuities, nor being sent in form aforesaid, shall simply preach in the churches where they have charge, only those things which are expressly contained in the provincial constitution set forth by John, our predecessor, of good memory, to help the ignorance of the priests, which beginneth, 'Ignorantia Sacerdotum.'"
   Article 3: "Moreover . . . we will and command, that the preacher of God's word . . . shall be of good behaviour . . . : and chiefly preaching to the clergy, he shall touch the vices,

tion of Pecham's Syllabus here (in article 1) is perhaps intended to imply that Arundel is returning the English church to a lost doctrinal purity: the Syllabus provided much of the impetus for the vernacular pastoralia of the fourteenth century by defining a minimum of religious knowledge that secular priests must teach their parishioners (incorporating the Creed, the Ten Commandments, the Lord's Prayer, the names of the deadly sins, the virtues, and so on) as part of the great educational drive initiated by the Fourth Lateran Council of 1215. Yet any suggestion that the Constitutions are simply reviving the force of earlier archiepiscopal legislation ignores a crucial difference: that here Pecham's *minimum* necessary for the laity to know if they are to be saved has been redefined as the *maximum* they may hear, read, or even discuss. This revisionist version of the Syllabus shows how much seemed, to Arundel in 1409, to have changed since 1281. No longer was it the ignorance of the laity and their priests (*ignorancia sacerdotum*) that was a matter for concern; it was the laity's too eager pursuit of knowledge.

So far, there is no mention of vernacular writing (as distinct from oral instruction), and it may well be that such writing was not as major a concern for Arundel as it is for us. Yet I think we can assume that written instruction was supposed to be included in the Constitutions' discussions of preaching and teaching. For the single article that does deal explicitly with vernacular writing imposes even severer constraints than are applied to preaching. Arundel never attempted to prevent preachers from translating and expounding biblical passages in their sermons, even though he did drastically restrict the topics such expositions could cover; given the liturgical context in which much preaching occurred, this would not have been practicable, even had it been desirable. But article 7 forbids anybody to make any written translation of a text of Scripture into English or even to own a copy, without diocesan permission, of any such

---

commonly used amongst them; and to the laity, he shall declare the vices commonly used amongst them; and not otherwise."

Article 4: "Forasmuch as the part is vile, that agreeth not with the whole, we do decree and ordain, that no preacher aforesaid, or any other person whatsoever, shall otherwise teach or preach concerning the sacrament of the altar, matrimony, confession of sins, or any other sacrament of the church, or article of the faith, than what already is discussed by the holy mother church; nor shall bring any thing in doubt that is determined by the church, nor shall, to his knowledge, privily or apertly pronounce blasphemous words concerning the same."

Article 5: "Forasmuch as a new vessel, being long used, savoureth after the head, we decree and ordain, that no schoolmasters and teachers whatsoever, that instruct children in grammar, or others whosoever, in primitive sciences, shall, in teaching them, intermingle any thing concerning the catholic faith, the sacrament of the altar, or other sacraments of the church, contrary to the determinations of the church; nor shall suffer their scholars to expound the holy Scriptures (except the text, as hath been used in ancient time); nor shall permit them to dispute openly or privily concerning the catholic faith, or sacraments of the church."

Article 8: "For that Almighty God cannot be expressed by any philosophical terms, or otherwise invented of man . . . we do ordain and specially forbid, that any manner of person, of what state, degree, or condition soever he be, do allege or propone [sic] any conclusions or propositions in the catholic faith, or repugnant to good manners (except necessary doctrine pertaining to their faculty of teaching or disputing in their schools or otherwise), although they defend the same with ever such curious terms and words." (Foxe, *Acts and Monuments*, 3:243–46.)

translation made since Wycliffe's time.[3] As Hudson has shown, the phrase "textum sacrae scripturae" used here was intended in the widest sense, to include even single verses translated in written form as well as the Wycliffite Bible itself, often thought of as its main target. Thus it would seem that vernacular writers (whose translations of biblical quotations, unlike those of preachers, would be permanent and thus possible to use and misapply) were forbidden to extend their discussion even to the limits allowed to preachers.

* * *

3. Article 7: "Item, It is a dangerous thing, as witnesseth blessed St. Jerome, to translate the text of the holy Scripture out of the tongue into another; for in the translation the same sense is not always easily kept, as the same St. Jerome confesseth, that although he were inspired, yet oftentimes in this he erred: we therefore decree and ordain, that no man, hereafter, by his own authority translate any text of the Scripture into English or any other tongue ['aliquem textum sacrae scripturae auctoritate sua in linguam Anglicanam, vel aliam transferat'], by way of a book, libel, or treatise ['per viam libri, libelli, aut tractatus']; and that no man read any such book, libel or treatise, now lately set forth in the time of John Wickliff, or since, or hereafter to be set forth, in part or in whole, privily or apertly, upon pain of greater excommunication, until the said translation be allowed by the ordinary of the place, or, if the case so require, by the council provincial. He that shall do contrary to this, shall likewise be punished as a favourer of error and heresy" (Foxe, *Acts and Monuments*, 3:245).

Selected Bibliography

MANUSCRIPT

British Library MS. Additional 61823. The manuscript was the property of Colonel William Erdeswick Ignatius Butler-Bowdon, whose family had possessed the manuscript since at least the mid-eighteenth century. The manuscript contains two bookplates, both those of Henry Bowdon, born in 1754. At the top of the verso of the binding leaf of the manuscript and written in a late-fifteenth-century hand is the sentence "This boke is of Mountegrace," indicating that earlier the manuscript belonged to the Carthusian monastery of Mount Grace in Yorkshire. In 1934, Hope Emily Allen identified the manuscript.

• indicates works included in or excerpted for this Norton Critical Edition.

TEXTS

Allen, Hope Emily. *Writings Ascribed to Richard Rolle*. London: Oxford UP, 1927.
Bokenham, Osbern. *Legendys of Hooly Wummen*. Ed. Mary Serjeantson. EETS 206. London: Oxford UP, 1938.
Guidebook to Palestine (ca. 1350), ed. J. H. Bernard. Palestine Pilgrim's Text Society, 6, no. 3. London, 1894.
Horstmann, C., ed. *Lives of Women Saints*. EETS 86. London: Trübner, 1886.
Horstmann, K., ed. *Prosalengendem Anglia* 7–8 (1884–85): 102–96.
• Jacques de Vitry. *The Life of Marie d'Oignies*. Trans. Margot H. King. *Two Lives of Marie d'Oignies*. Toronto: Peregrina Publishing, 1998.
John Poloner's Description of the Holy Land (ca. 1421). Trans. A. Stewart. Palestine Pilgrim's Text Society, 6, no. 4. London, 1894.
Meech, Sanford Brown, and Hope Emily Allen, eds. *The Book of Margery Kempe*. EETS 212. New York: Oxford UP, 1940, 1961.
Nichols, Francis Morgan, ed. and trans. *The Marvels of Rome. Mirabilia Urbis Romae*. 2nd ed. Intro. Eileen Gardiner. New York: Italica, 1986.
Petroff, Elizabeth Alvilda, ed. *Medieval Women's Visionary Literature*. Oxford: Oxford UP, 1986.
Raguin, Virginia, and Sarah Stanbury. *Mapping Margery Kempe: A Guide to Late Medieval Material and Spiritual Life*. http://sterling.holycross.edu/departments/visarts/projects/Kempe.
• Ragusa, Isa, and Rosalie Green, eds. and trans. *Meditations on the Life of Christ: An Illustrated Manuscript of the Fourteenth Century*. Princeton: Princeton UP, 1961.
Staley, Lynn, ed. *The Book of Margery Kempe*. Kalamazoo, MI: Medieval Institute Publications, 1996.
Stewart, Aubrey, trans. *Theoderich. Guide to the Holy Land*. 2nd ed. Introduction, Notes, & Bibliography by R. G. Musto. NY: Italica Press, 1986.
Windeatt, B. A., trans. *The Book of Margery Kempe*. New York: Penguin Books, 1985.
———, ed. *The Book of Margery Kempe*. Longman Annotated Texts. Harlow, Essex: Pearson Education Ltd., 2000.

STUDIES

• Aers, David. *Community, Gender, and Individual Identity: English Writing 1360–1430*. London: Routledge, 1988.

Ashley, Kathleen, and Pamela Sheingorn, eds. *Interpreting Cultural Symbols: Saint Anne in Late Medieval Society*. Athens: U of Georgia P, 1990.

• Ashley, Kathleen. "Historicizing Margery: *The Book of Margery Kempe* as Social Text." *Journal of Medieval and Early Modern Studies* 28 (1998): 371–88.

Aston, Margaret. *Lollards and Reformers: Images and Literacy in Late Medieval Religion*. London: Hambledon, 1984.

• Atkinson, Clarissa. *Mystic and Pilgrim: The Book and the World of Margery Kempe*. Ithaca: Cornell UP, 1983.

———, Constance H. Buchanan, and Margaret R. Miles, eds. *Immaculate and Powerful: The Female in Sacred Image and Social Reality*. Harvard Women's Studies in Religion Series. Boston, 1985.

Beckwith, Sarah. "A Very Material Mysticism: The Medieval Mysticism of Margery Kempe." *Medieval Literature: Criticism, Ideology, and History*. Ed. David Aers. New York: St. Martin's Press, 1986. 34–57.

• ———. *Christ's Body: Identity, Culture, and Society in Late Medieval Writings*. New York: Routledge, 1993.

———. "Problems of Authority in Late Medieval English Mysticism: Language, Agency, and Authority in *The Book of Margery Kempe*." *Exemplaria* 4 (1992): 171–200.

Blamires, Alcuin, and C. W. Marx. "Woman Not to Preach: A Disputation in British Library MS Harley 31." *Journal of Medieval Latin* 3 (1993): 34–63.

Bradley, Ritamary. "In the Jaws of the Bear: Journeys of Transformation by Women Mystics." *Vox Benedictina* 8 (1991): 17–75.

Brown, Peter. "The Saint as Exemplar in Late Antiquity." *Representations* 1 (1983): 1–25.

• Bynum, Caroline Walker. *Holy Feast and Holy Fast: The Religious Significance of Food to Medieval Women*. Berkeley: U of California P, 1987.

———. *Jesus as Mother: Studies in the Spirituality of the High Middle Ages*. Berkeley: U of California P, 1982.

———. "Women Mystics and Eucharistic Devotion in the Thirteenth Century." *Women's Studies* 11 (1984): 179–214.

Coletti, Theresa M. "'Paupertas est. donum dei': Hagiography, Lay Religion, and the Economics of Salvation in the Digby *Mary Magdalene*." *Speculum* 76 (2001): forthcoming.

Cross, Claire. "'Great Reasoners in Scripture': The Activities of Women Lollards." *Medieval Women: Essays Dedicated and Presented to Professor Rosalind M. T. Hill*. Ed. Derek Baker. Oxford: Basil Blackwell, 1978. 359–80.

Delany, Sheila. "Sexual Economics, Chaucer's Wife of Bath and *The Book of Margery Kempe*." *Writing Woman: Women Writers and Women in Literature Medieval to Modern*. New York: Schocken Books, 1983. 76–92.

Dickman, Susan. "Margery Kempe and the English Devotional Tradition." *The Medieval Mystical Tradition in England*. Ed. Marion Glasscoe. Exeter: Exeter UP, 1980. 156–72.

———. "Margery Kempe and the Continental Tradition of the Pious Woman." *The Medieval Mystical Tradition in England*. Ed. Marion Glasscoe. Cambridge: D. S. Brewer, 1984. 150–68.

Dinshaw, Carolyn. *Getting Medieval: Sexualities and Communities, Pre- and Post-Modern*. Durham: Duke UP, 1999.

Duffy, Eamon. *The Stripping of the Altars: Traditional Religion in England 1400–1580*. New Haven: Yale UP, 1992.

Ellis, Deborah S. "The Merchant's Wife's Tale: Language, Sex, and Commerce in Margery Kempe and in Chaucer." *Exemplaria* 2 (1990): 595–626.

Ellis, Roger. "'Flores ad Fabricandam . . . Coronam': An Investigation into the Uses of the Revelations of St. Bridget of Sweden in Fifteenth-Century England." *Medium Aevum* 51 (1982): 163–86.

———. "Margery Kempe's Scribes and the Miraculous Books." *Langland, the Mystics, and the Medieval English Religious Tradition*. Ed. Helen Phillips. Cambridge: D. S. Brewer, 1990. 161–76.

Feinberg, Nona. "Thematics of Value in *The Book of Margery Kempe*." *Modern Philology* 87 (1989): 132–41.

• Gibson, Gail McMurray. *The Theater of Devotion: East Anglian Drama and Society in the Late Middle Ages*. Chicago: U of Chicago P, 1989.

Goodich, Michael. "The Contours of Female Piety in Later Medieval Hagiography." *Church History* 50 (1981): 20–32.

Goodman, Anthony. "The Piety of John Brunham's Daughter of Lynn." *Medieval Women: Essays Dedicated and Presented to Professor Rosalind M. T. Hill*. Ed. Derek Baker. Oxford: Basil Blackwell, 1978. 347–58.

Gray, Douglas. "Popular Religion and Late Medieval English Literature." *Religion in the Poetry and Drama of the Late Middle Ages in England*. Ed. Piero Boitani and Anna Torti. Cambridge: D. S. Brewer, 1990. 1–28.

Green, Alice Stopford. *Town Life in the Fifteenth Century*. 1894. New York, 1971.

Hirsch, John C. *The Revelations of Margery Kempe: Paramystical Practices in Late Medieval England*. Leiden: E. J. Brill, 1989.

———. *Hope Emily Allen: Medieval Scholarship and Feminism*. Norman, OK: Pilgrim Books, 1988.

Holbrook, Sue Ellen. "Margery Kempe and Wynkyn de Worde." *The Medieval Mystical Tradition in England.* Ed. Marion Glasscoe. Exeter Symposium IV. Cambridge: D. S. Brewer, 1987. 27–46.

Hudson, Anne. *The Premature Reformation: Wycliffite Texts and Lollard History.* Oxford: Clarendon, 1988.

Justice, Steven, and Kathryn Kerby-Fulton. *Written Work: Langland, Labor, and Authorship.* Philadelphia: U of Pennsylvania P, 1997.

Kieckhefer, Richard. *Unquiet Souls: Fourteenth-Century Saints and Their Religious Milieu.* Chicago: U of Chicago P, 1984.

Knowles, David. *The English Mystical Tradition.* London: Burns and Oates, 1961.

• Lochrie, Karma. *Margery Kempe and Translations of the Flesh.* Philadelphia: U of Pennsylvania P, 1991.

McEntire, Sandra J., ed. *Margery Kempe, A Book of Essays.* New York: Garland Publishing, 1992.

McNiven, Peter. *Heresy and Politics in the Reign of Henry IV.* Woodbridge, Suffolk: The Boydell Press, 1987.

Middleton, Anne. "Acts of Vagrancy: The C Version 'Autobiography' and the Statute of 1388." Justice and Kerby-Fulton, pp. 208–318.

Mueller, Janel M. "Autobiography of a New 'Creatur': Female Spirituality, Selfhood, and Authorship in *The Book of Margery Kempe.*" *Women in the Middle Ages and Renaissance.* Ed. Mary Beth Rose. Syracuse: Syracuse UP, 1986. 155–72.

Newman, Barbara. *From Virile Woman to Woman Christ: Studies in Medieval Religion and Literature.* Philadelphia: U of Pennsylvania P, 1995.

Parker, Vanessa. *The Making of King's Lynn.* London: Phillimore, 1971.

Partner, Nancy F. "Reading the Book of Margery Kempe." *Exemplaria* 3 (1991): 29–66.

Riehle, Wolfgang. *The Middle English Mystics.* London, 1981.

Rubin, Miri. "Corpus Christi Fraternities and Late Medieval Piety." *Studies in Church History* 23 (1986): 97–110.

———. *Corpus Christi: The Eucharist in Late Medieval Culture.* Cambridge: Cambridge UP, 1991.

• Staley, Lynn. *Margery Kempe's Dissenting Fictions.* University Park, Pennsylvania: State UP, 1994.

Strohm, Paul. *England's Empty Throne. Usurpation and the Language of Legitimation 1399–1422.* New Haven: Yale UP, 1998.

Taylor, Charles. *Sources of the Self: The Making of Modern Identity.* Cambridge: Harvard UP, 1989.

Vance, Eugene. "Augustine's *Confessions* and the Grammar of Selfhood." *Genre* 6 (1973): 1–28.

Voaden, Rosalynn. *God's Words, Women's Voices: The Discernment of Spirits in the Writing of Late-Medieval Women Visionaries.* York, England: York Medieval Press, 1999.

Wallace, David. "Mystics and Followers in Sienna and East Anglia: A Study in Taxonomy, Class and Cultural Mediation." *The Medieval Mystical Tradition in England.* Ed. Marion Glasscoe. Cambridge: D. S. Brewer, 1984. 169–91.

Watson, Nicholas. *Richard Rolle and the Invention of Authority.* Cambridge: Cambridge UP, 1992.

• ———. "Censorship and Cultural Change." *Speculum* 70 (1995): 827–29.